Annual Franchise and Distribution Law Developments 2023

Anne P. Caiola
Charles S. Marion

AMERICAN**BAR**ASSOCIATION
Forum on Franchising

Cover Design by ABA Design.

The materials contained herein represent the opinions of the authors and/or the editors and should not be construed to be the views or opinions of the law firms or companies with whom such persons are in partnership with, associated with, or employed by, nor of the American Bar Association or the Forum on Franchising, unless adopted pursuant to the bylaws of the Association.

Nothing contained in this book is to be considered as the rendering of legal advice for specific cases, and readers are responsible for obtaining such advice from their own legal counsel. This book is intended for educational and informational purposes only.

© 2023 American Bar Association. All rights reserved.

No part of this publication may be reproduced, stored in a retrieval system, or transmitted in any form or by any means, electronic, mechanical, photocopying, recording, or otherwise, without the prior written permission of the publisher. For permission contact the ABA Copyrights & Contracts Department, copyright@americanbar.org, or complete the online form at
http://www.americanbar.org/utility/reprint.html.

27 26 25 24 23   5 4 3 2 1

Discounts are available for books ordered in bulk. Special consideration is given to state bars, CLE programs, and other bar-related organizations. Inquire at Book Publishing, ABA Publishing, American Bar Association, 321 N. Clark Street, Chicago, Illinois 60654-7598.

www.shopABA.org

TABLE OF CONTENTS

CHAPTER 1 1
    I.   Introduction.. 1
    II.   Essential Elements of a Franchise.................................... 1
    III.   Essential Elements of a Dealership................................... 4
    IV.   Accidental Franchises 5

CHAPTER 2 7
    I.   Introduction.. 7
    II.   Violations of Registration or Disclosure
          Requirements 7
    III.   Financial Performance Representations............................. 13
    IV.   Other Misrepresentations or Omissions............................ 13

CHAPTER 3 14
    I.   Introduction.. 14
    II.   Petroleum Marketing Practices Act 15
    III.   Automobile/Motor Vehicle Dealer Laws.......................... 19
    IV.   Beer and Wine Laws 30
    V.   Other Statutes.. 32

CHAPTER 4 36
    I.   Introduction.. 36
    II.   Performance and Termination Disputes Generally 36
          A.   Breach of Contract.. 36
          B.   Breach of Covenant of Good Faith and Fair Dealing 54
          C.   Tortious Interference 55
          D.   Fraud.. 57
          E.   Unfair and Deceptive Trade Practices 60
          F.   Violations of State relationship Statutes............. 62
          G.   Negligence... 68
          H.   Other Claims... 72
    III.   Non-Compete, Non-Solicitation Covenants 72

IV.	Encroachment	79
V.	Transfer Disputes	79
VI.	Injunctive Relief	82
VII.	Damages	94
VIII.	Attorneys' Fees	97
IX.	Other Issues	100

CHAPTER 5 103

I.	Introduction	103
II.	Unauthorized Use of Trademarks	104
III.	Copyright, Patent Infringement	113
IV.	Misappropriation of Trade Secrets	114
V.	Injunctive Relief	118
VI.	Other Trademark Issues	118

CHAPTER 6 122

I.	Introduction	122
II.	Antitrust	123
III.	Bankruptcy	128
IV.	RICO	132
V.	Civil Rights	133
VI.	Employment	134
VII.	Tax	142
VIII.	Insurance	142
IX.	Consumer Protection	144
X.	Constitutional	144
XI.	Trafficking Victims Protection Reauthorization Act	146
XII.	Other	154

CHAPTER 7 159

I.	Introduction	159
II.	Franchisor-Franchisee Liability to Franchisee's Employees	160
III.	Franchisor-Franchisee Liability to Third Parties	173
IV.	Other Franchisor Liability	182

CHAPTER 8 185

I.	Introduction	185
II.	Substantive and Personal Jurisdiction	186
III.	Venue and Choice of Forum	195

IV.	Choice of Law		207
V.	Amendment of Pleadings and Joinder of Claims and Parties		211
VI.	Arbitration		215
	A.	Enforceability	215
	B.	Binding Non-Signatories	225
	C.	Class/Collective Arbitration	228
	D.	Award Confirmation	228
	E.	Waiver	230
VII.	Mediation		230
VIII.	Statutes of Limitations		230
IX.	Collateral Estoppel/*Res Judicata*		231
X.	Class Actions		231
XI.	Discovery Issues		238
XII.	Default Judgment		245
XIII.	Settlements and Releases		251
XIV.	Enforcement and Collection		252
XV.	Withdrawal/Disqualification of Counsel		253
XVI.	Other Issues		253

CHAPTER 9 258

I.	Introduction	258
II.	Australia	258
III.	Cambodia	263
IV.	India	266
V.	Malta	272
VI.	New Zealand	277
VII.	Thailand	287
VIII.	Ukraine	292
IX.	Vietnam	298

TABLE OF CASES 304

TABLE OF AUTHORITIES 351

ABOUT THE AUTHORS

ANNE P. CAIOLA

Anne P. Caiola is a partner at Caiola & Rose, LLC in Atlanta, Georgia, a firm she co-founded with Elizabeth B. Rose. Annie started her career as a trial attorney at one of the largest international law firms in the world, before starting her own practice. She has tried hundreds of bench trials, jury trials, arbitrations and appeals of cases involving franchises, intellectual property, real estate, supply chain, leasing, lending, fiduciary duties, and corporate disputes. These days, Annie's practice is evenly balanced between trying cases and counseling clients on franchise sales practices, FDD preparation, corporate transactions, franchisee compliance, and marketing. Annie has also worked in-house for international franchisors where she has developed franchisee compliance programs and trained in-house attorneys, marketing teams and sales officers on best practices. She has also managed multidistrict and class action litigation involving foodborne illness, insurance rescission, and the TCPA.

At Caiola & Rose, Annie has enjoyed building a team of attorneys with similarly well-rounded practices that support franchisors and other business owners. She enjoys mentoring and developing attorneys to be problem solvers, fierce advocates and trusted partners for their clients. Annie has co-authored several articles and books for the ABA, the Forum on Franchising, the *Franchise Law Journal*, and the Georgia Bar Franchise & Distribution Section, that focus on franchising's intersection with real estate, advertising and other regulatory schemes. She has also received numerous awards and recognitions from *Franchise Times Magazine* (a "Legal Eagle"), *Super Lawyers Magazine* (a "Rising Star") and the Daily Report ("Top 40 Under 40" – which she received in the nick of time!).

Annie has served as Chair of the Franchise & Distribution Section of the Georgia Bar and has been a Member of the Women's Caucus and Nominating Committee for the ABA Forum on Franchising. She is a proud Double Tarheel from the University of North Carolina, and lives in Decatur, Georgia with her husband Greg (also a Tarheel), daughters Abby and Ellie (Tarheels in training), and dog Lacey (still figuring out what a Tarheel is).

ABOUT THE AUTHORS

CHARLES S. MARION

Charles S. (Chuck) Marion is a partner with the law firm of Blank Rome LLP, resident in its Philadelphia, Pennsylvania and Fort Lauderdale, Florida offices. Charles is an experienced litigator and trial attorney who focuses his practice in the areas of franchise litigation and counseling, complex business litigation, intellectual property litigation, and litigation and counseling regarding the Americans with Disabilities Act and similar state and local statutes.

Charles primarily represents franchisors in a wide variety of industries, including the quick-serve restaurant, hotel/hospitality, home improvement and automotive services industries. Charles' client-focused approach emphasizes creative problem-solving, risk minimization, and strategic counseling to achieve the best possible outcomes for his clients.

Charles has been an active member of the ABA Forum on Franchising, including writing articles for *The Franchise Law Journal* and *The Franchise Lawyer*, speaking at several of the Forum's annual conferences, and serving on certain committees. Charles has also been active in the ABA's Section of Litigation, in particular, the Intellectual Property Litigation Committee, for which he has co-chaired certain subcommittees. Charles has also long been active in the Philadelphia Bar Association, for which he currently co-chairs its Franchise Law Committee, and for which he previously served as chair of its Federal Courts Committee and led investigative teams for its Commission on Judicial Selection and Retention. Charles also previously served on the boards of the Young Lawyers Sections of both the Philadelphia and Palm Beach County Bar Associations.

Charles earned his law degree from the University of Pennsylvania ("Penn") and a Bachelor of Arts in History and a Bachelor of Science in Economics from Penn's College of Arts and Sciences and Wharton School of Business. Charles is the Immediate Past President of The Wharton Alumni Club of Philadelphia and has served as President and on the boards of a number of nonprofit and charitable organizations, including Delaware Valley Habitat for Humanity, The Chestnut Hill Community Fund and Settlement Music School.

Charles is an avid tennis player and plays keyboards in the rock band Lincoln Drive.

FOREWORD

The Forum's *Annual Franchise and Distribution Law Developments* book is a jewel in our Forum and its creation is one of the most challenging assignments for a Forum member to take on. Every year, the two authors of this book become familiar with and summarize the entire body of franchise-related law that our nation's courts issue for the year—generally at least hundreds of cases—as well as analyze international developments that are authored by our international contributors from select countries. This is no small endeavor, especially among competing client needs, business demands, and family and friend obligations. While this is a challenging assignment, it is also a very rewarding experience as the authors become all the more experts and scholars in our field. The authors' commitment and sacrifice ultimately benefits their clients, firms, and colleagues—and luckily all of us readers.

On behalf of the Governing Committee of the Forum, the 46th Annual Forum Co-Chairs Nicole Liguori Micklich and Heather Carson Perkins, and the entire membership of the Forum, I share our immense gratitude to the authors of the *Annual Franchise and Distribution Law Developments 2023* book, Annie Caiola of Caiola & Rose in Atlanta, Georgia and Chuck Marion of Blank Rome in Philadelphia, Pennsylvania and Fort Lauderdale, Florida. They dove into this assignment without hesitation to advance our Forum and improve the understanding and scholarship of franchise law. They embody our Forum's ideals of being the preeminent forum for the study and discussion of the legal aspect of franchising. Thank you, Annie and Chuck!

This year's book is again a strong example of the elevated scholarship that our Forum is known for. Our authors have covered cases across a wide span of topics, including developing law about misclassification of franchises, anti-poaching policies, the federal Trafficking Victims Protection Reauthorization Act, and motor vehicle dealer laws, as well as ongoing developments in vital topics such as performance, termination, and transfer disputes and non-competition and non-solicitation. Our members do not want to miss the signature plenary presentation by Annie and Chuck at our annual meeting in Dallas, where they will put their hard work and the year's legal developments into context.

I also thank Earsa Jackson, who edited the *Annual Franchise and Distribution Law Developments 2023* book. Earsa is a member of our Governing Committee and also authored her own book—the *Annual Franchise and Distribution Law Developments 2016* book—along with David

FOREWORD

Gurnick. Earsa knows the effort that goes into writing this book, and the editor's aid on this book is essential due to the wide-ranging topics and coverage. I also share our thanks to the Forum's International Division, led by Nicky Broadhurst, and the authors in this division who contributed sections for specific country developments in franchising. The Forum also thanks Ben Reed, the Forum's Publications Officer during the production of this book, and Sarah Orwig of the ABA publications staff and her team.

I hope you enjoy the *Annual Franchise and Distribution Law Developments 2023* book and use it to increase your knowledge and benefit your practice. It is a valuable addition to the Forum's scholarship. Thank you again to Annie and Chuck for their commitment and hard work on this important book.

Elizabeth M. Weldon
Chair, Forum on Franchising

ACKNOWLEDGMENTS

The African proverb "It takes a village to raise a child" could almost be applied to the production of this book. While perhaps not quite a village, it took a tremendous team effort to bring this volume to fruition, and Annie and Chuck are extremely and eternally grateful to all those who assisted and supported them along the way.

We would like to begin by thanking the co-chairs of this year's Annual Meeting, Nicole Liguori Micklich and Heather Carson Perkins, for entrusting us with this very important responsibility and for giving us the honor of presenting highlights from this book at the Forum's upcoming annual conference in Dallas. We appreciate the faith they have shown in us and the invaluable support and encouragement they have given us along the way. We are also grateful for the guidance and moral and other support provided along the way by our Program Director, Earsa Jackson.

The cover of this book should really list each and every person who helped us read and summarize the franchise and distribution cases decided in the last year. But alas, the cover is short and the list is long. The following colleagues of ours made various key contributions to the book (while at the same time continuing to handle their important client matters) and we truly could not have done this without them:

From Blank Rome: attorneys Greg Bailey, Alex Dondershine, Tom Dydek, Spencer Ebach, Devan McCarrie, Scarlett Montenegro Ordonez, Kevin Moran, Ben Reyes and Sabrina Rubis, law students/summer associates Rachel Finkelstein, Aria Janiszewski, Amanda Januszewski, Layla Najjar, Feven Negussie, Kira Pyne, Sarah Thorpe, and Deniz Tunceli, and a special shout-out to Chuck's Professional Assistant, Barb Evans, who day in and day out organized us, inputted cases into our master spreadsheet, assigned them to lawyers for review, and provided encouragement and many friendly reminders along the way!

From Caiola & Rose: Attorneys Elizabeth Rose, Jimmy Faris, Kimberly Reeves, Kathryn Rookes, Lindsay Henner, Leah Leipold, Setarah Jahid, Christen Morgan, Meredith Barnes and Drew

ACKNOWLEDGMENTS

Stevens, and a special shout-out to Tina Christensen and Amber Springer-Lamb, whose daily emails assigning cases for review were consistently met with smiles and eagerness to read another case!

We are also appreciative of the Forum's International Division which provided summaries of developments around the world, and in particular Australia (Iain Irvine and Riley Tully); Cambodia (Jay Cohen, Chanraksmey Sokun and Teo Pastor); India (Srijoy Das, Disha Mohanty, and Shivalik Chandan); Malta (Philip Formosa and Andrea Grima); New Zealand (Stewart Germann); Thailand (Sher Hann Chua and Alan Adcock); Ukraine (Anzhela Makhinova) and Vietnam (Tu Ngoc Trinh, Waewpen Piemwichai and Linh Thi Mai Nguyen).

Chuck and Annie would like to give a special thanks to Dan Oates and Susan Tegt, who quite literally descended the stage after their 2022 Annual Developments presentation and sat down and met with Chuck and Annie to tell and show them how they went about producing their edition of this book and help us begin preparing for our book and presentation. We also thank all of the past co-authors and co-presenters of Annual Developments, as it has been quite helpful to look back and build on what you did and because your examples and contributions made this daunting process far more organized and manageable.

Annie would also like to further recognize Elizabeth Rose – the first person Annie spoke to after receiving the phone call from the Forum's leadership asking her to co-present Annual Developments. While Annie's first reaction was concern about whether she had the capacity to make this commitment, Elizabeth's immediate response was: "This is not for you to do alone. We have built an A+ team, and our team is going to nail this." And nail it we did! Thank you, Elizabeth, for your unwavering support of me personally and your uncompromised commitment to our firm and our clients. Annie would also like to thank her husband Greg Caiola, for understanding the commitment this takes, for making sacrifices to be all-in with me, for keeping the wheels on the bus at home and in the office – and most importantly, for keeping me focused on what matters most!

Chuck also thanks his family - his amazing wife Mandy and his wonderful kids Daniel, Mia and Rachel - for being incredibly supportive and tolerant of his efforts, even when it took him away from family events and activities. Chuck dedicates his portions of the book to them.

And to you the reader, we hope this book is useful to your practice and helpful to your clients. Enjoy the read – it's a real page-turner!

INTRODUCTION

After reviewing several hundred franchise and distribution cases that were decided during the reporting period of August 1, 2022 through July 31, 2023, it's fair to say that if the reader is looking for clarity or predictability in outcomes to aid their law practice, those things won't be found here. The cases covered in this book go a variety of ways, even among very similar factual circumstances. On the down-side, this book doesn't reveal any easy answers or silver bullets. On the up-side, franchise and distribution lawyers continue to enjoy job security. This book is packed with discreet cases that rule on discreet issues, and it also includes the continuation of several cases that franchise and distribution lawyers have been following for years.

On that note, franchisor Jan-Pro continues to make headlines in what seems like never-ending litigation involving alleged misclassification of franchisees. In *Roman v. Jan-Pro Franchising International, Inc.* (discussed at length in Chapter 7), the Northern District of California ruled for a second time on the merits of the plaintiffs' claims after initially granting summary judgment in favor Jan-Pro, only to have that decision overturned and remanded by the Ninth Circuit, following the California Supreme Court's adoption of the "ABC test" in *Dynamex Operations W. v. Superior Court*, 4 Cal. 5th 903, 955, 416 P.3d 1, 34 (2018). On its second pass, the Northern District of California certified a limited class and then granted summary judgment, this time in favor of the plaintiffs on all class-certified claims. And as if franchisors of janitorial cleaning businesses have a target on their backs, a similar result was reached in *Jani-King of New York, Inc. v. Commissioner of Labor*, where the New York Supreme Court found that franchisees of Jani-King's regional divisions were liable for the franchisees' unemployment insurance contributions because an employer/employee relationship existed.

This year also presented a substantial volume of cases brought against hotel franchisors under the federal Trafficking Victims Protection Reauthorization Act ("TVPRA"). Most of these cases follow a similar trend (at least in the Middle District of Florida), where certain claims are dismissed on the basis that the complaint fails to state a plausible claim that the franchisor participated in the sex trafficking venture or had actual or constructive knowledge of the venture. However, many courts have found that

Introduction

factual questions exist as to the franchisor's control over the hotel. The Southern District of Ohio has taken a different view from the Middle District of Florida. In *A.R. v. Wyndham Hotels & Resorts, Inc.* the Ohio federal court denied the franchisor's motion to dismiss, concluding (among other things) that a franchisor's knowledge of sex trafficking generally at its hotels, and failure to adequately train staff, met the constructive knowledge requirement under the TVPRA. These cases are discussed in Chapter 6, Section XI.

During the reporting year, the Eleventh Circuit aligned with the Washington Attorney General when it reversed a trial court's decision regarding a "No-Hire Agreement" (a/k/a a "No-Poach Provision") which prevents franchisees from soliciting employees of other franchisees. While the trial court found that the "No Hire Agreement" did not violate the Sherman Act because the franchisor and franchisee constituted a single enterprise, the Eleventh Circuit reversed, finding that franchisees compete among one another and therefore are capable of engaging in the type of concerted activity required for claims under the Sherman Act. *Arrington v. Burger King Worldwide, Inc.* is discussed further in Chapter 6.

Finally, on the dealership side, Tesla once again found itself in the headlines, this time after the Delaware Division of Motor Vehicles denied its application for a new dealer license so that it could sell its electric vehicles directly to consumers. According to the Delaware DMV (and the Delaware Superior Court which affirmed the DMV's decision), the Delaware Franchise Act prohibits manufacturers from selling vehicles directly to consumers. The Delaware Supreme Court however reversed course, explaining that the legislative intent behind the Delaware Franchise Act was to regulate the relationship between manufacturers and dealers, and not to prohibit a direct sales model. So readers can rest comfortably knowing they can buy their self-driving cars directly from Tesla, at least in Delaware. *Tesla Inc. v. Delaware Division of Motor Vehicles* is discussed further in Chapter 3.

Before turning the page, the authors would like to note that they exercised discretion in determining which cases to include in this book. While they endeavored to summarize every franchise and distribution case decided during the reporting period, not all cases are summarized, particularly if the opinion had insufficient legal analysis, if the opinion was the result of a default or unopposed motion, or if the case involved other technicalities not germane to franchise and distribution law. Likewise, the summaries themselves are based on what the authors deemed appropriate in their judgment. The summaries are intended to give a very high overview of some, but not all, issues in a case. Since every case is different, practitioners should review the full case thoroughly before citing the case to a court or otherwise relying on the summary. In addition, readers should review the case history and

INTRODUCTION

procedural posture of the case to confirm the case is still good law. Finally, the authors did not designate unpublished opinions, and not every case summarized in the book can be cited as precedent.

CHAPTER 1

The Elements of a Franchise Relationship

I. Introduction

There was not an extensive amount of court opinions this year on the elements of a franchise relationship under federal or state law. Similarly, the amount of court opinions on whether a relationship between two parties constituted a dealership was slim. However, the court opinions that were issued shed light on the elements that influence whether a franchise or dealership relationship exists between parties. For instance, in a California case in which the plaintiff asserted violations of California Franchise Relations Act and the California Franchise Investment Law, the court concluded that while one element of the three-prong test was met, the other two were not. And therefore, the court concluded that a franchise relationship did not exist between the parties. Additionally, this year, there was a stand-out court opinion on an accidental franchise relationship based in Missouri, where New Jersey's franchise statute influenced claims brought under the Missouri Franchise Act, and the court found that a franchise relationship did exist between the parties.

II. Essential Elements of a Franchise

Absolute USA, Inc. v. Harman Professional, Inc., No. 221CV06410MEMFMAAX, 2023 WL 2064048 (C.D. Cal. Feb. 14, 2023). Absolute USA, Inc. ("Absolute") entered into a non-exclusive dealership agreement with Harman Professional, Inc. ("Harman") to sell Harman's

CHAPTER 1

audio-video equipment. Harman later terminated the dealership agreement, and as a result Absolute sued Harmon asserting not only breach of contract and related claims, but also violations of the California Franchise Relations Act ("CFRA") and the California Franchise Investment Law ("CFIL"). Harmon moved to dismiss Absolute's CFRA and CFIL claims, necessitating a determination as to whether the relationship between Harmon and Absolute was that of a franchisor/franchisee under California law.

Both the CFRA and the CFIL define a franchise as a contract, either express or implied, whether oral or written, by which (1) a franchisee is granted the right to engage in a marketing system substantially prescribed by the franchisor; (2) the business is substantially associated with the franchisor's trademark or other commercial symbol; and (3) the franchisee is required to pay a franchise fee.

Applying these three elements to the relationship between Absolute and Harmon, the court concluded that although Absolute's complaint alleged facts sufficient to satisfy the second element–the business's substantial association with the "franchisor's" trademark–it failed to allege sufficient facts to satisfy the other two elements–the existence of a marketing plan and the requirement of a franchise fee. These failures, coupled with the dealership agreement's express language that the agreement was to be "narrowly tailored to retail distribution only" and that "[n]othing stated in th[e] agreement shall be construed as creating the relationship of franchisor and franchisee," was more than sufficient for the court to find that a franchise relationship did not exist between the parties. The court consequently dismissed Absolute's CFRA and CFIL claims.

Fenix Group LLC v. GPM Investments, LLC, No. CV-18-6043242-S, 2023 WL 369986 (Conn. Super. Ct. Jan. 17, 2023). Fenix and GPM entered into three agreements which together allowed Fenix to operate a Valero gas station and convenience store. Under one of the agreements, the "Consignment Supply Agreement," GPM agreed to furnish petroleum products to Fenix. GPM was the sole provider and set the prices at which the products were to be sold, and Fenix paid security deposits for the rent due under the sublease agreement (subleasing the premises where the gas station was located) and for the gasoline provided under the Consignment Supply Agreement. Central to the opinion was Fenix's allegations that GPM violated the Connecticut Petroleum Franchise Act (CPFA), and the court proceeded to analyze whether the relationship constituted a franchise arrangement. GPM argued that it did not because Fenix did not *purchase* any of the petroleum products but rather received them from GPM on consignment. The court first noted the definitions of "franchisor" and "franchisee" under the CPFA and that both include reference to a retailer, but that the statute does not define the term "retailer." The court compared the CPFA to the Federal Petroleum Marketing Practices Act (PMPA), which includes a limitation on the definition of the word retailer, namely, that the entity must *purchase* petroleum to get the protection of the PMPA. In contrast to the limitation in the PMPA, the CPFA does not contain any requirement that the franchisee must *purchase* anything. Thus, the court concluded that the relationship was one of franchisor/franchisee and the CPFA and its protections applied, and denied the defendant's motion for summary judgment as to the plaintiff's claims for violations of the CPFA.

In ***Fluid Power Engineering Co., Inc. v. Cognex Corp.***, No. 22 CV 2707, 2022 WL 16856395 (N.D. Ill. Nov. 10, 2022), the district court of Illinois granted defendant Cognex Corporation's ("Cognex") motion to dismiss on the basis that plaintiff, Fluid Power Engineering Company, Inc. ("FPE"), failed to properly state its claim that Cognex violated the Illinois Franchise Disclosure Act ("IFDA").

The dispute arose out of a one-year strategic partnership agreement between FPE and Cognex under which Cognex granted FPE the right to sell its products in Illinois and Iowa (the "Agreement"). The Agreement explicitly stated that FPE acted as an independent purchaser and that a franchise relationship did not exist between the parties. Six years into their partnership, Cognex notified FPE that it would not be renewing their Agreement. FPE then sued Cognex for allegedly violating the IFDA, and Cognex removed the case to federal court and filed a motion to dismiss for failure to state a claim.

The district court found that the IFDA did not apply to the Agreement because FPE did not directly pay a franchise fee to FPE. Further, despite FPE's argument that it indirectly paid a franchise fee through purchasing demonstration equipment and hiring and training Cognex managers, the district court concluded otherwise. Rather, the district court found that their purchase of demonstration equipment was an agreement to purchase goods for which there is an established market, which is not considered a franchise under the IFDA. The court likened the requirement to purchase demonstration equipment to a sales quota, noting that the plaintiff was only required to purchase a small amount of equipment (sufficient to make an adequate demonstration) and that the plaintiff was not seriously disadvantaged by purchasing the equipment after the relationship ended.

Additionally, the district court found that the costs FPE incurred to hire and train Cognex managers were not an indirect franchise fee because these costs were not "substantial" and "unrecoverable" as the Seventh Circuit held in *Wright-Moore Corp. v. Ricoh Corp.*, 980 F.2d 432 (7th Cir. 1992).

Accordingly, the district court found that Cognex did not violate the IFDA because a franchise relationship did not exist between the parties. Therefore, the district court granted Cognex's motion to dismiss for FPE's failure to properly state a claim.

Good Times Restaurants, LLC v. Shindig Hospitality Group, LLC, No. 21-CV-07688-AGT, 2022 WL 16856106 (N.D. Cal. Nov. 10, 2022). Defendant asserted a counterclaim against plaintiff under California's Franchise Investment Law ("CFIL") and other state franchise laws. In response, plaintiff filed a motion to dismiss, arguing that the contract between the parties did not plausibly establish a franchise under the CFIL. The Court rejected this argument and denied the motion to dismiss.

In doing so, the court found that the defendant had plausibly alleged that the fee required to be paid to plaintiff in exchange for the right to use a trade name while operating a specific restaurant concept could plausibly be construed as a franchise fee under the CFIL. The court thus denied the motion to dismiss. Given that plaintiff failed to identify any reason why defendant's other state law claims should be treated any differently from its CFIL claim, the court denied the motion to dismiss as to the other state law claims, as well.

In ***Neff Group Distributors, Inc. v. Cognex Corp.***, No. CV 22-11270-NMG, 2022 WL 17156025 (D. Mass. Nov. 22, 2022), the district court held that the distributor plaintiff was not a franchisee under the Indiana Deceptive Franchise Practices Act, because the cost of the excess inventory the plaintiff had purchased from the defendant did not constitute a "franchise fee," as required by the statute. This case is discussed in Chapter 4, Section II.F.

III. Essential Elements of a Dealership

Track, Inc. v. ASH North America, Inc., No. 21-cv-786-jdp, 2023 WL 2733679 (W.D. Wis. Mar. 31, 2023) (denying manufacturer-defendant's motion to dismiss the complaint asserted claims for violation of Wisconsin's Fair Dealership Law, under which a dealership is defined as (1) a contract or agreement, (2) that grants a person the right to sell or distribute a product or use certain branding materials, (3) that demonstrates a community of interest in the business, and finding that plaintiff-dealer's claim was for the unlawful termination of its exclusive sales territories and the geographic exclusivity to sell large and costly snow removal vehicles under the agreement in question, which constituted a plausible community of interest).

The Elements of a Franchise Relationship

IV. Accidental Franchises

Good Times Restaurants, LLC v. Shindig Hospitality Group, LLC, No. 21-CV-07688-AGT, 2022 WL 16856106 (N.D. Cal. Nov. 10, 2022) (denying motion to dismiss for failure to state a claim under California's Franchise Investment Law and the FTC's Franchise Rule based on counterclaimant's plausible allegations that the contract between the parties established a franchise). This case is discussed in Chapter 1, Section II.

Major Brands, Inc. v. Mast-Jägermeister US, Inc., No. 18-CV-423-HEA, 2022 WL 3585605 (E.D. Mo. Aug 22, 2022). Major Brands, Inc. and Mast-Jagermeister US, Inc. ("Jagermeister") had a 40-year relationship whereby Major Brands sold Jagermeister products in the state of Missouri. Jagermeister terminated the relationship with Major Brands, and Major Brands filed a lawsuit in the Eastern District of Missouri, asserting claims against Jagermeister under the Missouri Franchise Act ("MFA").

Following a jury trial, damages were assessed against Jagermeister and the other defendants in an amount of $11,750,000. Jagermeister then moved for judgment as a matter of law or remittitur pursuant to Federal Rule of Civil Procedure 50 and 59(e). The court held that the record included sufficient evidence to support the verdicts and denied Jagermeister's motion.

Jagermeister argued that its relationship with Major Brands and others was merely a traditional distribution relationship and that the evidence at trial was insufficient to establish a franchise under the MFA. The court had previously held that for a franchise to exist under the MFA, Jägermeister must have granted Plaintiff a license to use its trade name, trademark, or service mark, and there must be a community of interest in the marketing of goods or services.

The court took up the community of interest requirement first to determine if the MFA applied. The court explained that the Missouri courts have not set forth a framework for determining a community of interest. Based on the similarities of the New Jersey franchise statute to the Missouri statute at issue, the court applied the Third Circuit's guidance on whether a franchise exists. The Third Circuit's two-part test for determining whether a community of interest exists analyzes whether (1) the distributor's investments were substantially franchise-specific, and (2) the distributor was required to make these investments by the parties' agreement or by the nature of the business. The court also relied upon the Seventh Circuit's analysis of a very similar Wisconsin Fair Dealership Law.

The court pointed to the following evidence to hold that a reasonable jury could find a community of interest: (1) Major Brands had a prominent

CHAPTER 1

role in marketing and promoting Jagermeister in Missouri and made investments in the local marketing fund in excess of the required contribution amount; (2) Major Brands agreed to send $2 per case of Jagermeister sold to Jagermeister headquarters for use in its national advertising; (3) Major Brands had a dedicated employee who only sold Jagermeister; and (4) Jagermeister asked Major Brands to stop selling product in 2017 to allegedly boost sales in 2018. Jagermeister argued that the revenue from Jagermeister sales for Major Brands was not a large enough proportion of its total revenue to have a community of interests. The court, however, held that a reasonable jury could conclude that Major Brands made the specialized type of investment in Jagermeister to find a community of interests. Having found that a reasonable jury could find a community of interest based on the evidence, the court turned to the jury's finding that Jagermeister granted Major Brands a trademark license. Evidence presented to the jury included that Major Brands had access to Jagermeister's trademarks, used Jagermeister's logos and images in its business, and had access to Jagermeister's password protected website. The court held that the jury had sufficient evidence to reasonably conclude that the public understood that there was a connection between Major Brands and Jagermeister and Jagermeister had granted Major Brands a trademark license.

As such, the court held the jury's determination that a valid franchise existed between the parties was reasonable based on the evidence presented and denied Jagermeister's motions. The court distinguished a 2014 distributor case that Jagermeister relied on heavily, *Bacardi U.S.A., Inc. v. Major Brands, Inc.*, 2014 WL 2200042 (S.D. Fla. Mar. 20, 2014). The court emphasized that the *Bacardi* court held that the MFA did not apply. Additionally, the court distinguished the *Barcardi* case by noting that the parties had written agreements which governed Major Brands's use of Bacardi's trademarks and which required prior specific permission from Bacardi to use Barcardi's marks.

In connection with the termination of Major Brands, Jagermeister entered into an agreement with Southern Glazers Wine & Spirits of Missouri for the Missouri territory. In this action, Major Brands also asserted claims against Southern Glazers for tortious interference and civil conspiracy to violate the MFA. With respect to the civil conspiracy claim, evidence was presented that Southern Glazers and Jagermeisters discussed that Missouri was a franchise state and Southern Glazers ultimately agreed to indemnify Jagermeisters for wrongful termination claims. The jury verdict against both Jagermeister and Southern Glazers was upheld.

CHAPTER 2

Registration and Disclosure

I. Introduction

Whether within or outside the bounds of a Franchise Disclosure Document, franchisees may assert claims against franchisors for alleged violations of federal and state disclosure requirements, negligent misrepresentations or omissions, and fraud. In one court opinion issued from the Eastern District of New York, the court explained that the New York Franchise Sales Act ("NYFSA") has a broad definition of a franchise, and allows for claims against officers of the company individually.

II. Violations of Registration or Disclosure Requirements

LG2, LLC v. American Dairy Queen Corporation, No. 22-cv-1044 (WMW/JFD), 2023 WL 171792 (D. Minn. Jan. 12, 2023). A Dairy Queen franchisee, LG2, brought an action against the franchisor American Dairy Queen ("ADQ") in the District Court of Minnesota. LG2 asserted claims for breach of contract and the implied covenant of good faith and fair dealing, violation of the Minnesota Franchise Act (MFA), and declaratory judgment.

LG2's franchise rights originated from a 1961 legacy agreement between ADQ and Bob Denny, which was assigned with ADQ's consent several times, including the 2019 assignment to LG2. The dispute arises from ADQ's refusal to permit LG2 to relocate its restaurant 1.5 miles from the approved location in Oklahoma. ADQ's headquarters are in Minneapolis.

ADQ moved to dismiss LG2's claim for violation of the MFA for failure to state a claim and to transfer venue to the Eastern District of Texas.

Registration and Disclosure

With respect to its motion to dismiss, ADQ asserted that the MFA does not apply because the MFA only applies to franchisees located in Minnesota. The court noted that courts disagree as to the application of the MFA to franchisees located outside of Minnesota. LG2 asserted that because ADQ's headquarters are in Minneapolis, the offer of franchise in connection with the 2019 transfer of the franchise agreement was made in the state of Minnesota.

The court granted ADQ's motion to dismiss the violation of MFA's claim because it found that ADQ's consent to the 2019 Assignment, Guaranty, and Consent Agreement, which granted LG2 its franchise rights from the prior franchisee was not an offer of sale under or purchase of a franchise within the meaning on the MFA. The court held that as a matter of law the MFA exempts a franchisor's consent to a franchise assignment from a sale or an offer to sale. The court explained that Section 80C.03(a) of the MFA clarifies that a sale is not effected by or through a franchisor merely because a franchise has a right to approve or disapprove a different franchisee.

The court denied ADQ's motion to transfer to the district court in which the restaurant was located and addressed each of the four transfer factors applied by 28 U.S.C. § 1404(a). The court noted that a defendant seeking transfer bears a heavy burden of proof to establish that the transfer is warranted. After reviewing each factor and finding one factor in favor of LG2, one factor in favor of ADQ and two factors being neutral, the motion to transfer was denied.

Lunt v. Frost Shades Franchising, LLC, No. 3:22-cv-00775, 2023 WL 3484202 (M.D. Tenn May 16, 2023). Bob Lunt signed a franchise agreement with Frost Shades Franchising, LLC ("Frost Shades") to operate the franchised business of selling and installing window tinting and films in South Carolina. Lunt later claimed that in addition to Frost Shades having never provided an operational manual or sufficient training, the FDD he was disclosed on was deficient as it related to Item 3. Specifically, two of Frost Shades' owners (Goldberg and Swanson) were previously involved with another franchisor (Patch Boys Franchising) which was subject to the following actions: 1) two private lawsuits brought by franchisees against the franchisor and both Goldberg and Swanson in the District of Minnesota; 2) an investigation by the Minnesota Department of Commerce, resulting in consent order whereby the franchisor and Goldberg acknowledged violation of the Minnesota Franchise Act; and 3) an investigation by the Attorney General of New York, resulting in assurance of discontinuance whereby the franchisor and Goldberger acknowledged they had failed to disclose Goldberg's 1999 felony conviction for credit card fraud. Nevertheless, in response to Item 3,

CHAPTER 2

Frost Shade's FDD stated: "No litigation is required to be disclosed in this Item."

Lunt brought claims in the United States District Court of the Middle District of Tennessee for fraudulent inducement, fraudulent concealment, fraudulent misrepresentation, restitution, recission and for an injunction, prohibiting Frost Shades from enforcing its noncompete. In response to Lunt's lawsuit, Frost Shades filed a motion to compel arbitration. Upholding the Federal Arbitration Act, the court stayed the proceedings while granting the motion to compel arbitration. However, the court retained jurisdiction over Lunt's claim for injunctive relief.

After examining the parties' conflicting choice of law arguments, the court ultimately found that Lunt had demonstrated a likelihood of success on the merits of the fraud claim because the prior actions involving Patch Boys likely should have been disclosed, which supports an "inference that the defendants were aware that they had improperly omitted items from the FDD and that they committed those omissions for the purpose of inducing Lunt's reliance." On the irreparable harm factor, the court found that while the showing of irreparable harm was not "overwhelming," Lunt had sufficiently demonstrated that his right to operate a business in the field of choosing was separate from his claim for damages. In analyzing the balance of equities, the court found that the harm Lunt would suffer by complying with the noncompete was worse than the harm Frost Shades would suffer if he did not comply with it. In terms of the public interest factor, the court found that public interest disfavors restraints on trade and interference with a person's livelihood. And while there is also a public interest in enforcing contracts, here, that circles back to the merits of the claim which favor Lunt. As a result, the court granted the injunction in favor of Lunt insofar as he was not required to comply with the non-compete, but the court declined to extend the injunction to prohibit Frost Shades from competing with Lunt which he had also requested.

In *Sea Tow Services International, Inc. v. Tampa Bay Marine*, No. 20-CV-2877(JS)(SIL), 2022 WL 5122728 (E.D.N.Y. Sept. 30, 2022), Sea Tow International, Inc. ("Sea Tow"), as the franchisor, was party to a franchise agreement with a Florida-based entity, Tampa Bay Marine Towing & Services ("TBM-Towing"), as the franchisee. TBM-Towing had operated a Sea Tow franchise since 2002. In 2015, Kathleen and Raul Moreno ("Morenos") purchased TBM-Towing and later entered into the-then current franchise agreement, which allowed for the continued operation of the franchise and provided an exclusive area of responsibility ("AOR") in a portion of Tampa Bay, Florida. The franchise agreement required customers pay certain annual

Registration and Disclosure

fees directly to Sea Tow, which were then shared between Sea Tow and the franchisee pursuant to a confidential formula.

The Morenos financed the purchase by obtaining a series of loans on which the Morenos subsequently defaulted. As a result of the Morenos' and TBM-Towing's defaults under the loans, one of its lenders initiated a collection action. Under the franchise agreement's default provisions, that collection action constituted a default that automatically terminated the franchise agreement. Following that automatic termination, Sea-Tow, TBM-Towing, and the Morenos entered into a termination agreement. As part of the termination agreement, and at the Morenos' request, Sea-Tow appointed Tampa Bay Marine Recovery, Inc. ("TBM-Recovery") and Erich and Abigail Jaeger ("Jeagers") as managers of the AOR. Under that management agreement, TBM-Recovery agreed to operate under the franchise agreement and to pay Sea Tow 15% of the gross revenues generated by the AOR, among other things. In the interim, TBM-Towing filed for bankruptcy, in which TBM-Towing asked the bankruptcy court to require Sea Tow to turn over the terminated franchise agreement, as well as certain membership fees. The bankruptcy filing was eventually dismissed before any ruling on the request to turn over the franchise agreement.

Thereafter, Sea Tow terminated the management agreement with TBM-Recovery and the Jaegers, based on alleged violations of both the management agreement and the franchise agreement. Sea Tow then filed suit against TBM-Towing, the Morenos (along with another entity owned by the Morenos), the Jaegers, and TBM-Recovery for a variety of claims including (1) fraud and related conspiracy claims; (2) trademark infringement; and (3) breach of the franchise agreement, breach of the termination agreement, and breach of the management agreement. The Jaegers filed a third-party complaint and counterclaims against Sea Tow, as well as its general counsel and chief executive officer alleging, in part, claims of (1) violation of the New York Franchise Sales Act ("NYFSA") and (2) violations of the Florida Business Opportunities Act.

Sea Tow moved for judgment on the pleadings as to the Jaegers' third-party complaint, and the defendants filed motions to dismiss Sea Tow's complaint, as amended. Certain of Sea Tow's fraud claims were premised upon TBM-Towing's bankruptcy filing for the alleged purpose of reinstating the terminated franchise agreement. The court dismissed those claims on the basis that filing a bankruptcy petition is a lawful right and, as such, cannot form the basis of a claim for fraud, even if the lawful act was done maliciously. The court ruled that the remaining fraud claims related to alleged concealments and misrepresentations as to the parties' intertwined underlying

CHAPTER 2

contracts were stated with the particularity required under New York law and denied the motion to dismiss those claims.

As for the Jaegers' counterclaim for violation of the NYFSA, the Jaegers argued that Sea Tow violated the NYFSA by (i) failing to register an offering prospectus with the state's attorney general's office; (ii) failing to make the required disclosures; and (iii) fraud-based violations under the NYFSA. Sea Tow argued that the management agreement was not a franchise agreement and therefore the NYFSA was inapplicable.

The court noted that the NYSFA's definition of a franchise is broad, and applies any time a franchisee is either: (1) granted the right to operate under the franchisor's marketing plan or system in exchange for a franchise fee; or (2) is granted the right to use the franchisor's "trademark, service mark, trade name, logotype, advertising, or other commercial symbol designating the franchisor" in exchange for a franchise fee. *Citing* N.Y. Gen. Bus. Law § 681(3)(a)(b) (McKinney). "Franchisee fee" is defined as "any fee or charge that a franchisee or subfranchisor is required to pay or agrees to pay directly or indirectly for the right to enter into a business under a franchise agreement or otherwise sell, resell or distribute goods, services, or franchises under such an agreement ...." *Id.* § 681(7).

The court found that the management agreement fell within the ambit of the NYFSA because the management fees paid to Sea Tow were paid for the right to enter into a business that was governed by the franchise agreement and for the right to use Sea Tow's marks. The management agreement also required compliance with the franchise agreement.

The court also rejected Sea Tow's arguments that: (1) the management agreement nevertheless fell within an isolated sales exemption, or (2) that even if the NYFSA applied, the Jaegers could not allege any harm or damages as a result of the failure to register and make the required disclosures. The court ruled that the isolated sales exemption is a narrow one, and only applies when the franchisor sells a single franchise. Because Sea Tow sold franchises to other entities, even if outside of New York, the exemption did not apply. Noting that this matter was at the pleading stage, the court found that the Jaegers' allegations that they had been damaged because the lack of disclosures caused these defendants to enter into the management agreement were sufficient to state a claim. In addition, the court noted that the NYFSA authorizes rescission of the franchise agreement where a violation is willful and material, and whether the Sea Tow's failure to comply with the NYFSA was willful and material was a question of fact.

The Jaeger defendants also alleged that Sea Tow's failure to comply with the registration and disclosure requirements was a violation of Section 687 of the NYFSA's prohibition on fraud and misrepresentation. Sea Tow

Registration and Disclosure

argued that the heightened pleading requirements for a fraud claim under New York law applied to any such claim under Section 687 of NYFSA and the Jaegers' allegations failed to meet this standard. The court noted that while the case law was unsettled, the growing consensus was to apply the heightened pleading standard to such claims and to require the plaintiff to sufficiently allege reliance to state a claim. The court then found that the Jaeger defendants could not plausibly allege reliance on any representations of Sea Tow or its representatives, because they had counsel to advise them as to the legal effect and nature of the transaction while entering into the management agreement.

The Jaegers also argued that the mere failure to register or to make disclosures was also tantamount to fraud under the NYFSA. The court rejected this argument, and found that to allow such a claim under the general disclosure requirements would render Section 687 superfluous, in violation of the rule of construction to interpret a statute to give effect to every provision. The sort of fraud claims that could be brought under the disclosure requirements were claims such as a misrepresentation of profitability or as to the training program, for example. Thus, the court granted Sea Tow's motion for judgment on the pleadings as to the fraud claims.

In addition to the claims against Sea Tow, the Jaegers also brought claims against Sea Tow's general counsel and chief executive officer, individually, for violating the NYFSA. Because the NYFSA also imposes sanctions on any corporate officer, director, or controlling persons, and because the Jaegers' provided detailed allegations as to these individuals' alleged participation in procuring the management agreement, the court allowed these claims to proceed against Sea Tow's general counsel and chief executive officer.

As noted above, the parties also alleged a variety of breach of contract claims. In analyzing these claims, the defendants asked the court to rule that the termination clause in the franchise agreement was invalid under New York law or was unconscionable, and therefore unenforceable. The court found that the termination clause was valid. The court noted that the NYFSA covers the formation of a franchise agreement, not the substance of the agreement or the termination of an agreement.

The court granted the motion to dismiss Sea Tow's claim to recover certain membership fees that it had collected and then shared with TBM-Towing and the Morenos. Under the franchise agreement, customers were to pay the fees directly to Sea Tow, which then divided between Sea Tow and the franchisee. When, however, a customer paid the fees directly to the franchisee, the franchisee had to hold those fees in trust and then send Sea Tow its share of the fees. There was nothing in the franchise agreement that required a franchisee to hold the fees Sea Tow provided to the franchisee in trust. Thus, there was no means to recover fees that had been previously disbursed by Sea Tow to the franchisee. However, the court also found that the Morenos and TBM-Towing were nevertheless liable for these fees under the terms of the parties' termination agreement.

The court also dismissed Sea Tow's claims for violation of the franchise agreement and related contracts' non-compete, non-disclosure requirements, as well as claims for trademark infringement. Sea Tow based these claims on disclosures that were made to the bankruptcy trustee and bankruptcy counsel in TBM-Towing's bankruptcy case, as well as court filings in that bankruptcy case. The defendants argued that these disclosures were protected by the attorney client privilege and the litigation privilege. The court granted the motion to dismiss these claims. The court also granted the motion to dismiss Sea Tow's claims that the Jaegers violated non-compete provisions. The court found that Sea Tow had not sufficiently pled any violation of the non-compete provisions.

The court denied Sea Tow's motion to dismiss the claims for violation of the Florida Business Opportunities Act. Sea Tow argued these claims were prohibited by the franchise agreement's New York choice of law provision. The court ruled that the choice of law provision did not preclude claims under other states' statutes.

III. Financial Performance Representations

Functional HIIT Fitness, LLC v. F45 Training Incorporated, No. 5:22-CV-10168, 2022 WL 17828930 (E.D. Mich. Oct. 26, 2022) (recommending the denial of the franchisor's motion to dismiss fraud and negligent misrepresentation claims based on allegedly false information in the Franchise Disclosure Document). This case is discussed in Chapter 8, Section IV.

IV. Other Misrepresentations or Omissions

The authors' review of cases decided during the reporting period did not reveal any significant decisions addressing this topic.

CHAPTER 3

Industry-Specific Statutes Affecting the Franchising Relationship

I. Introduction

As an added layer to the regulation of franchise sales, federal and state statutes offer an array of protections to dealers and distributors involved in the sale of petroleum, alcohol, and various types of equipment. During the reporting period, the bulk of the court opinions issued pertained to automobile and motor vehicle laws. Specifically, numerous alleged violations were brought under state specific statutes, such as South Carolina Code Ann. § 56-15, which prevents a franchisor from unreasonably withholding consent to the transfer of interest in a dealership and also prevents a franchisee from transferring its interest without required notice. Additionally, there were claims brought under the Automobile Dealers' Day in Court Act, which allows automobile dealers to "bring suit against any automobile manufacturer engaged in commerce... by reason of the failure of said automobile manufacturer... to act in good faith in performing or complying with any of the terms or provisions of the franchise...." 15 U.S.C. § 1222. In the beer and wine industry, during the reporting period, there was a notable court opinion from the Southern District of Ohio, where the court grappled with whether a party to the suit was a "a manufacturer" or "the manufacturer" in order to determine whether a franchise relationship existed.

Industry Specific Statutes Affecting the Franchising Relationship

II.   Petroleum Marketing Practices Act

ASA Enterprise, Inc. v. Stan Boyett & Son, Inc., No. 1:21-cv-00915-BAK, 2022 WL 4182188 (E.D. CA Sept. 13, 2022). In a case involving the termination of a franchise agreement to operate a gas station as a "76" brand station due to plaintiffs' failure to obtain passing scores of "mystery shop" inspections during which plaintiffs were found to have failed to comply with imaging standards, the court disagreed with plaintiffs' argument that Boyett's decision to terminate the agreement had to be in good faith and in the normal course of business. The court held that the Petroleum Marketing Practices Act ("PMPA") applies that standard to decisions to decline to renew a franchise agreement and that in the type of termination at issue in this case, Section 2802(b)(2)(E) of the PMPA applied. That Section provides that among the grounds for termination or non-renewal of a franchise were a failure by the franchisee to comply with any provision of the franchise agreement, which provision is both reasonable and of material significance to the franchise relationship, and that there was no basis or authority for implicitly reading into that termination provision the good faith and normal course of business standard. This case is discussed more fully in Chapter 8, Section XI.

Boca Gas Co. Holdings 2, LLC v. First Coast Energy, LLP, No. 3:23-CV-366-BJD-PDB, 2023 WL 3563460, at *1 (M.D. Fla. Apr. 26, 2023) (The court denied the plaintiff's request to enjoin the termination of a motor fuel franchise agreement on the basis that the plaintiff was entitled to ninety days' notice under the Petroleum Marketing Practices Act. The court noted that the plaintiff owed more than $2.7 million under the franchise agreement and that the franchisor had agreed to forebear, not waive its right to terminate, and had provided more than a year of advance notice it would terminate if the plaintiff did not cure its default. The court also found that the breaches of the franchise agreement, including plaintiff's sale of misbranded fuel, would justify termination on less than ninety days notice.)

In ***BP Products North America Inc., v. Blue Hills Fuels, LLC***, 2022 WL 16540804 (S.D.N.Y. Oct. 28, 2022), the U.S. District Court of the Southern District of New York largely denied the motions for summary judgment by each of Westward Service Station, Inc. ("Westward"), BP Products North America Inc. ("BP") and Blue Hills Fuels, LLC ("Blue Hills"). BP brought an action seeking a declaration that BP had lawfully terminated a lease for a gas station and the associated Dealer Agreement with Westward, following denial by the New York State Department of Transportation ("DOT") to withdraw its letter, which would require BP to remove two of the three curb cutouts present at the gas station.

BP argued that the Petroleum Marketing Practices Act ("PMPA") allowed BP to terminate the Dealer Agreement because the DOT's refusal to withdraw its letter was an "occurrence of an event which is relevant to the franchise relationship and as a result of which termination of the franchise [...] is reasonable, if such event occurs during the period the franchise is in effect." Westward responded that termination of the Dealer Agreement by BP was not reasonable because (1) the DOT issued their letter prior to BP and Westward entering into the Dealer Agreement and therefore the event had not occurred during the franchise relationship, and (2) BP did not meet the notice requirements outlined in the PMPA because it provided two alternative dates, not one specific termination date, in its notice of termination. On Westward's first argument, the court found that when BP requested reconsideration by the DOT and was rejected, a new event arose that could provide grounds for BP to reasonably terminate the Dealer Agreement. On Westward's second argument, the court found that so long as the notice of termination provided one, lawful date on which the termination could occur and so long as the termination did not occur prior to that date, the notice requirements under the PMPA were met.

BP also argued that the PMPA preempted Westward's counterclaims related to breach of contract and breach of the covenant of good faith and fair dealing. The court found that the Second Circuit has narrowly construed the preemption clause in the PMPA to mean that only laws that specifically address termination or non-renewal of franchises and conflict with the PMPA would be preempted. The court determined that one dispute of material fact remained concerning whether BP could safely operate the gas station if it complied with the DOT's letter. The court denied BP's motion for summary judgment, except with respect to Westward's counterclaim concerning breach of good faith and fair dealing because it was duplicative of Westward's claim for breach of contract. The court further denied Westward and Blue Hill's motion for summary judgment, except with respect to BP's claim of mutual mistake.

Nasreen v. Capitol Petroleum Group, LLC, No. 20-1867(TJK), 2023 WL 2734210 (D. D.C. March 31, 2023). Plaintiff operates a gas station under a franchise agreement with Anacostia Realty, LLC, which owns the lot the station is on. Capitol Petroleum Group, LLC helps Anacostia provide the gasoline services to plaintiff and issues invoices for Anacostia to plaintiff. After Anacostia tried to terminate the franchise agreement for failure to meet contractual obligations, plaintiff sued, claiming breach of contract and

Industry Specific Statutes Affecting the Franchising Relationship

violation of the Petroleum Marketing Practices Act ("PMPA"). The court granted the defendant's motion to dismiss on all claims. With respect to defendant Capitol Petroleum, the court found that Capital was not the franchisor and that only franchisors were governed by the PMPA. It further held that Capitol had no contract with the plaintiff.

As to defendant Anacostia, the court granted the motion to dismiss because the reasons given for Anacostia's termination of the contract were valid under the PMPA. Specifically, non-payment is one of the enumerated reasons in the PMPA for appropriate termination of a franchise agreement. Regarding the plaintiff's other breach of contract claims, the court dismissed them, finding that the plaintiff failed to comply with the payment provision, the minimum purchase provision, and that Anacostia's lease of awning space to Verizon was permissible under the lease (the lease included a provision that Anacostia could sublease to another party without sharing revenue so long as none of plaintiff's operations were interfered with, and plaintiff had no operations on the roof).

Sasoro 13, LLC v. 7-Eleven, Inc., No. 3:18-CV-03274-N, 2023 WL 2290788 (N.D. Tex. Feb. 27, 2023). This case arose out of defendant 7-Eleven's motion to dismiss all of plaintiff Sasoro's claims. Sasoro, owned by Henri and Ester Sas, operated a 7-Eleven gas station franchise in Las Vegas, Nevada. Under the parties' franchise agreement ("Agreement"), 7-Eleven had discretion to terminate the Agreement in several circumstances, including in the event that Sasoro failed to comply with its terms within a 2-year period. Between December 2021 and July 2022, 7-Eleven issued Sasoro ten notices of material breach for alleged noncompliance, including late and missing cash reports and refusing to permit 7-Eleven access to the premises. As a result, 7-Eleven notified plaintiffs that it was exercising its right to terminate the Agreement. The Sasoros initiated this litigation shortly thereafter, and 7-Eleven moved to dismiss.

First, the court dismissed the breach of contract claim. Sasoro's breach of contract claim was based on the implied covenant of good faith and fair dealing however, Texas courts only recognize an implied duty of good faith and fair dealing when intentionally created by express language in a contract *or* a special relationship of trust and confidence exists between the parties to the contract. Here, the Agreement lacked a provision incorporating the covenant, and Texas courts have held that the "special relationship" status does not extend to ordinary commercial contractual relationships, including in the franchisor-franchisee context. The court also held that Sasoro's allegations did not support its claim that 7-Eleven lacked authority to terminate the Agreement. The Agreement specifically stated that the occurrence of four instances of any noncompliance within two years is itself a material breach. Thus, post-notification corrections did not absolve Sasoro of noncompliance for purposes of the four-strike limit. The court held that because Sasoro had not sufficiently pled a term of the Agreement that 7-Eleven allegedly breached, its common law breach of contract claim failed.

Second, the court dismissed plaintiff's claim under Article 2 of the Texas Uniform Commercial Code ("UCC"). The court held that the heart of the transaction at issue was Sasoro's use of 7-Eleven's trademark, and that the essence of the Agreement was services, not goods. Though Sasoro purchased branded goods from 7-Eleven under the Agreement, it did so in connection with its contractual rights to use the 7-Eleven name. Thus, the court held that plaintiff's UCC claim failed.

Third, the court dismissed plaintiff's claim that defendant had violated the Petroleum Marketing Practices Act (PMPA), 15 U.S.C. § 2801. The court noted that the PMPA was enacted in "response to widespread concern over increasing numbers of allegedly unfair franchise terminations and nonrenewals in the petroleum industry" (citing *Mac's Shell Serv., Inc. v. Shell Oil Prods. Co.*, 559 U.S. 175, 178 (2010)). It protects covered franchisees by prohibiting early termination or nonrenewal except in specific circumstances. The PMPA applies to any contract between (i) a refiner and a distributor; (ii) a refiner and a retailer; (iii) a distributor and another distributor; or (iv) a distributor or a retailer, under which a refiner or distributor authorizes or permits a retailer or distributor to use, in connection with the sale, consignment, or distribution of motor fuel, a trademark which is owned or controlled by such refiner or by a refiner which supplies motor fuel to the distributor which authorizes or permits such use.

In order for Sasoro to invoke the protections of the PMPA, the court held that it had to satisfy the definition of either a retailer or a distributor. A covered retailer is "any person who purchases motor fuel for sale to the general public for ultimate consumption." 5 U.S.C. § 2801(7). Under the Consigned Gasoline Amendment ("Amendment") to the Agreement, Sasoro did not purchase fuel from 7-Eleven. Rather, 7-Eleven retained title to the gasoline until the moment of sale, and Sasoro earned a set commission. Thus, the court held that Sasoro is not a retailer within the meaning of the PMPA. A covered "distributor" is "any person" who "purchases motor fuel for sale, consignment, or distribution to another" or "receives motor fuel on consignment for consignment or distribution to his own motor fuel accounts or to accounts of his supplier." 15 U.S.C. §§ 2801(6)(A)–(B). Previous decisions clarify that this second definition of a distributor also does not encompass an entity that receives fuel on consignment for sale to the public.

Since Sasoro did not purchase gasoline from 7-Eleven, the court held that it also did not satisfy the first definition of a distributor.

Prior cases concluded that the structure of the PMPA considers the sale of fuel as separate and distinct from its distribution, and thus under the plain meaning of § 2801(B), a person is not a distributor if the person receives fuel on consignment for retail sale. Thus, the court held that Sasoro was a consignee rather than a purchaser of gasoline. The court further held that because the consignment was for retail sale rather than distribution to other fuel accounts, Sasoro did not satisfy the PMPA's second definition of a distributor. The parties' franchise agreement was thus not covered by the statute, and Sasoro's PMPA claim accordingly failed. The court dismissed Sasoro's claims, but granted Sasoro leave to amend.

Yogi Krupa, Inc. v. GLeS, Inc., No. 22-226-CFC, 2022 WL 16834164 (D. Del. Nov. 9, 2022). Plaintiff, a franchisee of a BP-branded gas station, sued its franchisor as well as its franchisors' landlords, the owners of the property on which the station was located, for violation of the PMPA. The franchisor had decided not to renew its lease of the property and the landlords rejected the franchisee's offer to purchase the property, instead accepting a higher offer from a third party that intended to operate the station itself. Plaintiff sued the franchisor and the franchisors' landlords for failing to provide it with an opportunity to renew its franchise relationship in violation of the PMPA. In granting the landlords' motion to dismiss, the court held that while the PMPA limits termination or nonrenewal of a motor fuel franchise to specified grounds and permits franchisees to bring causes of actions against franchisors for failure to renew the franchise relationship, the statute does not provide a cause of action against a franchisor's landlord. Such a claim would be beyond the scope of what the statute permits, and Congress granted courts limited authority under the PMPA. The court also considered plaintiff's argument that it was an intended third-party beneficiary of the lease, but found that the question had no bearing on whether the PMPA reached the franchisor's landlords, noting that the PMPA does not speak of third-party beneficiaries or offer protections for subtenants against master landlords.

III. Automobile/Motor Vehicle Dealer Laws

In ***Armstrong Ford, Inc. v. Ford Motor Co.***, No. 5:23-CV-167-D, 2023 WL 4585904, at *1 (E.D.N.C. July 18, 2023), franchisees of Ford Motor Company filed a petition with the Commissioner of the North Carolina Division of Motor Vehicles, claiming that the franchisor's electrical vehicle program violated the North Carolina Motor Vehicle Dealers and Manufacturers

Licensing Law. The franchisor removed the matter to the federal district court for the eastern district of North Carolina. The franchisees moved to remand the matter back to the Commissioner. The court granted the motion to remand. The court noted that there was diversity between the parties and the amount in controversy was satisfied even though the franchisees only sought injunctive relief because participating in the electric vehicle program would require each franchisee to invest more than $1,100,000. However, the court also found that the petition filed with the North Carolina Division of Motor Vehicles was not a civil action brought in a state court subject to removal.

Barber Group, Inc. v. New Motor Vehicle Board, No. C095058, 2023 WL 4699885 (Cal.App.3d July 24, 2023). Under California's Vehicle Code, section 3062, if a franchisor seeks to establish a new dealership, it must notify the California New Motor Vehicle Board (the "Board") and each existing franchisee within the "relevant market area" of its intent. Each notified franchisee then has 20 days in which to file an objection to the new franchise location, known as an "establishment protest." Under California's Vehicle Code, section 3065.3: "No franchisor shall establish or maintain a performance standard, sales objective, or program for measuring a dealer's sales, service, or customer service performance that is inconsistent with the standards set forth in section 11713.13(g)". Under section 11713.13(g), a manufacturer, manufacturer branch, distributor, or distributor branch may only impose performance standards on its dealers that are "reasonable" taking into account a dealer's local market. If a dealer wishes to challenge the reasonableness of a franchisor's performance standards under section 11713.13(g), it may file a protest before the Board under section 3065.3. Under section 3062, the dealer has the burden of proof in an establishment protest; under section 3065.3, the franchisor has the burden of proof. It is these conflicting burdens that gave rise to this appeal.

Barber Group, Inc. ("Barber"), in a section 3062 establishment protest, challenged a determination by the Board that American Honda Motor Co. Inc. ("Honda") could proceed with establishing an additional dealership within Barber's relevant market area. Barber alleged that the Board prejudicially erred when it relied on Honda's dealer performance standards at the section 3062 establishment hearing without first deciding whether those standards were reasonable (with Honda bearing the burden of proof on that question) under section 11713.13(g).

On appeal, the court was challenged with determining whether the two conflicting provisions could be reconciled in a proceeding in which an existing dealer was challenging the establishment of another dealership within its relevant market area under section 3062. Applying principles of statutory construction, the court determined that they could not be reconciled, finding that because the dealer has the burden of proof in a section 3062 establishment protest, and the franchisor has the burden of proof in a section 3065.3 proceeding, the statutes were irreconcilable when a dealer challenged the reasonableness of a franchisor's performance standards in a section 3062 establishment protest. The court determined that the two statutes could not be interpreted harmoniously without adding language to one or both statutes, which was essentially what Barber was asking the court to do, by imposing a burden of proof on the franchisor within the section 3062 hearing.

In ***Braman Motors, Inc. v. BMW of North America, LLC***, No. 17-23360-CV, 2023 WL 3509818 (S.D. Fla. Apr. 28, 2023), *report and recommendation adopted*, 1:17-CV-23360, 2023 WL 3496807 (S.D. Fla. May 17, 2023), the court denied the defendant BMW of North America, LLC's motion to dismiss three claims brought by franchisees under the Florida Motor Vehicle Dealer Act. The franchisees were BMW dealers in Florida. The court previously dismissed all claims but three, which sought injunctive relief under the Florida Motor Vehicle Dealer Act. The franchisor argued that the court lacked subject matter jurisdiction once the prior claims were dismissed because the court no longer had diversity jurisdiction and the claims for injunctive relief under the Florida Motor Vehicle Dealer Act stated that they must be brought in state court. At the hearing, the franchisor argued instead that the court had supplemental jurisdiction, but should decline to exercise that supplemental jurisdiction because there were complex issues of state law and exceptional circumstances.

    The court denied the motion on the basis that it had diversity jurisdiction because jurisdiction that exists at the time of filing is not divested by subsequent events, such as the change in the amount in controversy. The court also noted that under the Supremacy Clause of the Constitution, a state statute cannot discriminate against a party's right to resort to a federal forum. The court also found that there were no novel issues of law or exceptional circumstances that would warrant abstention or remand.

Continental Imports, Inc. v. Mercedes-Benz USA, LLC, No. 03-21-00377-CV, 2023 WL 114876 (Tex. App. Jan. 6, 2023). Swickard Austin, LLC ("Swickard Austin") filed an application to establish a new Mercedes-Benz dealership in Austin. Continental Imports, Inc. ("Continental") owns an existing Mercedes-Benz dealership in Austin and initiated a proceeding to protest Swickard Austin's application. Mercedes-Benz USA, LLC, the national distributor, intervened on behalf of Swickard Austin ("MB USA"). The State Office of Administrative Hearings (SOAH) conducted a hearing

CHAPTER 3

before two administrative law judges (the "Board") to determine whether to deny the application. Specifically, following a protest, an application may be denied if the applicant fails to prove good cause in establishing the dealership. The Board determined that Swickard Austin met its burden of demonstrating good cause for a new Mercedes-Benz dealership in Austin.

The single relevant issue in a protest proceeding is good cause. Swickard Austin had the burden of proving good cause with seven factors to consider: adequacy of representation, substantial compliance with dealer's franchise, desirability of a competitive marketplace, harm to protesting franchised dealer, public interest, harm to the applicant, and projections of economic conditions and the market.

For the first factor, the Board determined that in the specific context of Austin, Texas, Continental had below average sales and the preponderance of the evidence showed that Continental was not adequately representing the Mercedes-Benz brand. For the second factor, MB USA argued that Continental was not in compliance with its franchise agreement because it did not achieve 100 percent sales effectiveness, and Continental responded that MB USA recently renewed its franchise agreement and had not sent any noncompliance or cure notices. The Board stated that the franchise agreement was not introduced into evidence, and there was no support for MBA USA's claim. For the third factor, the Board decided that Continental is a highly profitable dealership that is in good position to compete with a new dealership. For the fourth factor, the Board found Continental's projections and experts unpersuasive. For the fifth factor, the Board found that the public interest would benefit from increased competition in the marketplace. For the sixth factor, the Board found that the evidence provided was too speculative and failed to establish harm to Swickard Austin. For the seventh and final factor, the Board noted extensive evidence on projected economic growth and high-income households in Austin.

In sum, the Board determined that five of the seven factors weighed in favor of establishing a new dealership. The court affirmed the final order because it was supported by substantial evidence and there was no abuse of discretion by the Board.

DeCozen Chrysler Jeep Corp. v. Fiat Chrysler Automobiles, LLC, No. 22-0068, 2022 WL 17094778 (D.N.J. Nov. 21, 2022). This dispute involved a dispute between plaintiff DeCozen Chrysler Jeep Corp., which operates a dealership in Verona, New Jersey that sells, markets, and distributes Chrysler, Jeep, Dodge, and Ram ("CJDR") vehicles throughout the U.S., and the defendant, that manufactures and supplies such vehicles to DeCozen. The parties entered into various dealer agreements, which they acknowledge created a franchise relationship, and pursuant to which defendant agreed to supply DeCozen with CJDR vehicles and Plaintiff agreed to sell and service those vehicles, along with other related products. In its lawsuit, plaintiff claimed that, during the course of the franchise relationship, defendant took several actions that were either unlawful under certain statutes or breached the dealer agreements. For instance, plaintiff contended that defendant failed to supply plaintiff with sufficient inventory and that it failed to enforce its dealer agreements with other CJDR dealers, for example, by allowing other dealerships to use non-franchised automobile brokers to sell CJDR vehicles to consumers. Plaintiff asserted claims against defendant for (1) violations of the New Jersey Franchise Practices Act; (2) breach of contract under New Jersey state law; (3) violations of the Automobile Dealers' Day in Court Act (ADDCA); (4) breach of the implied covenant of good faith and fair dealing under New Jersey state law; and (5) a declaratory judgment under 28 U.S.C. § 2201 and N.J.S.A. § 2A:16-51.

Defendant moved to dismiss plaintiff's claims. The court first reviewed the ADDCA claim and held that plaintiff had failed to sufficiently plead violations of the Act. The court provided background on the ADDCA, stating that the Act provides a cause of action for automobile dealers to "bring suit against any automobile manufacturer engaged in commerce... by reason of the failure of said automobile manufacturer... to act in good faith in performing or complying with any of the terms or provisions of the franchise..." The court then explained what constitutes a violation of the "good faith" requirement, including coercion, intimidation, and threats. It further held that to state an ADDCA claim, "the dealer must show more than that the manufacture was unfair;" there must be an actual and wrongful demand made on the dealer which will result in sanctions if not complied with. Because plaintiff's complaint only alleged that defendant failed to provide sufficient inventory, which was based on a one-new-vehicle-for-every-three-sold formula, the conduct at most was unfair and did not rise to the level of bad faith required to state a claim under the ADDCA. Moreover, plaintiff did not point to any of the terms or provisions of the franchise agreement itself to demonstrate that defendant had not acted in good faith. Thus, the court dismissed the claim.

Next, the district court looked at whether plaintiff adequately alleged diversity jurisdiction. It held that the plaintiff did not, because it failed to discuss the amount in controversy, and while plaintiff alleged general economic loss or injury, it did not describe that loss in such a way that would permit the court to deduce whether the amount in controversy requirement was satisfied. Since the court did not have original federal question jurisdiction (given its dismissal of the ADDCA), nor did it have diversity

CHAPTER 3

jurisdiction, the court declined to exercise supplemental jurisdiction over the remaining state law claims and dismissed such claims (including plaintiff's claim for a declaratory judgment).

Hyundai Motor America Corp. v. Efn West Palm Motor Sales, LLC, No. 20-82102-CV, 2022 WL 16968426 (S.D. Fla. Nov. 16, 2022). An automobile manufacturer filed suit against a distributor alleging warranty fraud, among other claims. The distributor-defendant asserted counterclaims against the manufacturer under the Florida Dealer Act. The distributor-defendant moved for summary judgment in its favor on its counterclaims. In denying the distributor-defendant's motion for summary judgment on its counterclaims, the court held that genuine issues of material fact precluded granting summary judgment as to the dealership. In particular, the court ruled that a determination as to whether the manufacturer had improperly refused to deliver vehicles in reasonable quantities was in violation of the Florida Dealer Act, was a jury question. Similarly, the court could not rule as a matter of law that the manufacturer acted with nefarious intent in connection with its discretionary allocation of vehicles to the dealership.

iMotorsports, Inc. v. Vanderhall Motor Works, Inc., No. 2-21-0785, 2022 IL App. (2d) 210785 (Ill. App. Dec. 1, 2022). iMotorsports, Inc., an auto dealer, sued Vanderhall Motor Works, Inc. ("Vanderhall"), an auto manufacturer, after Vanderhall appointed another dealer within 75 miles of iMotorsports' dealership after the parties' franchise agreement expired, allegedly violating an exclusivity provision.

The trial court dismissed iMotorsports' complaint in its entirety, and the appellate court affirmed this decision. The court found no valid contract existed at the time of the alleged breach because the agreement had expired, and therefore plaintiff's allegations could not support a breach of contract claim. The court also ruled that there was no implied contract with an exclusivity provision, as iMotorsports did not adequately allege a meeting of the minds regarding any exclusivity after the agreement's expiration.

The court also examined the notice requirements for termination or nonrenewal under the Illinois Motor Vehicle Franchise Act. That statute's unfair competition provision requires manufacturers to provide dealers with 60 days' notice of intent to terminate franchise agreements. Here, Vanderhall provided the requisite notice yet it continued to provide iMotorsports with new products, reimbursements for warranty service, and trademarked material and signage, and continued to list iMotorsports as an authorized dealer on its website past the date specified in the expiration provision. Nevertheless, because there was no longer a contract in place, the court found there was no breach that would support the statutory claim. The appellate court affirmed, agreeing with the trial court that no enforceable contract existed at the time of the alleged breach.

Liberty Ford Lincoln Mercury, Inc. v. Ford Motor Co., No. 1:21-CV-02085, 2022 WL 17417258 (N.D. Ohio Dec. 5, 2022). Plaintiffs, six Northeast Ohio Ford dealerships, brought claims against defendant Ford Motor Company ("Ford"), challenging, in part, Ford's allocation of vehicles to its dealers. Plaintiffs moved for a partial summary judgment, arguing that Ohio law obligates Ford to disclose certain information about its distribution. Ford's distribution process included an initial allocation of vehicles according to a formula and two discretionary offerings—one pre-allocation and one post-allocation. Plaintiffs twice requested a complete breakdown of the allocation (including discretionary offerings) and relevant methodology, which Ford did not provide, and sought a declaratory judgment that Ohio law requires Ford to disclose information regarding its system of new vehicle allocation. In its decision, the court considered how much disclosure Ford was legally required to provide.

More specifically, the court analyzed the Ohio Motor Vehicle Dealers Act, which regulates aspects of the manufacturer-dealer's franchise relationship, and in particular Ohio Revised Code §4517.59(A)(14), a provision of the Act that requires manufacturers to disclose information about their "system of allocation" of vehicles to franchisee dealers. This statute requires disclosure of the franchisor's "manner and mode" of distributing vehicles to dealers who handle the same line-make within the same county, and prohibits a franchisor from refusing to disclose to a dealer its "system of allocation." The statute further requires disclosure of "a concise listing of dealerships with an explanation of the derivation of the allocation system including its mathematical formula in a clear and comprehensible form."

In interpreting the statute, the court found it requires the manufacturer to disclose its method or procedure for allocating vehicles, but it does not require disclosure of the manufacturer's process for making discretionary allocations. The court based its interpretation on the repeated references to systems in the Act as well as its consideration of real-world industry practices. Ford was thus required to disclose to its dealers the system of initial allocation and a listing of dealerships, explaining how Ford derives the system of allocation and the mathematical formula used, but it was not required to disclose any information about its discretionary allocations. Accordingly, plaintiff's motion for partial summary judgment was denied.

CHAPTER 3

Mason Investment Group, LLC v. General Motors, LLC, No. CV 3:22-1940-MGL, 2023 WL 1451915 (D.S.C. Feb. 1, 2023). The dispute between Mason Investment Group, LLC ("Mason"), an auto dealership, and General Motors, LLC ("GM"), an auto manufacturer, centered on the parties' dealership agreement. Mason sued GM for violation of the South Carolina Dealer's Act, negligent misrepresentation, and for a declaratory judgment. In response, GM moved for judgment on the pleadings to dismiss the claims of negligent misrepresentation and declaratory judgment.

The court denied GM's motion regarding the negligent misrepresentation claim, finding that Mason had sufficiently alleged the elements of the claim. The court ruled that non-reliance clauses in the parties' contract did not automatically bar the claim. However, the court dismissed Mason's declaratory judgment claim without prejudice, stating Mason improperly asked the court to create new standards rather than interpret the contract. Mason was given leave to amend the declaratory judgment claim to properly seek interpretation of the dealership agreement. The court did not address Mason's Dealer Act claim, which remained intact.

McKinney Dodge Chrysler Jeep, Inc. v. Mazda Motor of America, Inc., No. 8:22-CV-00496-HMH, 2022 WL 3053766 (D.S.C. Aug. 3, 2022). Defendant-franchisor Mazda Motor of America, Inc. d/b/a Mazda North American Operations ("Mazda") moved for judgment on the pleadings after plaintiff-franchisee McKinney Dodge Chrysler Jeep, Inc. d/b/a McKinney Mazda ("McKinney") claimed that Mazda broke its dealer agreement and did not operate in good faith. The claims concerned a purported succession plan to transfer the franchised ownership interest to a different franchisee after the franchise owner was diagnosed with a terminal disease. Mazda terminated the dealer agreement after McKinney failed to properly renew its license with the state DMV. However, McKinney and Mazda disagreed as to whether McKinney's notice provided to Mazda regarding the illness and succession plans were sufficient under the dealer agreement and as required by the relevant statute.

McKinney claimed Mazda violated S.C. Code Ann. § 56-15, which both prevents a franchisor from unreasonably withholding the transfer of interest in a dealership and also prevents a franchisee from transferring its interest without the required notice. The notice provided by McKinney was the disagreed-upon fact and thus the court found the claim could not be decided at the pleading stage. McKinney also claimed Mazda violated the Automobile Dealers Suit Against Manufacturers or the Automobile Dealers Day in Court Act ("ADDCA") for failing to act in good faith. The court dismissed this claim because McKinney could not allege any specific coercion, intimidation, or threat as required to show a lack of good faith under the ADDCA.

New World Car Nissan, Inc. v. Hyundai Motor America, 658 S.W.3d 754 (Tex. App. 2022). Appellant New World Car Nissan, Inc. ("New World Car"), an automobile dealer, appealed a final order by the Texas Department of Motor Vehicles Board (the "Board") in favor of defendant Hyundai Motor America ("HMA"). New World Car alleged HMA violated provisions in the Texas Occupations Code relating to vehicle allocations and sales efficiency standards. After an Administrative Law Judge ("ALJ") held an evidentiary hearing and recommended denying New World Car's claims, the Board initially rejected the ALJ's conclusion but ultimately adopted the recommendation after remand.

The appellate court affirmed the Board's order, finding it supported by substantial evidence and not arbitrary, capricious, or an abuse of discretion. The court dismissed New World Car's procedural and evidentiary challenges to the Board's decision-making process. The court's analysis focused on the provisions of the Texas Occupations Code that regulate the franchise relationship between automobile manufacturers and authorized dealers. Specifically, the court cited provisions which stated a manufacturer, distributor, or representative may not discriminate unreasonably between or among franchisees in the sale of a motor vehicle owned by the manufacturer or distributor. The court also stated each party to a franchise agreement owes to the other party a duty of good faith and fair dealing.

The appellate court deferred to the Board's weighing of the evidence and credibility determinations, and upheld the administrative agency's decision against the automobile dealer, New World Car, on all issues raised relating to alleged statutory violations by the manufacturer, HMA.

Parker Powersports Inc. v. Textron Specialized Vehicles Inc., No. cv 122-054, 2023 WL 2695103 (S.D. Ga. Mar. 29, 2023). Plaintiff ("Parker") are powersports vehicle dealers and contracted to sell the defendant manufacturer's ("Textron") vehicles. After entering into the agreement with Parker, Textron manufactured a new line of vehicles similar to the ones Parker sold in their store, but under a different name. Parker eventually terminated the parties' agreement, and took a loss on their remaining inventory of Textron's vehicles. Parker then filed suit and asserted several claims, most of which alleged violations of Colorado's Dealer Act.

Parker claimed that Textron's new vehicle was essentially the same line-make of the vehicle that was the subject of their dealer agreement, and that Textron violated several provisions of the Dealer Act by selling the new vehicle. The court dismissed Parker's Colorado Dealer Act claim, finding that the two vehicles in question were not the same "line-make." The court found that vehicles having the same mechanical make-up is not relevant, only the brand identification. Parker could not claim Textron denied them line-makes because the two vehicles in question were marketed and labeled differently.

Reno Dealership Group, LLC v. General Motors, LLC, No. 21-55609, 2023 WL 234786 (9th Cir. Jan. 18, 2023). The U.S. Court of Appeals for the Ninth Circuit affirmed the district court's dismissal with prejudice of a dealership's complaint against a vehicle manufacturer.

The dealership had first asserted a breach of contract claim against the manufacturer based on the theory that the agreement between the parties imposed an obligation on the manufacturer to regulate or supervise false advertising or unfair competition by other dealerships. Applying Michigan law, the Ninth Circuit affirmed the district court's rejection of this argument based on the contract's plain language, which did not impose any obligation on the manufacturer to supervise or regulate the conduct of other dealerships.

The Ninth Circuit also rejected the dealership's argument that the manufacturer had breached the agreement by failing to deliver new motor vehicles to the dealership in a fair and equitable manner. On that issue, the court held that the manufacturer had complied with the specific text of the agreement to "endeavor" to distribute the vehicles in a fair and equitable manner, which was also subject to the manufacturer's discretion.

The dealership had also asserted a claim for negligence against the manufacturer based on the theory that the manufacturer owed its dealers a legal duty to supervise the promotional activities of the manufacturer's other dealers. The plaintiff dealership, however, did not cite to any authority to support the recognition of such a duty, and Michigan law (which applied by contract to the parties' relationship) does not recognize a tort-based duty among contractual parties to exercise reasonable care to avoid intangible economic losses.

Lastly, as support for its claim of negligence, the dealer also argued that statutory duties imposed on vehicle manufactures under Nevada and Michigan law created this duty. The Ninth Circuit, however, rejected these arguments, too. The court held that Nevada's motor vehicle dealer law prohibited a manufacturer from *causing* misleading advertising, but this statute did not impose an affirmative obligation to stop a dealer's misleading advertising. As to Michigan's Motor Vehicle Franchise Act, the Ninth Circuit held that the dealer had failed to demonstrate that this statute created a tort duty on a manufacturer to avoid economic harm to dealers. As a result, the Ninth Circuit held that the dealer had failed to state a claim based on

Industry Specific Statutes Affecting the Franchising Relationship

allegations that the manufacturer had failed to exercise reasonable care in the delivery of its vehicles.

Star Houston, Inc. v. Volvo Cars of North America, LLC, No. 03-21-00239-CV, 2023 WL 3639585 (Tex. App., May 25, 2023). The court denied Volvo's motion to overrule the finding of an administrative proceeding that two of its dealer incentive programs violated section 2301.467(a)(1) of the Occupations Code which prohibited distributors from "requir[ing] adherence to unreasonable sales or service standards." The programs were based in part on sales numbers and customer survey results. The court found that the evidence of record in the proceeding, particularly the statistical evidence and expert opinion evidence presented, provided a reasonable basis for finding that the programs were required and unreasonable and thus violated the code. The court further denied Volvo's motion to overrule the finding that it treated Star differently from other franchisees, relying on the first finding that the incentive programs at issue were violations themselves, the resulting differing treatment also constituted a violation and the administrative proceeding had a rational basis for so deciding.

Tesla Inc. v. Delaware Division of Motor Vehicles, No. 375, 2022, 2023 WL 3470406 (Del. May 15, 2023). Tesla designs, develops and manufactures new electric vehicles. But unlike most other car manufacturers, Tesla sells its vehicles directly to consumers without using independent franchise dealers. Tesla filed an application with defendant Delaware Division of Motor Vehicles ("DMV") for a new dealer license so that it could sell its cars directly to Delaware consumers. The application was rejected by the DMV, which took the position that Delaware's Licensing Act requires that the applicant comply with Delaware law, and that Tesla was not in compliance with Delaware's Franchise Act, because that statute prohibits a new motor vehicle manufacturer from selling its vehicles directly to Delaware consumers. Tesla requested an administrative hearing and the officer upheld the DMV's denial of a dealer license. Tesla then appealed to the Delaware Superior Court, which also affirmed the denial.

On appeal, the Delaware Supreme Court reversed the Superior Court's judgment upholding the DMV's denial of Tesla's new dealer license application and remanded the case for further proceedings. While the court first acknowledged that the DMV can deny a dealer license for a violation of the Franchise Act, it then considered the legislative intent of the Franchise Act, and found that it was intended to regulate the relationship between motor vehicle dealers and manufacturers, and that its purpose was to protect dealers from a manufacturer's unfair practices. Indeed, the Franchise Act addresses

CHAPTER 3

such issues as termination, cancellation, nonrenewal, and succession to ownership of franchises between manufacturers and dealers. The court found that the Franchise Act was not intended to prohibit the direct sales model, which does not involve such a relationship (it also noted that other states, such as Arizona, had reached similar conclusions and excluded the direct sales model from franchising restrictions). The court also found that Tesla did not fit the Franchise Act's definition of a "manufacturer," as that definition is a manufacturer that sells new motor vehicles *to a new motor vehicle dealer*, and Tesla does not sell its cars to dealers.

IV. Beer and Wine Laws

Block v. Canepa, No. 22-385, 2023 WL 4540523 (6th Cir. July 14, 2023). Plaintiffs challenged the constitutionality of Ohio liquor laws that prevented out-of-state wine retailers from shipping wine directly to Ohio consumers (the "Direct Ship Restriction") and prohibiting individuals from transporting more than 4.5 liters of wine into Ohio during any 30-day period (the "Transportation Limit"). Plaintiffs asserted that the Direct Ship Restriction and the Transportation Limit discriminated against interstate commerce, protected local economic interests, and violated the Commerce Clause. This case is discussed in Chapter 6, X.

Cavalier Distributing Company, Inc. v. Lime Ventures, Inc., No. 1:22-cv-121, 2023 WL 2384440 (S.D. Ohio Mar. 7, 2023). Cavalier Distributing Company, Inc. ("Cavalier") distributed beer produced by Belgian breweries Brouwerij 3 Fonteinen ("3F") and De La Senne (collectively, "the Breweries") and acquired through an importer, Shelton Brothers, in Ohio. When Shelton Brothers went bankrupt, Lime Ventures, Inc. ("Lime") became the importer for the Breweries, and ultimately began selling the beers to one of Cavalier's competitors. Cavalier filed a complaint centered on Ohio's beer franchise statute, Ohio Revised Code §§ 1333.82–87. Cavalier alleged that since it distributed the beer for more than ninety days, it enjoyed a franchise relationship with the Breweries pursuant to § 1333.83. It also alleged that Lime, acting as an agent of the Breweries, terminated the Breweries' franchise relationship with Cavalier in violation of § 1333.85. Cavalier moved for a preliminary injunction against Lime. The court applied the traditional four-factor test in evaluating Cavalier's motion: (1) whether the movant has a strong likelihood of success on the merits; (2) whether the movant would suffer irreparable injury without the injunction; (3) whether issuance of the injunction would cause substantial harm to others; and (4) whether the public interest would be served by the issuance of the injunction.

Industry Specific Statutes Affecting the Franchising Relationship

The court focused on "whether, under Ohio's alcoholic beverage franchise law, Shelton Brothers was 'a manufacturer' or 'the manufacturer.'" It emphasized that "if Cavalier had a franchise relationship only with Shelton Brothers (i.e., Shelton Brothers was the sole 'manufacturer'), then Shelton Brothers' bankruptcy, not Lime, terminated the relationship with Cavalier . . . But if the Breweries were also separately 'manufacturers' under the statute, and thus also had a franchise relationship with Cavalier, then Lime's conduct could be construed as terminating that existing franchise relationship between the Breweries and Cavalier." The Ohio franchise law does not limit the term "manufacturer" to entities that brew the beer, but instead includes those who supply it to distributors. A "distributor" is "a person that sells or distributes alcoholic beverages to retail permit holders." Ohio Rev. Code § 1333.82. Critically, under the law, "[w]hen a distributor of beer ... for a manufacturer ... distributes the beer ... for ninety days or more without a written contract, a franchise relationship is established." Ohio Rev. Code § 1333.83. Once that relationship is established, the law limits the ability of the manufacturer to confer another franchise for the sale of the beer brand within the same sales territory. Notably, "no manufacturer or distributor shall cancel or fail to renew a franchise ... without the prior consent of the other party for other than just cause and without at least sixty days' written notice," unless a specific statutory exception applies. *See* Ohio Rev. Code § 1333.85.

The issue here was whether Cavalier had a franchise relationship with the Breweries as well as Shelton. The court discussed the ability of a given party to control the beverages being sold, stating that "if the unilateral ability to control product distribution matters in deciding who is a manufacturer for purposes of Ohio's alcoholic beverage franchise law, then Shelton Brothers (and now Lime), not the Breweries, appears to qualify for that role on the facts here." Ultimately, the court stated that the Ohio beer franchise statute could be interpreted to mean that where "the brewer relinquishes its say over all distribution decisions and the importer takes exclusive control over those decisions, the brewer would not incur franchise obligations under Ohio law." For that reason, the court found that Cavalier did not show that it had a substantial likelihood of success on the merits. Separately, the court found that: (1) Cavalier may suffer irreparable harm absent a preliminary injunction; (2) that third party distributors and beer sellers would be harmed by the issuance of a preliminary injunction; and (3) that the "Ohio beer-consuming public's interest favor[ed] the continued availability of these products, whether delivered though Cavalier or" one of its competitors. On these grounds, the court denied Cavalier's motion for a preliminary injunction.

CHAPTER 3

Eskimo Hut Worldwide, Ltd. v. South Plains Sno, Inc., No. 07-22-00259-CV, 2023 WL 177684 (Tex. App. Jan. 9, 2023) (court allowed interlocutory appeal of partial summary judgment in case involving possible conflicts between the parties' franchise agreement's requirements and restrictions with respect to the Defendant franchisee's sale of certain types of alcoholic beverages and the Texas Alcoholic Beverage Code). This case is also discussed in Chapter 8, Section XVI.

Ste. Michelle Wine Estates, LLC v. Tri County Wholesale Distributors, Inc., No. 4:22 CV 1702, 2022 WL 17617319 (N.D. Ohio Dec. 13, 2022) (court found that, in light of the termination of a distributorship relationship by the plaintiff wine manufacturer due to a change in its control, under applicable Ohio law, the manufacturer had to pay a fee to the defendant in order to be able to transfer the distribution rights to a new distributor).

V. Other Statutes

In ***A.B. Corp. v. Dunkin' Donuts Franchising, LLC***, No. 3:22-CV-1474 (SVN), 2022 WL 17337756 (D. Conn. Nov. 30, 2022) A.B. Corp ("A.B. Corp") alleged that Dunkin' Donuts Franchising, LLC ("Dunkin' Donuts") improperly terminated the parties' twenty-year franchise agreement in violation of the Connecticut Franchise Act (the "CFA"), after the franchisee had failed three food safety inspections.

The CFA allows a franchisee to bring an action for damages and injunctive relief against a franchisor for a substantive or procedural violation of the CFA. (Conn. Gen. Stat. § 42-133g(a).) In this case, A.B. Corp demonstrated some degree of success on the merits of the claim that Dunkin' Donuts failed to comply with the CFA's sixty-day notice requirement. However, the court noted that the remedy for such violation is generally limited to franchisee's lost profits for the time period the termination was in effect without proper notice. Accordingly, on the present record, the injury suffered by A.B. Corp was not truly "irreparable" as required to warrant an issuance of a temporary restraining order because it could be monetarily remedied. As such, the court denied A.B. Corp's motion for a temporary restraining order.

Francois v. Victory Auto Group LLC, No. 22-cv-04447 (JSR), 2023 WL 4534375 (S.D.N.Y. July 13, 2023). Plaintiff alleged that a Mitsubishi dealership facilitated the theft of her identity by her brother-in-law, who purchased a car in plaintiff's name from the defendants. After the dealership ran credit checks on plaintiff's brother-in-law and then his friend, both of which had insufficient credit, it ran a credit check on plaintiff which came back as satisfactory. Plaintiff's brother-in-law then purchased the car in plaintiff's name even though she never consented to the sale. Plaintiff asserted claims for negligence and violation of the Fair Credit Reporting Act ("FCRA") against defendants. Defendants moved for summary judgment, which the court granted on plaintiff's negligence claim due to its finding that plaintiff had not introduced any evidence or actual damages or injury. But it denied summary judgment on the FCRA claim, noting that under that statute, a plaintiff can recover for emotional damages, and plaintiff created a genuine issue of fact as to whether defendants' conduct caused her significant emotional distress. It also denied defendants' motion for partial summary judgment on the question of whether their violation of the FCRA was willful, finding that the overall sequence of events, in particular the evidence that the dealership ran three different individuals' credit information until they finally found someone who qualified to make the car sale, sufficed to create a genuine issue of fact as to whether the dealership acted willfully.

G.F.B. Enterprises, LLC v. Toyota Motor Sales U.S.A, Inc., No. 23-CV-20392-RAR, 2023 WL 2631467 (S.D. Fla. Mar. 24, 2023) (The United States District Court for the Southern District of Florida denied Defendant, Toyota Motor Sales U.S.A., Inc.'s ("TMS") motion to dismiss plaintiff's complaint, holding that TMS cited no authority that would allow this court to dismiss plaintiff's complaint. TMS only provided unsupported representations that plaintiff did not submit compliant repair orders per Section 320.696 of the Florida Statutes required to receive increased compensation from TMS. Accordingly, TMS' motion to dismiss was denied.)

Innovative Sports Management, Inc. v. Gutierrez, No. 22-CV-05793-BLF, 2023 WL 4157627 (N.D. Cal. June 23, 2023) (court granted in part plaintiff's motion for default judgment in case alleging that the defendants violated the Federal Communications Act, Cable and Television Consumer Protection Act, and the California Unfair Competition Law by airing a soccer match in a public restaurant without first obtaining the appropriate sublicense from the plaintiff).

Patel v. 7-Eleven, Inc., 489 Mass. 356, 183 N.E.3d 398 (Mar. 24, 2022). 7-Eleven franchisees ("Patel" or the "Plaintiffs") filed a putative class action against 7-Eleven, Inc. ("7-Eleven" or "Defendant") for misclassifying franchisees as independent contractors instead of employees. A federal judge had previously allowed summary judgment in favor of 7-Eleven, stating that the independent contractor statute does not apply to franchisee-franchisor relationships because there is a conflict between the independent contractor statute and FTC Franchise Rule. Thus, the Plaintiffs appealed, and the question before the court was whether the three-pronged test for independent contractor status set forth in the independent contractor statute is applicable in a relationship between a franchisor and franchisee, where the franchisor must comply with FTC Franchise Rule.

The independent contractor statute, under the court's view, set a presumption that an individual performing a service for a putative employer shall be considered an employee for the purposes of the wage statute. Then, the alleged employer may rebut by establishing each of the three-prongs (known as the "ABC test"). The court expressed no opinion as to how the ABC test applied to the facts of the present case. Additionally, the plain language of the independent contractor statute does not expressly include or exclude franchisees, therefore the court inferred that the legislature intended that the criteria for identifying independent contractors to be applied in the context of the franchise relationship.

Next, the court considered whether a conflict existed between federal regulations and the first prong of the state independent contractor statute, by analyzing under the principles of preemption. Under the preemption doctrine, the FTC Franchise Rule preempts the independent contractor statute only if the latter actually conflicts with the former, which would mean it would be impossible for a private party to comply with both state and federal requirements. The court concluded that no such conflict existed; therefore, the independent contractor statute applied to the franchisor-franchisee relationship and was not in conflict with franchisor's disclosure obligations in the FTC Franchise Rule.

South Shore D'Lites LLC v. First Class Products Group, LLC, 215 A.D.3d 412, 187 N.Y.S.3d 185 (2023) (The Supreme Court, Appellate Division, First Department, New York affirmed the lower court's ruling that franchisee was entitled to summary judgment because franchisor violated New York's Franchise Sales Act by failing to provide the required pre-sale written disclosures and that the individual owners of franchisor were control persons jointly and severally liable for any Franchise Sales Act violations by franchisor.)

United States ex rel. Hart v. McKesson Corp., No. 15-CV-0903 (RA), 2023 WL 2663528 (S.D.N.Y. Mar. 28, 2023) (The United States District Court for the Southern District of New York granted defendant McKesson's motion to dismiss plaintiff Hart's complaint without prejudice, finding that Hart failed to plausibly allege that McKesson provided the Margin Analyzer and

Regimen Profiler tools to oncology practices free of charge with the requisite scienter that could constitute unlawful inducement under the federal Anti-Kickback Statute and the False Claims Act.)

Wirtgen America, Inc. v. Hayden-Murphy Equipment Company, No. 3:22-CV-00308, 2023 WL 123499 (M.D. Tenn. Jan. 6, 2023). The parties had a distribution sales and service agreement whereby Hayden-Murphy agreed to be a nonexclusive dealer of various Wirtgen products in Minnesota. Wirtgen sought a declaratory judgment that it could not renew or could terminate the parties' agreement due to a change in the management and/or control of Hayden Murphy. Hayden-Murphy argued that Wirtgen had acquiesced to the change in control. The court denied Hayden-Murphy's motion to dismiss. It held that Tennessee law applied given the parties' express agreement to that state's law governing in their agreement. It then cited to the relevant section of Tennessee's equipment dealer law, Tenn. Code. Ann. Section 47-25-1302, which relates to failure to renew a renewable dealer agreement, and found that at this stage of the case, there was a factual question as to whether good cause existed to terminate the agreement.

CHAPTER 4

Disputes Regarding Performance, Termination, and Transfers

I. Introduction

Not surprisingly, there has been ample case law during the reporting period on disputes regarding performance, termination, and transfer. For instance, in a South Dakota case, the court analyzed whether terminating a dealer agreement on the basis of the discontinuation of distribution of a certain vehicle in the United States constituted "good cause," and the court turned to the construction of the specific state statute, SDCL § 32-6B-45, in its evaluation of the claim. Similarly, in a Washington case, the court considered a motion for preliminary injunction following the termination to a distribution agreement. Additionally, the courts also considered claims arising from covenants of non-competition and non-solicitation.

II. Performance and Termination Disputes Generally

A. BREACH OF CONTRACT

360 Painting, LLC v. Misiph, No. 3:22-CV-00056, 2023 WL 4533932 (W.D. Vir. July 13, 2023). The court granted the defendant franchisee's motion to dismiss a breach of contract claim brought by the franchisor. The franchisor had terminated the franchise agreement and then filed suit, attempting to recover certain amounts the franchisee had not paid, and claiming that non-

CHAPTER 4

payment constituted a breach by the franchisee. The court disagreed, noting that an addendum to the franchise agreement signed by both parties amended the contract to preclude the franchisor from collecting the types of damages it was seeking in the case.

Amaro Oilfield Automation, LLC v. Lithis CM, Inc., 661 S.W.3d 477, No. 08-21-00013-CV (Tex. App. Jan. 23, 2023). The court reviewed the lower court's decision granting summary judgment to Lithis. Lithis was an auto dealership that accepted a trade-in of an old truck and sold a new truck to a managing member of Amaro who used Amaro funds to purchase the vehicle. Amaro alleged that the managing member did not have actual authority to enter into the purchase and that Lithis had made false representations regarding attempts to recover the trade-in vehicle. Thus, Amaro brought claims for breach of contract, violation of the Texas Deceptive Trade Practices Act, and common law fraud against Lithis.

As to the breach of contract claim, the court determined that because Amaro judicially admitted that the purchaser did not have actual authority to enter into the transaction, Amaro effectively undermined its argument that a contract could be formed and existed. Since there was no valid contract, the court determined that Amaro could not establish a claim for breach of contract and affirmed the lower court's grant of summary judgment to Lithis on that claim.

In ***Baim v. Dukart***, No. CV 21-1696, 2023 WL 2330410 (E.D. Pa. Mar. 2, 2023), the United States District Court for the Eastern District of Pennsylvania held that plaintiff, Edward Baim's ("Baim") decision to honor Grant and George Skylasses' right of first refusal to purchase Baim's remaining Philadelphia McDonald's locations, (the "Restaurants") did not breach Baim's contract with defendants Joel and Michael Dukart (the "Dukarts").

This dispute arose out of a Purchase and Sale Agreement (the "Agreement") between Baim and the Dukarts. Under the Agreement, Baim agreed to sell the Dukarts the Restaurants if the Skylasses decided to not exercise their right of first refusal, and if there was no threatened or pending litigation against the Agreement. The Skylasses threatened to sue if Baim failed to honor their right of first refusal. However, the Skylasses ultimately agreed to purchase the Restaurants and Baim entered a contract with them to do so.

Baim sought a declaration from the court blessing the sale of the Restaurants to the Skylasses. However, the Dukarts asserted counterclaims contending that the Skylasses' threatened litigation rendered the Agreement illusory and that Baim's sale of the Restaurants to the Skylasses breached the Agreement.

The court held that the Agreement was not illusory because Baim would have been obligated to sell the Restaurants to the Dukarts had the Skylasses not exercised their right of first refusal. Further the Court held that the Skylasses threat to sue violated a necessary condition to closing under the Agreement and that Baim did not breach the Agreement because the Dukarts knew of the prospective sale to the Skylasses and still willingly entered into the Agreement despite the risks.

In ***Cajunland Pizza, LLC v. Marco's Franchising, LLC***, 2022 WL 4353345 (N.D. Ohio Sept. 20, 2022), the court denied the counter-defendants' motion to dismiss the defendant's counterclaims for damages in the form of lost royalties. The court found that it would have required the court to make a factual determination that the defendant's actions had been wrongful and precluded the plaintiffs in question from complying with their contractual obligations, which the court concluded was inappropriate at the motion to dismiss phase.

Choice Hotels International, Inc. v. C & O Developers, L.L.C., 199 N.E.3d 1 (Oh. App. Sept. 15, 2022). Franchisor Choice Hotels and franchisees Frank and David Crisafi, entered a franchise agreement for a Cambria Suites hotel. The agreement included an arbitration clause for disputes under the agreement or related agreements. The franchisees assigned the franchise agreement to their LLC, C&O Westfield, LLC ("C&O"). Subsequently, Choice Hotels provided financing to C&O through a loan agreement and related loan documents, which specified that disputes would be litigated in court.

After a default on the loan, the franchisor brought an action against the assignors of the franchise agreement, the owner of the assignee, and the guarantors of the loan agreement for a confessed judgment, breach of contract based on a promissory note issued pursuant to the loan agreement, and breach of the guarantee agreement. Defendants filed motion to stay pending arbitration pursuant to the franchise agreement, The trial court denied the motion, holding the clause did not apply to the loan documents, as they were separate, later agreements with their own jurisdiction clauses specifying litigation in court.

The appellate court found the dispute arising from the alleged default under the loan agreement was not subject to arbitration under the separate franchise agreement, as the franchise agreement and the loan were separate transactions subject to different dispute resolution clauses. The appellate court therefore affirmed the denial of the motion to compel arbitration. The court further noted that the Crisafis had assigned the franchise agreement to C&O and were no longer parties to that contract; therefore, they did not have standing to enforce the arbitration clause.

Cici Enterprises, LP v. TLT Holdings, LLC, No. 3:21-CV-02121-S-BT, 2022 WL 17657576 (N.D. Tex. Nov. 18, 2022). Cici Enterprises, LP ("CE"), the franchisor of CiCi's brand restaurants, and Yes Caps, LLC, the owner of the trademarks associated with the franchise system (the "Marks"), sued one of its franchisees and the individual who personally guaranteed the franchisee's obligations under the franchise agreement signed by the parties (the "Franchise Agreement"), alleging breach of contract, trademark infringement and unfair competition. The plaintiffs alleged that the defendants failed to make required payments for royalties and the cost of food products purchased from CE and its affiliates, and that the defendants continued to operate their restaurant using the Marks after CE terminated the Franchise Agreement. The magistrate court granted the franchisor-plaintiffs' motion to strike privileged settlement communications from the record and recommended that the district court grant plaintiffs' motion for summary judgment on all claims.

The magistrate court rejected the defendants' argument that they had complied with their obligations under the Franchise Agreement by engaging in negotiations with CE over the amounts owed and by tendering payment to CE. The magistrate court noted that evidence of the negotiations was stricken from the record as privileged and the defendants only sent checks to CE after the lawsuit was filed. CE returned these checks to defendants and, therefore, the magistrate court held that the defendants' failed to cure their breach and plaintiffs were entitled to summary judgment on the breach of contract claims.

In response to the Lanham Act claims, the defendants argued that (i) the plaintiffs had consented to defendants' continued use of the Marks after the Franchise Agreement was terminated by engaging in negotiations with defendants, and (ii) the plaintiffs should be equitably estopped from recovering on their claims because, by engaging in negotiations with defendants after the termination of the Franchise Agreement, plaintiffs led the defendants to believe that they could continue to operate their restaurant using the Marks. The magistrate court rejected the defendants' arguments because they relied solely on the privileged settlement communications, which were inadmissible.

Coldwell Banker Real Estate LLC v. Bellmarc Group, LLC, No. 21-2862, 2022 WL 3644183 (3d Cir. Aug. 24, 2022). Following a bench trial, the U.S. Court of Appeals for the Third Circuit affirmed the judgment of the district court that the franchisor had not breached the franchise agreements, on the

Disputes Regarding Performance, Termination, and Transfers

one hand, but that the franchisee had breached the franchise agreements by failing to pay royalty fees, on the other. According to the evidence presented at the trial, the franchisee had stopped paying royalties to the franchisor to, among other reasons, seek reimbursement for advertising costs that the franchisee believed to be owed by the franchisor.

The district court rejected the franchisee's arguments and ruled that the franchise agreement did not provide for reimbursement to the franchisee for advertising costs. The district court further ruled that the franchisor had not committed any breach of the franchise agreement. Finding no errors, the court of appeals affirmed the trial court's ruling.

D3 International, Inc. v. AGGF Cosmetic Group S.p.A., No. 21-cv-06409 (S.D.N.Y. March 7, 2023). Plaintiff and defendant had a distribution agreement wherein plaintiff was granted the exclusive right to distribute defendant's products in the U.S. The court granted the defendant's motion to dismiss the plaintiff's breach of contract claim, finding that the defendant had properly issued a six-month notice of its intention to cancel the contract pursuant to the termination provision of the agreement. Plaintiff also argued that an oral contract was created which granted it distribution rights in perpetuity. However, the court disagreed, finding the plaintiff did not meet its burden of establishing there was an oral contract and that even if it did, there was no showing that the distribution rights were granted in perpetuity.

The court further granted the defendant manufacturer's claim for account stated, finding that the plaintiff had agreed to pay the defendant a sum of money that the parties agreed to serve as compensation for amounts due under the contract.

Dana Innovations v. Trends Electronics International Inc., No. 8:22-cv-02155-FWS-ADS, 2023 WL 3335909 (C.D. Cal. Apr. 21, 2023). Plaintiff Dana Innovations, a California corporation, entered into an agreement with Trends Electronics International Inc. ("Trends"), a Canadian electronics company, for Trends to be the exclusive distributor of plaintiff's electronic audio equipment in Canada. In relevant part, the agreement provided that it was "effective from the date of its execution to June 30, 1998, unless earlier terminated hereunder. Notwithstanding the foregoing, should [defendant] not receive a written letter of termination from [plaintiff] by the termination date hereof, the Agreement shall be deemed renewed for one year from the date of such renewal, with all terms and conditions hereof remaining in full force and effect." In 2022, plaintiff sent defendant a written letter seeking to terminate the agreement after plaintiff learned defendant was selling or agreed to sell competing products and failed to pay plaintiff for delivered goods. The instant

CHAPTER 4

case asserting claims for breach of contract and for a common count ensued, as did a separate case in Canada brought against plaintiff by defendant.

Defendant sought to dismiss plaintiff's claim for breach of contract under FRCP Rule 12(b)(6) for failure to state a claim. Defendants alleged that the agreement expired in 1999 after the initial term and one-year renewal, and thus plaintiff's claim was time-barred under California's statute of limitations. The court determined that the language of the agreement was ambiguous as to whether it would only automatically renew for one year or would continue to renew each year absent a written notice of termination. Thus, the court denied the motion to dismiss after finding the renewal provision to be ambiguous.

Eddie's Truck Center, Inc. v. Daimler Vans USA LLC, No. 5:21-CV-05081-VLD, 2023 WL 3388503 (D.S.D. May 11, 2023). Plaintiffs Eddie's Truck Center, Inc. ("Floyd's Rapid City") and Four Open A Trucks, Inc. ("Floyd's Belgrade") entered franchise and service agreements with defendants Daimler Vans USA LLC ("DVUSA") and Mercedes-Benz USA, LLC ("MBUSA") for the service and distribution of Freightliner Sprinter vehicles. Floyd's Rapid City's Commercial Vehicle Dealer Agreement with DVUSA, a wholly owned subsidiary of MBUSA, granted it a franchise to sell and service new Freightliner Sprinter motor vehicles and to use the Sprinter trademark. In August 2020, DVUSA notified Floyd's Rapid City that it was terminating their dealer agreement effective December 31, 2021, because it was discontinuing distribution of the Sprinter vehicles in the United States. Floyd's Rapid City asserted that this was a termination without "good cause" while Sprinter vehicles would continue to be distributed by MBUSA for resale to other dealers.

Floyd's Belgrade had entered into a service provider agreement with DVUSA under which it would service Freightliner Sprinter vehicles and purchase parts, accessories, and tools, which was extended through either October 31, 2021, or the execution of a new agreement. DVUSA sent notice to Floyd's Belgrade in October 2021 that the agreement would be extended through December 31, 2021, then terminated at that time pursuant to the discontinuation of the Freightliner Sprinter, but extended through December 31, 2026, for the purposes of the activities authorized under the original agreement. Floyd's Belgrade asserted that this termination and refusal to formally continue the service agreement constituted a termination without "good cause" under Montana law. The plaintiffs filed suit for damages and defendants moved for a judgment on the pleadings pursuant to Fed. R. Civ. P. 12(c).

In evaluating Floyd's Rapid City's claim for damages based on its argument that a "line-make discontinuation" does not constitute good cause, the court considered the construction of SDCL § 32-6B-45, the statute under which the claim was brought. The statute specifically notes that a franchisor may not terminate, cancel, fail to renew, or substantially change a vehicle dealership agreement without good cause, which means failure by a vehicle dealer to substantially comply with essential and reasonable requirements imposed upon the dealer by the agreement. The statute also lists additional specific examples of good cause, none of which include a line-make discontinuation circumstance. The court ultimately held that the statute's specific examples are not exclusive, because (1) the statute itself does not include any exclusivity language with respect to the examples; (2) a reading of the examples as exclusive would render another statute, SDCL § 32-6B-49, which lists circumstances which are not good cause for termination, as superfluous; and (3) interpreting the statute's examples as exclusive would give rise to a dormant Commerce Clause problem where out-of-state vehicle producers would be burdened in favor of local businesses. There were additional considerations for the court on this claim, particularly whether DVUSA's termination of the dealer agreement was itself based on a line-make discontinuation. The court ultimately held that material factual disputes arising from the pleadings barred the motion for judgment on the pleadings, and denied defendants' motion.

The defendants also challenged Floyd Belgrade's claim on the basis that it lacked standing to sue. The court noted that to have standing, a plaintiff must have (1) suffered an injury in fact, (2) that is fairly traceable to the channeled conduct of the defendant, and (3) that is likely to be redressed by a favorable judicial decision. MONT. CODE ANN. § 61-4-205(1) states that a franchisor may not terminate a franchise unless the franchisor has cause for termination, while standing to sue under the statute is outlined by Mont. Code Ann. § 61-4-217, which states that only a new motor vehicle dealer (or its affiliates) may file suit. The court noted that Floyd's Belgrade's agreement with DVUSA only allowed it to service vehicles, not buy or sell them. Furthermore, the original agreement specifically stated that it was not a franchise or dealer agreement authorizing Floyd's Belgrade to sell new Freightliner vehicles. Accordingly, the court held that Floyd's Belgrade did not have standing to assert a claim under Mont. Code Ann. § 61-4-217 and granted defendants' motion for judgment on the pleadings.

EFN West Palm Beach Motor Sales, LLC v. Hyundai Motor America Corp., No. 21-80348-CIV-CANNON/Matthewman, 2023 WL 2825920 (S.D. Fla. March 7, 2023). Plaintiffs were two authorized Hyundai dealerships in Florida. The dealerships were part of a group of motor vehicle dealerships owned or controlled by North American Automotive Services ('NAG') that

CHAPTER 4

provides centralized services to the dealerships. NAG is run by Edward Napleton ("Napleton"), who is also the "Dealer-Principal" and Chairman and majority owner of the Plaintiffs.

The two dealer agreements contain an identical clause allowing defendant Hyundai Motor America Corp. ("Hyundai") to terminate the agreements on 60 days' notice if it learns of any events which, "in its sole discretion," it determines require termination, including any conduct which in Hyundai's opinion impairs the reputation of Hyundai or the dealer. In early 2019, Napleton was arrested and charged with sexual battery on a helpless person. The victim then filed a civil lawsuit against Napleton. The incident and lawsuit received a lot of media attention. Napleton subsequently pleaded guilty to the sexual battery charge. Shortly thereafter, Hyundai served notices of default to the plaintiffs for impairment of and harm to Hyundai's and the dealerships' reputation. After some additional correspondence between the parties, Hyundai sent plaintiffs notices of termination which referenced, among other reasons, Napleton's sexual battery criminal charge and civil lawsuit

Plaintiffs sued defendant for unlawful termination. They argued that defendant was not authorized to terminate plaintiffs for the actions of an affiliated corporation (NAG) or employee, neither of whom are parties to the dealer agreements or officers, employees or agents of the plaintiffs. In granting defendant's motion for summary judgment, the court found that defendant had reasonably exercised its discretion under the termination provision at issue. The court recognized that when one party to a contract has "sole discretion," that party, in exercising its discretion, must act in good faith and in accordance with the contracting parties' expectations. However, the court noted that this good-faith limitation on a party's exercise of its sole discretion "is not great," and that, unless no reasonable party would have made the same discretionary decision, it is unlikely the party's decision would violate the covenant of good faith. The court reviewed the record facts and evidence and concluded that defendant had reasonably exercised its discretion in determining that Napleton's sex crime and plaintiffs' response to it had harmed Hyundai's and the dealerships' reputations, and in therefore terminating the dealer agreements. The court also rejected plaintiffs' argument that defendant could not terminate based on the actions of a non-party, finding that the termination clause relied on by defendant did not limit action that could impair the reputation of the parties to only the conduct of the parties to the agreement, rather they allowed termination for "any conduct" which in defendant's opinion impaired the reputation of defendant or the dealerships.

Disputes Regarding Performance, Termination, and Transfers

Flawless Style LLC v. Saadia Group LLC, No. 23 Civ. 2354 (JHR), 2023 WL 3687782 (S.D.N.Y. May 26, 2023). The district court held that Saadia lost the right to terminate a license agreement for plaintiffs' alleged breach when Saadia continued performing under the license agreement after the alleged breach. This case is discussed in Chapter 5, Section II.

Greentree Hospitality Group Inc. v. Mullinix, No. CV-22-00088-PHX-DJH, 2022 WL 17832782 (D. Ariz. Dec. 21, 2022) (granting plaintiff franchisor's motion for entry of default judgment for breach of contract against the defendant and scheduling a hearing on damages, where the defendant personally guaranteed a loan from the plaintiff franchisor to the franchisee's business, the court had jurisdiction, the defendant failed to appear, and entry of a default judgment was otherwise warranted).

Hickory Hills Foodmart, Inc. v. Equilon Enterprises, LLC, No. 22 C 5393, 2023 WL 4273664 (N.D. Ill. June 29, 2023) (court found plaintiff franchisee adequately asserted a claim against defendant franchisor for breach of a written and oral franchise agreement arising from defendant's authorizing a competing gas station which resulted in the franchisee losing half of its gross sales, but dismissed plaintiff's remaining claims for lack of standing or failure to state a claim).

Hopp v. Leistad Systems, Inc., No. 22-0056, 2023 WL 383002 (Iowa Ct. App. Jan. 25, 2023). Leistad Systems, Inc. ("Leistad") distributed Safeguard Business Systems, Inc. ("Safeguard") products using a network of associate distributors. Leistad's contracts with its associate distributors contained provisions for payments to the associate distributors after termination of the agreements if various conditions precedent were met—including a specified length of time. Leistad later sold itself to Safeguard. The associate distributors claimed their right to the payments was lost because Leistad had persuaded them to sign new agreements that did not have the payment-after-termination provisions. The court, in affirming the district court's grant of summary judgment for the defendants, noted that the associate distributors could not prove they were damaged because they terminated their old contracts early, and in any event they had not satisfied the conditions precedent necessary to receive the termination payments under those contracts.

Howard Johnson International, Inc. v. Kunwar, No. 21-19287, 2023 WL 3199174 (D.N.J. May 1, 2023). Franchisor Howard Johnson sued former franchisee Ram Kunwar for breach of a hotel franchise agreement. Franchisee unilaterally terminated the agreement and ceased the operation of a Howard

CHAPTER 4

Johnson hotel. Howard Johnson sought outstanding recurring fees, liquidated damages for early termination, interest, and attorneys' fees. As Kunwar did not respond, the court deemed a default judgment appropriate. The court awarded Howard Johnson the requested recurring fees plus interest, as well as liquidated damages for the early termination, plus interest, pursuant to the franchise agreement.

iMotorsports, Inc. v. Vanderhall Motor Works, Inc., No. 2-21-0785, 2022 WL 210785 (Ill. App. Ct. Dec. 1, 2022) (court dismissed plaintiff-dealer's claims against defendant vehicle manufacturer for breach of contract, breach of implied-in-fact contract, and violation of Section 4(b) of the Illinois Motor Vehicle Franchise Act because, even though the parties continued to do business together after their franchise agreement expired, the dealer failed to provide any evidence that it or the manufacturer intended to continue to be bound by the terms of the agreement after its expiration, therefore plaintiff's claims were all based on the breach of a nonexistent contractual obligation).

Innovare, Ltd. v. Sciteck Diagnostics, Inc., No. 21-CVS-2180, 2023 WL 325141 (N.C. Super. Ct. Jan. 19, 2023) (plaintiff distributor's counterclaims under the Lanham Act and for breach of contract were upheld against defendant's motion to dismiss on the basis of the scope of the distributor agreement between the parties).

Integrity Real Estate Consultants v. Re/Max of NewYork, Inc., 213 A.D.3d 815 (2023). Plaintiff Integrity Real Estate Consultants ("Integrity") entered into a franchise agreement with Re/Max of New York (Re/Max) to operate a Re/Max real estate office, but Integrity relocated the office without the consent of Re/Max as required under the franchise agreement. Re/Max deemed the relocation a breach under the agreement, and Integrity responded by filing suit against Re/Max for breach of contract and violation of antitrust law. Re/Max countersued for unpaid franchise fees and legal fees under the agreement.

The trial court ruled in favor of Re/Max, finding Integrity breached the agreement by relocating and failing to pay fees, and awarded Re/Max $521,240 in unpaid franchise fees and attorneys' fees. However, on appeal, the court found that Re/Max breached the agreement by excluding Integrity from its advertising (by, among other things, refusing to include plaintiff in its list of offices on its website), which excused plaintiff from continuing to perform. The appellate court modified the judgment and dismissed Re/Max's claims against Integrity and its guarantors, finding no basis to award Re/Max fees as the prevailing party.

JTH Tax LLC v. Irving, No. CV RDB-21-3000, 2023 WL 1472021 (D. Md. Feb. 1, 2023) (court granted summary judgment in favor of the defendant former franchisee on the plaintiff franchisor's claim to collect on a series of promissory notes it issued to the franchisee, holding that Maryland's three-year statute of limitations for contractual claims applied and barred the plaintiffs' claims).

JTH Tax, LLC v. Shahabuddin, No. 21-2031, 2023 WL 3002736 (4th Cir. Apr. 19, 2023) (affirming trial court's decision that found that franchisor expressly waived its right to assignment of certain leases under the franchise agreement when it repeatedly told the franchisee that it would not take over the leases and then waited three years to request assignment of the leases).

Jumping Jack Retail II, Inc. v. 7-Eleven, Inc., No. 23-CV-60460, 2023 WL 2987666 (S.D. Fla. Apr. 18, 2023) (The United States District Court for the Southern District of Florida granted the franchisor defendant 7-Eleven's motion to dismiss the plaintiff's ("Jumping Jack") breach of contract claim, finding that Jumping Jack failed to adequately plead a breach of contract claim because it failed to specify any provision of the allegedly breached franchise agreement and because Jumping Jack was not a party to the franchise agreement at issue.)

KAM Development, LLC v. Marco's Franchising, LLC, No. 3:20-CV-2024, 2023 WL 3251216 (N.D. Ohio May 4, 2023). Plaintiff KAM Dev., LLC ("KAM") entered into two Area Representative Agreements with Defendant Marco's Franchising, LLC ("Marco's"). When Marco's declined to renew one of KAM's Area Representative Agreements, KAM sought a declaratory judgment that it was not in default under either agreement. The Court denied KAM's motions for preliminary injunctions, and Marco's then terminated both agreements. After Marco's terminated both agreements, KAM filed an amended complaint, which asserted breach of contract claims against Marco's for its termination of the two agreements.

Marco's filed a motion for summary judgment on KAM's breach of contract claims, which the court granted in part and denied in part. The court found that genuine disputes of material fact existed as to whether the parties had modified one of the Area Representative Agreements, which would have altered KAM's development obligations under that agreement. And because the court could not conclude as a matter of law that the modification was enforceable, it could not conclude on summary judgment whether KAM had fully performed its contractual obligations sufficient to permit it to maintain a

CHAPTER 4

breach of contract action against Marco's. Fact issues also existed as to whether KAM could properly claim certain credits against its development obligations under the two agreements.

Keshav Convenience Store, LLC v. G & G Oil, Inc., 573 MDA 2022, 2023 WL 142551 (Pa. Sup. Ct. Jan. 10, 2023) (appellate court affirmed summary judgment in favor of defendant, supplier of Sunoco gas to plaintiff, who complained that defendant began selling Sunoco gas to a nearby competitor in violation of the parties' contract, however the court held that the contract was clear and did not place any restrictions on defendant's ability to sell Sunoco gas to others in the vicinity of plaintiff's gas station).

Le Fort Enterprises, Inc. v. Lantern 18, LLC, 491 Mass. 144 (2023). This case involved a breach of contract dispute between the plaintiff franchisor, Le Fort Enterprises, Inc. ("Le Fort"), and the defendant franchisee, Lantern 18, LLC, along with its owners. The disagreement arose over Lantern 18's failure to pay the full purchase price for a cleaning services franchise owned by Le Fort. In 2015, Lantern 18 purchased the franchise from Le Fort under an asset purchase agreement and promissory note that required monthly payments over several years. However, during the COVID-19 pandemic in 2020, Lantern 18 defaulted on the monthly payments.

Lantern 18 argued that its payment obligations were excused due to impracticability and frustration of purpose because the pandemic and subsequent shutdown orders had prevented the franchise from operating and generating revenue. Despite this argument, the Massachusetts Supreme Court affirmed summary judgment for Le Fort, finding no evidence that the pandemic had made Lantern 18's performance impracticable or frustrated the purpose of the contract. The court further noted that the contract did not condition payment on franchise revenue, and the parties had allocated the risk of changing financial conditions to Lantern 18.

Nasreen v. Capitol Petroleum Group, LLC, No. 20-1867(TJK), 2023 WL 2734210 (D. D.C. March 31, 2023). Plaintiff operates a gas station under a franchise agreement with Anacostia Realty, LLC, who owns the lot where the station is situated. Capitol Petroleum Group, LLC helps Anacostia provide the gasoline services to plaintiff as well as issues invoices for Anacostia to plaintiff. After Anacostia tried to terminate the franchise agreement for failure to meet contractual obligations, plaintiff sued, claiming breach of contract and violation of the Petroleum Market Practices Act ("PMPA"). The court granted the defendant's motion to dismiss on all claims. As to defendant Capitol

Disputes Regarding Performance, Termination, and Transfers

Petroleum, the court found that Capitol had no contract with the plaintiff. This case is discussed in Chapter 3, Section II.

Peterbrooke Franchising of America, LLC v. Miami Chocolates, LLC, No. 21-10242, 2022 WL 6635136 (11th Cir. Oct. 11, 2022). Franchisor requested that its franchisees upgrade the Point-of-Sale ("POS") system they were required to use, relying on a provision of the franchise agreement providing the franchisor with broad discretion to require such upgrades. Despite multiple requests from the franchisor, however, the franchisee refused to install the new system. As a result, the franchisor terminated the franchise agreement, citing the franchisee's failure to upgrade the POS system as a breach of contract. Franchisor subsequently sued the franchisee for breach of contract and unfair competition. The district court granted summary judgment in favor of the franchisor, however, on appeal, the Eleventh Circuit vacated the summary judgment, finding there were certain unresolved factual disputes regarding whether the franchisee's refusal to upgrade the POS system constituted a material breach permitting termination.

Peterson Motorcars, LLC v. BMW of North America, LLC, No. 3:19-cv-277-DJH-RSE, 2022 WL 4125102 (W.D. Ky. Sept. 9, 2022). Plaintiff, a MINI vehicle dealer, asserted claims against the defendant for breach of the parties' franchise agreement, contending that BMW had not adequately supported plaintiff and other MINI dealers because BMW had not conducted an adequate amount of advertising and marketing of the vehicles and it had failed to introduce new models over the years that customers would want to purchase. The court granted BMW's motion for summary judgment on plaintiff's breach of contract (and breach of the implied covenant of good faith and fair dealing) claims. It held that the franchise agreement gave BMW discretion as to how to conduct its advertising, and that the evidence showed BMW did do a substantial amount of advertising related to the MINI vehicles during the years in question. The court also held that the defendant BMW entity was not the actual manufacturer of the MINI vehicles, therefore the claim that it did not make desirable models of the cars was without merit.

Philadelphia Indemnity Insurance Co. v. Markel Insurance Co., No. 1:20-cv-00669-JRR, 2023 WL 113748 (D. Md. Jan. 5, 2023) (finding a breach of the franchise agreement where the franchisee failed to indemnify franchisor for a settlement arising from an underlying personal injury action arising from an incident that occurred at the franchisee's location). This case is also discussed in Chapter 6, Section VIII.

CHAPTER 4

Pinnacle Foods of California, LLC v. Popeyes Louisiana Kitchen, Inc., No. 21-21555-CIV, 2022 WL 17736190 (S.D. Fla., Dec. 16, 2022). The plaintiff-franchisee ("Pinnacle") filed this suit after its franchisor, Popeye's Louisiana Kitchen, Inc. ("Popeye's") terminated Pinnacle's exclusive territory under the development agreement between the parties due to Pinnacle's failure to (i) develop the requisite number of restaurants according to the schedule in the agreement, (ii) pay certain fees due under the agreement, and (iii) meet Popeye's operational standards in Pinnacle's operating restaurants. Pinnacle alleged the Popeye's (i) breached the development agreement by failing to consider plaintiff's proposed site packages under the same criteria it used to evaluate sites in comparable markets, and (ii) breached the duty of good faith and fair dealing by failing on the same grounds, as well as by terminating plaintiff's exclusive territory. The court denied Popeye's motion to dismiss the breach of contract claim based on Popeye's argument that Pinnacle failed to allege recoverable damages. In dismissing the implied duty of good faith and fair dealing claim, the court noted that, as alleged in the complaint, Pinnacle's claim relating to Popeye's failure to appropriately consider its sites was duplicative of the breach of contract claim and Pinnacle failed to allege that Popeye's failed to observe the reasonable limits of its discretion in terminating the exclusive territory.

Plaintiff also bought a claim against Popeye's and the other defendant, Restaurant Brand International, Inc. ("RBI"), for violation of the Florida Deceptive and Unfair Trade Practices Act ("FDUTPA"); however, the court granted defendant' request for dismissal of these claims, noting that Pinnacle's allegations amounted to, at most, intentional breach of the development agreement, which is not sufficient to support a FDUTPA violation. Finally, plaintiff brought additional claims against RBI for tortious interference with contract and tortious interference with business relationship. The court did not reach the merits of these claims; and, instead held that it lacked personal jurisdiction over RBI, a Canadian corporation, under the Florida long-arm statute because (i) RBI submitted evidence that plaintiff's references to "'RBI's headquarters, offices, or operations" in the U.S. referred to RBI's affiliates and subsidiaries, none of which were a party to the action, and (ii) Pinnacle's allegations were insufficient to justify piercing the corporate veil or to show that Popeye's was RBI's agent.

Pizza Inn, Inc. v. Odetallah, No. CIV-21-00322-PRW, 2022 WL 4473621 (W.D. Okla. Sept. 26, 2022). (The court granted plaintiff-franchisor's motion for summary judgment on its claims for trademark infringement and breach of contract as well as on the franchisee-defendant's counterclaims for breach of contract, fraud, conversion, and negligence. The court disagreed with the franchisor's calculation of damages based upon the franchisee's breach of his post-termination obligations under the franchise agreement because the franchisor included breaches of franchisee's pre-termination obligations in the calculation.)

Qdoba Restaurant Corp. v. Zurich American Insurance Co., No. 120CV03575DDDNRN, 2023 WL 2725875 (D. Colo. Mar. 30, 2023). (The United States District Court for the District of Colorado granted the insurer defendant's motion for judgment on the pleadings for plaintiff Qdoba's breach of contract lawsuit and dismissed Qdoba's claims with prejudice.)

Reno Dealership Group, LLC v. General Motors, LLC, No. 21-55609, 2023 WL 234786 (9th Cir. Jan. 18, 2023) (affirming dismissal of breach of contract claim based on the theory that the agreement between the parties imposed an obligation on a vehicle manufacturer to regulate or supervise false advertising or unfair competition by other dealerships). This case is discussed in Chapter 3, Section 3.

Road King Development, Inc. v. JTH Tax, LLC, No. 2:21-cv-55, 2023 WL 2090280 (E.D. Va. Feb. 17, 2023). Plaintiffs Road King Development, Inc. ("Road King") and ZeeDee, LLC ("ZeeDee") had area development agreements with Defendant JTH Tax, franchisor of Liberty Tax Service franchises ("Liberty"). The agreements required the Plaintiffs to develop candidates to become franchise owners and provide support services to franchisees in certain territories. In November 2020 and January 2021, respectively, Liberty sent letters to Road King and ZeeDee advising them that Liberty would not renew their area development agreements due to each Plaintiff's failure to meet the development goals as set forth in the agreements. The two franchisees sued Liberty for breach of the area development agreements.

In determining the parties' cross motions for summary judgment, the court first held that Liberty's agreement with Road King provided for both termination with and without cause. It then found that Liberty's stated reason for terminating the Road King contract, that Road King had failed to meet its development goals as set forth in the agreement, was not one of the stated bases pursuant to which Liberty could terminate the agreement without first providing Road King with an opportunity to cure. Therefore, the court held that Liberty had breached the parties' contract by improperly terminating Road King without first providing the proper notice and opportunity to cure.

In ZeeDee's situation, however, the court held that Section 7.2 of the parties' area development agreement gave ZeeDee the opportunity to enter

CHAPTER 4

into a new agreement with Liberty if ZeeDee was in compliance with the area development agreement, gave 180 days written notice, and executed a general release. The court first held that ZeeDee had not met the minimum development requirements in the contract, thus it was not in compliance with the area development agreement. It further held that ZeeDee did not give proper notice of its intention to renew or enter into a new area development agreement because, instead of providing the notice in writing to Liberty's CEO as the contract required, ZeeDee sent a message through Liberty's Issue Tracker system that was not addressed to anyone in particular. The court therefore held that ZeeDee had not established a prima facie breach of contract claim for wrongful termination. It further rejected ZeeDee's argument that Liberty had waived the notice requirement by replying to ZeeDee through the Tracker portal that it would "start working on AD renewal", finding this was not an intentional or express waiver of the notice requirement by Liberty.

SC America, LLC v. Marco's Franchising, LLC, No. 3:22-cv-919, 2023 WL 2229654 (N.D. Ohio Feb. 23, 2023) (denying motion to dismiss when release agreement executed between the franchisor and franchisee was broad and the intent of the parties had to be resolved by the trier of fact.)

Synlawn of Northern Nevada LLC v. Synthetic Turf Resources Corp., C.A. No. 4:22-CV-116-MHC, 2022 WL 18460632 (N. D. Ga. Nov. 3, 2022) (dismissing breach of contract claim based on a distribution agreement that was specifically disavowed by a later executed supply agreement that expanded plaintiff's distribution territory).

Terrier, LLC v. HCA Franchise Corporation, No. 222cv01325GMNEJY, 2022 WL 4280251 (D. Nev. Sept. 2022). Plaintiff entered into a franchise agreement with defendant in December of 2006. The agreement contained a post-term covenant not to compete and the plaintiff had an option to renew the agreement, contingent on the plaintiff executing the franchisor's then-current standard form franchise agreement, which included a provision allowing the franchisor to include terms which were different than what was in the original franchise agreement. Plaintiff formed Terrier, LLC and transferred its contractual obligations to that entity in May of 2019. When the plaintiff exercised its conditional right to renew, the defendant provided a demand agreement which would serve as the new franchise agreement. The demand agreement included a compulsory sale provision and the plaintiff refused to sign it. The plaintiff brought suit seeking, among other things, injunctive relief and a declaratory judgment concerning the post-term non-compete. Plaintiff also asserted claims that Defendant breached the contract and its implied covenant of good faith and fair dealing. The court held that there was no breach of the contract, because the express terms of the original franchise agreement allowed the defendant to introduce substantially different terms in a renewal agreement than in the original agreement. The court further held that defendant's conditional renewal requiring the acceptance of the new terms did not constitute bad faith.

Travelodge Hotels, Inc. v. Durga, LLC, No. 15-8412, 2023 WL 314313 (D.N.J. Jan. 19, 2023). Travelodge Hotels, Inc. ("Travelodge") entered into a franchise agreement with Durga, LLC ("Durga") pursuant to which Durga would operate a Travelodge hotel. Travelodge claims to provide customers with access to a "guest lodging facility" franchise network, and its franchise system is based on and utilizes federally-registered trade names, service marks, logos, and derivations thereof, as well as a proprietary reservation platform.

Under the franchise agreement, Travelodge could terminate the agreement early under two circumstances, one of which was if Durga discontinued operating the facility as a Travelodge hotel. If the agreement was terminated early, Durga would pay Travelodge liquidated damages and reimburse Travelodge for any outstanding recurring fees and associated costs. Durga stopped operating the hotel as a Travelodge facility and Travelodge informed Durga it was terminating the agreement early and that Durga was required to pay liquidated damages, fees, and costs. Durga did not pay the amounts Travelodge claimed it was owed, therefore Travelodge filed suit, seeking damages for breach of contract and unjust enrichment.

Travelodge moved for partial summary judgment on three of the six counts it asserted: to recover liquidated damages, to recover recurring fees, and for breach of the guaranty agreement. Durga argued the contract was voidable because Travelodge fraudulently induced it to enter into the franchise agreement, and therefore no breach occurred. Durga also argued Travelodge materially breached the contract when it delayed providing Durga with access to its reservation system. The court found that in a breach of contract claim, where a genuine dispute of fact regarding fraudulent inducement exists, granting summary judgment is inappropriate because, if fraudulent inducement is proven, the contract would be voidable. The court further noted that Durga had presented testimony and other evidence that raised genuine issues of material fact regarding whether Durga had been fraudulently induced to enter into the franchise agreement and whether it had been denied access to Travelodge's reservation system. For these reasons, the court denied Travelodge's motion for partial summary judgment.

CHAPTER 4

Vital Distributions, LLC v. Pepperidge Farm, No. 2:22-cv-00319-MCE-KJN, 2023 WL 2433362 (E.D. Cal. Mar. 9, 2023). In 2017, plaintiff entered into an exclusive distributor agreement with defendant to supply Pepperidge Farm products to retail stores in Yolo and Sacramento County in California. Plaintiff managed to enter into the agreement without having to sign an acknowledgement preventing plaintiff from supplying e-commerce accounts in the region. The unsigned acknowledgement stated, in part, that e-commerce accounts were not retail stores as contemplated by the agreement.

When COVID hit, the market shifted and there was a significant increase in e-commerce transactions. Defendant was unable to meet all of plaintiff's requirements for re-stocking physical retail locations. However, even as production stabilized, defendant still did not meet plaintiff's supply requirements. At the same time, defendant had established an online retail site with Amazon to directly supply consumers. Plaintiff initiated this action for breach of contract, among other claims.

At issue with respect to the breach of contract claim was whether what was a retail store was ambiguous in the agreement between plaintiff and defendant. Defendant argued that the agreement only contemplated brick and mortar retail locations. Plaintiff argued that Amazon has brick and mortar facilities within the territory that are responsible for fulfilling retail orders placed through the Amazon website, thus bringing the sales within the scope of the agreement. The court determined that the term retail store was ambiguous in the agreement and susceptible to plaintiff's interpretation. The court found that online sales through brick and mortar locations located within plaintiff's territory were no different than online sales made through traditional grocery store websites, which are fulfilled by brick and mortar grocery stores and delivered directly to a customer. Such sales through a grocery store were indisputably covered by the agreement. Thus, the court determined that plaintiff's interpretation was sufficiently plausible and denied defendant's motion for summary judgment.

Waters Edge Wineries, Inc. v. Wine Vibes, LLC, No. 5:22-cv-01883-SB-SHK 2023 WL 4297563 (C.D. Cal. June 29, 2023). The court denied the plaintiff franchisor's motion for summary judgment because the record did not show the franchisor exercised reasonable business judgment (as was required by the parties' franchise agreement) in refusing to allow the defendants to build their store without using the construction management firm named in the franchise agreement. The court also noted that the franchisor's desired and approved construction management firm terminated the contract with the defendant.

Disputes Regarding Performance, Termination, and Transfers

Wesdem, L.L.C. v. Illinois Tool Works, Inc., No. 22-50769, 70 F. 4th 285 (5th Cir. June 9, 2023) (court affirmed summary judgment in favor of defendant manufacturer on plaintiff's claim that defendant breached a distributorship agreement because, under Texas' statute of frauds, there had to be a writing with a quantity term in it - even if, as plaintiff contended, the agreement was a requirements contract - and the email plaintiff relied on in which defendant welcomed plaintiff "to the Auto Magic family" did not specify any quantity of goods or even state that plaintiff would purchase Auto Magic products exclusively from defendant). This case is also discussed in Section II(D) of this Chapter.

Wistron Neweb Corporation v. Genesis Networks Telecom Services, LLC, No. 22-cv-2538-LJL, 2022 WL 17067984 (S.D.N.Y. Nov. 17, 2022) (court denied defendants' motions to dismiss plaintiff's claim that defendants had breached the parties' distributor agreement, finding that plaintiff had complied with the procedures set forth in the distribution agreement, including its requirement that the parties engage in a three-step mediation process before a lawsuit could be filed).

Wistron Neweb Corporation v. Genesis Networks Telecom Services, LLC, No. 22-CV-2538 (LJL), 2023 WL 4493542 (S.D.N.Y. July 12, 2023). Taiwanese manufacturer of telecommunications equipment sued its U.S. distributor to recover for unpaid invoices totaling $9,232,256.94 for products manufactured and delivered pursuant to a distributor agreement. Distributor defendants attempted to defend against the manufacturer's breach of contract claim on the ground that an assignment of the distribution agreement had relieved them of liability. The court, however, ruled that the assignment of the distribution agreement did not act to relieve defendants' of liability absent evidence of a novation, which defendants had failed to show. The court therefore granted plaintiff manufacturer's summary judgment motion with respect to defendants' liability on the $9,232,256.94 in unpaid invoices.

B. BREACH OF COVENANT OF GOOD FAITH AND FAIR DEALING

José Santiago, Inc. v. Smithfield Packaged Meats Corp., 66 F.4th 329 (1st Cir. 2023). Plaintiff, José Santiago Inc. ("JSI"), alleged it had an exclusive dealership contract with the defendant, Smithfield Packaged Meats Corp. ("Smithfield"). Puerto Rico's Law 75 governed the dealer-supplier relationship, and the court sought to determine the course of dealing between JSI and Smithfield. The court found that JSI held a non-exclusive right to have

CHAPTER 4

its orders filled by Smithfield because of the parties' course of dealing. However, Law 75 provided protections against unfair contract terminations, including that suppliers could only terminate contracts for "just cause" during a genuine impasse in negotiations. The court ruled that Smithfield had just cause to cease filling JSI's orders due to a deadlock over exclusivity following a brand consolidation. The court adopted a flexible interpretation of Law 75 to balance the interests of dealers and suppliers, taking into account legitimate business decisions such as brand consolidations.

Keshav Convenience Store, LLC v. G & G Oil, Inc., 573 MDA 2022, 2023 WL 142551 (Pa. Super. Ct. Jan. 10, 2023) (The Superior Court of Pennsylvania affirmed the trial court's order granting summary judgment in Defendant's favor because Defendant did not grant Plaintiff an exclusive territory in which no other Sunoco stations could operate under their distribution contract (the "Contract"). Accordingly, no genuine issue of material fact existed because Defendant's branding of a competitor gas station as "Sunoco" and Defendant's sale of Sunoco fuel to this competitor did not constitute a breach of Defendant's good faith under the Contract or UCC. This case is also discussed in Section II.A of this Chapter.

Pinnacle Foods of California, LLC v. Popeyes Louisiana Kitchen, Inc., No. 21-21555-CV, 2022 WL 17736190 (S.D. Fla., Dec. 16, 2022) (dismissing franchisee-plaintiff's claim that franchisor breached duty of good faith and fair dealing by allegedly failing to appropriately consider plaintiff's site packages for new restaurant locations because these allegations were identical to the basis for plaintiff's breach of contract claim. The court also dismissed plaintiff's contention that the franchisor breach its duty of good faith and fair dealing by terminating plaintiff's exclusive territory under its development agreement because plaintiff to allege that the franchisor capriciously exercised its discretion when setting criteria by which the franchisor found plaintiff in default of the development agreement. This is discussed in Chapter 4, Section II.A.)

Terrier, LLC v. HCAFranchise Corporation, No. 222cv01325GMNEJY, 2022 WL 4280251 (D. Nev. Sept. 2022). This case is discussed in Section II.A of this Chapter.

C. TORTIOUS INTERFERENCE

Arnone v. Burke, 211 A.D.3d 998, 181 N.Y.S.3d 311 (2022) (The Appellate Division of the Supreme Court of New York affirmed the lower court's order which denied the franchisor Defendants' motion to dismiss the franchisee Plaintiffs' causes of action for tortious interference with contract and promissory estoppel, finding that Plaintiffs sufficiently pled these claims.)

Branco v. Hull Storey Retail Group, LLC, No. 2021-000233, 2023 WL 3614244 (S.C. May 24, 2023) (The Supreme Court of South Carolina reversed a court of appeals decision overturning a damages award to the plaintiff, a former Great American Cookie Co. franchisee, for tortious interference by the defendant landlord for the franchise location. The plaintiff entered an asset purchase agreement ("APA") for the franchise at the end of plaintiff's lease term that was contingent on the buyers securing a lease from the same landlord. The landlord improperly claimed that the APA amounted to a lease assignment entitling the landlord to the entire APA purchase price as an assignment fee, which led the buyers to walk away from the sale).

Corvallis Hospitality, LLC. v. Wilmington Trust, No. 2017-LC26, 6:22-CV-00024-MC, 2023 WL 3170438 (D. Or. Apr. 28, 2023) (The United States District Court for the District of Oregon granted in part and denied in part defendants' motion to dismiss plaintiff's amended Complaint (the "Motion"). The court granted defendants' Motion on plaintiff's Oregon Trust Deed Act and tortious interference claims because the foreclosure sale never occurred, and because plaintiff did not sufficiently allege facts showing that defendants intentionally interfered with plaintiff's economic relations. Additionally, the court found that plaintiff sufficiently pled its breach of contract and breach of covenant of good faith and fair dealing claims and dismissed defendants' Motion on both of these claims.)

Good Clean Love, Inc. v. Epoch NE Corporation, Civ. No. 6:21-cv-01294-AA, 2023 WL 2709653 (D. Or. March 30, 2023). If a defendant is not a third party, but rather acting as a party to the contract (as, for instance, a corporate employee or agent of a contracting party), then the defendant cannot be liable for intentional interference with that contract. This case is discussed in Chapter 8, Section II.

JTH Tax LLC v. Anderson, No. CV-23-00209-PHX-DJH, 2023 WL 3499645 (D. Ariz. Apr. 18, 2023) (The court denied a motion to dismiss the franchisor's first amended complaint for failure to state a claim against defendants who were office managers of prior franchisees, finding that the franchisor met pleading standard to state a claim for tortious interference and other claims.) This case is discussed in Chapter 5, Section IV.

CHAPTER 4

Planet Fitness International Franchise v. JEG-United, LLC, No. 20-cv-693-LM, 2022 WL 4484477 (D.N.H. Sept. 27, 2022). Court granted summary judgment in favor of Planet Fitness on JEG's claim that Planet Fitness and its Chief Development Officer had tortiously interfered with JEG's prospective contractual relationships with three different entities JEG had communicated and negotiated with in connection with its efforts to develop Planet Fitness franchises in Mexico. With respect to one of the entities, JEG had sought to include Planet Fitness in the proposed transaction, and there was no evidence that Planet Fitness or its executive did anything to prevent JEG from entering into the contractual relationship on its own. With respect to the second entity, JEG had only engaged in "high level" conversations about a possible lease of real estate, which the court held did not create the "reasonable expectation of economic advantage" necessary to sustain a tortious interference claim. Regarding the third entity, Planet Fitness and its executive actually helped arrange JEG's meeting with the entity and a possible transaction. This case is discussed more fully in Chapter 4, Section VII.

Shandong Luxi Pharmaceutical Co., Ltd. v. Camphor Technologies, Inc., No. 8:21-CV-942-CEH-AEP, 2023 WL 2499157 (M.D. Fla. Mar. 14, 2023) (The United States District Court for the Middle District of Florida granted in part plaintiff's motion to dismiss Defendant's Amended Counterclaims (the "Motion") finding that Defendant failed to adequately plead its injunction and tortious interference claims. However, the Court denied in part Plaintiff's Motion, finding that Defendant adequately pled its breach of contract and misappropriation of trade secrets claim. The Court also gave Defendant the option to file a Second Amended Counterclaim within 14 days to address the deficiencies addressed in the Court's order.)

D. FRAUD

Amaro Oilfield Automation, LLC v. Lithis CM, Inc., 661 S.W.3d 477, No. 08-21-00013-CV (Tex. App. Jan. 23, 2023). The court affirmed the lower court's granting of Lithis's motion for summary judgment on Amaro's claim that Lithis committed common law fraud, because it found Amaro had not presented sufficient evidence to establish that Lithis had made a false representation regarding attempts to recover a trade-in vehicle. This case is discussed in Chapter 4, Section II.A.

Lunt v. Frost Shades Franchising, LLC, No. 3:22-cv-00775, 2023 WL 3484202 (M.D. Tenn May 16, 2023). The court found the franchisee plaintiff had a likelihood of success of the merits for purposes of granting injunctive relief based on the franchisor's omission of disclosures from Item 3 of the FDD. This case is discussed in Chapter 2, Section 2.

BASF Corp. v. Stoutenger, No. 5:22-CV-00281 (MAD/ML), 2023 WL 3624680 (N.D.N.Y. May 24, 2023) (The District Court for the Northern District of New York denied plaintiff manufacturer's motion to dismiss counterclaims by the defendant owner of an automotive repair shop for anticipatory repudiation, breach of contract, unjust enrichment, and fraudulent inducement. The defendant alleged a bait and switch scheme in which an authorized distributor of the plaintiff contracted with the defendant to supply products, but the plaintiff manufacturer subsequently misled the defendant into signing another agreement with a higher purchase requirement.).

Cipercen, LLC v. Morningside Texas Holdings, LLC, No. N19C-12-074 EMD CCLD, 2022 WL 4243687 (Super. Ct. Del. Sept. 14, 2022). In this case, the franchisee claimed that it was fraudulently induced to enter into an agreement to sell the franchised location to franchisor's preferred purchaser in exchange for a waiver of certain franchise fees. The court dismissed the claim for failure to state a claim, with no leave to amend, because franchisor's offer to waive the franchise fees was expressly conditioned upon the closing of the sale and other matters that did not occur. The court also dismissed both the franchisee's claim that the franchisor tortiously interfered with a prospective economic advantage and the franchisor's counterclaim for breach of contract, based on franchisee's failure to pay franchise fees, as time-barred. The court held that both the tortious interference and breach of contract claims were subject to a three-year statute of limitations under North Carolina law, which governed pursuant to the franchise agreement's choice-of-law provision.

Hyundai Motor America Corp. v. EFN West Palm Motor Sales, LLC, 343 F.R.D. 230 (S.D. Fla. 2022) (granting in part and denying in part defendant automobile dealership's motion for sanctions for spoliation of evidence in plaintiff automobile manufacturer's fraud action alleging dealership fraudulently collected warranty funds, where the plaintiff manufacturer failed to preserve all engines it received from the dealerships despite a clear and longstanding duty to preserve).

SBFO Operator No. 3, LLC v. Onex Corp., No. 4:19-CV-0321-JAR, 2023 WL 2631521 (E.D. Mo. Mar. 23, 2023). Plaintiff SBFO Operator No. 3, LLC, operated ten Save-A-Lot grocery stores as an independent licensee and defendant Onex Corp. ("Onex") acquired Save-A-Lot from its parent

CHAPTER 4

company in 2016. Plaintiff alleged Save-A-Lot and Onex conspired to induce plaintiff to invest into a failing business based on false representations and inaccurate projections, and that the parties skimmed plaintiff's profits by inflating wholesale prices.

The court analyzed the agreement to determine whether Save-A-Lot's model constituted a hidden franchise and evaluated the differences between franchises and license agreements. However, the agreement in question explicitly said that it would not be construed to create a franchise relationship. Further, plaintiff pointed to no evidence that Onex charged a wholesaler's mark-up beyond a certain percentage to constitute a franchise fee. The court ultimately found no evidence of intentional misrepresentation by Save-A-Lot and Onex. The court further concluded that Save-A-Lot's pricing structure did not transform the license model into a franchise.

Additionally, the parties involved had counsel review the differences between a franchise and licensee model before finalizing the agreement. The court found the plaintiff had signed several disclaimers and anti-reliance releases that barred their claims unless induced by fraud. Moreover, the court found no evidence showing Save-A-Lot continued a fraudulent scheme after acquiring Save-A-Lot. Therefore, plaintiff's RICO and conspiracy claims failed. The court also found the economic loss doctrine barred claims related to pricing.

As a result, the court ruled plaintiff failed to establish fraudulent inducement or other unlawful acts that would invalidate the disclaimers in the agreement with Save-A-Lot. The court therefore granted the defendants' motion for summary judgment on all claims.

Wesdem, L.L.C. v. Illinois Tool Works, Inc., No. 22-50769, 70 F. 4th 285 (5th Cir. June 9, 2023). Defendant manufactures automotive products. Plaintiff discussed with Defendant becoming a distributor of defendant's products by purchasing an existing distributor. That distributor sold defendant's products through Amazon and similar companies, and plaintiff claimed defendant assured plaintiff it could continue to sell defendant's products on Amazon and similar sites "for as long as it wanted." Plaintiff purchased the existing distributor and, for the next two years, sold defendant's products on Amazon and other online marketplaces. Then, however, defendant sent plaintiff and other of its distributors a notice advising them of a new policy that prohibited distributors from selling defendant's products on any online marketplace.

Plaintiff sued defendant for fraud. The district court granted defendant's motion to dismiss plaintiff's fraud claim and the appellate court affirmed. It found that plaintiff's alleged facts did not support a reasonable inference that defendant's representation prior to plaintiff purchasing the existing distributor was false and that defendant knew it was false when it made the representation. The court found that the alleged misrepresentation was a promise of future performance and that defendant's later prohibition of online sales was not evidence of defendant's intent not to perform when the promise was made. The court further held that plaintiff's successfully selling defendant's products online for two years undermined its claim of fraud.

Yarber v. Kia America, Inc., No. 22-cv-03411-HSG, 2023 WL 2654186 (N.D. Cal. March 27, 2023) (in vehicle defect case, court granted defendant's motion to dismiss plaintiff's fraudulent concealment claim and request for punitive damages, finding that the claims was barred by the economic loss rule (as plaintiff had only suffered economic losses), plaintiff's allegations did not plausibly support an inference that the Defendant knew about the specific alleged defect, and punitive damages cannot be recovered for contract claims).

E. UNFAIR AND DECEPTIVE TRADE PRACTICES

Amaro Oilfield Automation, LLC v. Lithis CM, Inc., 661 S.W.3d 477, No. 08-21-00013-CV (Tex. App. Jan. 23, 2023). The court affirmed the lower court's granting of Lithis's motion for summary judgment on Amaro's claim that Lithis violated the Texas Deceptive Trade Practice Act because the court determined that Amaro provided no evidence that it was a consumer with respect to Lithis. Amaro had judicially admitted that the Amaro employee who had purchased the truck from Lithis did not have actual authority from Amaro to enter into the transaction, thus Amaro could not be a consumer for purposes of the statute. This case is discussed in Chapter 4, Section II.A.

CajunLand Pizza, LLC v. Marco's Franchising, LLC, No. 3:20-cv-536-JGC, 2022 WL 3960574 (N.D. Ohio Aug. 31, 2022). Plaintiff franchisee, CajunLand Pizza, brought suit against defendant franchisor, Marco's Franchising, LLC, alleging that defendant had made misrepresentations about profitability and the right to sell franchises to induce the franchisee to invest in the franchisor. The franchisor asserted counterclaims for attorney's fees after franchisee's claims were dismissed, invoking provisions in the franchise agreement that allowed for fees for "successfully defending" claims that it committed fraud or that the agreement's terms were unfair. The court held that the franchisor was entitled to fees for defending the dismissed claims under Ohio's Deceptive Trade Practices Act and the Ohio Business Opportunity Act. The court held these statutes applied to the claims because the franchisees alleged that the franchisor misrepresented contractual rights, which amounted to fraud in the inducement. However, the court denied fees for other dismissed claims that were not covered by the contractual provisions.

Calabasas Luxury Motorcars, Inc. v. BMW North America, LLC, No. CV 21-8825-DMG (ASX), 2022 WL 17350921 (C.D. Cal. Sept. 19, 2022). Plaintiff Calabasas Luxury Motorcars, Inc. ("CLM") operates a luxury used vehicle dealership in California. CLM filed a complaint against BMW North America, LLC and BMW Financial Services, LLC (collectively, "BMW"), alleging that BMW's policy of not honoring payoffs from third-party dealers for its leased vehicles violates California's Unfair Competition Law ("UCL"). BMW filed a motion to dismiss, arguing that the claims fail as a matter of law.

The court granted the motion to dismiss. As an initial matter, the court held that the proper test for whether a business practice is unfair as between competitors is whether "conduct threatens an incipient violation of an antitrust law or violates the policy or spirit of one of those laws because its effects are comparable to or the same as a violation of the law, or otherwise significantly threatens or harms competition." The court then concluded that BMW's policy choice to implement an exclusive dealing arrangement is a unilateral act permitted under the antitrust laws. Because BMW was permitted under antitrust laws to franchise only with certain dealers, its policy of only honoring payoffs from its franchised dealers was likewise permissible under the UCL.

Havtech, LLC v. AAON Inc., No. CV SAG-22-00453, 2023 WL 200117 (D. Md. Jan. 17, 2023) (defendant manufacturer's motion to dismiss was denied in distributor's suit alleging violation of Oklahoma Fair Practices of Equipment Manufacturers, Distributors, Wholesalers, and Dealers Act because the Act was constitutional, the parties' dealer agreement did not contain a forum selection clause, and discovery is required to determine whether the Act applies to the type of equipment that was the subject of the parties' transaction).

Queen v. Wineinger, No. 21-cv-378-wmc, 2022 WL 3017004 (W.D. Wis. Aug. 1, 2022). Plaintiff operated a Dairy Queen since 1998 governed by a franchise agreement which allowed for the sales of non-system food. Dairy Queen no longer allowed such provisions in its current franchise agreement and required that a transferee of the store sign a current franchise agreement. Plaintiff argued that Dairy Queen violated the Wisconsin Fair Dealership Law ("WFDL") by making a "substantial change" to the competitive circumstances of the original 1952 franchise agreement which governed the restaurant. The Court disagreed, noting that Dairy Queen's move to prohibit the sale of non-system food was "essential, reasonable and non-discriminatory" given its "objectively ascertainable need for uniformity in updating its franchise agreements for new dealers" and the franchisor's applying the new franchise agreements in a non-discriminatory manner.

F. VIOLATIONS OF STATE RELATIONSHIP STATUTES

Central Jersey Construction Equipment Sales, LLC v. LBX Co., LLC, No. 22-5581, 2023 WL 3093575 (6th Cir. Apr. 26, 2023). Plaintiff Central Jersey Construction Equipment Sales ("Central") contracted with Defendant LBX Company ("LPX") to become a dealer of LBX's construction equipment. According to Central's complaint, LBX allegedly asked Central to open an additional facility and promised a new dealer agreement if Central did so. Central alleged that it invested in the costly expansion but never received the promised contract. LBX instead terminated the parties' existing agreement a few years later.

Central claimed that LBX's conduct violated the Kentucky statute (Ky. Rev. Stat. §§ 365.800-.840) that requires a manufacturer to have "good cause" to terminate a contract with a retailer. Central also raised a promissory-estoppel claim and argued that Central had opened the additional location in reliance on LBX's unfulfilled promise of a new agreement.

On appeal, the Sixth Circuit Court of Appeals affirmed the district court's dismissal of both claims. As for its statutory claim, the parties' agreement gave Central one year to file any action pertaining to the agreement. But Central waited over a year before filing its suit under the Kentucky law that required "good cause" for its termination. The court therefore affirmed the district court's enforcement of this contractual limitation period under Kentucky law. As for Central's promissory-estoppel claim, the court held that the Kentucky Supreme Court would enforce only definite promises in promissory-estoppel cases. Therefore, according to the court, the abstract promise of a future "agreement" without reference to any of its terms was insufficient to state a promissory-estoppel claim.

In ***City Beverages LLC v. Crown Imports LLC***, 2022 WL 17582370 (W.D.Wash, December 12, 2022), plaintiff City Beverages LLC d/b/a Olympic Eagle Distributing ("Olympic") filed a motion for preliminary injunction to stop defendant Crown Imports LLC d/b/a/ Constellation Beer Brands Division ("Constellation") from terminating the Distribution Agreement between Olympic and Constellation. Constellation moved for reconsideration of the court's temporary restraining order.

Olympic was the long-time distributor for Constellation's beer brands in the Pierce and King Counties, under a Distribution Agreement

CHAPTER 4

between the parties. On September 8, 2022, Constellation notified Olympic of its intention to terminate the Distribution Agreement and required Olympic to transfer all of its rights to one of its competitor distributors. The notice did not provide a reason for the termination.

The court discussed the legal standard for a preliminary injunction, noting that the Ninth Circuit developed a sliding scale approach under *Winter v. Natural Res. Def. Council, Inc.*, 555 U.S. 7 (2008), under which two factors, likelihood of success on the merits and the balance of equities, could be evaluated on a sliding scale, so long as the other two factors, a likelihood of irreparable harm and an injunction is in the public interest, are met. The court first discussed the likelihood of success on the merits by focusing on the application of two Washington statutes to the facts of the case: The Wholesale Distributor/Supplier Equity Agreement Act (the "Act") and the Washington Franchise Investment Protection Act ("FIPA").

Olympic argued that the Act does not allow termination of a Distribution Agreement without cause, while Constellation argued the Act contemplates certain non-cause terminations and in any event, the Distribution Agreement allowed for a termination without cause. With respect to the Act, the court ultimately determined that the most likely reading of the Act is that it precludes termination without cause and that Olympic would have a high likelihood of success on the merits.

Olympic further argued that it was a franchisee under the FIPA and therefore the franchisor/franchisee relationship between Olympic and Constellation could not be terminated without good cause. A 'franchise' is established under the FIPA if an agreement establishes that "(i) a person is granted the right to engage in the business of offering, selling, or distributing goods or services under a marketing plan prescribed or suggested in substantial part by the grantor or its affiliate; (ii) The operation of the business is substantially associated with a trademark, service mark, trade name, advertising, or other commercial symbol designating, owned by, or licensed by the grantor or its affiliate; and (iii) The person pays, agrees to pay, or is required to pay, directly or indirectly, a franchise fee." The term "substantially associated" under the second prong of the franchise definition is not defined under the FIPA, but has been interpreted to mean that a plaintiff must show substantial association with the trade name or trademarks. Olympic argues that it meets this prong because it had the right to use Consellation's trademarks for distribution and advertising purposes, however, the court concluded that it did not prove customers associated Olympic with Constellation, and therefore the court could not conclude Olympic would have a high likelihood of success on the merits based on the FIPA claim. The court found that Olympic met the remaining factors necessary and granted

Olympic's preliminary injunction and denied Constellation's motion for reconsideration.

CJ Consultants, LLC v. Window World, Inc., No. 22-CV-3, 2022 WL 4354265 (W.D. Mich. Sept. 20, 2022). The U.S. District Court for the Western District of Michigan granted defendant franchisor's motion to dismiss, including claims under the Michigan Franchise Investment Law ("MFIL"). Franchisee, CJ Consultants, first entered into a franchise agreement with franchisor, Window World, in 2012. Again, in 2017, CJ Consultants entered into a franchise agreement for a 10-year period. Approximately three years into that 10-year term, Window World required more onerous financial reporting requirements. When CJ Consultants failed to comply with the enhanced financial reporting requirements, Window World terminated CJ Consultant's franchise agreement.

Thereafter, CJ Consultants initiated a lawsuit against Window World, bringing six claims, including breach of contract, wrongful termination, and breach of the MFIL. Window World successfully moved to dismiss all claims.

With respect to the MFIL claims, the court found that CJ Consultants was unable to state a claim under the disclosure requirements of Section 8 (Section 445.1508) because the court determined that the 2017 franchise agreement was a renewal of the 2012 franchise agreement. The renewal determination was material because the MFIL does not apply to the renewal or extension of an existing franchise where there is no interruption in the operation of the franchised business by the franchisee. In determining that the 2017 franchise agreement was a renewal, the court pointed to the waiver of the initial franchise fee waiver and an addendum to the franchise agreement making reference to a "Renewal Franchise Agreement." As such, the Section 8 MFIL claim was dismissed for failure to state a claim.

The court also dismissed CJ Consultants' MFIL claim under Section 28 (Section 445.1527), which voids franchise agreement provisions that allow for termination without good cause. The court held that CJ Consultants could not make out this claim because Section 445.1527 does not provide a private right of action. The Michigan Supreme Court has not determined whether MFIL provides a private right of action for wrongful termination without good cause. As such, the district court analyzed and agreed with the 1997 Michigan Court of Appeals case of *Franchise Management Unlimited, Inc. v. America's Favorite Chicken*, 561 N.W.2d 123 (Mich. Ct. App. 1997), which held that there was no private right of action. In doing so, the court elected not to follow the Sixth Circuit's 1990 ruling in *Geib v. Amoco Oil Co*, 29 F.3d 1050 (6th Cir. 1994), which held a private right of action was available under Section 445.1527. The court reasoned that CJ Consultants' reliance on the Sixth

CHAPTER 4

Circuit case did not satisfy the applicable standard of "a strong showing" that the Michigan Supreme Court would decide the issue differently, and the court dismissed the claim under Section 28 of the MFIL.

EFN West Palm Beach Motor Sales, LLC v. Hyundai Motor America Corp., No. 21-80348-CIV-CANNON/Matthewman, 2023 WL 2825920 (S.D. Fla. March 7, 2023). Defendant Hyundai terminated the plaintiffs' dealer agreements pursuant to a clause in the agreements allowing Hyundai to terminate if it determined, in its sole discretion, that conduct occurred which damaged Hyundai's and the dealers' reputational harm. Plaintiffs sued for wrongful termination and asserted, among other things, that defendant had not shown that it complied with the termination requirements of Florida's Dealer Act (specifically, Fla. Stat. Sec. 320.641(3)). Under the statute, defendant has the burden of proving that its termination is fair and is not prohibited by the parties' franchise agreement. The court first rejected plaintiffs' contention that defendant was also required under the statute to demonstrate, as a prerequisite to termination, a "material and substantial breach" of the parties' dealer agreement. The court noted that defendant was terminating pursuant to a discretionary reputational harm provision and not for breach of the agreement. It held that the statute contemplates terminations that are clearly permitted by the dealer agreement irrespective of a breach (in addition to terminations that *are* based on alleged breaches of the dealer or franchise agreement). Reviewing the record, the court found there was no triable issue of fact as to whether defendant acted in bad faith or in a manner that was not uniform and consistent, and granted defendant's motion for summary judgment on plaintiffs' wrongful termination claims.

This case is discussed in further detail in Section II(A) of this Chapter.

Golden Fortune Import & Export Corporation v. Mei-Xin Limited, No. 22-1710, 2022 WL 3536494 (3d Cir. Aug. 5, 2022). Plaintiff Golden Fortune Import & Export Corporation ("Golden Fortune"), a United States-based Asian grocery distributor, contracted with Mei-Xin Limited ("Mei-Xin"), a Hong Kong-based manufacturer of pre-packaged bakery products, to distribute Mei-Xin's products in the United States. The parties entered into their most recent distribution agreement in 2021. The agreement provided that Mei-Xin could terminate the agreement for any reason upon 30 days' written notice, or for breach immediately without notice. Mei-Xin emailed Golden Fortune two separate written notices of termination on January 21, 2022 and March 3, 2022. Golden Fortune sued Mei-Xin, arguing the termination was invalid under the New Jersey Franchise Practices Act ("NJFPA"), while Mei-

Xin contended that the NJFPA was inapplicable. The United States District Court for the District of New Jersey granted Golden Fortune's motion for a preliminary injunction. However, the Third Circuit reversed.

On appeal, Mei-Xin argued that Golden Fortune had failed to establish either a likelihood of success on the merits or irreparable harm. The Third Circuit agreed. First, the court held that Golden Fortune failed to establish that it was likely to succeed on the merits of its claim, because the NJFPA likely does not apply to the parties' relationship. The NJFPA requires that a "community of interest in the marketing of goods and services" exist between a franchisor and franchisee. The court held that no such community of interest existed, because Mei-Xin did not exercise sufficient control over Golden Fortune, Golden Fortune was not economically dependent on Mei-Xin, and there was no great disparity in the parties' bargaining power. Moreover, the NJFPA only applies where "20% of the franchisee's gross sales are intended to be or are derived from the franchise," and Golden Fortune derived only about 8.6% of its gross sales from the sale of Mei-Xin's products over a 12-month period. Second, the court held that Golden Fortune failed to establish irreparable harm because it merely alleged lost sales and profits, which are quantifiable and amenable to monetary damages.

JB Brothers, Inc v. Poke Bar GA Johns Creek I, LLC, No. 2:21-cv-01405-CBM-MRWx 2022 WL 17080158 (C.D. Cal. Sept. 29, 2022). Plaintiff, the owner and franchisor of Poke Bar Dice & Mix restaurants, sued the defendant franchisee for breach of the parties' franchise agreement. In response, the franchisee asserted several counterclaims, including for (1) violation of the California Franchise Investment Law ("CFIL"), (2) intentional misrepresentations (fraud); (3) violations of California's Unfair Competition Law (UCL); and (4) unjust enrichment. The court granted the franchisor's motion to dismiss these claims.

Regarding the first claim, the franchisee argued that the franchisor violated the CFIL because, at the time the parties entered into the franchise agreement, the franchisor was not registered as a franchisor and did not own the trademark rights to "Poke Bar." The court disagreed, noting that the law contained a provision which excluded transfers of interest in a franchise to residents of another state from the CFIL's registration requirements. Specifically, where the locations were all physically outside of California, as they were here (they were in Georgia), the registration requirements did not apply and thus there was no violation of the CFIL. The court also noted that the claim was outside of the CFIL's one-year statute of limitations period because the franchisee had inquiry notice more than four years prior.

CHAPTER 4

The court ruled that the CFIL preempted the franchisee's other counterclaims due to Section 31306 of the CFIL, which forecloses "civil liability in favor of any private party ... as a result of the violation of any provision of this law or any rule or order hereunder." The court went on to elaborate that "only claims independent of CFIL violations are not preempted under the statute," and that the franchisee's counterclaims here all stemmed from the same alleged misrepresentation which was argued to be a violation of the CFIL (the first counterclaim).

Neff Group Distributors, Inc. v. Cognex Corp., No. CV 22-11270-NMG, 2022 WL 17156025 (D. Mass. Nov. 22, 2022). On January 1, 2021, Neff Group Distributors, Inc. ("Neff") entered into three separate, nonexclusive distribution agreements with Cognex Corp. ("Cognex"), under which Neff was authorized to sell Cognex's products in Wisconsin (the "Wisconsin Agreement"), Indiana (the "Indiana Agreement"), and Ohio, Pennsylvania, and West Virginia (the "Ohio Agreement"). All three agreements included sales quotas, express disclaimers of reliance on any extra-contractual representations, and a specific and limited geographic territory. In addition, all three agreements automatically expired on December 31, 2021, unless the parties mutually agreed to renew them.

Cognex notified Neff on November 2, 2021 that it intended to terminate its relationship with Neff, and that it would therefore not be renewing the Wisconsin, Indiana, and Ohio Agreements. Neff subsequently sued Cognex in Wisconsin state court, asserting claims for violations of the Wisconsin Fair Dealership Law ("WFDL") and the Indiana Deceptive Franchise Practices Act ("IDFPA"), as well as claims for promissory estoppel and unjust enrichment. Cognex removed the case to the U.S. District Court for the District of Wisconsin based on diversity jurisdiction and subsequently filed a motion to dismiss and a motion to transfer to the District of Massachusetts, as the parties' agreements contained Massachusetts forum selection and choice of law provisions. The District of Wisconsin found the forum selection clauses controlling and transferred the case to the District of Massachusetts, which subsequently considered Cognex's motion to dismiss.

With respect to Neff's claims under the WFDL, the court found that although that statute may apply to the Wisconsin Agreement, it does not apply to the Indiana and Ohio Agreements, as those agreements do not permit business transactions in the State of Wisconsin. The court therefore dismissed Neff's WFDL claims as they applied to the Indiana and Ohio Agreements. As for Neff's claims under the IDFPA, the court found that the relationship between Neff and Cognex was not a "franchise" as defined under that statute, because Neff did not pay a franchise fee to Cognex. In so finding, the court reasoned the cost of the excess inventory Neff had purchased from Cognex did not constitute an "indirect" franchise fee, because Neff was free to sell that inventory subject to reasonable restrictions provided under the relevant agreements. The court therefore dismissed Neff's claims under the IDFPA. As for Neff's promissory estoppel and unjust enrichment claims, the court found that the agreements' integration clauses were sufficient to dismiss the former, and that the latter was a quasi-contract claim that could not be maintained given the existence of an enforceable contract between the parties.

Ramos v. Willert Home Products, Inc., No. 22-1247 (RAM), 2023 WL 234758 (D.P.R. Jan. 18, 2023) (The United States District Court for the District of Puerto Rico dismissed the plaintiff sales representative's improper termination suit against the defendant principal merchant for failure to state a claim under the Puerto Rico Sales Representative Act and failure to state a claim for breach of contract. The plaintiff failed to plead the Puerto Rico Sales Representative Act's statutory requirement of an exclusive relationship with the principal merchant, sought to improperly apply the statute retroactively and extraterritorially, and could not plead breach of contract for improper termination because the contract was terminable at will.).

G. NEGLIGENCE

Estate of Zamarie Chance v. Fairfield Inn & Suites, 287 N.C. App. 393, 2022 WL 17985662 (N.C. Ct. App. Dec. 29, 2022). This case arose from a fatal assault upon decedent by his mother, Crystal Matthews, in a Fairfield Inn & Suites by Marriott hotel room located in Fayetteville, N.C. while the decedent and Matthews were guests there in 2017. Another hotel guest, who was staying in the room directly below Matthews's room, "heard repetitive thuds, stomping[,] and muffled cries for help," and called the hotel front desk twice to complain about the noises. After the second call to the front desk, the guest also phoned 911 to report the incident and the police department responded to the room, where they found decedent and transported him to the hospital. The decedent was later pronounced dead due to blunt force trauma.

Plaintiff filed a complaint against the defendants entities and an individual Plaintiff believed to be the owner, operator, franchisee, and/or in control of the hotel at the time of decedent's death. Plaintiff alleged that defendants were liable in tort for decedent's death on the grounds they did not properly prevent and respond to the incident after being notified of the disturbance in Matthews's room. Plaintiff further contended that defendants were negligent and breached their duties to decedent as a lawful guest and business invitee of defendants by failing to do several things, including

CHAPTER 4

providing adequate safety, responding and intervening in time, properly training their employees to respond to a report of suspected physical violence in a hotel room, and properly respond to complaints regarding noise from hotel guests.

Defendant Fairfield Inn & Suites by Marriott filed a motion to dismiss on the basis it is a trade name and not a legal entity. Defendants Newport Ramsey, LLC; ATC Manager, LLC; MLP Manager, LLC; Newport Hospitality Group, Inc.; Marriott International, Inc.; and Adam K. Collier each filed an answer to Plaintiff's complaint.

In 2021, defendants filed a motion for summary judgment and amended motion for summary judgment. Defendants asserted in their motion that Marriott International, Inc. is merely a franchisor of the Hotel and has no agency relationship with any other defendant and does not manage or exercise any control over the day-to-day operations of the hotel. Defendants argued that therefore Marriott International, Inc. was not subject to liability for alleged torts on the hotel's property. They also argued that the other named corporate entities did not exercise the requisite control for tort liability. The defendants further argued that the "intentional criminal act" that had been committed was unforeseeable and there was no causal link between any negligence and the decedent's death.

The lower court denied plaintiff's motion for summary judgment and granted defendants' motion for summary judgment after considering the parties' briefing and the evidence of record. Plaintiff appealed the decision. The North Carolina Court of Appeals considered whether the trial court properly granted defendants' motion for summary judgment, and concluded that it had been properly granted.

The appellate court broke down the duty plaintiff claimed the defendant entities owed into two separate duties of care: (1) the duty of an innkeeper to keep the premises and hotel rooms in reasonably safe condition; and (2) the duty of an innkeeper to respond to and provide aid to a guest who the innkeeper knows, or should know, is injured. As for the first duty, the test in determining when a proprietor has a duty to safeguard his invitees from injuries caused by the criminal acts of third parties is one of "foreseeability," and the court held that the murder of the decedent in a hotel room was not foreseeable by the hotel operator, and there was no reasonable safety measure the hotel owner could have implemented to prevent the crime. Since the plaintiff did not plead any facts indicating the hotel owner was on notice of Matthews's violent nature, the court concluded that Matthews's criminal act was an independent and intervening act, breaking any causal chain flowing from defendants' failure to provide reasonable safety or security measures.

Disputes Regarding Performance, Termination, and Transfers

As for the second duty, the court noted that this was a case of first impression, as it concerned whether defendants, in their role as innkeeper, had a duty to take affirmative action to provide aid or protection to a guest. The North Carolina Supreme Court has recognized that a special relationship exists between an innkeeper and its guests, and under such circumstances, the law imposes a duty on the innkeeper "to take reasonable action ... to give [the guest] first aid after its knows or has reason to know that [the guest is] ill or injured, and to care for [the guest] until [he or she] can be cared for by others." The court concluded that while plaintiff presented evidence that there was a duty created by the special relationship between the hotel's owner and operator, an innkeeper, and the decedent (who was a guest of the hotel), the plaintiff nevertheless failed to produce evidence demonstrating that defendants breached that duty of care to the decedent (among other things, plaintiff failed to show any responsive measures taken by the hotel owner after it received the phone calls). Because "breach" is an essential element of the negligence claim and was required for plaintiff's claim to survive summary judgment, the appellate court held that the trial court had not erred in granting defendant's motion for summary judgment.

In ***Flynn v. Anytime Fitness, LLC***, No. C.A. 2022-0742, 2022 WL 17982922 (La. Ct. App. 1st Cir. Dec. 29, 2022), a Louisiana appellate court affirmed the dismissal of Plaintiff William Flynn's ("Flynn") claims against Defendant Anytime Fitness, LLC ("Anytime") on a motion for summary judgment.

While exercising at Thornhill Brothers Fitness, LLC ("Thornhill"), an Anytime franchisee, Flynn began using an inversion table that came apart, causing severe injury to his cervical spine. The subject inversion table was purchased secondhand by Thornhill on Craig's List, which was in direct violation of the franchise agreement that required all equipment to be purchased new and from a designated vendor.

Flynn initiated suit against Anytime, Thornhill, and others, and pursued claims for general negligence, custodial or premises liability, and vicarious liability or *respondeat superior*. The appellate court affirmed dismissal of the plaintiff's claims against Anytime, finding that the franchisor did not owe a duty to the plaintiff because Anytime did not exert day-to-day control over its franchisee's management procedures, have custody or "garde" of the franchisee's premises, nor select, approve, maintain or require purchase of the defective equipment. The Court concluded that when the franchisor's role is limited to offering the franchisee company trademarks and support, that relationship is insufficient to confer control over the day-to-day operations of the franchise. As a result, the plaintiff was unable to maintain an action against Anytime for Thornhill's alleged negligence.

CHAPTER 4

Reno Dealership Group, LLC v. General Motors, LLC, No. 21-55609, 2023 WL 234786 (9th Cir. Jan. 18, 2023) (affirming dismissal of negligence claim based on the theory that a vehicle manufacturer owed its dealers a legal duty to supervise the promotional activities of the manufacturer's other dealers). This case is discussed in Chapter 3, Section 3.

Sai Nath, LLC v. Patel, 660 S.W.3d 474 (Mo. Ct. App. 2023) (Plaintiff, a majority shareholder of a Days Inn, brought an action against Girakumari Patel ("Geera"), a former managing member of the Days Inn and her husband for conversion and breach of fiduciary duty. Geera filed a cross claim for breach of fiduciary duty. The Missouri Court of Appeals, Southern District, reversed in part and remanded this matter to the circuit court to enter an amended judgment that removed Respondent, Shailesh Patel's ("Sonny") name from the damages awarded on Respondent Geera's crossclaim because Sonny was not a party to that claim and was not a member of Sai Nath LLC ("Nath LLC"). The Court also reduced the damages awarded to Geera to correspond with her personal investments in Nath LLC and her percentage ownership in Nath LLC.)

Toth v. Subway Restaurants, LLC, No. 21 MA 0084, 2022 WL 4351090 (Ohio Ct. App., Sept. 16, 2022). Toth sued Subway Restaurants, LLC after she was injured when a display case fell on her foot at a Subway franchise location. Toth argued that Subway Restaurants, LLC exercised "remarkable control" over the franchise location and therefore owed Toth a duty such that Toth could bring a negligence claim against it. Subway Restaurants, LLC filed a motion for summary judgment, supported by unrefuted affidavits, arguing that it is not the franchisor entity and has no franchise or other relationship with the franchisee, but rather is merely a service provider to the Subway franchisor entity.

As a result, the court concluded that the plaintiff had improperly named Subway Restaurants, LLC which was not the franchisor; was not a party to the franchise agreement; had no contractual relationship with the franchisee; and had no involvement with the restaurant operations. The court noted that the plaintiff did not raise an apparent agency theory of liability, and instead made arguments based solely on a negligence theory. The appellate court affirmed the trial court's grant of summary judgment in favor of Subway Restaurants, LLC.

Disputes Regarding Performance, Termination, and Transfers

H. OTHER CLAIMS

Happy Tax Franchising LLC v. Hill, No. 19-24539-CIV-MORENO/Louis, 2023 WL 2664261 (S.D. Fla. Jan. 25, 2023). Among other complaints regarding application of a contractual statute of limitations, plaintiff-counterdefendant franchisor argued that the general release in the franchise agreement released it from claims for federal securities law violations and Florida Deceptive and Unfair Trade Practices Act violations. The court denied summary judgment, holding that general releases are only effective against acts occurring before the release, and the at issue text messages and conversations the franchisees relied on occurred after the agreement containing the general release was signed.

In *Innovative Solutions & Technology, LLC v. Pro Spot International, Inc.*, No. CV 21-17302, 2023 WL 3260031 (D. N.J. May 4, 2023), plaintiff, a distributor of defendant's welders, sued the defendant manufacturer for breach of contract, tortious interference and promissory estoppel after defendant terminated plaintiff as a distributor and factory authorized service and repair center for defendant's products, and refused to supply plaintiff with replacement parts. The court denied defendant's motions to dismiss and strike, finding, among other things, that plaintiff is permitted under the Federal Rules of Civil Procedure to plead alternative and inconsistent claims, plaintiff adequately pleaded the elements of a promissory estoppel claim, and defendant's claim that the complaint contained unsubstantiated factual allegations was better determined on a motion for summary judgment.

III. Non-Compete, Non-Solicitation Covenants

In *Advantage Payroll Services, Inc. v. Rode*, No. 2:21-CV-00020-NT, 2022 WL 17737878 (D. Me. Dec. 16, 2022), plaintiff Advantage Payroll Services, Inc. ("Advantage") filed a motion for partial summary judgment concerning its breach of contract claim against defendant Ronald Rode ("Rode"), a former franchisee of Advantage. Following a licensing dispute between Rode and Advantage, Advantage purchased Rode's franchise as part of a settlement agreement, under which Rode signed a Non-Solicitation and Non-Servicing Agreement (the "NS Agreement"). Based on the financial and substantive assistance Rode provided to a new, competitive entity to Advantage during the four-year restrictive period under the NS Agreement, the court found that Rode violated the NS Agreement and granted Advantage's motion for partial summary judgment on the breach of contract claim, but denied Advantage's request for liquidated damages.

CHAPTER 4

Brow Art Management, LLC v. Idol Eyes Franchise, LLC, No. CV 23-11434, 2023 WL 4665357 (E.D. Mich. July 20, 2023) The District Court for the Eastern District of Michigan granted in part and denied in part plaintiff franchisor's motion for a preliminary injunction against two former employee defendants and the competitor franchise defendant that hired the former employee defendants. The court found that the plaintiff likely had not acquired the former employee defendants' restrictive covenant agreements in an asset purchase agreement with the plaintiffs' predecessor in interest. As a result, the plaintiff could not prevent the former employee defendants from working for a competitor. However, the court enjoined the defendants from soliciting the plaintiff's customers to the defendants' competing business under the plaintiff's tortious interference claim.

In *Doan Family Corp. v. Arnberger*, 522 P.3d 364 (Kan. Ct. App. 2022), the Kansas Court of Appeals found that a two-year non-compete clause in a franchisee's employment agreement was reasonable and that a tolling agreement in the non-compete clause was unreasonable. The appeals court therefore reversed in part and remanded the case with instructions for the district court to reconsider the damages, attorneys' fees, and expenses in light of its new findings.

Appellant, an H&R Block franchise, brought action against Appellee, a former employee, for violating the two-year, noncompete clause of her employment agreement (the "Agreement") by filing tax returns for Appellant's former clients less than one year after leaving her employment with Appellant. Appellant moved for summary judgment which was granted. However, the district court reduced the duration of the non-compete clause from two years to one year and limited Appellant's damages to that one-year period. The district court also declined to enforce the tolling provision of the non-compete clause which extended the non-compete restrictions for as long as Appellee breached the Agreement.

Appellant appealed, arguing that a two-year non-compete is reasonable because this is the length of time that it typically takes to build a client relationship. The appeals court reversed the district court's ruling in part, finding that the district court erred when it reduced the term of the non-compete clause but upheld the district court's decision to not enforce the clause's tolling provision because it could restrict Appellee's postemployment activities in perpetuity. The appeals court remanded the case with instructions that the district court determine Appellant's damages for both the 2017 and 2018 tax seasons and to not just restrict it to one year as it did previously.

Disputes Regarding Performance, Termination, and Transfers

Gimex Properties Corp., Inc. v. Reed, 205 N.E.3d 1 (Ohio App. Dec. 29, 2022). Plaintiff-franchisor Gimex Properties Corp., Inc. ("Gimex") brought an action against its former franchisees, Thomas and Ashley Reed (collectively, "Reed"). Gimex accused the Reeds of breaching their franchise agreement by working at a competing auto shop after terminating the parties' franchise agreement.

The underlying franchise agreement contained non-compete and confidentiality clauses that prohibited the Reeds from competing (or disclosing trade secrets) within a 5-mile radius of any Gimex location for two years. The trial court granted a permanent injunction enforcing the non-compete clause, deeming it reasonable and necessary to prevent irreparable harm to Gimex's franchise system.

On appeal, the Reeds contended they were unjustly denied the opportunity to testify at the injunction hearing. However, the appeals court found the Reeds had been granted the opportunity to testify but failed to do so. Additionally, the Reeds challenged the finding of irreparable harm. The appeals court upheld the injunction, citing substantial evidence that the Reeds possessed trade secrets, as former franchisees, that could potentially harm Gimex if used for or by a competitor.

Got Docs, LLC v. Kingsbridge Holdings, LLC, No. 19 C 6155, 2023 WL 2078450 (N.D. Ill. Feb. 17, 2023). While Defendant Mendecina worked for Got Docs, he entered into an employment agreement with the company that was governed by California law. Plaintiffs alleged that when Mendecina went to work for defendant Kingsbridge, he violated the restrictive covenants in the employee agreement (non-competition, non-disclosure, and non-solicitation). As to non-solicitation, the court determined that the non-solicitation agreement was enforceable under California law and that there was a genuine issue of material fact because defendants' internal communications discussed hiring former Got Docs employees. As to non-disclosure, the court dismissed defendants' contention that the non-disclosure provision was invalid as a matter of law because trade secrets were implicated in the case.

The court, however, did grant summary judgment in favor of Mendecina as to the non-competition provision, because he had not signed the operating agreement that contained the applicable provision. Defendants also alleged that the restrictive covenants at issue were unenforceable because plaintiffs breached their contract by failing to pay defendant a salary, which plaintiffs countered by alleging that defendant breached first by embezzling funds. The court determined that there were genuine issues of material fact and denied summary judgment. This case is discussed in Chapter 5, Section IV.

CHAPTER 4

H-1 Auto Care, LLC v. Lasher, No. 21-18110 (ZNQ) (TJB), 2022 WL 13003468 (D.N.J. Oct. 21, 2022) (court denied franchisor's motion for preliminary injunction against two franchisees who had started competing auto care businesses after terminating their franchise agreements because franchisor waited nearly one year before filing its motion, and therefore failed to demonstrate irreparable harm). This case is discussed in Chapter 4, Section VI.

In *H.H. Franchising System, Inc. v. CareSmart Solutions, Inc.*, No. 1:21-CV-575, 2022 WL 4274278 (S.D. Ohio Sept. 15, 2022), the court granted plaintiff-franchisor H.H. Franchising System, Inc.'s ("HHFS") motion for a preliminary injunction where the defendant-franchisee CareSmart Solutions, Inc. ("CareSmart") allegedly breached the franchise agreement's non-compete clause by operating a similar in-home care enterprise. First, the court found that HHFS had a likelihood of success on the merits for breach of the non-compete clause, which provided that CareSmart could not operate in-home care services within 15 miles of HHFS's territory for two years following the termination of the franchise agreement. The court found this non-compete clause protected HHFS's legitimate business interest and was reasonable both in length and scope.

The court next found that HHFS would suffer irreparable injury not fully compensable by monetary damages without a preliminary injunction, due to loss of goodwill, loss of customers, and inability to refranchise the territory. The court also determined that substantial harm to others would not occur and that the public interest would be served, as the public would not lose a necessary provider of in-home care, as there were several other similar providers of in-home care services in the area.

In re EllDan Corp., No. 22-31870, 2023 WL 3394917 (Bankr. D. Minn. May 11, 2023). EllDan Corp., a hair salon franchisee, operated seven Fantastic Sams salons pursuant to a franchise agreement with the franchisor, Fantastic Sams Franchise Corp. ("FSFC"). EllDan filed for bankruptcy but continued operating four salons that were unrelated to FSFC, under the name Sota-Styles. FSFC argued this constituted a violation of the non-compete clause in the franchise agreements.

The court held the non-compete clause was valid and enforceable under Minnesota law because the clause served FSFC's legitimate interest in protecting its brand and goodwill. The court granted summary judgment to FSFC, finding that EllDan had breached the non-compete clauses by operating salons within prohibited areas.

Disputes Regarding Performance, Termination, and Transfers

The court also ruled EllDan's rejection of the franchise agreement constituted a breach of contract, not a rescission, allowing FSFC to retain its contractual right to seek injunctive relief for the breach. The court issued an injunction prohibiting EllDan from operating salons in violation of the non-compete clauses until January 2025.

FSFC also claimed Lanham Act violations and related claims. However, these became moot when the parties agreed to a permanent injunction on the use of FSFC's trademarks. As such, the court denied any further injunctive relief on those claims.

JTH Tax, LLC v. Agnant, No. 22-1229-cv, 62 F.4th 658, 2023 WL 2467363 (2d Cir. Mar. 13, 2023) (in affirming district court's denial of franchisor JTH's motion for preliminary injunction to enforce post-termination non-compete and non-solicitation covenants, appellate court held that there is no automatic assumption of irreparable harm in breach of covenant cases, rather the determination of whether irreparable harm has been established "depends upon the factual particulars in each case"). This case is discussed in further detail in Section VI of this Chapter.

JTH Tax LLC v. Anderson, No. CV-23-00209-PHX-DJH, 2023 WL 2072496 (D. Ariz. Feb. 17, 2023) (court denied motion for temporary restraining order seeking to enjoin defendants from offering tax preparation services within twenty-five miles of their former franchise territories due to failure to demonstrate all necessary elements for such relief).

In ***JTH Tax LLC v. Gause***, No. 3:21-CV-00543-FDW-DCK, 2023 WL 3081300 (W.D.N.C. Apr. 25, 2023), the court granted the franchisor's motion for summary judgment on nearly all of its claims, which involved the plaintiff's former franchisee's operating a tax preparation business, which was prohibited by the post-termination covenants and obligations in the parties' franchise agreements. The court noted that, in defense, the franchisee had only argued that he "did not intentionally breach any agreement" and "was not aware of any breach until [he] received the lawsuit," and held that the record was clear that the franchisee had breached several provisions of the franchise agreements.

In ***JTH Tax LLC v. Pierce***, No. 1:22-CV-1237-SEG, 2022 WL 4122215 (N.D. Ga. Sept. 8, 2022) the court denied defendants' motion to dismiss finding that plaintiff, JTH Tax LLC ("JTH") adequately pled its claim that defendants, Leslie N. Pierce ("Pierce"), James E. Axley ("Axley"), LNPA Services LLC ("LNPA"), AX Holdings, Inc., and Nest Financial Services

CHAPTER 4

LLC ("Nest Financial") (collectively, "Defendants") breached the post-termination non-compete covenant of their franchise agreement.

The dispute arose out of a franchise agreement between JTH and defendants Pierce and Axley (the "Franchise Agreement"). In 2012, Pierce and Axley began operating a Liberty Tax franchise in Roswell, Georgia (the "Franchised Business"). In 2013, Pierce and Axley amended the Franchise Agreement to name LNPA as the franchisee and themselves as guarantors. The Franchise Agreement expired on October 31, 2017. Notwithstanding the expiration of the Franchise Agreement, LNPA continued operating the Franchised Business and continued paying commissions to JTH until 2019, at which time Pierce and Axley began operating Nest Financial, a tax preparation and financial services business located within six miles from the Franchised Business.

JTH filed suit against Defendants alleging that by operating Nest Financial, Defendants violated the post-termination non-compete covenant of the Franchise Agreement which provides that the franchisee cannot prepare or electronically file tax returns for a fee within 25 miles of the Franchised Business's territory for a two-year period following termination or expiration of the Franchise Agreement. JTH alleges that the Franchise Agreement was not terminated until it sent Defendants a termination notice on May 15, 2020, therefore, the post-termination covenants did not go into effect until after that date. However, Defendants allege that the Franchise Agreement expired on October 31, 2017 and was not renewed. Therefore, the post-termination non-compete covenant had no force after October 31, 2019.

The district court applied Virginia law based on the choice of law clause of the Franchise Agreement, finding that although the Franchise Agreement expired in 2017, JTH and LNPA entered an implied contract that they had continuing obligations to one another under the Franchise Agreement. This implied contract was evident based on their mutuality of assent where Defendants continued paying their regular commissions to JTH until 2019 and JTH did not sue Defendants for operating the Franchised Business after the Franchise Agreement expired. The court also found that the post-termination non-compete provisions applied to the implied contract. Accordingly, the district court denied Defendants' Motion to Dismiss.

In *JTH Tax, LLC v. Shahzad*, 199 N.E.3d 1257 (E.D. Wis. Jan. 23, 2023), the court entered an order requiring the parties to submit a joint report in preparation for a possible evidentiary hearing on Plaintiff's motion for an injunction. Plaintiff and franchisor JTH Tax, LLC ("Liberty Tax"), which sold franchises for tax preparation services, sought an injunction against its former franchisee, Yasmeen Shahzad. Liberty Tax claimed that Shahzad was violating a non-compete agreement in the franchise agreement by preparing tax returns. It sued her for breach of contract and misappropriation of trade secrets and also filed a motion for a temporary restraining order and preliminary injunction against the defendants. The court determined that an evidentiary hearing was required because the defendants' response raised genuine issues of material fact.

Kava Culture Franchise Group Corp. v. Dar-Jkta Enterprises LLC, No. 2:23-cv-278-JLB-KCD, 2023 WL 3121893 (M.D. Fla. April 27, 2023). Plaintiff, franchisor of Kava Culture Kava Bars, entered into two separate franchise agreements with defendants to operate Kava Culture Bars in Texas. One location was opened but, in March 2023, defendants notified plaintiff they were putting the other location "on hold." That same day, however, defendants created a website for a competing Kava bar business and began operating a business called "The Kava Bar." Plaintiff sent defendants notices of termination of the franchise agreements and then moved for a temporary restraining order, arguing that defendants were breaching the agreements' non-compete covenants by, among other things, operating competing Kava bars within the geographic (75-mile) area covered by the covenants and continuing to use plaintiff's Kava Culture mark, recipes, methods, color scheme, franchise system, and various other aspects of plaintiff's Kava Culture Kava Bars. In granting in part plaintiff's motion for a temporary restraining order, the court found plaintiff was likely to succeed on the merits of its breach of contract claim and that, under Eleventh Circuit law, the violation of an enforceable restrictive covenant creates a presumption of irreparable injury, therefore plaintiff was entitled to such presumption.

Luxottica of America, Inc. v. Brave Optical, Inc., No. 4:22-CV-244, 2023 WL 4589222 (E.D. Tex. July 18, 2023). The non-compete in this case is discussed in Chapter 5, Section II.

Madison Auto Center, LLC v. Lallas, No. 2022AP1376, 2023 WL 3880300 (Wis. Ct. App. June 8, 2023). On appeal, the court affirmed the lower court's grant of summary judgment in favor of a former employee of an automotive dealership, finding that the dealership's non-compete agreement was unenforceable against the employee as it was broader than necessary to protect the dealership's interest.

Powerlift Door Consultants, Inc. v. Shepard, No. 21-CV-1316 (WMW/ECW), 2023 WL 2976031 (D. Minn. Apr. 17, 2023). Defendant Shepard owned and operated a metal supply store and was a licensee of

CHAPTER 4

products from plaintiff Power Lift Door Consultants, Inc. Defendant sent an email to other licensees of plaintiff's products making many derogatory remarks, including about plaintiff and its products. Plaintiff then terminated the distribution agreement between the parties, and defendant continued to, among other acts, sell plaintiff's product. Plaintiff's complaint alleged that defendants breached the distribution agreement between the parties (including that agreement's non-compete provision), and that defendants were improperly using plaintiff's trademarks and confidential information. The court granted plaintiff's motion for partial summary judgment, determining that plaintiff breached the distribution agreement both before and after termination of the agreement, and infringed on defendant's trademarks. This case is also discussed in Chapter 5, Section II.

Terrier, LLC v. HCAFranchise Corporation, No. 222cv01325GMNEJY, 2022 WL 4280251 (D. Nev. Sept. 2022) (court found post-termination covenant not to compete to be valid and enforceable under both Nevada ("reasonable restrictions are those that are "reasonably necessary to protect the business and goodwill of the employer." *quoting Jone v. Deeter*, 913 P.2d 1272, 1275 (Nev. 1996)) or New Mexico law ("reasonable limits of time and space" *see Bowen v. Carlsbad Ins. & Real Estate, Inc.*, 724 P.2d 223, 225 (N.M. 1986)). This case is discussed in more detail in Section II.A of this Chapter.

IV. Encroachment

The authors' review of cases decided during the reporting period did not reveal any significant decisions addressing this topic.

V. Transfer Disputes

Choice Hotels International, Inc. v. C & O Developers, L.L.C., 199 N.E.3d 1 (Oh. App. Sept. 15, 2022). Assignee of franchise agreement which had an arbitration provision entered into and then subsequently defaulted on separate loan documents with the franchisor. The appellate court affirmed the lower court's denial of Defendant's motion to compel arbitration, finding the loan documents, which provided for litigation of any disputes, were for a separate transaction than the franchise agreement. This case is discussed further in Chapter 4, Section II.A.

K.C. Company, Inc. v. Pella Corp., No. DKC 20-0227, 2022 WL 3716537 (D. Md. Aug. 29, 2022). Plaintiff K.C. was a longstanding franchise and

Disputes Regarding Performance, Termination, and Transfers

distributor of Defendant Pella's windows and doors. K.C. and Pella operated pursuant to two sets of distribution contracts, the "Trade Agreements" and the "Sales Branch Agreements." The contracts gave K.C. distribution rights for Pella products in certain regions, and provided that K.C. could not sell, transfer or assign those rights without securing Pella's prior written consent. Pella agreed its consent would not be unreasonably withheld, however it reserved the right to accept or reject a proposed replacement distributor based on certain factors, which Pella in the "exercise of its business judgment," deemed relevant, including Pella's marketing needs and the proposed replacement's financial and other qualifications.

In 2014-2015, Pella revamped its marketing strategy, and asked K.C. to split up one of its regions so that it could focus on one metropolitan area and sell the other in the territory to a new owner. Pella ultimately agreed that K.C. could sell its entire region to a single buyer and it and K.C. entered into a memorandum of understanding ("MOU") for how such sale effort would proceed, including the deadlines for each step or phase of the process. K.C. hired a business broker and marketed its sale. It elicited bids from three potential buyers, and Pella subsequently provided K.C. with the name of another potential buyer. K.C. submitted for Pella's approval the highest bid it received from a buyer named Parksite. Pella investigated Parksite and its business and rejected Parksite for a number of reasons, including that it did not fit with Pella's business model because it was not an owner-operator and it was selling various other competitors' door and window products so would not be fully focused on and committed to Pella's product line and growth in the market.

Pella said it was open to other potential candidates and noted it had recommended one to K.C. K.C. subsequently submitted a bid by a group of K.C. employees. Pella evaluated the employees but they did not earn a passing score. Pella also had an issue with the structure of this proposed ownership group, as it had found having multiple owners for the same business not to be a tenable business model. K.C. was eventually purchased by a company controlled by someone who had been involved in the candidate Pella had introduced to K.C.

K.C. sued Pella for breach of contract, arguing that Pella withheld consent to the transfer of K.C.'s distributions rights to Parksite unreasonably, that its withholding consent was based on a pretext, that Pella had interfered with the sale process, and Pella breached the MOU. The court granted Pella's motion for summary judgment on K.C.'s contract claim, finding that "multiple officers of Pella identified multiple objective business reasons for its rejection of Parksite" and that these reasons were explained to K.C. Pella also presented an expert opinion supporting its position that Parksite's business structure was not compatible with Pella's marketing and distribution model and plans, and the court noted that K.C. did not oppose the expert's report with evidence or an expert of its own. Regarding K.C.'s claim that the reasons Pella gave for its rejection of Parksite were pretextual and Pella really wanted to transfer the rights to the candidate it introduced, the court noted that Pella simply identified and provided information to K.C. about the other candidate and did not pressure K.C. to sell to that candidate, rather it simply asked K.C. to consider the candidate. K.C. did not present evidence that Pella interfered with the sale process. The court finally held that Pella had not breached the MOU, which in any event was non-binding and did not add any additional obligations to the parties' rights in their two sets of agreements.

Queen v. Wineinger, No. 21-cv-378-wmc, 2022 WL 3017004 (W.D. Wis. Aug. 1, 2022). Plaintiff, which had been operating a Dairy Queen franchise since 1998 pursuant to a franchise agreement originally entered into in 1952. Since commencing operation plaintiff sole non-system food, a, tried to transfer its franchise to a new owner. But Dairy Queen required the new owner to sign a new franchise agreement it was now using and which, unlike the original franchise agreement, contained a provision prohibiting the franchisee's use or sale of non-system food. Plaintiff contended this change violated Wisconsin's Fair Dealership Law, however the court disagreed, finding that the franchise agreement unambiguously gave Dairy Queen the right to withhold approval of any proposed franchise transfer in whole or in part.

Singh v. Wireless Vision, LLC, No. 2:22-CV-01018-JDP, 2023 WL 275284 (E.D. Cal. Mar. 31, 2023). Plaintiffs Paul Singh ("Singh") filed a breach of contract against Wireless Vision, LLC and Ameritel Management, Inc ("Ameritel"). Singh entered into a T-Mobile Operating Agreement ("Agreement") with Ameritel who held a master license from T-Mobile to sell, license and operate T-Mobile retail shops. Singh invested over $160,000 in the store based on the Agreement to purchase equipment and build the store. Singh was paid a commission of the sales, but the Agreement did not include how commissions would be determined. Wireless Vision eventually assumed oversight of the business from Ameritel and subsequently terminated the Agreement with Singh, evicting him from the store and equipment. Singh then sued Wireless Vision for breach of contract and violation of the California Franchise Relations Act ("CFRA").

The defendants sought to transfer the venue under the agreement's forum selection clause which provided for litigation to be filed and determined in New York. However, the court found that the agreement constituted a franchise agreement under the CFRA. The court analyzed CFRA's definitions and determined Singh's payments under the Agreement constituted a "franchise fee." The court therefore found the CFRA provision voiding the forum selection clause applied to the Agreement, and denied defendant's motion to transfer.

Sonate Corp. v. Dunkin' Brands Group, Inc., No. 6:22-CV-812-WWB-EJK, 2023 WL 2624756 (M.D. Fla. Mar. 24, 2023) (The United States District Court for the Middle District of Florida granted Defendants Motion to Transfer Venue to the United States District Court for the District of Massachusetts finding that despite plaintiffs' objections, the Court had jurisdiction over the subject matter of the action, venue was proper there and defendants were amenable to process issuing out of the transferee court.)

Wistron Neweb Corporation v. Genesis Networks Telecom Services, LLC, No. 22-cv-2538-LJL, 2022 WL 17067984 (S.D.N.Y. Nov. 17, 2022) (court denied defendant's motion to transfer, holding that the choice of forum clause in the parties' distributor agreement was controlling and determined the appropriate venue of the litigation). This case is also discussed in Chapter 4, Section II.

VI. Injunctive Relief

In *Arnone v. Burke*, 211 A.D3d 998 (N.Y. App. Div. Dec. 28, 2022), the court affirmed the order of the Supreme Court, Richard County, which denied the portions of the defendants' motion to dismiss that asked for dismissal of claims alleging tortious interference with contract and promissory estoppel, on the grounds that not enough discovery had been completed to dismiss the tortious interference with contract claim at this point in the litigation, and that the promissory estoppel claim should move forward because the defendants dispute whether a valid contract was ever entered into.

Brow Art Management, LLC v. Idol Eyes Franchise, LLC, No. CV 23-11434, 2023 WL 4665357 (E.D. Mich. July 20, 2023) The district court denied a preliminary injunction for claims based on a restrictive covenant but granted a preliminary injunction for a tortious interference claim where a competitor franchise and former employees of the plaintiff were soliciting the plaintiff's customers. This case is discussed in Chapter 4, Section V.

Bruce-Terminix Company v. Terminix International Company Limited Partnership, No. 1:20-CV-962, 2023 WL 2974080 (M.D.N.C. Apr. 17,

CHAPTER 4

2023). Plaintiff Bruce-Terminix Company ("Bruce"), a pest control company, successfully moved for summary judgment for breach of a license agreement against Defendant Terminix International Company Limited Partnership ("Terminix"). The license agreement gave Bruce exclusive rights to use the Terminix name, brand, and system in a defined territory of seventeen counties in North Carolina. Under the license agreement, Terminix agreed that it would not establish or license another to establish within the defined territory a location for a Terminix system or a business similar to the Terminix system. Terminix's parent company acquired two companies involved in pest control within the Agreement's exclusive territory, Copesan and Gregory Pest Solutions ("Gregory"). Gregory employed technicians who provided services to customers within Bruce's exclusive territory and used programs, materials and pest control methods that were part of the Terminix system, while Terminix handled the company's recruiting needs. Meanwhile, Copesan used the Terminix name to solicit a contract to be performed by Gregory in competition with Bruce. Bruce offered evidence of harm to reputation and customer confusion caused by these breaches of the license agreement, but no evidence of actual damages. Following the grant of summary judgment, Bruce filed for a permanent injunction against Terminix, seeking to enjoin it from permitting the use of the Terminix System, brand, and related marks and trade dress by other entities engaged in a pest control business, including Gregory and other Terminix affiliates, in the exclusive service territory. It also sought to enjoin Terminix from operating competing pest control businesses within the service area.

The court applied North Carolina law to Bruce's request for injunctive relief. Under North Carolina law, the moving party for injunctive relief must show: (1) an irreparable injury; (2) that damages not reasonably obtainable; and (3) that the injury is of such continuous and frequent recurrence that no reasonable redress can be had in a court of law. The court found that Bruce suffered irreparable harm as a result of Terminix allowing Copesan and Gregory to use the Terminix name, brand, and system in Bruce's service area, "undermining Bruce's competitive advantage and causing customer confusion in the area." Furthermore, the court stated that damages were not reasonably obtainable because recovery for these non-monetary harms were not available under applicable Tennessee law (which governed under the license agreement) and damages are extremely difficult to prove given the nature of the breach. The injury was found to be continuous such that an injunction would be appropriate because Terminix itself stated that it did not authorize the use of its brand or system in the service area, while evidence at trial showed Gregory's extensive access to the system and use of the brand in recruiting. Terminix continued to argue at the preliminary injunction stage that it was permitted to share its confidential information, part of the Terminix System, with whatever entity it chose to. The court disagreed, finding this assertion to be further evidence in support of Bruce's concerns of irreparable injury, and granted Bruce's motion for a permanent injunction for the remainder of the license agreement.

On Bruce's request to enjoin Terminix from operating competing pest control businesses within the service area, the court found in favor of the defendant. Terminix's parent company had merged with another pest control business, Rentokil, and the court determined that its continued operation without permission to use the Terminix name, brand and system in the exclusive territory did not violate the terms of the license agreement. This request for injunctive relief was denied on the grounds that it was overbroad.

In *CiCi Enterprises, LP v. Fogel Enterprises, Inc.*, No. 3:22-CV-1202-E, 2023 WL 2731048, at *1 (N.D. Tex. Mar. 30, 2023) the court issued a preliminary injunction in favor of the plaintiffs, Cici Enterprises, LP, the franchisor, and Yes Caps, LLC, the owner of the franchisor's intellectual property used in connection with the franchise system. The court enjoined the former franchisee and its owners from continuing to use the plaintiffs' marks and from continuing to operate a competitive pizza business for two years within ten miles of the formerly approved location. The court noted that it was undisputed that the franchisor terminated the franchise agreement after sending six notices of default to the franchisee and its owners. The undisputed evidence showed that the franchisee had materially breached the franchise agreement; therefore, the franchisor properly terminated the franchise agreement and it was undisputed that the defendants continued to operate a pizza restaurant and to use the plaintiffs' marks after the franchise agreement was terminated. Thus, the plaintiffs had established a likelihood of success on the merits, the balance of harm weighed in favor of protecting the market goodwill of the plaintiffs, and the public interest would not be disserved by issuing the injunction. The court denied the plaintiffs' for attorneys' fees without prejudice noting that the plaintiffs could move the court for fees, but would need to identify the claims for which fees were sought, the legal authority to award fees, and documentation of the fees.

City Beverages, LLC, dba Olympic Eagle Distributing v. Crown Imports, LLC dba Constellation Brands Beer Division, No. 23-359 (9th Cir. July 20, 2023) (The Ninth Circuit Court of Appeals vacated a preliminary injunction entered by the United States District Court for the Western District of Washington where the plaintiff distributor was unlikely to succeed on its claim under the Washington Wholesale Distributor/Supplier Equity

CHAPTER 4

Agreement Act because the distribution agreement granted the defendant supplier the express right to terminate without cause, and the Washington Franchise Investment Protection Act was unlikely to apply given the more specific statute covering distributorships.).

Doctor's Associates LLC v. Khononov, C.A. No. 22-cv-7637, 2023 WL 184389 (E.D.N.Y. Jan. 13, 2023), the court held that the franchisor, Subway, was not entitled to a preliminary injunction seeking to bar the continuation of a sandwich business at the same location that previously operated as a Subway franchise, and to prevent the former franchisee, defendant Khononov, from using any names, décor, or slogans associated with Subway. The court denied the motion for a preliminary injunction because it found the plaintiff had not established it would be irreparably harmed if the injunction were not entered. Among the reasons the court gave for its decision were:

First, the franchise agreement contemplated a liquidated damages provision in the event the franchisee breached the non-compete covenant by opening a new store or using Subway secrets and materials, and therefore, the franchisor had a legal remedy available.

Second, the plaintiffs' "loss of goodwill" argument failed because there were several other Subway franchise locations within a three-mile radius described in the non-compete agreement which permitted Subway to "continu[e] to have a presence and build goodwill in the territory."

Third, denial of the preliminary injunction motion was not likely to harm the entire franchise system because Subway could still pursue an ordinary civil breach of contract action based on the franchise agreement.

For these reasons, the court held that the plaintiffs had not met their burden of establishing irreparable harm, and therefore it denied plaintiffs' motion for a preliminary injunction.

D.Q.S.A. LLC v. American Dairy Queen Corporation, No. CV-22-00335-TUC-JGZ, 2023 WL 4365332 (D. Ariz. July 6, 2023). Plaintiff, D.Q.S.A. LLC ("DQSA"), is a Dairy Queen Territory Operator with over 54 authorized Dairy Queen subfranchisees within its territories in Arizona. DQSA sued American Dairy Queen Corporation ("ADQ"), the United States master franchisor for the Dairy Queen franchise system, seeking a declaratory judgment that ADQ could not compel DQSA and its subfranchisees to immediately replace their existing electronic point-of-sale cash register systems with a new "Integrated Technology Platform" ("ITP"). In opposing DQSA's requested relief, defendant ADQ sought an order that would require DQSA to compel ITP installation at two types of its subfranchisees: those operating under a new form operating agreement and those authorized to sell

Disputes Regarding Performance, Termination, and Transfers

food. The parties agreed that interpretation of the relevant contracts was a legal issue appropriate for resolution on summary judgment, and they filed cross motions for summary judgment with respect to that interpretation.

DQSA operates under agreements between its predecessors and ADQ's predecessors that date back to the 1940s, though a number of DQSA's subfranchisees have entered into agreements similar to ADQ's current form operating agreement. In addition, DQSA subfranchisees that offer food (as opposed to just dairy products) are subject to a Food Service Agreement ("FSA"). A third category of DQSA subfranchisees, those that operate under older form operating agreements and that do not offer food, were not at issue in this lawsuit.

The parties agreed that ADQ can require that DQSA compel its subfranchisees to install the ITP, but their dispute concerned when ADQ can require that installation. Specifically, DQSA argued that the parties' agreements only permit ADQ to require that subfranchisees install new equipment, like the ITP, when specific triggering events occur, such as a 10-year remodel, a franchise renewal, or a franchise transfer. ADQ, on the other hand, argued that the newer form operating agreement and the FSA permit it to determine and periodically modify what equipment subfranchisees may use, such that it can immediately require that DQSA compel its subfranchisees to replace their existing point-of-sale system with the new ITP.

The court first looked at the newer form operating agreement and found that its plain terms permitted ADQ to set and periodically update its mandatory system standards, including its standards for approved equipment like the ITP. In so finding, the court noted that DQSA's contrary interpretation–which focused exclusively on the section of the agreements concerning modernization and replacement–failed to account for and was inconsistent with other provisions of the agreements that plainly authorized ADQ to periodically update and otherwise modify system standards and equipment. According to the court, reading those other provisions in conjunction with the section dealing with modernization and replacement made clear that the triggering events in the modernization section merely establish the baseline duty of modernization for subfranchisees–those triggering events do not limit ADQ's authority to require equipment replacement at other times.

The court similarly found that the language of the FSA authorized ADQ to demand immediate installation of the ITP equipment with respect to DQSA subfranchisees that offer food. As a result, the court granted summary judgment in ADQ's favor and entered an order directing DQSA to require that subfranchisees that fall under the FSA and the newer form operating agreement immediately install the ITP.

CHAPTER 4

E. Moran, Inc. v. Tomgal, LLC, (D.P.R. May 2, 2023). Plaintiff E. Moran, Inc.'s ("EMI") requested a preliminary injunction against Defendant TomGal, LLC. d/b/a Robin Ruth ("Robin Ruth"), a global brand of high-quality fashion accessories for the tourism industry, under the Puerto Rico Dealer's Act, and the U.S. Magistrate Judge recommended that the request be denied.

EMI alleged that it was the distributor of Robin Ruth in Puerto Rico and that Robin Ruth undermined, breached, and impaired the parties' exclusive distribution agreement without just cause when it delayed shipments to EMI in 2021, failed to deliver purchase orders in 2022, and withheld payment over pending invoices from Walmart stores in Puerto Rico in 2022. EMI claims that Robin Ruth's actions constitute a violation of the Puerto Rico Dealer's Act. EMI thus moved the court for a preliminary injunction requesting that Robin Ruth cease, desist and refrain from impairing the parties' exclusive distribution agreement.

The court denied EMI's request, however, because it found: 1) that EMI's evidence was not sufficient to show that it was likely to succeed on the merits of it claim; 2) that EMI did not demonstrate that it would suffer irreparable harm in the absence of the requested injunction; and 3) the balance of interests weighed against EMI's request.

H-1 Auto Care, LLC v. Lasher, No. 21-18110 (ZNQ) (TJB), 2022 WL 13003468 (D.N.J. Oct. 21, 2022). Franchisees of two auto care centers terminated their franchise agreements, claiming that due to the COVID-19 pandemic, they were struggling financially and could not meet their obligations and commitments under the agreements. The franchise agreements contained post-termination "non-solicit covenants", which the court noted were essentially non-compete agreements, and strict confidentiality agreements. The parties entered into mutual termination agreements for the locations, but the franchisor subsequently discovered that, just before entering into the agreements, the franchisees had formed two new corporations which then opened up competing auto care facilities at the former franchise locations. The franchisor filed a Complaint seeking injunctive relief and monetary damages, claiming the franchisees used the franchisor's business resources and employees to start competing businesses in violation of the franchise agreements. Seven weeks later, and nearly one year after the franchisees terminated their franchise agreements and opened the competing businesses, the franchisor filed a motion for a preliminary injunction. The court denied the motion on the grounds that the franchisor failed to show it would suffer irreparable harm if the injunction were not granted. The court held that demonstrating irreparable harm is the most important prerequisite for issuing a preliminary injunction and that the party seeking injunctive relief must make "a clear showing of immediate irreparable injury." The court found the fact that the franchisor waited 11 months to seek a preliminary injunction to be fatal to its claim, as its delay was evidence that speedy, urgent relief was not needed. The court further noted that the franchisor did not make any effort to explain why it had not acted sooner.

In *Jani-King of Miami, Inc. v. Leicht*, No. 3:23-CV-0389-B, 2023 WL 2335658, at *1 (N.D. Tex. Mar. 2, 2023), Jani-King of Miami, Inc., the franchisor, obtained a temporary restraining order and an order authorizing expedited discovery from a state court in Texas against former franchisees who were allegedly violating their post-expiration covenants. The franchisees removed the matter to federal court. The federal court extended the temporary restraining order to allow time for briefing by the parties, but dissolved the order for expedited discovery, finding that the franchisor had not shown sufficient "good cause" to expedite the discovery procedures. Good cause was lacking because the motion and order did not explain what information the franchisor needed or why it was needed on an expedited basis, and the order imposed too great a burden on the respondents, by requiring them to provide written responses and appear for depositions in three days.

JTH Tax, LLC v. Agnant, No. 22-1229-cv, 62 F.4th 658, 2023 WL 2467363 (2d Cir. Mar. 13, 2023). Franchisor JTH Tax, LLC, doing business as Liberty Tax Service ("Liberty"), appealed the district court's denial of its motion for preliminary injunction. Liberty terminated its franchise agreements with Agnant, which had authorized Agnant to operate four pre-existing franchise locations in Brooklyn under Liberty's name and mark, for alleged violations of federal tax laws and regulations in preparing tax returns for its customers. Liberty also demanded that Agnant comply with various post-termination obligations, including non-compete and non-solicitation covenants.

The court first held that the district court had applied the correct standard in denying Liberty's motion. It found that the case fell within one of the two circumstances in which a plaintiff seeking a preliminary injunction must meet a heightened standard, by showing a "clear or substantial likelihood of success on the merits," and making a strong showing of irreparable harm. This was because the injunction Liberty was seeking would provide Liberty with all of the relief it sought in the litigation and could not be meaningfully undone in the event that Agnant ultimately prevailed at trial on the merits. As the court noted, "Liberty does not explain, nor can we divine, how a court could undo the effect of a wrongfully imposed injunction that would effectively put Agnant out of business." The court found Liberty had not met

CHAPTER 4

its heightened burden. The district court credited Agnant's testimony that her franchises had not committed any material violations of the law in preparing returns over the testimony of JTH's witness, and found that Liberty did not have a basis to terminate the franchise agreements, and the appellate court found that the district court had not clearly erred in crediting Agnant's testimony. The court also agreed with, and affirmed, the district court's finding that Liberty had not presented evidence that Agnant's ongoing operations (which, post-termination, were being conducted under the name Rocket Tax and did not use Liberty's name or mark) would irreparably harm Liberty's goodwill, client relationships, or ability to compete in Brooklyn.

Just Between Friends Franchise Systems, Inc. v. Samone Gibson Enterprises, LLC, No. 23-CV-098-JFH-JFJ, 2023 WL 2496584 (N.D. Okla. Mar. 14, 2023). The franchisor of a children's clothing consignment concept sued a former franchisee for trademark infringement and related claims as a result of the franchisee's failure and refusal to transfer control of certain franchise-branded social media accounts back to franchisor. The franchisor moved for a temporary restraining order mandating the transfer and enjoining further use of franchisor's trademarks, which the court granted.

Kia America, Inc. v. Rally Auto Group, Inc., No. 822CV00109JVSJDE, 2022 WL 17185011 (C.D. Cal. Oct. 20, 2022). Kia sued one of its authorized dealers, Rally, for trademark infringement and breach of contract, based upon Rally entering into an agreement (the "Consulting Agreement") with a third party, Dalia, that effectively transferred ownership or management of Rally's Kia dealership from Rally to Dalia, without Kia's authorization, in violation of Rally's dealer agreement with Kia.

The district court entered a preliminary injunction that enjoined Dalia from using the Kia trademarks in any way and that prohibited Rally from contributing to that use. Kia then moved to enforce the preliminary injunction to (1) compel Rally and Dalia to terminate or unwind the Consulting Agreement, (2) withdraw any capital contributions Dalia had made to Rally pursuant to that Consulting Agreement, and (3) restrain Dalia from taking any financial interest in Rally's Kia dealership. The district court denied Kia's motion to enforce, concluding that its preliminary injunction order prohibiting Dalia from using Kia's trademarks did not require that Dalia terminate the Consulting Agreement, withdraw capital contributions, or otherwise take a financial interest in Rally's Kia dealership.

Disputes Regarding Performance, Termination, and Transfers

Pizza Inn, Inc. v. Allen's Dynamic Food, Inc., No. CIV-23-00164-PRW, 2023 WL 3015297 (W.D. Okla. Apr. 19, 2023). Fawzi "Allen" Odetallah entered into a franchise agreement with Pizza Inn to operate a restaurant in Ponca City, Oklahoma (the "Ponca City Restaurant"). Allen's Dynamic Food, Inc. ("Allen's") entered into a separate franchise agreement with Pizza Inn to operate a restaurant in McAlester, Oklahoma (the "McAlester Restaurant"), and Odetallah personally guaranteed the McAlester Restaurant agreement. In an earlier lawsuit between Pizza Inn and Odetallah, the court found that Odetallah infringed Pizza Inn's trademarks and breached the franchise agreement, ruled that Pizza Inn properly terminated the Ponca City Restaurant franchise agreement, and entered judgment in favor of Pizza Inn on its contract and trademark infringement claims. Pizza Inn separately sent a notice of deficiencies and demand to cure to Allen's with respect to the McAlester Restaurant. After Allen's failed to respond to the notice or cure the deficiencies, Pizza Inn terminated that franchise agreement. However, both franchisees continued to operate their restaurants. Despite Pizza Inn's sending Odetallah a cease-and-desist letter, the franchisees still did not cease operations. Pizza Inn then moved for a preliminary injunction, seeking to stop the franchisees from continuing to operate the restaurants, use Pizza Inn's trademarks in connection with the restaurants, and sell pizza and other Pizza Inn menu items at the restaurants.

The court held that Pizza Inn established all of the elements necessary to obtain preliminary injunctive relief on its trademark infringement claim. First, Pizza Inn established that it was likely to succeed on the merits, because despite properly terminating the franchise agreements, the Defendants continued using Pizza Inn's trademarks at both restaurants, and such unauthorized use was likely to deceive, or cause confusion or mistake on the part of the general public. Second, under the Trademark Protection Act of 2020, when the evidence shows a likely infringement, a rebuttable presumption of irreparable harm arises, and the burden shifts to the Defendants to prove that the consumer confusion was unlikely to cause irreparable harm. The court found the franchisees failed to offer any such evidence, therefore they did not overcome the rebuttable presumption. Third, the court found that the Defendants did not even address the balance-of-harms element, therefore Pizza Inn established that its threatened injury outweighed any potential injury to the franchisee. The court also noted that any harm to the franchisees was self-inflicted, because they failed to comply with the terms of the franchise agreements and cease operating the restaurants. Lastly, the court found that Pizza Inn showed that the injunction would not be adverse to the public interest—in fact, it would serve the public interest—because the unauthorized use of a trademark risks deceiving consumers. The court granted

CHAPTER 4

Pizza Inn's motion for preliminary injunctive relief. It also waived the security (bond) requirement, because Defendants did now show a likelihood of harm without the security.

Roleo Beverage Corp. v. Pepsi-Cola Bottling, No. 1:22-CV-6921 (MKV), 2022 WL 3974465 (S.D.N.Y. Sept. 1, 2022). Plaintiffs Roleo Beverage Corp. ("Roleo") and Leonard Costa sued Pepsi-Cola Bottling Co. of New York, Inc. ("Pepsi") for breach of contract and filed a motion for a preliminary injunction to prevent Pepsi from terminating its Distributor Agreement with Roleo or otherwise disrupting Roleo's business. Pepsi filed a motion to compel arbitration according to the terms of the Distributor Agreement.

The court granted both motions. First, the court reasoned that Roleo demonstrated a high likelihood of success on the merits of its claims, that the loss of its distributor agreement with Pepsi would constitute irreparable harm, that balance of equities was clearly in favor of Roleo's continued distribution of Pepsi products, and that the public interest is promoted by adhering to the terms of the distributor agreement. The court therefore granted the preliminary injunction. However, the court also found that the distributor agreement's arbitration clause governed the dispute and that the action belonged in arbitration, and therefore granted Pepsi's motion to compel arbitration.

Sonic Industries, LLC v. Olympia Cascade Drive Ins LLC, No. CIV-22-449-PRW, 2022 WL 3654748 (W.D. Okla. Aug. 24, 2022) (The court granted the plaintiff-franchisor's motion for temporary restraining order in a lawsuit brought by the franchisor against a former franchisee where the defendant continued to operate its restaurant using the franchisor's trademarks after the defendant's franchise agreement had been terminated. In doing so, the court rejected defendant's argument that the termination failed to comply with the notice and termination provisions of the Washington Franchise Investment Protection Act ("WFIPA"). The court noted that WFIPA does not address the content of the notices of default.)

Sr. Ozzy's Franchising LLC v. Morales, No. CV-23-00238-PHX-GMS, 2023 WL 2601258 (D. Ariz. Mar. 22, 2023). In May 2022, the parties entered into a Franchise Agreement for defendant to open a Sr. Ozzy's restaurant in Phoenix, Arizona. But before the restaurant opened, the defendant stopped communicating with the franchisor (Plaintiffs SR Ozzy's LLC and Sr. Ozzy's Franchising LLC's ("Sr. Ozzy's")). Sr. Ozzy's then terminated the Franchise Agreement, but—according to Sr. Ozzy's—the defendant continued to operate the restaurant and to improperly use the Sr. Ozzy's trademarks, all in violation of the post-termination obligations under the Franchise Agreement.

Disputes Regarding Performance, Termination, and Transfers

As a result, Sr. Ozzy's moved for a temporary restraining order and preliminary injunction to stop the defendant's violations of the post-termination obligations, which was granted in part and denied in part. The court first ruled that Sr. Ozzy's was likely to succeed on the merits of its trademark infringement claims, and thus granted the preliminary injunction on that claim and ordered the defendant to cease use of the franchisor's trademarks.

The court, however, ruled that Sr. Ozzy's had failed to present evidence to sufficiently show that the defendant was in fact in violation of its post-termination non-compete. Instead, the court ruled that the franchisor had produced mere speculation that the defendant intended to breach its post-termination non-compete. The court therefore did not grant the preliminary injunction on Sr. Ozzy's claim related to defendant's breach of the post-termination non-compete. Rather, the court granted Sr. Ozzy's request for a preliminary injunction on its breach of contract claims only to the extent it was not based on the alleged breach of the non-compete (i.e., the court granted the requested relief as to the remaining post-termination obligations in the Franchise Agreement).

Lastly, the court ruled that Sr. Ozzy's had failed to present evidence to sufficiently show that the defendant intended to misuse the franchisor's confidential manual—and therefore, the court denied the franchisor's request for a preliminary injunction on its claim for trade secrets misappropriation under Arizona law.

Terrier, LLC v. HCAFranchise Corporation, No. 222cv01325GMNEJY, 2022 WL 4280251 (D. Nev. Sep. 15, 2022). Plaintiff entered into a franchise agreement with defendant in December of 2006. The agreement contained a post-termination covenant not to compete and the plaintiff had an option to renew the agreement, contingent on the plaintiff executing the franchisor's then-current standard form franchise agreement, which included a provision that allowed the franchisor to include terms which were different than what was in the original franchise agreement. Plaintiff formed Terrier, LLC and transferred its contractual obligations to it in May of 2019. When the plaintiff exercised its conditional right to renew, the defendant provided a demand agreement that would serve as the franchise agreement. The demand agreement included a compulsory sale provision and the plaintiff refused to sign it. The plaintiff brought suit against defendant, seeking, among other things, injunctive relief and a declaratory judgment concerning the post-termination non-compete and asserting claims for breach of contract and its implied covenant of good faith and fair dealing.

CHAPTER 4

The court found for the defendant on all counts, holding that the plaintiff failed to meet its burden of proving the *Winter* factors (1. Likelihood of success on the merits; 2. Irreparable Harm; 3. Balance of Equities; and 4. Public Interest) in order to obtain a temporary restraining order or a preliminary injunction. The court found the plaintiff failed to articulate which claims it was seeking injunctive relief on and thus failed to meet its burden of establishing a likelihood of success on the merits. Regarding the second factor, the court held that plaintiff had not established irreparable harm, since any alleged harm was caused by the express terms of the agreement, which allowed the renewal terms to contain different provisions than what was in the original agreement, and which permitted the franchisor to include the compulsory sale provision. The court further held that the interest of parties having freedom to contract weighed in favor of denying the motion. Moreover, the plaintiff had agreed to these terms, despite their now causing plaintiff to have to make a difficult choice if it wanted to renew the franchise agreement. This case is also discussed in Section II.A. of this Chapter.

In **TRBR, Inc. v. General Motors, LLC**, No. 20-11269, 2022 WL 16758482 (E.D. Mich. Nov. 8, 2022), auto dealerships (collectively, "TRBR") filed two motions: (1) an injunction to pause the expiration of state dealer licenses and to prohibit the manufacturer and distributor of the cares ("GM") from terminating TRBR's franchise, and (2) a temporary restraining order directing GM to cease any efforts to terminate the Franchise Agreement. The court denied the request for an injunction to pause the expiration of the license because the state which issued the license was not a party to the case. The court also denied the request for an injunction prohibiting the termination of the franchise on the basis that there were no remaining claims in the case that would have an effect on the franchise. The court further noted that because TRBR had already sold the land its dealership operated on, any irreparable harm was in the past, and therefore not an adequate basis for a preliminary injunction.

Washburn v. One Hour Air Conditioning Franchising, SPE, LLC, No. 3:21-CV-235, 2022 WL 4481416 (S.D. Ohio Sept. 27, 2022). Plaintiff, a former franchisee of Defendant One Hour Air Conditioning Franchising SPE, LLC ("One Hour"), filed a lawsuit against One Hour.. One Hour filed counterclaims, including for breach of a post-termination non-competition covenant and trademark infringement, and sought a preliminary injunction to prevent Washburn from operating in the territory covered by the non-competition covenant and from using One Hour's proprietary marks and trade names. The court entered the preliminary injunction and ordered Washburn to comply with the post-termination non-competition covenant and cease the use of One Hour's trademarks. In support of its decision, the court found that there was a high likelihood One Hour would succeed on the merits because the non-competition covenants were enforceable under applicable law and One Hour had demonstrated an infringement of its trademark. The court further found that One Hour would suffer irreparable harm if Washburn continued to ignore the non-competition covenant and use One Hour's trademarks, the balance of the equities weighed in favor of One Hour, and the public interest in favor of freedom of contract and enforcing federal trademark law also supported the injunction.

Zest Anchors, LLC v. Geryon Ventures, LLC, No. 22-CV-230 TWR (NLS), 2022 WL 16838806 (S.D. Cal. Nov. 9, 2022). The court previously preliminarily enjoined plaintiff's competitor and plaintiff's former distributor (who were now working together) from using the trade dress of plaintiff's products or importing into the United States any products using such trade dress. Plaintiff moved the court to find defendants in civil contempt for engaging in an "end-run around" the preliminary injunction by selling non-infringing individual components to foreign distributors, because defendants knew those parts would be combined into an infringing whole for sale to customers in the United States who the court found would be confused by the products' similarity to plaintiff's products. The court granted plaintiff's motion and awarded plaintiff the disgorgement of any profits earned by the defendants in violation of the preliminary injunction and their attorney's fees incurred in filing the motion.

VII. Damages

In ***Cajunland Pizza, LLC v. Marco's Franchising, LLC***, 2022 WL 4353345 (N.D. Ohio Sept. 20, 2022), the court dismissed the counter-defendants' motion to dismiss the defendant's counterclaims for damages in the form of lost royalties. This case is discussed in Chapter 4, Section II.A.

Chilli Associates Limited Partnership v. Denti Restaurants Inc. d/b/a/ Max & Erma's, No. 22CA30, 2023 WL 4004578 (Ohio Ct. App. June 13, 2023). Defendant spent approximately $2 million to build a restaurant to operate a Max & Erma's franchise. However, defendant then defaulted under its lease for the building premises, and plaintiff, the landlord of the property, sued for breach of contract and to recover amounts owed by defendant under the lease. The appellate court affirmed the trial court's granting of summary judgment in favor of the landlord on its breach of contract claim, and rejected

CHAPTER 4

defendant's argument that it was entitled to an offset against the amounts owed under the lease for the improvements defendant made to the property, finding that the lease expressly provided that the landlord could keep all such improvements if the lease was terminated.

Greenspire Global, Inc. v. Sarasota Green Group, LLC, No. 2D22-2653, 2023 WL 4139142 (Fla. 2nd DCA June 23, 2023). Sarasota Green Group ("SGG"), a distributor of defendant Greenspire Global, Inc.'s ("Greenspire") bactericide and fungicide compounds, sued defendant for fraudulent inducement, negligent misrepresentation, fraud, violation of Florida's Deceptive and Unfair Trade Practices Act, and unjust enrichment. Greenspire appealed the Manatee County Circuit Court's order permitting SGG to amend its complaint to seek punitive damages. The appellate court reversed, finding that what SGG relied on to support its punitive damages claim was inadequate under Florida law.

The court began by noting that, in Florida, punitive damages are authorized and governed by statute, in particular, by Fla. Stat. § 768.72. Under the statute, SGG was required to produce evidence that Greenspire's conduct, knowledge and intent reached the level of "intentional misconduct" or "gross negligence" in order to be able to assert a claim for punitive damages. The court held that SGG did not meet that burden. Rather, it relied solely on the unverified allegations of and attachments to its complaint as well as an affidavit from its managing member. The court first noted that the complaint itself was not evidence. Similarly, the court could not rely on the unauthenticated attachments to the complaint. Regarding the managing member's affidavit, the court noted that it represented that the statements made therein were "correct to the best of my personal knowledge, information, and belief," and a verification based on information and belief is insufficient to entitle the verifying party to relief due to the verification or affidavit being qualified in that way.

Pizza Inn, Inc. v. Odetallah, 2022 WL 4473621 (W.D. Okla. Sept. 26, 2022). (The court granted plaintiff-franchisor's motion for summary judgment on its claims for trademark infringement and breach of contract as well as on the franchisee-defendant's counterclaims for breach of contract, fraud, conversion, and negligence. The court disagreed with the franchisor's calculation of damages based upon the franchisee's breach of his post-termination obligations under the franchise agreement because the franchisor included breaches of franchisee's pre-termination obligations in the calculation.)

Disputes Regarding Performance, Termination, and Transfers

In *Pizza Inn, Inc. v. Odetallah*, 2022 WL 17475784 (W.D. Okla. Dec. 6, 2022), the court granted plaintiff franchisor's motion for summary judgment on the issue of damages on plaintiff franchisor's trademark infringement and breach of contract claims. The court found that plaintiff franchisor's proved its estimate of damages for its breach of contract claim with a reasonable degree of certainty and the defendant failed to show there was a genuine dispute of fact as to the damages. The court further found that because the defendant continued to operate its restaurant in violation of the plaintiff franchisor's franchise agreement after the court ruled in favor of the plaintiff franchisor on its breach of contract and trademark infringement claims, disgorgement of profits was the correct standard for damages under the Lanham Act.

Planet Fitness International Franchise v. JEG-United, LLC, No. 20-cv-693-LM, 2022 WL 4484477 (D.N.H. Sept. 27, 2022). JEG-United ("JEG") entered into letter agreements with Planet Fitness International Franchise ("Planet Fitness") to negotiate an Area Development Agreement ("ADA") to open various Planet Fitness franchises in Monterrey and other parts of Northern Mexico. JEG opened two franchises but contended that Planet Fitness and its Chief Development Officer did not negotiate in good faith to complete the ADA, and tortiously interfered with JEG's prospective business relationships with certain third parties that either had real estate JEG was interested in for opening more franchises or had existing gyms they wanted to sell to JEG which would be converted into Planet Fitness franchises. In its counterclaims, JEG sought damages for (1) the money it expended developing Planet Fitness franchises in Mexico in reliance on Planet Fitness's promise to negotiate in good faith, which was approximately $20 million, and (2) the profits JEG lost for not entering into an ADA with Planet Fitness, which JEG's experts opined would have been approximately $46 million if JEG had opened 20 franchises and about $232 million if JEG had opened 100 franchises.

Regarding the first category, the court found that while JEG did invest $20 million in its Mexican Planet Fitness franchises, those franchises were now worth $40 million, therefore JEG had profited or would profit from its investment. Regarding the second category, the court held that a plaintiff in a breach of contract case can only recover lost profits if they were a foreseeable consequence of the breach and a particular amount of lost profits were reasonably certain to result from the breach. The court cannot, however, award lost profits for speculative and hypothetical future business dealings. But the court noted that, on the other hand, proving a precise amount of future losses with absolute certainty is not necessary, because "a degree of uncertainty is inherent in any projection of future profits." The court found

CHAPTER 4

that it was too speculative to conclude that JEG and Planet Fitness would at some unknown point in the future contract for a 100-franchise ADA, but that a 20-franchise development schedule was contemplated during the parties' negotiations. Because the record evidence would support a jury finding that, had there been good faith negotiations of an ADA, Planet Fitness and JEG were reasonably certain to agree to a 20-store development schedule, Planet Fitness was not entitled to summary judgment on JEG's lost profits claim for a 20-franchise ADA.

In *Soderholm Sales & Leasing, Inc. v. BYD Motors, Inc.*, No. 21-16778, 2022 WL 16847543 (9th Cir. Nov. 10, 2022), the Ninth Circuit affirmed the district court's award in franchisee's favor of its ongoing business value due to franchisor's bad faith discontinuance of the franchisee's franchise agreement, which the district court calculated by multiplying the franchisee's average daily income (taken from its tax returns) by the number of days franchisor had acted in bad faith.

VIII. Attorneys' Fees

CajunLand Pizza, LLC v. Marco's Franchising, LLC, No. 3:20-cv-536-JGC, 2022 WL 3960574 (N.D. Ohio Aug. 31, 2022). The court awarded attorney's fees to the franchisor for its successful defense of the franchisee's claims of breach of the franchise agreement and certain Ohio statutes. The parties' franchise agreement provided for the prevailing party to recover its attorney's fees for certain claims brought under or in relation to the agreement. This case is discussed in Chapter 4, Section II.E.

Integrity Real Estate Consultants v. Re/Max of New York, Inc., 213 A.D. 815, No. 2019-06925, 2019-07405, 2019-07406, 2019-09360, 8794/07 (N.Y. App. Div. Feb. 15, 2023). The franchise agreement between plaintiff franchisee Integrity Real Estate Consultants ("Integrity") and defendant franchisor Re/Max of New York, Inc. ("Re/Max") included a provision that granted the franchisor the right to recover attorneys' fees incurred while enforcing the terms of the agreement. Although the lower court awarded Re/Max its attorney's fees, the appellate court overturned the award after it determined that Re/Max had breached the franchise agreement before the conduct by plaintiff that Re/Max had complained of. However, because the franchise agreement included a provision regarding attorney's fees, the court analyzed the provision to determine whether an award of attorney's fees was warranted. The court strictly construed the provision and determined that Re/Max was neither a prevailing party, nor was the litigation in connection

Disputes Regarding Performance, Termination, and Transfers

with plaintiff's failure to comply with the franchise agreement. The court determined that the initial litigation was for the grant of a temporary restraining order and preliminary injunction in the plaintiff's favor. Thus, Re/Max was not entitled to an award of attorney's fees. This case is discussed in Chapter 4, Section II.A.

Kentucky Peerless Distilling Co. v. Fetzer Vineyards Corp., No. 3:22-CV-037-CHB, 2023 WL 2160851 (W.D. Ky. Feb. 22, 2023). In a dispute concerning an exclusive wine distribution agreement, the court denied the wine manufacturer's motion for nearly half-a-million dollars in attorneys' fees, finding that it lacked jurisdiction to award such fees under the parties' agreement, as that agreement contained a mandatory arbitration provision.

ME SPE Franchising LLC v. NCW Holdings LLC, No. CV-21-00458, 2023 WL 269162 (D. Ariz. Mar. 29, 2023). Plaintiff franchisor sued defendant franchisee, alleging federal trademark infringement, federal and common law unfair competition, breach of the parties' two franchise agreements, and breach of a guaranty agreement relating to both agreements. After the district court entered default judgment in favor of plaintiff, plaintiff filed a motion for attorneys' fees and expenses pursuant to an attorney's fees provision in the franchise agreements and an Arizona statute. Defendant opposed plaintiff's motion, arguing that plaintiff's recovery was limited to work associated with the two breach of contract claims. The court granted plaintiff's motion for attorneys' fees associated with all five claims, finding that because all five claims were interwoven, each claim directly depended on defendant's obligations under the franchise agreements.

In *NFVT Motors, LLC v. Jupiter Chevrolet, L.P.*, No. 05-21-01031-CV, 2022 WL 16959260 (Tex. App. Nov. 16, 2022), a car dealership sued its former employee and that employee's new employer for violating a noncompetition clause. Upon finding in favor of the employee and the new employer, the trial court awarded attorneys' fees in favor of the new employer, despite that new employer not being a party to the employment agreement that contained both the noncompetition clause and the "prevailing party" fee-shifting provision. The appeals court reversed the trial court's ruling, as there was nothing in the employment agreement to suggest that the car dealership and its former employee intended for the fee-shifting provision to benefit persons or entities other than themselves.

Patel v. 7-Eleven, Inc., No. CV 17-11414-NMG, 2023 WL 35357 (D. Mass. Jan. 4, 2023). Following nearly five years of litigation between a class of

CHAPTER 4

franchisees and franchisor 7-Eleven, which included a certified question to the Massachusetts Supreme Judicial Court as to whether there was a conflict between the Massachusetts Independent Contractor Law and the disclosure requirements of the FTC Franchise Rule, the U.S. District Court for the District of Massachusetts awarded summary judgment to 7-Eleven on the franchisees' misclassification claim. The court held that franchisees were independent contractors and not employees. With that classification ruling, the only remaining claims in the case were 7-Eleven's counterclaims for breach of the franchise agreements and indemnification. 7-Eleven's counterclaims were before the court on the parties' cross motions for summary judgment.

As to the breach of contract claim, 7-Eleven asserted that franchisees breached the franchise agreements by holding themselves out as employees. 7-Eleven asserts that its measure of damages was $3.4 million in attorney fees. The court rejected 7-Eleven's assertion of damages and held that, in the absence of a controlling contractual provision regarding the allocation of attorneys' fees, the American Rule only entitles 7-Eleven to costs, not attorneys' fees. Additionally, the court also rejected 7-Eleven's position that the third-party exception to the American Rule was applicable to these facts. As such, the court determined that 7-Eleven was not entitled to recover its attorneys' fees as damages resulting from its breach of contract claim.

Next, 7-Eleven asserted that its attorneys' fees constitute indemnifiable losses under the indemnification provision of the franchise agreements. The relevant provision provided that each franchisee agreed to indemnify 7-Eleven "from all losses arising out of or relating to your Store and its operation" up to $500,000. The franchisees successfully argued that the language of the indemnification provision did not make any reference to defense costs or attorneys' fees, so 7-Eleven's request for fees would also not be covered by indemnity. As such, 7-Eleven's motion for summary judgment was denied and franchisees' motion for summary judgment was granted.

Pizza Hut, LLC v. Ronak Foods, LLC, No. 5:21-CV-00089-RWS, 2022 WL 18456981 (E.D. Tex. Dec. 22, 2022). In this case, the Court awarded attorneys' fees and costs to the franchisor, Pizza Hut, LLC, against the defendants. In a prior order, the court found the franchisor to be the prevailing party following a five-day bench trial. The underlying case involved claims and counterclaims related to breach of contract, violations of the Lanham Act, fraud, and tortious interference with prospective business relations. In addition to an award of damages, the court also found that the franchisor was entitled to recover its reasonable and necessary attorney fees', costs, and

Disputes Regarding Performance, Termination, and Transfers

expenses. Texas law governed, which allows a prevailing party to obtain fees and costs where a contract or statute allows recovery of fees.

The franchisor sought fees in the amount of $4,332,504.24, based on the lodestar method. The court rejected defendants' arguments that the fees were unreasonable, and also declined to adjust the lodestar rate upwards or downwards. The defendants also argued that because the franchisor did not recover its future royalties, the amount of fees was excessive based on the results obtained. The court noted that the franchisor prevailed on all of its claims and on the counterclaims raised by defendants. The recovery of future royalties is an element of damages related to a claim on which the franchisor did prevail and for which the work would be too inextricably intertwined to decrease the fee award on that basis.

IX. Other Issues

North American Specialty Flooring, Inc. v. Humane Manufacturing Company, LLC, No. 22-CV-244-JDP, 2023 WL 4762592 (W.D. Wis. July 26, 2023). Beginning in 2019, plaintiff North American Specialty Flooring, Inc. ("NASF"), a specialty flooring installer with an exclusive distributorship agreement with a flooring manufacturer in Taiwan, began negotiating with defendant Humane Manufacturing Company, LLC (Humane) about a possible acquisition of NASF by Humane, including acquisition of NASF's rights under its exclusive distribution agreement with the Taiwanese flooring manufacturer. The parties hoped to close on that acquisition in early 2020, but the closing was delayed by the COVID-19 pandemic. The parties ultimately entered into an agreement in May 2020 that contemplated an eventual acquisition, and contained an option in Humane's favor to that effect, but which was primarily a distribution agreement.

Humane ultimately decided not to exercise its purchase option under the parties' agreement, and NASF sued for breach of contract and for breach of the duty of good faith and fair dealing. Specifically, NASF argued that the contract required Humane to purchase NASF, and that the "option" language in the contract was really a memorialization of the parties' prior conversations and agreements that closing on the acquisition was being delayed for a year. NASF argued that this memorialization was made clear by the fact that the distribution terms of the agreement were so favorable to Humane, and so unfavorable to NASF, that the agreement and the "option" language in that agreement were patently absurd if not understood to obligate Humane to purchase NASF.

Humane moved for judgment on the pleadings, which the court granted, finding that the plain language of the contract unambiguously granted

CHAPTER 4

Humane the option to purchase NASF, and an option is merely an offer to contract and not an obligation to do so.

RJS Distributors, LLC v. Pepperidge Farm, Inc., No. 21 C 2125, 2022 WL 16836383 (N.D. Ill. Nov. 9, 2022). The plaintiff, Richard J. Straube, Jr. ("Straube"), and defendant Pepperidge Farm, Inc. entered a consignment agreement pursuant to which plaintiff was granted the exclusive right to distribute certain Pepperidge Farm products within a defined territory. Later, with defendant's consent, plaintiff assigned his rights in the agreement to plaintiff RJS Distributors, LLC, of which Straube and his wife are the only members. The consignment agreement contained a description and a map of the relevant territory, and identified which establishments were "fronting" the boundary or the territory.

Plaintiffs sought a declaration from the court that a Target store was within their exclusive territory, and accused defendant of breaching the consignment agreement by excluding the Target store at issue from the territory. The court applied traditional rules of contract interpretation to determine whether the Target store was within, or was excluded from, the territory of plaintiff's distributorship. It reviewed the plain meaning of the contract's words and the overall contract, and found that "in light of the map, [it] is clear, as a matter of law, where the boundary is." The court found that the agreement was not ambiguous and ruled that the undisputed facts showed that the Target store in question was excluded from plaintiff's territory. The court held that plaintiffs could not show that defendant breached the agreement, and entered summary judgment in defendant's favor.

Stauffer v. Innovative Heights Fairview Heights, LLC, No. 3;20-CV-00046-MAB, 2022 WL 3139507 (S.D. Ill. Aug. 5, 2022). Plaintiff Madisyn Stauffer filed suit against defendants Innovative Heights, CenterEdge Software, and Sky Zone Franchise Group, alleging violations of the Illinois Biometric Information Privacy Act ("BIPA"). Stauffer claimed the defendants collected employees' fingerprints for timekeeping purposes without obtaining the necessary consent, thereby violating BIPA. Defendants moved to dismiss the claim, arguing that they had not taken any "active step" to collect their franchisee's employees' biometric data as required for a BIPA violation. The court examined the parties' franchise agreement to determine which party had obligations when it came to using the Point-of-Sale (POS) system required to be used by franchisees for data collection purposes. The court agreed with defendants' position that mere access to biometric data is insufficient to state or establish a BIPA violation - a defendant must take an active step to acquire

Disputes Regarding Performance, Termination, and Transfers

the data. The court therefore granted defendants' motion to dismiss plaintiff's claims, however it granted her leave to file an amended complaint.

CHAPTER 5

Intellectual Property Disputes

I. Introduction

Intellectual property, and in particular, trademarks, has long been one of the most important - if not the most important - components of a franchise agreement and relationship, and it is typically of great importance in distribution agreements as well. Indeed, it is well-established that one of the key elements of a franchise is the granting by the franchisor of the right for the franchisee to operate a business that is associated or identified with the franchisor's trademark, or to offer, sell, or distribute goods, services or commodities that are identified or associated with the franchisor's trademark. The trademark is the franchisor's most valuable asset and what really makes its brand identifiable by consumers and the general public.

Because its trade market and other intellectual property are so important to the franchisor's business, franchisors often seek immediate relief in the form of a temporary restraining order or a preliminary injunction to stop a franchisee or other party from infringing its trademark, misappropriating its trade secret(s), or engaging in other conduct that violates the franchisor's legal rights and interests. There were several cases this year in which franchisors, or parties to a distribution agreement, sought such relief to enforce their intellectual property rights. In several cases, this occurred when a franchisee or a former distributor continued using the plaintiff's trademarks after the franchise or distribution agreements terminated, as such conduct could adversely impact the plaintiff's business model and brand, and cause customer

CHAPTER 5

confusion. This does not mean, however, that the plaintiffs in these cases were always successful - as discussed below, the courts normally require the moving party to prove all of the required elements to obtain injunctive relief, and the plaintiffs did not always meet their burden of proof.

The courts have also held franchisors and former parties to distributor agreements to strict burdens of proof when they sue to protect their purported trade secrets. Among other things, courts this year scrutinized whether the plaintiffs had, in fact, taken steps to ensure that the alleged trade secrets they were seeking to protect were kept secret.

This was a light year in terms of copyright and patent claims involving or relating to a franchise or distribution relationship or agreement.

II. Unauthorized Use of Trademarks

Achieve 24 Fitness Limited Liability Co. v. Alloy Personal Training Solutions, LLC, No. CV 21-12085 (GC), 2023 WL 2264129 (D.N.J. Feb. 28, 2023) (The United States District Court for the District of New Jersey, denied in part Alloy Personal Training Solutions, LLC's ("Alloy") motion to dismiss against Achieve 24 Fitness Limited Liability Company's ("Achieve") trademark infringement and unfair competition claims finding that Achieve adequately stated these claims and that the issue of whether Alloy used its "STRONGER TOGETHER" mark before Achieve's "STRONG TOGETHER" mark remains a factual dispute. The Court therefore denied Alloy's motion to dismiss on this basis. This case is also discussed in Chapter 6, Section XII.)

Bahia Bowls Franchising LLC v. DJS LLC, No. 2:23-CV-94-JLB-NPM, 2023 WL 2303048 (M.D. Fla. Mar. 1, 2023). Bahia Bowls Franchising LLC ("Bahia Bowls"), the franchisor, sued its former franchisee DJS LLC for continuing to operate an acai café under Bahia Bowls' trademarks after their franchise agreement was terminated. Bahia Bowls sought a temporary restraining order ("TRO") to stop DJS from using its marks and violating the agreement's non-compete clause.

The court found that Bahia Bowls demonstrated a likelihood of success on its claims for breach of contract and trademark infringement based on DJS's unauthorized continued use of Bahia Bowls trademarks. It held that the non-compete clause was reasonable and enforceable under Florida law, and that DJS was presumed to be causing irreparable harm by violating it.

As a result, the court issued a TRO prohibiting DJS from operating a competing business within 25 miles, as provided in the agreement, of any Bahia Bowls or using Bahia Bowls' trademarks until the preliminary injunction hearing. DJS was ordered to cease operations and trademark usage in compliance with the franchise agreement. The court found that the public interest favored enforcing trademarks and contracts, and the balance of harms weighed in Bahia Bowls' favor.

Cici Enterprises, LP v. TLT Holdings, LLC, No. 3:21-CV-02121-S-BT, 2022 WL 17657576 (N.D. Tex. Nov. 18, 2022). The magistrate court recommended the district court grant the franchisor plaintiffs' motion for summary judgment on claims for trademark infringement and unfair competition. In so doing, the magistrate court rejected the franchisee defendants' argument that the franchisor was equitably estopped from bringing its claims, or that franchisor consented to the franchisee's continued use of the franchisor's trademarks after the franchise agreement was terminated by engaging in negotiations. The court determined that defendants' arguments relied solely on communications that were privileged and inadmissible. This case is discussed in Chapter 4, Section II.

Home-Grown Industries of Georgia, Inc. v. Mellow Mushroom of Tom's River, LLC, No. 1:22-CV-04919-SCJ, 2023 WL 2179474 (N.D. Ga. Jan. 3, 2023). The court granted plaintiff Home-Grown Industries of Georgia Inc. d/b/a Mellow Mushroom's motion for a preliminary injunction against defendant Mellow Mushroom of Tom's River, LLC after defendant continued to operate its business and use plaintiff's federally registered marks following termination of the parties' franchise agreement. The court determined that defendant's continued use will cause irreparable harm since plaintiff could no longer control defendant's impact to plaintiff's own brand, the threatened injury outweighed any threatened harm, and plaintiff had a likelihood of success on the merits.

In *Exel Industries SA v. Sprayfish, Inc.*, No. 2:22-CV-00691-RAJ, 2022 WL 17141201 (W.D. Wash. Nov. 22, 2022), the district court denied plaintiff Sames Kremlin Inc.'s ("Kremlin") motion for preliminary injunction on the basis that Kremlin failed to meet its burden of establishing that defendant, Sprayfish, Inc., et. al., ("Sprayfish") unlawfully used Kremlin's federally-registered trademarks, KREMLIN® and XCITE® and unregistered marks, ATX™ and AVX™ (collectively, the "Marks").

Kremlin moved for an injunction, alleging that Sprayfish unlawfully used its Marks to sell replacement parts for Kremlin's paint spraying equipment and that Sprayfish's use of these Marks confused customers into believing that Sprayfish was affiliated with, or endorsed by, Kremlin.

CHAPTER 5

Accordingly, Kremlin claimed that Sprayfish was liable for trademark infringement under the Lanham Act.

To bring a trademark infringement claim under the Lanham Act, Kremlin was required to show, among other things, that the alleged infringer used the plaintiff's valid trademark and that the use is likely to cause confusion as to the source of the product. The district court found that Kremlin met their burden of proving the validity of the Marks. However, to assess whether use of the Marks caused confusion, the district court applied the nominative fair use analysis and found that Kremlin failed to meet its burden of showing that the Marks caused confusion.

Specifically, Kremlin failed to meet this burden because it did not explain whether their paint spraying equipment would be readily identifiable without the use of the Marks. Kremlin also failed to explain how Sprayfish's use of the Marks went beyond a minimal or necessary level. Finally, Kremlin also failed to show how Sprayfish falsely suggested Kremlin's endorsement, when it has a disclaimer on its website specifying that Sprayfish's replacement parts for Kremlin were not manufactured by Kremlin. As a result, the district court denied Kremlin's motion for preliminary injunction.

In *FIMIC, S.r.L. v. ADG Solutions, Inc.*, No. 1:19-CV-05636-SDG, 2022 WL 4715685 (N.D. Ga. Sept. 30, 2022), the district court denied defendant ADG Solutions, Inc.'s ("ADG") renewed summary judgment motion and allowed plaintiff FIMIC, S.r.L ("FIMIC) to proceed on its trademark and trade dress infringement claims, holding that the similarity of the machines designed by FIMIC and its former distributor, ADG, presents a genuine issue of material fact that the jury must resolve. This case is discussed in Chapter 5, Section IV.

Flawless Style LLC v. Saadia Group LLC, No. 23 Civ. 2354 (JHR), 2023 WL 3687782 (S.D.N.Y. May 26, 2023). Plaintiff entities are wholly owned by actress and author Gabrielle Monique Union-Wade. Plaintiffs filed for a temporary restraining order and preliminary injunction after termination of a License and Spokesperson Agreement for the GABRIELLE UNION line of clothing ("License Agreement") when Defendant Saadia Group LLC ("Saadia") continued to sell the branded clothing. Saadia had defaulted under the License Agreement, which plaintiffs terminated when Saadia failed to cure the default. Plaintiffs filed claims for breach of contract, infringement and for false designation of origin. A temporary restraining order was entered, and Saadia opposed the request for preliminary injunction.

Saadia alleged that plaintiffs had breached the License Agreement first, which would have allowed Saadia a right of sell-off of remaining merchandise that was not available if the License Agreement was terminated due to Saadia's breach. The court rejected this argument, noting that Saadia had never sent a written notice of default to plaintiffs, as required by the License Agreement, and continued to perform as if the License Agreement had not been terminated. The court found that Saadia had relinquished its right to terminate the License Agreement when Saadia continued to perform after the alleged default. The court then determined that plaintiffs had terminated the License Agreement due to Saadia's breach.

On the infringement and false designation of origin claims, the plaintiffs needed to establish that the mark was entitled to protection and that Saadia's use of the mark was likely to cause consumers confusion as to the origin or sponsorship of the goods. The court found that the GABRIELLE UNION mark was entitled to protection, as its certificate of registration was prima facie evidence that the mark was so entitled. The court pointed out that, in the licensing context, a likelihood of confusion is presumed when an ex-licensee continues to use the mark after the license expires. Based on the resolution of these two issues in plaintiffs' favor, the court found that plaintiffs had a strong likelihood of success on the merits of their infringement claim. This finding automatically entitled plaintiffs to a rebuttable presumption of irreparable harm. The court rejected Saadia's rebuttal to this presumption that plaintiffs could not show that plaintiffs were actually harmed, as its continued sale of the clothing included only merchandise that plaintiffs had previously approved. The court held that proof of actual harm was not required, as the mere possibility that Saadia could depart from the previous approvals was sufficient to warrant issuance of the preliminary injunction. The court noted that the loss of control constituted irreparable harm in the licensing context.

Saadia then claimed that the balance of the hardships warranted denial of the preliminary injunction, since, if issued, Saadia would lose millions of dollars and have to lay off at least 35 employees. The court also rejected this argument, noting that the law does not protect from the consequences arising from the loss of the chance to promote infringing products.

Hillstone Restaurant Group Inc. v. Houston's Hot Chicken Inc., No. CV-22-02004-PHX-MTL, 2023 WL 110926 (D. Ariz. Jan. 4, 2023) (court granted in part motion for preliminary injunction by plaintiff, which owns and operates several Houston's restaurants and registered the Houston's mark in 1979, against defendant which failed to abide by a previous settlement agreement pursuant to which it agreed to cease using its Houston's Hot Chicken mark in connection with their restaurants, several of which are operated by franchisees, by a certain date).

CHAPTER 5

Kava Culture Franchise Group Corp. v. Dar-Jkta Enterprises LLC, No. 2:23-cv-278-JLB-KCD, 2023 WL 3121893 (M.D. Fla. April 27, 2023). Plaintiff, franchisor of Kava Culture Kava Bars, owns the mark "Kava Culture," which simply consists of those words in "standard characters without claim to any particular font, style, size or color." Plaintiff's former franchisees opened a competing business named "The Kava Bar" and plaintiff moved for a temporary restraining order ("TRO"), arguing, among other things, that defendants were infringing and diluting plaintiff's "Kava Culture" trademark by using "a colorable imitation of the registered mark in connection with the sale, offering for sale, distribution and advertising of foods and services in a manner likely to cause confusion . . . ." In denying plaintiff's motion for a TRO on the trademark infringement claim, the court noted that plaintiff's registered mark was simply "Kava Culture" without claim to any particular font style, size or color, and its registration made clear that it was not making any claim to the exclusive right to use "Kava" apart from the mark as shown. Because defendants did not use the word "culture", the court concluded that plaintiff had not established Defendants were using a colorable imitation of its mark and plaintiff failed to establish a substantial likelihood of success on the merits of its trademark claim. This case is also discussed in Chapter 4, Section III.

Luxottica of America, Inc. v. Brave Optical, Inc., No. 4:22-CV-244, 2023 WL 4589222 (E.D. Tex., July 18, 2023). Luxottica of America, Inc. ("Luxottica"), the franchisor of the Pearl Vision franchise system, brought this action against its former franchisee, Brave Optical, Inc. and its owners, Jeffrey and Dawn Gray (the "Grays") (collectively, the "Brave Parties") alleging trademark infringement and violation of the Brave Parties' two license agreements' non-competition provisions, among other claims. The Brave Parties had purchased two Pearl Vision stores from a previous franchisee in 2016. One of the license agreements expired in 2022, and Luxottica defaulted and subsequently terminated the other in late 2016 for failure to pay royalties and other fees.

In a separate state court action in 2017, the Brave Parties had filed suit against the former franchisee from whom they purchased their stores, alleging fraudulent misrepresentation. In 2019, the Brave Parties added Luxottica to that action, alleging that Luxottica knowingly assisted the fraud by making affirmative misrepresentations and concealing material facts to induce the Brave Parties into the sales transactions. In February 2022, the Brave Parties requested and received, a temporary injunction against Luxottica that only prevented Luxottica from attempting to close down the store that was the subject of the expired license agreement, that would continue until the trial in that action. At a September 2022 trial, the Brave Parties won on claims of fraud, fraud by non-disclosure, and conspiracy to defraud. The final judgment noted that Luxottica had withdrawn its interim appeal of the issuance of the temporary injunction, such that the temporary injunction remained in effect. After this trial, the Brave Parties de-identified both stores and rebranded them as "Brave Optical," removing all indicia of a Pearl Vision store, except for the stores' light-colored wood wall panels, desk furniture, shelving, and accents.

In April 2022, Luxottica filed for a temporary injunction in the instant action, which the court denied finding that the Anti-Injunction Act, which prohibits federal courts from issuing injunctions that countermand a state court injunction, prevented the court from granting the injunction without directly risking interfering with active state proceedings. In December 2022, Luxottica renewed its request for an injunction on its claims for trademark infringement, trade dress infringement, and violation of the non-compete provision.

As to Luxottica's claims for trade dress infringement, the court found that Luxottica had not proven that its trade dress was protected. The court noted that Luxottica had to show that its trade dress was distinctive and nonfunctional. Luxottica had described its trade dress as "a distinctive design and layout of a retail store featuring a clean modern appearance, consisting of light-colored wood wall panels and desk furniture, light-colored wood shelving and accents, and beige seating and flooring with the interior marked by square décor panels above square multitiered shelving, incorporating distinctive department and header graphics and brand and storytelling fixtures." In response, the Brave Parties presented evidence of a number of other optical stores that contained many of the same elements as in the claimed Pearl Vision trade dress. Given the similarities in the examples provided, the court determined that there were significant factual disputes that prevented the court from determining that Luxottica was likely to succeed in showing that the intrinsic nature of the Pearl Vision trade dress served to identify Pearle Vision as the particular source. The court also noted that Luxottica has not shown that its trade dress had acquired any secondary meaning, that would provide it with the necessary distinctiveness as it had failed to present any evidence of the seven factors used to determine secondary meaning: (1) length and manner of use of the trade dress; (2) volume of sales; (3) amount and manner of advertising; (4) nature of use of the trade dress in newspapers and magazines; (5) consumer survey evidence; (6) direct consumer testimony; and (7) the defendant's intent in copying the trade dress.

CHAPTER 5

Next, the court addressed Luxottica's claims for trademark infringement. The court acknowledged that Luxottica had proven that it was the owner of the PEARL VISION trademark and that it was the senior user of that mark. However, the court declined to grant the injunction, as Luxottica had not proven that the Brave Parties' use of the mark was likely to cause confusion about the defendant's mark. The court noted that the applicable test required evaluation of the following factors: (1) strength of the mark; (2) mark similarity; (3) product or service similarity; (4) outlet and purchaser identity; (5) advertising media identity; (6) defendant's intent; (7) actual confusion; and (8) care exercised by potential purchasers. The court believed that there were factual disputes that prevented the court from determining that Luxottica was likely to succeed in showing a likelihood of confusion. In addition, the court pointed out that Luxottica was unlikely to show that it had suffered irreparable harm as the Brave Parties had already rebranded the stores, noting that "the court will not issue a preliminary injunction when the only evidence presented shows that any harm done to Luxottica has likely ended – past injury is usually compensable through monetary damages."

The final issue the court addressed was whether an injunction should be granted due to the Grays' violation of the non-competition provisions in the license agreements. The Grays defended by arguing that the judgment that they had received in the state court action establishing fraud rendered the license agreements invalid and unenforceable. However, the court pointed out that a contract found to be procured by fraud was voidable, not void. The license agreements were therefore voidable, entitling the Grays to rescind them. However, in the state court action the Grays had elected to obtain money damages rather than rescinding the license agreements, thereby leaving the license agreements valid and enforceable. After finding the non-competition restrictions to be reasonable limitations on time, geographical area and scope, the court granted the preliminary injunction.

Makina Ve Kimya Endustrisi v. Kaya, No. 3:20-cv-00072, (W.D. Va. Feb 17, 2023). Plaintiff is a Turkish company that manufactures firearms and other military equipment under a trademark registered in Turkey. Defendant and plaintiff entered into an agreement whereby defendant was to be the exclusive U.S. distributor of plaintiff's products. Plaintiff claims that defendant wrongfully registered its own trademark that was substantially similar to the plaintiff's mark. The defendant filed a motion to dismiss the claim for lack of standing because the defendant had already voluntarily surrendered use of the trademark. The court denied the motion, holding that the plaintiff did have standing for at least the period leading up to the time the defendant surrendered the trademark and that the plaintiff had adequately alleged that it was damaged by the defendant's registration.

Nakava LLC v. The South Pacific Elixir Company, No. 22-13567, 2023 WL 4364502, (11th Cir. July 6, 2023). This case is one more in a saga of cases between three former partner litigants. Nakava LLC ("Nakava") is the owner of a trademark registration for the mark NAKAVA. During more peaceful times, Nakava had permitted The South Pacific Elixir Company ("SPEC") to use the NAKAVA mark to identify a bar that SPEC owned, with the partners' hopes that this bar would be the first franchise in the parties' attempts to create a franchised system identified by the NAKAVA mark. The parties did not enter into a written license agreement for this use. When the franchise pursuit failed to materialize, Nakava switched its focus to selling its signature NAKAVA product, a beverage made from the kava root, while SPEC continued to operate its NAKAVA bar. After much intervening litigation on other claims between the former partners, Nakava eventually notified SPEC that it was terminating SPEC's rights to use the NAKAVA mark. When SPEC failed to discontinue use of the mark, this litigation followed. SPEC's defense was that Nakava had abandoned the NAKAVA trademark through non-use and through naked licensing, where a mark is licensed but without maintaining any control over how the mark is used. After a two-day bench trial, the lower court ruled in favor of Nakava. This appeal followed.

As to the abandonment claim, the court noted that SPEC had to establish two elements to succeed: (1) that Nakava had ceased using the mark, and (2) that Nakava had no intention to resume using the mark. If a mark is not used for three consecutive years, there is *prima facie* evidence of abandonment, which creates a rebuttable presumption of an intent not to resume use. SPEC claimed that Nakava had abandoned the mark for three years. Due to the pendency of the previous litigation between the parties, Nakava had suspended its retail sales of its NAKAVA beverage for three years, but had continued to sell the product at wholesale. The court noted that SPEC had presented no evidence at all about Nakava's alleged non-use, and in fact, its corporate representative admitted that he lacked "any knowledge of anything Nakava has done other than what's in the public domain and on the internet. Nakava on the other hand, had presented evidence of its wholesale distribution of the NAKAVA beverages, thereby establishing the required use. The court therefore affirmed the lower court's finding that Nakava had not abandoned its NAKAVA mark.

The court also affirmed the lower court's ruling that Nakava had not abandoned its mark through the use of a naked license, noting that a licensee is estopped from contesting the validity of the licensor's title to the mark

CHAPTER 5

during the term of the licensing arrangement. Therefore, SPEC could only succeed using evidence that arose after Nakava had terminated the license. After termination of the license, Nakava was pursuing enforcement of its rights through the filing of the instant case.

Pizza Inn, Inc. v. Allen's Dynamic Food, Inc., No. CIV-23-00164-PRW, 2023 WL 3015297 (W.D. Okla. Apr. 19, 2023) (in granting Plaintiff franchisor's motion for a preliminary injunction to stop the Defendants from continuing to use Plaintiff's trademarks after Plaintiff had terminated their franchise agreements, the court found that Plaintiff had established a likelihood of success of the merits of its trademark infringement claim because Defendant's continued, unauthorized use of Plaintiff's marks was likely to deceive or cause confusion among customers, and Defendants failed to overcome the rebuttable presumption of irreparable harm provided by the Trademark Protection Act of 2020). This case is discussed more fully in Chapter 4, Section VI.

Powerlift Door Consultants, Inc. v. Shepard, No. 21-CV-1316 (WMW/ECW), 2023 WL 2976031 (D. Minn. Apr. 17, 2023). Defendant Shepard owned and operated a metal supply store and was a licensee of products from plaintiff Power Lift Door Consultants, Inc. Defendant sent an email to other licensees of plaintiff's products making many derogatory remarks, including about plaintiff and its products. Plaintiff then terminated the distribution agreement between the parties, and defendant continued to, among other acts, sell plaintiff's product. Plaintiff's complaint alleged that defendants breached the distribution agreement between the parties (including that agreement's non-compete provision), and that defendants were improperly using plaintiff's trademarks and confidential information. The court granted plaintiff's motion for partial summary judgment, determining that plaintiff breached the distribution agreement both before and after termination of the agreement, and that plaintiff infringed on defendant's trademarks. This case is also discussed in Chapter 4, Section III.

Powerlift Door Consultants, Inc. v. Shepard, No. 21-CV-1316 (WMW/ECW), 2023 WL 3012037 (D. Minn. Apr. 18, 2023) (Following plaintiff Powerlift Door Consultants, Inc.'s ("Powerlift") termination of a distribution agreement, the United States District Court for the District of Minnesota granted Powerlift's motion for partial summary judgment on its breach of contract and trademark infringement claims against the licensee defendants on the basis of the defendants' breach of the post-termination non-compete and their continued use of Powerlift's trademarks after termination of the agreement.)

Sea Tow Services International, Inc. v. Tampa Bay Marine, No. 20-CV-2877(JS)(SIL), 2022 WL 5122728 (E.D.N.Y. Sept. 30, 2022). The court dismissed the franchisor's claims for violation of the franchise agreement's non-compete, non-disclosure requirements, and dismissed the franchisor's claims for trademark infringement. The franchisor based these claims on disclosures that were made in the franchisee's bankruptcy filing. The defendants argued that these disclosures were protected by the attorney client privilege and the litigation privilege. The court agreed, and the court also noted that filing a bankruptcy petition is a lawful right.
See Chapter 2, Section II for complete case summary.

III. Copyright, Patent Infringement

F45 Training Pty Ltd. v. Body Fit Training USA Inc., No. 20-1194-WCB, 2022 WL 17177621 (D. Del. Nov. 17, 2022). Plaintiff sued defendants, franchisors of fitness gyms, claiming that they were infringing plaintiff's patent, which involved methods of remotely configuring and directing the operation of a fitness studio from a central server. Defendants moved for summary judgment that the patent was invalid and thus incapable of infringement. On the latter issue, the defendants argued that it was the franchisees' conduct that arguably violated the patent. Plaintiff claimed that defendants controlled the franchisees' operations and required in their franchise agreements that the franchisees utilize the accused product in their businesses. The court reviewed the language of the defendants' franchise agreement and found that there was a factual issue regarding whether the defendant franchisor had direct control over the conduct of its franchisees that was alleged to infringe plaintiff's patent. It therefore denied, in part, the defendants' motion for summary judgment of non-infringement.

Got Docs, LLC v. Kingsbridge Holdings, LLC, No. 19 C 6155, 2023 WL 2078450 (N.D. Ill. Feb. 17, 2023). The court found that the defendants only offered a perfunctory defense against plaintiffs' copyright claim by simply and conclusorily stating that "there is no evidence that [Kingsbridge] copied Got Docs' website or website content." While the court noted that it was unclear whether plaintiffs' claims that the websites looked similar rose to the level of copyright infringement, since defendants made "no effort to demonstrate that copyright infringement had not occurred," the court denied

CHAPTER 5

summary judgment as to the issue. This case is discussed in Chapter 5, Section IV.

IV. Misappropriation of Trade Secrets

In *FIMIC, S.r.L. v. ADG Solutions, Inc.*, No. 1:19-CV-05636-SDG, 2022 WL 4715685 (N.D. Ga. Sept. 30, 2022), the court denied defendant ADG Solutions, Inc.'s ("ADG") renewed summary judgment motion and allowed plaintiff FIMIC S.R.L ("FIMIC") to proceed on its claim that ADG, a former distributor of its products, violated the Defend Trade Secrets Act of 2016, 18 U.S.C. § 1836(b), *et seq* ("DTSA") and the Georgia Trade Secrets Act O.C.G.A. § 10-1-760, *et seq.* ("GTSA"). The court also denied ADG's renewed summary judgment motion regarding FIMIC's trademark and trade dress infringement claims against ADG.

This dispute arose out of an oral agreement between FIMIC and ADG under which FIMIC made ADG the North American representative and exclusive distributor of its products including the RAS filter (the "Agreement"). ADG operated as FIMIC's North American distributor from 2010 up until FIMIC terminated the Agreement in 2015. However, FIMIC alleges that after the Agreement terminated, ADG sold replacement parts for FIMIC machines and also used FIMIC's confidential information and trade secrets without authorization. ADG admits that it used reverse engineering to create a copycat machine (the "CFO Machine") and sold at least five CFO Machines since April 2015.

Among other claims, FIMIC alleged that ADG violated the DTSA and GTSA (the "Trade Secrets Claims") and that ADG was liable for trademark and trade dress infringement (the "Trademark Claims"). The court denied ADG's motion for summary judgment as to FIMIC's Trade Secrets Claims finding that although the RAS Filter's mechanical components were visible, FIMIC's patent filings include renderings of the RAS filter, FIMIC displayed the RAS filter at trade shows and FIMIC never stamped information shared with ADG as confidential, the question of whether FIMIC took reasonable measures to protect the trade secret information it shared with ADG under the Agreement, was one for the jury.

The court also denied ADG's renewed summary judgment motion regarding the Trademark Claims, finding that the issues of whether: (1) the CFO Machine looks like the RAS Filter, (2) the shape and appearance of the RAS Filter is functional versus non-functional, and (3) customer confusion exists regarding the similarity of the RAS Filter and the CFO Machine, are genuine issues of material fact that a jury should sort out.

Foundation Building Materials, LLC v. Conking & Calabrese, Co., Inc., No. 23 CVS 9285, 2023 WL 4561583 (N.C. Super. Ct. July 7, 2023). Plaintiff sought a preliminary injunction against defendant to enjoin defendant's alleged misappropriation of plaintiff's trade secrets. The court considered the alleged trade secrets and determined that the only confidential information of plaintiff that qualified as a trade secret was certain detailed information regarding the plaintiff's vendor rebate program. The court found that to be the only confidential information the misappropriation of which would cause irreparable harm to plaintiff if a preliminary injunction were not granted.

Gimex Properties Corp., Inc. v. Reed, 205 N.E.3d 1 (Ohio App. Dec. 29, 2022). The trial court granted a permanent injunction enforcing a franchise agreement's post-termination non-compete clause, deeming it reasonable and necessary to prevent irreparable harm to Gimex's franchise system due to the trade secret knowledge former franchisees, who were now working for Gimex's competitor, possessed. This case is discussed in Chapter 4, Section III.

Got Docs, LLC v. Kingsbridge Holdings, LLC, No. 19 C 6155, 2023 WL 2078450 (N.D. Ill. Feb. 17, 2023). Plaintiff Got Docs, LLC ("Got Docs"), a Xerox dealer, sued its former Chief Executive Officer, Mendecina and a competitor dealer Kingsbridge Holdings ("Kingsbridge"). In 2017, Mendecina left Got Docs and went to work for Kingsbridge after Got Docs ceased operations. At Kingbridge, Mendecina developed a software system for the company called BridgeConnect, and Got Docs alleged the defendants' software misappropriated Got Docs' proprietary software called IQ Connect. Got Docs asserted a multitude of claims, including for violations of the Defend Trade Secrets Act, 18 U.S.C. § 1836 et seq. ("DTSA") and the Illinois Trade Secrets Act, 765 ILCS 1065 ("ITSA").

While defendants contended that IQ Connect did not qualify as a trade secret and noted that plaintiffs did not have a current copy of the IQ Connect software, the court commented that defendants failed to engage in any analysis of the surrounding circumstances to determine whether IQ Connect qualified as a trade secret. Accordingly, the court assumed for the purposes of summary judgment that plaintiffs' software qualified as a trade secret under both DTSA and ITSA. Defendants argued that they had not misappropriated plaintiffs' software because there was no evidence that they "used, disclosed, or acquired" the software. Plaintiffs asserted that defendants took over the cloud hosting services, lured employees who had access to the source codes, and worked with the same software developers plaintiff used to develop the software. Furthermore, they pointed to a report where defendants

CHAPTER 5

discussed the cost of keeping the site active to keep the source code. Thus, the court determined that the report created a genuine issue of material fact, which, when combined with the court's determination that the plaintiff sufficiently pled that they were harmed by defendants' actions, justified the court's denial of defendants' motion for summary judgment on this issue. The court also held that several of plaintiffs' other claims, including for conversion, unjust enrichment and breach of fiduciary duty, were preempted by the trade secret statutes to the extent they were based on evidence involving the use of trade secrets or other protected information.

In *JTH Tax LLC v. Anderson*, No. CV-23-00209-PHX-DJH, 2023 WL 3499645 (D. Ariz. Apr. 18, 2023) the court denied a motion to dismiss the franchisor's first amended complaint for failure to state a claim against defendants who were office managers of prior franchisees. The court found that while the allegations against the non-franchisee defendants did not meet the stringent standard for a temporary restraining order, the allegations met the lenient standard under Rule 12 alleging violation of the Defend Trade Secrets Act, as well as claims for conversion, unjust enrichment, tortious interference, and the Computer Fraud and Abuse Act.

Smash Franchise Partners, LLC v. Kanda Holdings, Inc., No. 2020-0302-JTL, 2023 WL 4560984 (Del. Ch. July 14, 2023). The franchised business of plaintiff Smash Franchise Partners, LLC ("Smash") involves smashing trash in dumpsters using a rotating drum attached to a hydraulic boom mounted on a SMASH-branded truck, which allows customers to pack more trash into each dumpster truck load so they can save on the per-pickup fees that waste management companies charge for hauling away dumpsters. Defendant Todd Perri expressed interest in becoming a Smash franchisee, and he attended multiple informative sessions hosted by Smash to that end. Perri ultimately decided, however, that with his experience as an engineer and an entrepreneur, and because he became convinced that Smash did not have any patents or other intellectual property that could pose a threat to a competing business, he would create his own mobile trash compaction company.

Despite deciding not to purchase a Smash franchise, Perri continued to feign interest in doing so and he continued to gather information from Smash about the mobile trash compaction business, though he purposely avoided attending any of Smash's discovery days at which he knew he would have been required to sign a non-disclosure agreement that would contractually prohibit him from moving forward with his competing business.

Ultimately, Perri and his college fraternity brother, defendant Kevin McLaren, formed defendant Dumpster Devil, LLC to sell trash compacting equipment, and on their website they compared their Dumpster Devil equipment and the economic returns a buyer could generate with Smash's equipment and the economic returns a franchisee might expect.

Smash filed suit against Perri, McLaren, and Dumpster Devil and sought a preliminary injunction against them that would have shut down Dumpster Devil's business. The court refused to enter the business-stopping injunction, opting instead to enter a more limited injunction that barred Dumpster Devil pending trial from making certain comparisons to Smash on its website. In its order on injunctive relief the court held that Smash had demonstrated a reasonable likelihood of success on only two of its eight claims against the defendants: for fraud based on Perri misrepresenting his interest in a franchise, and for violations of the Delaware Uniform Deceptive Trade Practices Act (DUDTPA) based on certain of the comparisons to Smash on Dumpster Devil's website.

Over the course of the next two years of litigation Smash ended up dropping all of its claims except for the fraud and DUDTPA claims, and the parties had a bench trial on those two claims.

On the fraud claim, Smash sought to prove that Perri fraudulently induced it to reveal information by falsely representing that he was interested in a franchise, and as a remedy Smash asked for $3,427,091 in lost profits stemming from the head start that Dumpster Devil allegedly obtained by surreptitiously receiving "training" from Smash. According to Smash, it would have taken Perri and McLaren sixteen more months to get Dumpster Devil off the ground without the training that Perri received, and that during those sixteen months Smash would have sold five more franchises.

The court ultimately found that Smash's fraud claim failed because it was preempted by the Delaware Uniform Trade Secrets Act (DUTSA), which preempts all common law claims based on conduct that otherwise would give rise to a DUTSA claim if the misappropriated information qualified as a trade secret. The court concluded that Smash had tried to sidestep DUTSA preemption by inaccurately characterizing the information Perri obtained as training. However, what Perri received was not training, but rather participation in telephone calls designed to encourage prospects to buy a franchise. Absent preemption, the court found that Smash's fraud claim nevertheless failed because Smash had not carried its burden of providing causally related damages.

As for the DUDTPA claim, the court found that Smash had succeeded in proving that two of the comparison statements on Dumpster Devil's website violated the DUDTPA, but it nevertheless found that the grounds did not exist for permanent injunctive relief and there were no proven damages stemming from those violations.

CHAPTER 5

The court ultimately ruled that neither side in the case deserved any relief, as Smash had pursued an aggressive lawsuit that made overblown claims in an effort to destroy a nascent competitor, and as Perri had indeed engaged in fraudulent behavior in his dealings with Smash, albeit fraud that did not cause any compensable damages.

V. Injunctive Relief

Legendary Strikes Mobile Bowling, LLC v. Luxury Strike, LLC, No. 1:22-cv-05065-ELR, 2023 WL 4401541 (N.D. Ga. May 15, 2023) (denying motion for preliminary injunction based on trademark infringement claim because plaintiff failed to show it was likely to succeed on the merits due to unresolved and contested factual disputes which needed to be determined regarding which party first used the contested mark in commerce).

VI. Other Trademark Issues

Cynthia Gratton LLC v. Original Green Acres Café LLC, No. 2:20-cv-02085-MHH, 2023 WL 1070606 (N.D. Ala. Jan. 27, 2023) (granting default judgment in a case involving allegations of trademark infringement under the Lanham Act, trademark dilution, and false designation of origin, which allegedly caused customer confusion, damaged Green Acres's goodwill, and damaged the value of the marks and brand). This case is discussed in Chapter 8, Section XII.

Good Clean Love, Inc. v. Epoch NE Corporation, Civ. No. 6:21-cv-01294-AA, 2023 WL 2709653 (D. Or. Mar. 30, 2023). Oregon courts do not recognize a claim for conversion of a trademark, as this would displace federal trademark law. This case is discussed in Chapter 8, Section II.

Hofbräuhaus of America, LLC. v. Oak Tree Management Services, Inc., No. 2:22-cv-000421, 2023 WL 24179 (D. Nev. Jan. 3, 2023). Oak Tree Management Services ("Oak Tree"), a Missouri corporation, entered into several franchise agreements with Hofbräuhaus of America, LLC ("Hofbräuhaus"), a limited liability company with its principal place of business in Nevada, under which Oak Tree had a limited license to use Hofbräuhaus's copyrights, trade names, trademarks, and trade dress. Oak Tree operated a Hofbräuhaus-branded franchise in Illinois which used these trade names, marks, logos, and branding throughout the building. Oak Tree allegedly defaulted on its financial and operational obligations under the franchise agreements and, when its attempt to cure the defaults through a receivership action failed, Hofbräuhaus took the position that these defaults caused the expiration of the franchise agreement and it told Oak Tree's receiver to shut down operations and remove all indicia of its brand. The receiver refused and Hofbräuhaus asserted claims for trademark, trade dress, and copyright infringement and for a declaratory judgment against Oak Tree regarding its continued operation. Hofbräuhaus filed its lawsuit in Nevada state court and Oak Tree moved to dismiss, stay, or transfer venue.

The franchise agreements contained a choice of law provision applying Nevada law and a forum selection clause requiring any litigation to be brought in the United States District Court for the District of Nevada or the state court in Clark County. The court held that it had specific personal jurisdiction over Oak Tree because Oak Tree created a continuous relationship with a Nevada company, bound itself to contractual obligations in Nevada through the franchise agreements, and therefore purposefully directed its activities at Nevada. The court also held Oak Tree's alleged unauthorized use of materials protected by federal trademark law and copyright law were intentional acts that caused foreseeable injuries to Hofbräuhaus in Nevada. However, the court ultimately concluded that venue should be transferred to the Southern District of Illinois because the material events giving rise to the lawsuit took place in Illinois and the franchise in question was located in Illinois. It held that in trademark infringement cases, the place where the infringing activity occurs is generally the correct venue.

Joseph v. TGI Friday's, Inc., No. 21-CV-1340, 2022 WL 17251277 (N.D. Ill. Nov. 28, 2022). Plaintiff initiated a putative class action against the franchisor of the "TGI Fridays" restaurant chain, arguing that the "TGI Fridays Mozzarella Stick Snacks," which were manufactured by the named co-defendant, were misbranded and misleading, because the stick snacks did not contain actual mozzarella cheese. Plaintiff thus brought claims for deceptive trade practices in all fifty states.

In response, TGI Friday's filed a motion to dismiss on the basis that it could not be liable under Plaintiff's allegations because its conduct was that of "a mere trademark licensor." The court agreed and granted TGI Friday's motion and dismissed it from the litigation. As explained by the court: "an allegation that a party has licensed its trademark to appear on a product is not, by itself, sufficient to state a claim for liability for misleading representations that appear on the product."

LVDV Holdings, LLC v. Shelton, No. CV 22-5921-RSWL-PD X, 2023 WL 3258437 (C.D. Cal. May 2, 2023) (The United States District Court for the Central District of California granted in part and denied in part defendant's

CHAPTER 5

motion to dismiss plaintiff's Amended Complaint (the "Motion"). The court granted defendant's Motion on plaintiff's counterfeiting claim, finding that plaintiff failed to adequately show that defendant used counterfeit marks. Whereas, the court denied defendant's motion on plaintiff's trademark infringement, false designation of origin and unfair competition claims, finding that plaintiff adequately stated these claims in its Amended Complaint.)

Marina Group LLC v. Shirley May International US Inc., No. 2:21-cv-19951, 2022 WL 17622066 (D.N.J. Dec. 13. 2022). Plaintiff brought an action against defendants for infringement of plaintiff's trademark which was used in connection with a variety of personal care and fragrance products. Defendants were a distributor of plaintiff's products under the SWISSARABIAN brand and operated websites and an Amazon storefront using the mark. Defendants failed to provide access to the websites and accounts to plaintiff as required by the distributorship agreement, and plaintiff therefore terminated the distributorship, moved for a preliminary injunction against defendants to enjoin them from using the mark, and requested access to the website and accounts. Plaintiffs also alleged that defendants had filed trademark applications for marks similar to plaintiff's mark with the intent to deceive. The court denied the motion for preliminary injunction, finding that plaintiff failed to establish defendant's infringement created a likelihood of confusion as to the origin of its products, as it was unclear whether the defendant's conduct involved merely distributing genuine SWISSARABIAN product pursuant to the agreement or infringing products. The court also found plaintiff's claim–that defendant's infringing and fraudulent conduct was especially harmful because they sold identical products failed to establish irreparable injury because the distributorship already authorized defendants to sell such products.

R Journey, LLC v. Kampgrounds of America, Inc., No. CV 22-48-BLG-SPW, 2023 WL 2373352 (D. Mont. Mar. 6, 2023) (denying motion to dismiss counterclaims for common law trademark infringement and false designation of origin/false advertising on the basis that defendant had adequately pleaded its counterclaims).

San Juan Products, Inc. v. River Pools & Spas, Inc., No. 8:21-CV-2469-TPB-JSS, 2023 WL 1994087 (M.D. Fla. Feb. 14, 2023) (The United States District Court for the Middle District of Florida granted in part defendants' motion for summary judgment, finding that some of the statements in the franchisor defendants' business publication were not defamatory against plaintiff and therefore no genuine issue of material fact existed. However, the court also denied, in part defendants' summary judgment motion on plaintiff's trademark infringement claim, finding that a genuine issue of fact existed concerning the likelihood of consumer confusion about defendants usage of plaintiff San Juan's trademarks.

SoClean, Inc. vs. Sunset Healthcare Solutions, Inc., No. 2021-2311, 2022 WL 16826171, 52 F. 4th 1363 (Fed. Cir. Nov. 9, 2022). The court affirmed the lower court's preliminary injunction against Plaintiff's former distributor, which was selling knock-off replacement filters for Plaintiff's continuous positive airway pressure ("CPAP") machines. Plaintiff federally registered the trade dress of its products that it sued defendant for infringing. The court held that such registration was prima facie evidence of the validity of the registered mark and, once the lower court found SoClean was likely to succeed on the merits of its trade dress infringement claim, under the Trademark Modernization Act of 2020, SoClean was entitled to a presumption of irreparable harm.

Zest Anchors, LLC v. Geryon Ventures, LLC, No. 22-CV-230 TWR (NLS), 2022 WL 16838806 (S.D. Cal. Nov. 9, 2022). In a trade dress infringement case, the court held it was appropriate to apply the Lanham Act extraterritorially when plaintiff's former distributor and plaintiff's competitor were making an "end-run around" the court's preliminary injunction by selling non-infringing individual components to foreign distributors who defendants knew would then combine those parts and then sell infringing whole products to customers in the U.S. who would be confused by their similarity to plaintiff's products. This case is also discussed in Chapter 4, Section VI.

CHAPTER 6

Other Federal and State Law Issues

I. Introduction

Beyond the Federal Trade Commission's Rule and certain states' registration and other franchise-related statutes, franchises, like all businesses, are subject to and must comply with a wide variety of federal and state laws. These include antitrust laws, which in recent years have been used by state and federal authorities to target anti-poaching provisions in franchise agreements and other anti-competitive policies and clauses. In the automotive industry, Tesla's unique approach to selling its vehicles - directly to customers rather than through the traditional dealership model - gave rise to some interesting litigation this year regarding whether the company should be granted a dealer license or is even bound by state dealership and/or franchise laws.

While not as trendy or hot a topic, issues always arise (and this year was no exception) when a franchisee or licensee - or, not as commonly but in at least one case this year, a franchisor - files for bankruptcy protection, including what impact the bankruptcy filing has on the debtor's franchise or distribution agreement and relationship. Sadly, but not surprisingly, this year saw a number of bankruptcy cases involving hotel operators who were adversely impacted by the COVID-19 pandemic.

Franchise systems continue to be subject to claims by visually impaired, disabled individuals, who use screen readers to access content on the Internet, that franchisor's websites are not compatible with such screen readers, and therefore the websites are in violation of the Americans with

CHAPTER 6

Disabilities Act. See, for example, the *Ariza v. Coffee Beanery, Ltd.* decision, No. 22-61516-CIV, 2022 WL 17333106 (S.D. Fla. Nov. 29, 2022).

In the employment context, the alleged misclassification of workers (as independent contractors rather than employees) by franchisors or companies working with distributors continues to be a source of litigation, as does whether a franchisor exercises a sufficient level of control over a franchisee's hiring and employment practices to make it a joint employer (which is also discussed in Chapter 7).

And this year saw a continuation of the trend in recent years of victims of sex trafficking trying to hold hotel owners and franchisors responsible for the horrible circumstances they were subjected to and the damages they suffered under the federal Trafficking Victims Protection Reauthorization Act, and of there being insurance coverage disputes regarding such claims.

II. Antitrust

In *Arrington v. Burger King Worldwide, Inc.*, 47 F.4th 1247 (11th Cir. Aug. 31, 2022), plaintiffs, employees of Burger King franchise restaurants, sued the defendant franchisor, arguing that the franchisor's agreements with its franchisees constituted a violation of the Sherman Act. To obtain a Burger King franchise, a prospective franchisee was required to sign a standard franchise agreement that contained a "No-Hire Agreement," under which each franchisee agreed not to hire any employees of another Burger King franchisee for at least six months after the employee left the employment of the other Burger King franchise.

The district court initially dismissed the complaint on the basis that the franchisor and its franchisees constituted a single economic enterprise and therefore were not capable of engaging in the concerted action that a violation of Section 1 of the Sherman Act requires. The appellate court disagreed with that finding and instead held that each Burger King franchisee competed with all other Burger King franchisees, that they were all acting for their own interests, and that each was independently responsible for much of its own operations, including hiring decisions. Accordingly, the court reversed and remanded, finding that the plaintiffs had plausibly alleged that the franchisor and its separate franchisees were capable of engaging in the type of concerted action required for a finding of violation of Section 1 of the Sherman Act.

Calabasas Luxury Motorcars, Inc. v. BMW North America, LLC, No. CV 21-8825-DMG (ASX), 2022 WL 17350921 (C.D. Cal. Sept. 19, 2022). Defendants BMW North America, LLC and BMW Financial Services, LLC (collectively, "BMW") maintained policies of not permitting consumers to sell used BMW vehicles to non-BMW franchise dealerships and not permitting non-BMW franchise dealerships to purchase such vehicles as trade-ins. Plaintiff Calabasas Luxury Motorcars, Inc. ("CLM") challenged the policies as a violation of California's Unfair Competition Law ("UCL"). The court held that for an alleged unfair business practice to be actionable under the UCL, the conduct must threaten to violate an antitrust law or otherwise significantly impair competition. The court found that the antitrust laws do not preclude a unilateral act such as this exclusive dealing arrangement, and thus granted BMW's motion to dismiss.

Dexon Computer, Inc. v. Cisco Systems, Inc., No. 5:22-cv-53-RWS-JBB, 2023 WL 2941414 (E.D. Tex. Feb. 7, 2023). Plaintiff Dexon Computer, Inc. ("Dexon") alleged that defendant Cisco Systems, Inc. ("Cisco) acted as a monopolist in several worldwide and U.S. markets with respect to networking equipment and services for networking equipment. Dexon claimed that Cisco engaged in anticompetitive behavior by employing fear, uncertainty, and doubt ("FUD") tactics to foreclose purchases of competitive products. Dexon also alleged that Cisco conspired with defendant CDW Corporation ("CDW") to sell Cisco equipment and exclude resellers like Dexon through a monopolistic distribution agreement. Dexon asserted that the agreement between the two defendants constituted an unreasonable restraint of trade and a conspiracy to monopolize in violation of Sections 1 and 2 of the Sherman Act. Additionally, Dexon claimed that Cisco violated the Act by *per se* 'tying' in the Relevant Products Market and by unlawfully monopolizing the Relevant Networking Equipment Markets and the Relevant Product Markets.

In denying both defendants' 12(b)(6) motions to dismiss, the court—viewing Dexon's allegations collectively and in the light most favorable to Dexon—found that Dexon sufficiently pled plausible *per se* tying and monopolization claims under Sherman Act Section 1 and monopolization claims under Sections 1 and 2 of the Sherman Act. The court found that Dexon's allegations of Cisco's FUD strategies and "lock-in" tying-related conduct, involving using market power to force consumers to buy one product in order to receive another (such as threatening to cut network service when a customer went with a different brand's relevant product), plausibly alleged sufficient facts of anticompetitive conduct. The court found that such a theory of tying liability did not require a showing of substantial market foreclosure of competitor sales. The court also found that even though Dexon did not allege sufficient specific intent by CDW to monopolize as a conspiracy under Section 2 of the Sherman Act, an amended complaint could survive a motion to dismiss based on case law that intrabrand restrictions on distributor

CHAPTER 6

competition can entail a substantial adverse effect on consumer welfare. Furthermore, the court noted that while a manufacturer can choose who to use as a distributor, the agreement can still be unlawful when it is anticompetitive.

Tesla, Inc. v. Louisiana Automobile Dealers Association, No. CV 22-2982, 2023 WL 4053438 (E.D. La. June 16, 2023). As part of its efforts to challenge Louisiana's refusal to allow it to sell vehicles directly to consumers, Tesla, Inc. ("Tesla") brought suit against the Louisiana Automobile Dealers Association ("LADA"), a trade association representing nearly 350 new motor vehicle and heavy truck dealers in Louisiana), eighteen commissioners of the Louisiana Motor Vehicle Commission (the "Commission"), and ten dealerships that are owned by individual commissioners. Tesla's complaint alleged that Tesla's competitors took the position that Tesla's unique approach to selling, leasing, and servicing new vehicles threatened the traditional franchised dealership model, and as a result, Tesla's competitors in Louisiana had pursued protectionist legislation and coopted state regulatory authority.

Specifically, Tesla alleged that its competitors successfully lobbied the Louisiana Legislature to prohibit manufacturers like Tesla from selling vehicles directly to consumers, and that they abused their control of state regulatory power, through the Commission, by forming a "cartel" that conspired to prevent Tesla from leasing its vehicles and providing warranty repairs and services in Louisiana. As a result, Tesla brought antitrust claims under both federal and state law against all of the defendants, including the commissioners in both their individual and official capacities, as well as three constitutional claims against the commissioners in their official capacities for alleged violations of their rights under the Fourteenth Amendment's Due Process Clause, the Fourteenth Amendment's Equal Protection Clause, and the Commerce Clause.

The defendants moved to dismiss all of Tesla's claims, asserting that Tesla's lawsuit was a frivolous attempt to bypass the legislative process.

With respect to Tesla's claim under the federal Sherman Act, which forbids unreasonable restraints of trade, the defendants argued and the court agreed that the private defendants named in Tesla's complaint were immune from liability under the *Noerr-Pennington* doctrine, which permits joint efforts by individuals to influence public officials even though those intended efforts are intended to eliminate competition. The court therefore dismissed Tesla's Sherman Act claim against the private defendants pursuant to the *Noerr-Pennington* doctrine.

The court also dismissed Tesla's Sherman Act claim as to all of the defendants on the ground that Tesla's allegations had failed to give the court plausible grounds to infer an anticompetitive agreement to drive Tesla out of the Louisiana market had been entered into by any of the commissioners, much less by all of them, nor did Tesla's allegations demonstrate an intention on the part of the commissions to engage in a conspiracy for the purpose of unreasonably restraining trade.

The court similarly dismissed Tesla's state-law antitrust and unfair trade practices act claims, first because those claims were barred by the Eleventh Amendment's sovereign immunity protections to the extent they asserted claims against the commissioners in their official capacities, and second because those claims were untimely under the applicable one-year statute of limitation.

As for Tesla's constitutional claims against the defendants, the court concluded that Tesla did not have a constitutional right to a Commission that was sympathetic to its business model, and it was not persuaded by Tesla's allegations that the commissioners had an economic stake in their regulation of Tesla's leasing and warranty repairs activities sufficient to constitute a violation of due process. With respect to equal protection, the court found that the legislation at issue was rationally related to several legitimate interests. For example, limiting the entities that can perform warranty repairs could help assure that all entities providing these services meet the same basic requirements for special tools, technician certification, and training procedural

Finally, Tesla alleged that the legislation at issue violated the dormant Commerce Clause, which prevents the states from adopting protectionist measures and thus preserves a national market for goods and services. The court found, however, that the challenged legal restrictions were facially neutral, as they did not expressly favor in-state interests over out-of-state interests, and that Tesla had not plausibly alleged that the laws were enacted with a discriminatory purpose or had a discriminatory effect on interstate commerce.

As a result, the court dismissed the entirety of Tesla's complaint with prejudice.

U.S. Wholesale Outlet & Distribution, Inc. v. Innovation Ventures, LLC, No. 21-55397, 2023 WL 4633263 (9th Cir. July 20, 2023). U.S. Wholesale Outlet & Distribution, Inc., among other wholesalers (collectively, the "Wholesalers") brought claims against Living Essentials, LLC ("Living Essentials") and its parent company alleging that Living Essentials violated the Robinson-Patman Price Discrimination Act when it sold the 5-hour Energy drinks that it manufactured to Costco Wholesale Corporation ("Costco") at a lower price than it sold to the Wholesalers, in violation of what

CHAPTER 6

is known as "secondary-line discrimination." To establish secondary-line discrimination, a plaintiff must show that (1) the challenged sales were made in interstate commerce; (2) the items sold were of like grade and quality; (3) the seller discriminated in price between the disfavored and the favored buyer; and (4) the effect of such discrimination may be to injure, destroy, or prevent competition to the advantage of a favored purchaser. The Wholesalers won summary judgment on the first three elements. The fourth element was the subject of a jury trial. The fourth element does not ban all price discrimination, rather it only bans price discrimination to the extent that it threatens to injure competition. Therefore, the Wholesalers had to establish that they were in competition with Costco and that there was competitive injury. The jury returned a defense verdict. The Wholesalers then appealed, challenging various jury instructions and the court's denial of an injunction after the verdict.

The Wholesalers first challenged the jury instruction that indicated that the Wholesalers were required to show that Living Essentials made "reasonably contemporaneous" sales to the Wholesalers and to Costco at different prices. The Wholesalers' objection to this instruction was that "there was literally no evidence to suggest that Living Essentials' sales of 5-Hour Energy to Costco and Plaintiffs occurred at anything other than the same time over the entire 7-year period." The Wholesalers provided spreadsheets that contained literally thousands of sales transactions over a 7-year period involving the Wholesalers, Costco and other purchasers of the 5-hour Energy product. However, the spreadsheets were not presented to the jury and the Wholesalers did not present to the jury specific instances in which sales were made to the Wholesalers and to Costco on reasonably contemporaneous dates. As a result, the court found that with only the Wholesalers' conclusory assertions that all the sales were reasonably contemporaneous, an unexplained mass of spreadsheets, and Living Essentials' evidence of changing market conditions before it, the district court did not abuse its discretion in instructing the jury on this disputed element.

The second jury instruction provided that the Wholesalers had to prove that any difference in prices could not be justified as "functional discounts" to compensate Costco for marketing or promotional functions that it performed. The Wholesalers' objection to this instruction was that "there was 'a complete absence of evidence' of any savings for Living Essentials or costs for Costco in performing the alleged functions justifying the discount. Living Essentials had put forth a defense that any price differentials were the result of "functional discounts." Functional discounts are permissible to compensate a buyer for performing some marketing and promotional functions that the buyer undertakes at its own expense. The defense only applies to the extent that a buyer actually performs certain functions and cannot be used when the discount is completely unrelated to either the seller's savings from not providing the services or the buyer's costs for performing the services. The court found that there was adequate evidence to support the jury instruction.

As to the court's denial of the injunction, the court found that the district court had erred in finding that the Wholesalers and Costco were not in competition. The district court believed that Costco only sold to consumers, however, the 5-hour Energy products were only sold at Costco's Business Centers, which primarily sold to other businesses, such as mom and pop retailers who purchased from Costco to resell in their own retail stores.

III. Bankruptcy

In re Buck, No. 19-34052-SWE-7, 2023 WL 3394938 (Bankr. N.D. Tex. May 11, 2023). The franchisor of Nestle Toll House Café ("Plaintiff") entered into a franchise agreement with Healthy Goods & Stuff, LLC ("Company") in March 2018. The franchise agreement listed an owner of Company ("Debtor") as a guarantor to plaintiff. Company closed the franchise in July 2019, which constituted an event of default under the franchise agreement. The parties presented differing facts surrounding the closure and notice to plaintiff. Debtor filed for bankruptcy in December 2019 but did not list plaintiff as a creditor in the case. Plaintiff had no notice of Debtor's bankruptcy suit and filed a lawsuit against Debtor in state court to recover damages resulting from Company's default on the franchise agreement. After plaintiff filed the suit in state court, Debtor responded by filing a *Suggestion of Bankruptcy* and added plaintiff to the bankruptcy action. Plaintiff failed to participate in the bankruptcy action and instead attempted to pursue the state court action against Debtor again. The court held that plaintiff's claim was dischargeable under Section 523(a)(3) of the bankruptcy code, because Debtor had a reasonable explanation for not originally including plaintiff in the bankruptcy action, and, once plaintiff had notice of the bankruptcy action, the parties should have settled the damages dispute in the bankruptcy action, not state court.

In re Conte, No. 21-13189, 2022 WL 17096645 (Bankr. N.D. Ohio Nov. 21, 2022) (denying plaintiff's motion for summary judgment seeking to have judgment plaintiff obtained against defendants deemed "nondischargeable" under the Bankruptcy Code, where the defendants failed to repay a loan the plaintiff extended to them in order to purchase a pizza franchise, because questions of material fact existed as to whether the plaintiff relied on the

CHAPTER 6

defendants' misrepresentations on their financial statements and whether the defendants intended to deceive the plaintiff).

In re EllDan Corp., No. BR 22-31870-KLT, 2023 WL 175195 (Bankr. D. Minn. Jan. 12, 2023). A franchisee filed for bankruptcy protection and then moved to reject seven franchise agreements it had with the franchisor, Fantastic Sams Franchise Corporation, and to rebrand its existing franchised salons and resume operations post-bankruptcy. The franchisor objected to the franchisee/debtor's motion to reject the franchise agreements, because such rebranding and resumption of operations would violate the franchise agreements' covenants not to compete. The bankruptcy court granted the franchisee/debtor's motion to reject the franchise agreements, but held that the rejection resulted in a breach of the agreements on the part of the franchisee/debtor, and did not effectuate a rescission of the agreements or void the franchise agreements. Thus the franchisor was left to determine its rights and remedies following a breach based on non-bankruptcy law. The bankruptcy court declined to rule on the remaining issues raised by the parties related to performance under the franchise agreements and the enforceability of the non-compete provisions on procedural grounds.

In re Golden Seahorse LLC, No. 22-11582 (PB), 2023 WL 2472970 (Bankr. S.D.N.Y. Mar. 10, 2023). Debtor owns the hotel known as the Holiday Inn Manhattan Financial District (the "Hotel"), which is a 50-story, 492-room hotel touted as the tallest Holiday Inn in the world. As a result of COVID-19, the Hotel's performance suffered, and Debtor's inability to continue to pay interest on a $137 million debt (secured by the Hotel and its revenue) resulted in the Debtor filing for bankruptcy in November 2022.

In January 2023, Debtor entered into an agreement with the New York City Health & Hospitals Corporation ("HHC") pursuant to which, for a period of 15 months, HHC would house approximately 1,000 asylum seekers, which was expected to boost the Debtor's net revenues by more than $10 million. Debtor filed a motion with the bankruptcy court to approve the agreement, which Debtor's senior secured lenders strenuously opposed, citing a host of possible downsides that will gravely harm the value of the Hotel, which is their collateral. Specifically, the lenders contended that the agreement could result in significant potential physical damage to the premises, the difficulties the Hotel might have resuming normal operations after the HHC agreement ended, and the possible impairment of the Debtor's ability to sell or refinance as a result of and following the HHC agreement.

The bankruptcy court held an almost seven-hour hearing on the motion to approve the HHC agreement, which it ultimately granted because, at bottom, the court found that the lenders had failed to prove that the possible harms they identified were likely to occur, much less that those possible harms would result in an amount approaching the agreement's undisputed significant financial benefits. In so finding the court relied in large part on testimony from a top HHC official concerning the agency's experience housing about 7,000 asylum seekers at other New York City hotels over the prior four months, which had not resulted in the harms the lenders contended were likely to occur at the Hotel.

In re Start Man Furniture, LLC, No. 20-10553, 2023 WL 2717662 (Bankr. D. Del. Mar. 30, 2023). The debtors in these bankruptcy proceedings were franchisors of furniture stores. The case was filed on March 8, 2020. In May 2022, the chapter 7 trustee administering the case filed several adversary proceedings against franchisees seeking royalty payments and payments for furniture that the franchisor provided to the franchisees. All of the amounts sought were owed from 2019 to 2020. The franchisees moved to dismiss the adversary proceedings on the basis that they were untimely. The franchise agreement had a requirement that all claims be brought within a year, so that timeline expired in 2020 and 2021. The bankruptcy code provides an additional two years from the date of filing the bankruptcy in which a debtor or a trustee may bring a claim after expiration of the statute of limitations. Here, that deadline expired on March 8, 2022 and the trustee did not initiate these actions until May 2022. The court granted the motions to dismiss without prejudice should the trustee find claims under the franchise agreements that were not time barred.

In re Times Square JV, LLC, No. 22-11715-JPM, 2023 WL 1786408, (Bankr. S.D.N.Y. Feb. 4, 2022). Debtor, a licensee, owns a mixed-use building in Times Square that includes hotel space, office space, retail space, billboards and a parking garage. The hotel portion is subject to a license agreement with Holiday Hospitality Franchising ("HHF") and branded as a Crown Plaza Times Square Manhattan Hotel.

In 2016, prior to the bankruptcy filing, the licensee alleged a breach under the license agreement and sent HHF a notice of default and, one month later, sent HHF a purported termination notice. Contemporaneous with sending the termination notice, the licensee filed an action in New York Supreme Court with a declaratory judgment claim, asserting that the License Agreement was terminated and unenforceable. HHF filed a separate action in New York State Courts with its own declaratory judgment claim asserting that the License Agreement was not terminated. In 2018, a preliminary injunction was issued – to preserve the status quo – and barred the licensee from

CHAPTER 6

terminating the License Agreement until the pending cases were resolved. Licensee appealed the preliminary injunction, and the preliminary injunction was upheld and remains in place.

In 2022, the licensee filed a Chapter 11 bankruptcy petition and sought to sell its assets in bankruptcy without the License Agreement, arguing that the assets would yield a higher return for creditors without the requirement to continue to operate under the brand. Licensee filed a motion to authorize rejection of License Agreement pursuant to Section 365 of the Bankruptcy Code.

The basis of HHF's opposition to the motion is that the License Agreement was not an executory contract and, therefore, the right to reject was not available. The Bankruptcy Court explained the general *Countryman* test for determining whether a contract is executory – a contract is executory if both parties have performance obligations and if such obligations were not performed by one party, then there would be a material breach of the contract excusing performance of the other party. The Bankruptcy Court also explained that franchise agreements are generally considered executory.

HHF argues that License Agreement is rendered (i) non-executory by the preliminary injunction, (ii) allowing rejection would violate principles of comity and (iii) rejection would be contrary to the Rooker-Feldman doctrine.

First, HHF argues that the preliminary injunction, requiring continued performance by the licensee, renders the license agreement non-executory. The Bankruptcy Court rejected this position, distinguishing cases relied upon by HHF by the fact that such cases involved a final order entered on the merits. Here, the preliminary injunction was only a temporary order intended to preserve the status quo until the case could be fully litigated.

Second, the Bankruptcy Court held that authorizing rejection of the license agreement under Section 365 does not violate the doctrine of comity because the relief licensee seeks is available under the Bankruptcy Code.

Third, the Bankruptcy Court explained that *Rooker-Feldman* is a jurisdictional doctrine that bars cases brought by state-court losers complaining of injuries caused by state-court judgments rendered before the district court proceedings commenced and inviting district court review and rejection of those judgments. The Bankruptcy Court held that *Rooker-Feldman* did not apply because there was no state court loser because no final judgment had been entered.

The Bankruptcy Court granted the licensee's motion and authorized rejection of the license agreement, holding that the license agreement is an executory contract and the licensee properly exercised its business judgment under Section 365 of the Bankruptcy Code.

In re Vecchio, No. 6:20-AP-00117-LVV, 2022 WL 16828243 (Bankr. M.D. Fla. Oct. 3, 2022). Debtor Vecchio, who was in the business of selling franchises, borrowed money from Joseph Russo ("Russo") but defaulted on the loan. Russo obtained a judgment against Vecchio for the amounts he was owed plus attorney's fees and costs. Vecchio filed for bankruptcy protection and Russo sought to deny the debtor a discharge of this debt, arguing, among other things, that Vecchio had transferred or concealed assets before and after the bankruptcy filing, made a false oath and failed to maintain adequate records. The court, however, noted that the Bankruptcy Code provides that a discharge "shall" be granted unless the debtor committed one of the enumerated exceptions, and that the reasons for denying a discharge must be "real and substantial." It found that Russo had failed to meet his burden of proving that the exception in the Code allowing a court to deny a discharge when a debtor, "with intent to hinder, delay or defraud a creditor . . . transferred, removed, destroyed . . . or concealed" property of the debtor or his estate.

IV. RICO

In *Energium Health v. Gabali*, No. 3:21-CV-2951-S, 2022 WL 16842660 (N.D. Tex. Nov. 9, 2022), the court held, consistent with the decisions of other Courts of Appeal and district courts that have considered the issue, that 18 U.S.C. § 1965(b) requires that plaintiff must establish personal jurisdiction over at least one defendant under § 1965(a) before other RICO defendants could be subject to nationwide service of process under § 1965(b). This case is discussed in Chapter 8, Section II.

Hyundai Motor America Corp. v. Efn West Palm Motor Sales, LLC, No. 20-82102-CIV, 2022 WL 16968426 (S.D. Fla. Nov. 16, 2022). An automobile manufacturer filed suit against a distributor alleging violations of the Racketeer Influenced and Corrupt Organizations Act (18 U.S.C. § 1962) based on allegations of warranty fraud. The distributor-defendant moved for summary judgment against the manufacturer's RICO claims. The court, however, denied the distributor-defendant's motion for summary judgment against the manufacturer's RICO claims.

According to the court, disputes of material fact could not be resolved on summary judgment as to whether the manufacturer had failed to present sufficient evidence to show that defendants operated as an "enterprise" and whether the defendants had the intent to defraud the manufacturer.

CHAPTER 6

Paul Hobbs Imports Inc. v. Verity Wines LLC, 21 CIV. 10597 (JPC), 2023 WL 374120 (S.D.N.Y. Jan. 24, 2023) (The United States District Court of Southern District of New York, dismissed plaintiffs' RICO violation claims against defendants because plaintiffs' complaint failed to adequately plead that defendants engaged in a pattern of racketeering activity or that an enterprise existed pursuant to 18 U.S.C. § 1962(c).)

V. Civil Rights

Ariza v. Coffee Beanery, Ltd., No. 22-61516-CIV, 2022 WL 17333106 (S.D. Fla. Nov. 29, 2022). Plaintiff Victor Ariza ("Ariza") sued franchisor Coffee Beanery, Ltd. ("Coffee Beanery") and its franchisee Dolphin De Auberet, Inc. ("Dolphin") in the United States District Court for the Southern District of Florida asserting violation of Title III of the Americans with Disabilities Act ("ADA"). Ariza is blind and visually disabled and relies on a screen reader software and a specialized keyboard to use his computer and access content on the Internet. Ariza alleged that the defendants violated the ADA because Coffee Beanery's website, which links to the website for the cafe owned by its franchisee Dolphin, was not compatible with his screen reader software and keyboard. Coffee Beanery filed a motion to dismiss on the grounds that Coffee Beanery's website is not a place of public accommodation, Ariza failed to allege that Coffee Beanery owns, leases, or operates a place of public accommodation, and Ariza failed to allege facts sufficient to show that the website is an intangible barrier to any goods and services offered at the physical cafe.

The court denied the motion to dismiss. First, the court noted that Ariza never contended that the website itself was a place of public accommodation; rather, Ariza claimed that the website was an access barrier to the related physical places of public accommodation for blind and visually impaired individuals such as himself. Second, the court held that Coffee Beanery could be held liable, even though it was merely the franchisor, rather than the owner, of the cafe owned by Dolphin, because Coffee Beanery owned and operated the website that was alleged to be the intangible barrier preventing blind and visually impaired disabled individuals from accessing the cafe. Third, the court noted that the Eleventh Circuit had recently held that an inaccessible website could create an intangible barrier to access to physical goods and services.

Other Federal and State Law Issues

VI. Employment

Acuff v. Dy N Fly, LLC, No. 22-cv-12329, 2023 WL 3293278 (E.D. Mich. May 5, 2023) (court denied defendant-franchisor's motion to dismiss claims brought under Title VII of the Civil Rights Act of 1964 and the Elliot-Larson Civil Rights Act for a sexually hostile work environment and retaliatory termination, on the grounds that it did not possess sufficient control over its franchisee's day-to-day employee supervision to be considered a "joint employer," but where defendant-franchisor was involved in the hiring of certain plaintiff-employees, communicated with the franchisee about inappropriate workplace behavior, offered one plaintiff a small severance payment in exchange for an agreement not to sue the franchisor, and exerted control over the terms and conditions of employment with the franchisee).

In ***Canales v. CK Sales Co., LLC***, 67 F.4th 38 (1st Cir. 2023), the First Circuit held that the plaintiff distributors' claims against the defendants, alleging that the defendants misclassified the plaintiffs as independent contractors, were not subject to arbitration because the plaintiffs qualified as transportation workers engaged in interstate commerce and were thus exempt from the Federal Arbitration Act. This case is discussed in Chapter 8, Section VI.A.

Carpenter v. Pepperidge Farm, Inc., No. 20-CV-3881-GJP, 2023 WL 4552291 (E.D. Pa. July 14, 2023). Plaintiffs worked as "independent direct-store-delivery partners" ("IDPs") facilitating product distribution for Pepperidge Farm. Plaintiffs sought via a putative class action to be classified as employees rather than independent contractors so that they could claim violations of Pennsylvania's Wage Payment and Collection Law ("WPCL"). Pepperidge Farm moved for summary judgment on plaintiffs' WPCL claims on the grounds that plaintiffs were independent contractors and not covered by the WPCL.

The District Court for the Eastern District of Pennsylvania granted Pepperidge Farm's motion for summary judgment, finding that plaintiffs were independent contractors after weighing the following factors:

- Lack of control: The plaintiff IDPs had control over their own work, such as setting their schedules, purchasing territories they believed were profitable, and selling their routes when needed.
- Nature of work: The plaintiff IDPs engaged in sales and distribution, exercising judgment and sales strategies, which is distinct from employee-like menial tasks.
- Tools and equipment: The plaintiff IDPs owned and provided their trucks, devices, and other essential tools.

CHAPTER 6

- Payment: The plaintiff IDPs were paid on commission, typical of independent contractors.
- Business independence: Although there was some cooperation with Pepperidge Farm, IDPs could also distribute other non-competing products, and their businesses were not inextricably intertwined with Pepperidge Farm.
- Type of business: Distribution was a regular part of Pepperidge Farm's business, which was the lone factor that weighed in favor of an employment relationship.
- Termination rights: Pepperidge Farm had limited rights to terminate IDPs.

Carts v. Wings Over Happy Valley MDF, LLC, No. 4:17-CV-00915, 2023 WL 373175 (M.D. Pa., Jan. 24, 2023) (The United States District Court for the Middle District of Pennsylvania granted in part the franchisee defendants' motion for summary judgment, holding that the material facts undisputedly show that a portion of the former-employee plaintiff class was time barred from bringing a claim under the Fair Labor Standards Act ("FLSA") more than three years after their last date of employment. The court also denied in part the franchisee defendants' motion for summary judgment, finding that some of the FLSA claims were not time barred and that a genuine dispute of material facts existed for these claims.)

Doe v. Golden Krust Caribbean Bakery & Grill, Inc., No. 18-cv-05734, 2023 WL 2652264 (E.D.N.Y. Mar. 27, 2023) (court granted franchisor-moving defendants' motion to dismiss a complaint under Title VII for workplace harassment and retaliation, holding that plaintiff did not adequately allege facts under the joint employer doctrine where the moving defendants were not directly involved in plaintiff's hiring, firing, training, promotion, discipline, supervision, handling of records, insurance or payroll.)

Hicks v. Colorado Hamburger Company, Inc., No. 22-CA-0968, 2022 WL 17982947 (Col. Ct. App. Dec. 29, 2022) (appellate court reversed in part trial court's denial of plaintiff's (an employee of the defendant, a McDonald's franchisee) motion for class certification, finding that common questions did predominate over individual ones when it came to plaintiff's claim that defendant violated a Colorado regulation requiring that hourly employees be provided with rest breaks). This case is discussed in detail in Chapter 8, Section X.

Other Federal and State Law Issues

In *In re Lager*, No. 22-30072-MVL-11, 2023 WL 4676067 (Bankr. N.D. Tex. July 20, 2023), PIRTEK USA, LLC, the franchisor, filed an adversary proceeding against a former franchisee and his company, in the former franchisee's bankruptcy case. The franchisor moved for summary judgment on its claims that the franchisee breached the parties' prior settlement agreement, which obligated the franchisee to refrain from disparaging the franchisor or from making any public statement referencing the franchisor. The settlement agreement also contained a confidentiality provision preventing the parties from disclosing the existence or the terms of the settlement agreement. After the parties entered into the settlement agreement, the former franchisee proceeded to post a number of articles online accusing the franchisor of being racist. The former franchisee also shared the settlement agreement with the owner of a website entitled unhappyfranchisee.com and filed complaints with various entities such as the Federal Trade Commission.

The former franchisee filed for bankruptcy the night before an arbitration hearing was scheduled. The franchisor proceeded with the arbitration hearing as to the non-debtor company owned by the former franchisee. The former franchisee's company subsequently also filed bankruptcy and the franchisor initiated this adversary proceeding. The bankruptcy court granted summary judgment to the franchisor on its claims for breach of the parties' settlement agreement and awarded liquidated damages pursuant to the terms of the settlement agreement. The court denied summary judgment as to the attorneys' fees sought by the franchisor, without prejudice, finding that the fee request was not supported by sufficient evidence of reasonableness because there were no detailed billing records admitted into evidence.

The bankruptcy court also granted summary judgment to the franchisor on its claim that the debt owed to it as a result of the former franchisee should be exempted from discharge in the former franchisee's bankruptcy case. The bankruptcy court noted that while tort claims are more typically found to be non-dischargeable, the record was replete with evidence of the former franchisee's intent to harm the franchisor. For this same reason, the bankruptcy court also granted summary judgment as to the franchisor's request for a permanent injunction to enforce the non-disparagement provisions of the settlement agreement.

The bankruptcy court also granted summary judgment to the franchisor on its motion to dismiss the former franchisee's affirmative defenses and claims for violation of the Florida Unfair and Deceptive Trade Practices Act, tortious interference with prospective business relations, and defamation and slander. The franchisor also moved for summary judgment on the former franchisee's claim that the franchisor violated the automatic stay

CHAPTER 6

imposed by the former franchisee's bankruptcy filing when it proceeded with an arbitration hearing against the former franchisee's business. The bankruptcy court found that there were disputed issues of fact as to whether the former franchisee's business would have been considered property of the former franchisee's bankruptcy estate. For this same reason, the bankruptcy court also denied summary judgment as to the former franchisee's right to offset the franchisor's claim against the franchisee because of the possibility that the former franchisee prevailed on its counterclaim for violation of the automatic stay.

Jani-King of New York, Inc. v. Commissioner of Labor, 214 A.D.3d 1088, 184 N.Y.S.3d 473 (N.Y. App. Div. 2023) Jani-King of New York, Inc. ("JKNY") and Jani-King of Buffalo, Inc. ("JKB") appealed from a decision of the New York Unemployment Insurance Appeal Board finding them liable for additional unemployment contributions on remuneration paid to their franchisees. JKNY and JKB are regional divisions of Jani-King, an international sales and marketing company that sells commercial cleaning and janitorial franchises to corporate or individual franchisees. Following an administrative audit, the New York Department of Labor found that individual franchisees of JKNY and JKB who performed janitorial services were employees, and therefore JKNY and JKB were liable for additional unemployment insurance contributions. After appealing to the Unemployment Insurance Appeal Board, JKNY and JKB appealed to the New York Supreme Court, Appellate Division, which also affirmed.

The court found that the Unemployment Insurance Appeal Board did not err in finding that an employer-employee relationship existed because franchisees are subject to a criminal background check, must complete mandatory training, must follow manuals and policies provided by the franchisor, are subject to billing rates set by the franchisor, must maintain certain types of insurance, must wear clothing with the franchisor's logo, must submit monthly invoices to the franchisor for billing and collection, and are subject to inspection by the franchisor.

Lirette v. Sonic Drive-In Corp., No. CV 22-3594 DIV. (2), 2023 WL 3092984 (E.D. La. Apr. 26, 2023) (The United States District Court for the Eastern District of Louisiana granted defendant Sonic Drive-In Corp.'s ("Sonic") motion to dismiss, finding that plaintiff Lirette (a former employee of a Sonic franchisee) had failed to state a claim against Sonic under Title VII and the Equal Pay Act. Specifically, plaintiff had failed to allege any facts to support a claim that Sonic was either her direct employer or a joint employer of the Sonic franchisee.)

Other Federal and State Law Issues

Patel v. 7-Eleven, Inc., No. CV 17-11414-NMG, 2022 WL 4540981 (D. Mass. Sept. 28, 2022), on remand following the Massachusetts Supreme Judicial Court's answer to a certified question, the district court held that the plaintiff franchisees had not been misclassified as independent contractors instead of employees in violation of the Massachusetts Independent Contractor Law. This case is discussed in Chapter 7, Section II.

Quiroz v. DCT Enterprises of New Mexico, LLC, No. 221CV01197MISKRS, 2023 WL 1765383 (D.N.M. Feb. 3, 2023) (court denied plaintiff employee's motion for default judgment in a Fair Labor Standards Act lawsuit against employer defendant who owned Papa John's franchises because of ineffective service, and required plaintiff to show cause by a date certain why the case should not be dismissed for failure to timely serve the defendant).

Salinas v. Cornwell Quality Tools Co., No. 5:19-CV-02275-FLA (SPX), 2022 WL 16735359 (C.D. Cal. Oct. 17, 2022). Plaintiff, a dealer of defendant distributor Cornwell Quality Tools Company's ("Cornwell") products, filed a putative class action alleging that Cornwell improperly classified its dealers as independent contractors rather than employees, despite Cornwell's retaining and exercising control over the dealers. Plaintiff asserted nine claims against Cornwell, and Cornwell asserted forty-two affirmative defenses. Plaintiff moved for summary judgment on Cornwell's fifth and thirty-fifth affirmative defenses–that the plaintiff and putative class members were not employees of Cromwell, but rather were at all times independent contractors under California law. The court denied plaintiff's motion, holding that genuine issues of material fact existed as to whether plaintiff qualified as an employee under California law. First, the court noted that California law recognizes two tests for determining whether a worker is an employee or an independent contractor: the so-called "ABC" test established in *Dynamex Operations West, Inc. v. Superior Court*, 416 P.3d 1 (Cal. 2018) and the multi-factor test explained in *S. G. Borello & Sons, Inc. v. Dept. of Industrial Relations*, 769 P.2d 399 (Cal. 1989) (the "*Borello* Test"). The court first ruled that the ABC Test, rather than the *Borello* Test, applied to plaintiff's claims because the California legislature adopted the ABC test for all claims arising under the California Labor and Unemployment Insurance Codes, including plaintiff's. Next, the court held that the FTC's Franchise Rule, 16 C.F.R. § 436.1 et seq., did not preempt application of the ABC Rule because the Franchise Rule did not directly conflict with any provision of California law. Finally, the court held that genuine disputes of material fact existed as to

CHAPTER 6

whether plaintiff could satisfy prongs A and B of the ABC Test because a genuine dispute existed as to whether Cornwell reserved the requisite degree of control and direction over plaintiff and whether plaintiff performed work necessary rather than merely incidental to Cornwell's business. This case is also discussed in Chapter 7, Section II.

Spikes v. Schumacher Auto Group, Inc., No. 21-81223-civ-SMITH, 2022 WL 18402565 (S.D. Fla. Dec. 20, 2022). Plaintiffs were employed by Schumacher Auto Group. Schumacher Auto Group owns and operates a variety of automobile dealerships, with each dealership also named as a defendant. Plaintiffs worked at a call center known as the Business Development Center (BDC), which was located nearby one dealership but at a separate premise. BDC employees worked to drive sales to the respective dealerships and set up appointments for potential customers at the dealerships. Plaintiffs were not authorized to engage in the sale of any vehicles. All vehicle sales took place at the defendants' dealerships. The plaintiffs did not show cars, did not meet with customers, did not accept deposits from potential customers, and did not deliver vehicles to customers. There were no vehicles or other products for sale which were located at the BDC.

As compensation, plaintiffs received a flat monthly salary. Additionally, they received a set dollar amount for each appointment that they set that actually showed up at a dealership. Plaintiffs also received a flat rate commission based on the number of vehicles sold as a result of the appointments scheduled by that BDC sales agent.

At some point during their employment, plaintiffs received a notice that all overtime without prior approval would cease and they were directed to stop tracking their hours. After this notice, the plaintiffs no longer received overtime pay.

Plaintiffs brought this action and alleged a single count for violation of the FLSA's overtime provisions. This matter came before the court on cross-motions for summary judgment. Defendants seek summary judgment against plaintiffs based on two statutory exemptions to the FLSA, commonly known as the Automobile Sales Exemption and the Retail Sales Exemption (7(i)). Conversely, plaintiffs argue that they are entitled to summary judgment as they are not exempt employees under either the Automobile Sales Exemption or the Retail Sales Exemption. The court determined that neither exemption applied to plaintiffs and denied defendants' motion for summary judgment and granted plaintiffs' motion for summary judgment as to the application of the exemptions.

The court explained that the Automobile Sales Exemption excludes from the FLSA's overtime requirements "any salesman, partsman, or mechanic primarily engaged in selling or servicing automobiles, trucks, or farm implements, if he is employed by a nonmanufacturing establishment primarily engaged in the business of selling such vehicles or implements to ultimate purchasers." Based on the undisputed factual record, the court determined that plaintiffs' job duties do not fall within the definition of "salesman" as a matter of law because Plaintiffs do not "sell," as the FLSA defines that term. The court further explained that plaintiffs provide very limited information about the automobiles defendants have for sale, and they make appointments for customers to meet with the sales manager, who then assigns the customer to a salesperson. In determining that the Automobile Sales Exemption does not apply to plaintiffs, the court distinguished cases relied upon by the defendants by noting that plaintiffs do not provide for the eventual disposition of the products that defendants sell.

With respect to the FLSA's Retail Sales Exemption asserted by defendants, the court explained that this exemption requires that an employer must establish three things: (1) the employee was employed by a retail or service establishment; (2) the employee's regular rate of pay exceeded one and one-half times the minimum hourly rate; and (3) more than half of the employee's compensation for a representative period (not less than one month) represented commissions on goods or services. The court also referred to the regulations to further help explain what makes an establishment "retail or service," citing to the exact text of the regulation that provided "[t]ypically a retail or service establishment is one which sells goods or services to the general public... at the very end of the stream of distribution." Since no cars were sold at the BDC and the BDC was a distinct physical place of business from the dealerships, the court concluded that the BDC was its own "establishment" and held that the Retail Sales Exemption did not apply.

As a result of the court's holdings on the inapplicability of the asserted FLSA exemptions by defendants, plaintiffs' motion for summary judgment on the FLSA violation was granted and defendants' motion for summary judgment was denied. The calculations for overtime differed for each plaintiff with the ultimate overtime award to be determined by the jury.

Streedharan v. Stanley Industrial & Automotive, LLC, No. 5:22-cv-0322-MEMF (KSx), 630 F.Supp.3d 1244 (C.D. Cal. Sept. 27, 2022). Plaintiff operated FLM Enterprises, LLC, which entered into a franchise agreement with the defendant to be a distributor of its products. Plaintiff was required to sign the franchise agreement in his individual capacity and it contained provisions holding him to the same requirements as his company. Plaintiff filed a putative class action against defendant, alleging that defendant had misclassified him and others similarly situated as independent contractors

CHAPTER 6

rather than employees and was thus denying them the protections afforded under California's employment laws.

The defendant moved for judgment on the pleadings, but the court ultimately agreed with plaintiff's argument that, at this point in the proceeding, he had adequately alleged an employment relationship. In considering several important facts and factors, the court first concluded that the existence of a franchise agreement did not preclude a finding of an employment relationship. The second factor the court took into account was the level of control defendant exerted over plaintiff and his company. Another factor the court considered was the way the franchise agreement was written and its provisions stipulating that if the signatory was an LLC, the defendant had the right to terminate the agreement if the individual who signed the agreement ceased to oversee the distributor's operations. This case is also discussed in Chapter 8, Section VI(A).

Teague v. 7 Eleven, No. 4:21-cv-04097-SLD-JEH, 2023 WL 2072404 (C.D. Ill. Feb. 16, 2023) (denying defendant 7-Eleven's motion to dismiss that asserted 7-Eleven exercised insufficient control or supervision over the plaintiff to be considered an employer for the purposes of a Title VII claim). This case is discussed in Chapter 7, Section II.

Weiss v. Premier Technologies, No. 22-CV-6349DGL, 2023 WL 3314691 (W.D.N.Y. May 9, 2023) (denying defendant AT&T's motion to dismiss a claim for discrimination under Title VII of the Civil Rights Act of 1964, based on its argument that defendant-dealer Premier Technologies was plaintiff's sole employer, because it was plausible that AT&T was plaintiff's joint employer where the AT&T brand was displayed prominently throughout Premier's locations and operations and AT&T employees provided sales training and worked directly with plaintiff in developing sales strategies).

Winesburg v. Stephanie Morris Nissan, LLC, No. 2:22-CV-04157-MDH, 2023 WL 3901483 (W.D. Mo. June 8, 2023) (The District Court for the Western District of Missouri denied defendant car dealership owners' motion to dismiss class action claims for violation of the Fair Labor Standards Act and the Missouri Minimum Wage and Hour Law and held that former employee plaintiff sufficiently alleged that defendants were her "employer" under both statutes and that defendants were unjustly enriched by failure to pay overtime.).

Other Federal and State Law Issues

VII. Tax

The authors' review of cases decided during the reporting period did not reveal any significant decisions addressing this topic.

VIII. Insurance

A.W. v. Red Roof Inns, Inc., No. 2:21-CV-4934, 2022 WL 17585249 (S.D. Ohio Dec. 12, 2022). An alleged sex trafficking victim sued a hotel franchisee under the Trafficking Victims Protection Reauthorization Act ("TVPRA"). The insurance carrier that had been defending the hotel franchisee in the lawsuit moved to intervene in the case, in order to adequately protect its interests. The court denied the insurance carrier's motion, finding that its interest in the case is merely contingent because its stake in the litigation is dependent on a determination as to the hotel franchisee's liability and an adjudication on the insurance contract, which were separate and apart from the plaintiff's TVPRA claim.

Jani-King of New York, Inc. v. Commissioner of Labor, 214 A.D.3d 1088, 184 N.Y.S.3d 473 (2023). Jani-King of New York, Inc. and Jani-King of Buffalo, Inc. ("Appellants") appealed the decision of the Unemployment Insurance Appeal Board ("Board") that found Appellants liable for additional unemployment insurance contributions on remuneration paid to certain franchisees. Appellants contended that their franchisees had autonomy f and control over the day-to-day operations of their franchises, and therefore the franchisor was not part of an employer-employee relationship. The court found from the franchise agreement and the testimony that an employment relationship existed within the meaning of unemployment insurance law because franchisor/Jani-King provided to franchisees/Appellants manuals, procedures, advertising, initial client accounts, billing rates, insurance requirements, logo requirements, and revenue reporting requirements.

K.C. v. Choice Hotels International, Inc., No. 22-CV-2683, 2023 WL 2265214 (S.D. Ohio Feb. 28, 2023). The court denied an insurance carrier's motion to intervene in a case alleging that Choice Hotels International and Wyndam Hotels & Resorts were liable to the plaintiff under the Trafficking Victim Protection Reauthorization Act. The insurance carrier sought to intervene seeking a declaratory judgment that the insurance carrier had no obligation to defend or indemnify one of the defendants. The court denied the motion to intervene, finding that the insurance carrier failed to establish the showing required for mandatory or permissive intervention. The insurance

CHAPTER 6

carrier did not share any common question of law or fact with the existing parties. The insurance carrier's obligations depending on the language of the insurance policy, which is wholly separate from the Trafficking Victim Protection Reauthorization Act claims.

Philadelphia Indemnity Insurance Co. v. Markel Insurance Co., No. 1:20-CV-00669-JRR, 2023 WL 113748 (D. Md. Jan. 5, 2023). Daycare franchisor Kiddie Academy Domestic Franchising, LLC ("KADF"), Essential Brands, Inc. ("Essential"), and their insurance company Philadelphia Indemnity Insurance Co. ("Philadelphia Indemnity") sued franchisee Bullocks Bright Beginnings, LLC ("Bullocks"), KA Broadway, and their insurance company Markel Insurance Company ("Markel"). Prior to this suit, the parties settled a lawsuit filed on behalf of a child who was injured at KA Broadway. The parties settled for $6 million, with Philadelphia Indemnity contributing $2 million on behalf of KADF and Essential, and Markel contributing $4 million on behalf of KA Broadway. KADF, Essential, and Philadelphia Indemnity then brought this action seeking a declaratory judgment that Markel owed an additional $1 million toward the settlement, that Bullocks and KA Broadway owed KADF and Essential indemnification for the amount that Philadelphia Indemnity contributed to the settlement, as well as a claim for equitable subrogation, pursuant to an indemnification provision in the parties' franchise agreement. The parties then cross-moved for summary judgment.

The court denied the defendants' motions, and granted the plaintiffs' motions with respect to the defendants' insurance policy coverage limits and on the indemnification and equitable subrogation claims. First, the court analyzed the insurance policy documents and concluded that the defendants had not yet reached their insurance coverage limits and that there were still insurance funds available to contribute to the settlement. Second, the court concluded that the franchise agreement required the franchisee defendants to indemnify the franchisor plaintiffs for their contribution to the settlement, and that equitable subrogation was appropriate.

Westfield National Insurance Co. v. Quest Pharmaceuticals, Inc., 57 F.4th 558 (6th Cir. 2023) (opioid distributor's insurance policies did not cover RICO, state law, public nuisance and negligence claims because the plain language of the policies indicated that defense and indemnification of the distributor had to "derive from a particular bodily injury to a person.").

IX. Consumer Protection

Parker Powersports Inc. v. Textron Specialized Vehicles Inc., No. cv 122-054, 2023 WL 2695103 (S.D. Ga. Mar. 29, 2023). The court dismissed plaintiff's claim for violation of the Colorado Consumer Protection Act because although the court found the defendants made promises to other vehicle dealers, the complaint did not allege that such promises affected any other dealer. The court also determined that being required to sign a dealer agreement is a private transaction, and thus does not support the public impact needed to show a Consumer Protection Act violation. This case is discussed in Chapter 3, Section III.

X. Constitutional

Block v. Canepa, No. 22-385, 2023 WL 4540523 (6th Cir. July 14, 2023). Plaintiffs Kenneth M. Miller and House of Glunz, Inc. challenged the constitutionality of Ohio liquor laws that prevented out-of-state wine retailers from shipping wine directly to Ohio consumers (the "Direct Ship Restriction") and prohibited individuals from transporting more than 4.5 liters of wine into Ohio during any 30-day period (the "Transportation Limit"). Plaintiffs asserted that the Direct Ship Restriction and the Transportation Limit discriminated against interstate commerce, protected local economic interests, and violated the Commerce Clause. The district court held that: (1) plaintiffs lacked standing to challenge the Transportation Limit, as they could not show that they were in actual or imminent danger of being subjected to injury, as required under the "Cases and Controversies Doctrine;" (2) the Director of the Ohio Department of Public Safety was entitled to Eleventh Amendment immunity from plaintiffs' claims; and (3) the Direct Ship Restriction was constitutional under binding Sixth Circuit precedent.

Plaintiffs, a wine enthusiast and an Illinois wine retailer, challenged the Transportation Limit, but neither had been prosecuted, or threatened with prosecution, under the applicable statute. Under Article III's standing requirements, a plaintiff must show: (1) it has suffered an "injury in fact" that is (a) concrete and particularized and (b) actual or imminent, not conjectural or hypothetical; (2) the injury is fairly traceable to the challenged action of the defendant; and (3) it is likely, as opposed to merely speculative, that the injury will be redressed by a favorable decision. The court noted that when a plaintiff brings a pre-enforcement challenge, an allegation of future injury may suffice to show an injury in fact if the threatened injury is certainly impending, or there is a substantial risk that the harm will occur. The court also noted that the "substantial risk" requirement can be met if there is a credible threat of

CHAPTER 6

prosecution. Plaintiffs had provided evidence of several arrests and one administrative citation for violation of the Transportation Limit during the past few years, although the cases involved the subsequent resale of the alcoholic beverages or spiritous liquor rather than wine. The court found that these arrests and citation were sufficient to establish that Plaintiffs fear of prosecution was neither unreasonable nor imaginary or wholly speculative and therefore met the "injury in fact" requirement.

Plaintiffs also had challenged the lower court's finding that the Director of the Department of Public Safety had immunity from plaintiffs' claims. Ironically, as to this claim, the court agreed with the lower court that the Director had immunity, finding that plaintiffs had not provided sufficient evidence that there existed a "realistic possibility" that the Director would take legal or administrative actions against Plaintiffs.

The court then addressed the Direct Ship Restriction, which it evaluated under the Twenty-First Amendment and the Constitution's dormant Commerce Clause, which prohibits states from taking actions that adopt protectionist measures for their own citizens, thereby inhibiting a national market for goods and services. In this case, the court impliedly accepted that the Direct Ship Restriction did discriminate against out-of-state citizens as its analysis focused on whether the restriction was "narrowly tailored to advance a legitimate local purpose," not on whether it discriminated against out-of-state citizens. The court noted that while there often is tension between the Twenty-First Amendment and the dormant Commerce Clause, established precedent had never permitted the Twenty-First Amendment cases to violate the nondiscrimination requirements of the dormant Commerce Clause. Therefore, to uphold the law, the court would have to find that the law was justified as a public health or safety measure or qualifies for some other non-protectionist ground, and the law's predominant effect was the protection of public health or safety rather than protectionism. The lower court had upheld the statute based on an out-of-state case that had upheld a similar law in Michigan, without taking into account the evidence the parties to this case had presented on the subject Direct Ship Restriction. The court found this lack of evaluation of the evidence to be reversible error.

Jones v. Embassy Suites, Inc., No. 2:21-CV-5, 2023 WL 113056 (S.D. Ga. Jan. 5, 2023). This case arises out of the alleged unauthorized entry into the plaintiff's hotel room by hotel employees at the Embassy Suites by Hilton Hotel located in Brunswick, Georgia on October 17, 2018. The Plaintiff filed this lawsuit in 2020 against Embassy Suites, Inc., Embassy Suites Employer, LLC, Embassy Suites Franchise, LLC, Embassy Suites Management LLC, Hilton Worldwide, Inc., Hilton Worldwide Holdings, Inc., and John Doe.

Plaintiff asserted various Georgia state law claims, including invasion of privacy; infliction of emotional distress; breach of contract; tortious assault; and Fourth Amendment invasion of privacy. Defendants Embassy Suites Franchise, LLC, Hilton Worldwide, Inc., and Hilton Worldwide Holdings, Inc. filed a notice of removal based on the well-pleaded complaint rule because plaintiff pleaded a violation of the Fourth Amendment of the U.S. Constitution. Defendants moved for summary judgment, arguing that plaintiff sued the wrong party because none of the named defendants had any ownership interest in, business connection with, or management authority over the hotel. Plaintiff, in turn, argued that the federal court did not have subject matter jurisdiction over the case and sought to have it remanded to state court.

The court held that, because plaintiff alleged that defendants violated his expectation of privacy under the Fourth Amendment, the claim implicated federal-question subject-matter jurisdiction. Defendants relied upon plaintiff's Fourth Amendment claim as the basis for removal. But the court noted it is black letter law that plaintiffs are permitted to challenge unconstitutional actions of only *state* actors, not *private* citizens or businesses. As the court further found, the plaintiff did not allege, nor did it appear, that any of the defendants were state actors acting under color of state law. The court further held that, in fact, plaintiff conceded in his response brief that defendants were not state actors. Because defendants were neither private businesses nor private citizens, plaintiff could not assert a constitutional violation claim against them under § 1983. Thus, the court found that plaintiff's Fourth Amendment claim was "wholly insubstantial and frivolous" and insufficient to establish federal question subject matter jurisdiction. Because there was no federal question or diversity subject matter jurisdiction present, the court concluded that it was not authorized to hear the case, and remanded it to the Glynn County, Georgia Superior Court.

XI. Trafficking Victims Protection Reauthorization Act

A. D. v. Best Western International, Inc., No. 2:22-CV-650-JES-NPM, 2023 WL 2955711 (M.D. Fla. Apr. 14, 2023) the United States District Court for the Middle District of Florida, Fort Myers Division granted defendant Bonita Springs Hotel 1, LLC's ("Bonita Hotel") motion to dismiss the plaintiff's complaint brought pursuant to the Trafficking Victims Protection Reauthorization Act ("TVPRA"). The court also granted in part and denied in part, defendant Best Western International Inc.'s ("BWI") motion to dismiss and dismissed the plaintiff's complaint without prejudice with leave to amend within 21 days of the court's order.

CHAPTER 6

Plaintiff alleged that she was trafficked for commercial sex throughout Lee, Hillsborough, and Collier Counties in Florida, including at the BW Bonita Springs hotel. Plaintiff further alleges that BWI owns, supervises and/or operates the BW Bonita Springs hotel and that Bonita Hotel was involved in the staffing and operation of the BW Bonita Springs Hotel. Accordingly, plaintiff claims that BWI and the Vocisano Defendants (collectively, the "Defendants") knowingly benefitted from, participated in and had actual or constructive knowledge that the sex trafficking venture violated the TVPRA.

The court granted the Bonita Hotel's motion to dismiss finding no plausible statement of a claim against this party. The court also granted in part BWI's motion to dismiss, finding that Plaintiff failed to sufficiently plead all the components of her TVPRA claim. Specifically, plaintiff did not sufficiently plead that BWI participated in the sex trafficking venture, and she did not sufficiently plead that BWI had actual or constructive knowledge of the venture. However, the court also denied in part BWI's motion to dismiss, finding that the factual disputes regarding BWI's control of its hotel and its agency relationship with Bonita Hotel cannot be resolved on a motion to dismiss. Further, the court partially denied BWI's motion because plaintiff sufficiently pled that BWI knowingly benefitted from the sex trafficking and that this venture violated the TVPRA.

In ***A.D. v. Best Western International, Inc.***, No. 2:22-CV-651-JES-NPM, 2023 WL 2955712 (M.D. Fla. Apr. 14, 2023) the United States District Court for the Middle District of Florida, Fort Myers Division granted defendant Apex's motion to dismiss the plaintiff's complaint brought pursuant to the Trafficking Victims Protection Reauthorization Act ("TVPRA"). The court also granted in part and denied in part, defendant Best Western International Inc.'s ("BWI") motion to dismiss and dismissed the plaintiff's complaint without prejudice with leave to amend within 21 days of the court's order.

Plaintiff alleges that she was trafficked for commercial sex throughout Lee, Hillsborough, and Collier Counties in Florida, including Apex and BWI's (collectively "Defendants") hotel property. Plaintiff further alleges that BWI owns, supervises and/or operates the Best Western Fort Myers Inn & Suites (the "BW Fort Myers Hotel") and that Apex was involved in the staffing and operation of the BW Fort Myers Hotel, the hotel where plaintiff alleges she was trafficked. Accordingly, plaintiff claims that defendants knowingly benefitted from, participated in and had actual or constructive knowledge that the sex trafficking venture violated the TVPRA.

The court granted Apex's motion to dismiss finding no plausible statement of a claim against Apex. The court also granted in part BWI's

Other Federal and State Law Issues

motion to dismiss, finding that Plaintiff failed to sufficiently plead all the components of her TVPRA claim. Specifically, plaintiff did not sufficiently plead that BWI participated in the sex trafficking venture, and she did not sufficiently plead that BWI had actual or constructive knowledge of the venture. However, the court also denied in part BWI's motion to dismiss, finding that the factual disputes regarding BWI's control of its hotel and its agency relationship with Apex cannot be resolved on a motion to dismiss. Further, the court partially denied BWI's motion because plaintiff sufficiently pled that BWI knowingly benefitted from the sex trafficking and that this venture violated the TVPRA.

In *A.D. v. Best Western International, Inc.*, No. 2:22-CV-652-JES-NPM, 2023 WL 2955832 (M.D. Fla. Apr. 14, 2023) the United States District Court for the Middle District of Florida, Naples Division granted defendants Robert Vocisano and Mario Vocisano (the "Vocisano Defendants") doing business as the Best Western Naples Plaza Hotel's ("BW Naples") motion to dismiss the plaintiff's complaint brought pursuant to the Trafficking Victims Protection Reauthorization Act ("TVPRA"). The court also granted in part and denied in part, defendant Best Western International Inc.'s ("BWI") motion to dismiss and dismissed the plaintiff's complaint without prejudice with leave to amend within 21 days of the court's order.

Plaintiff alleges that she was trafficked for commercial sex throughout Lee, Hillsborough, and Collier Counties in Florida, including at the BW Naples hotel. Plaintiff further alleges that BWI owns, supervises and/or operates the BW Naples hotel and that the Vocisano Defendants own, operates and manages the hotel. Accordingly, Plaintiff claims that BWI and the Vocisano Defendants (collectively, the "Defendants") knowingly benefitted from, participated in and had actual or constructive knowledge that the sex trafficking venture violated the TVPRA.

The court granted the Vocisano Defendants' motion to dismiss finding no plausible statement of a claim against these parties. The court also granted in part BWI's motion to dismiss, finding that plaintiff failed to sufficiently plead all the components of her TVPRA claim. Specifically, plaintiff did not sufficiently plead that BWI participated in the sex trafficking venture, and she did not sufficiently plead that BWI had actual or constructive knowledge of the venture. However, the court also denied in part BWI's motion to dismiss, finding that the factual disputes regarding BWI's control of its hotel and its agency relationship with the Vocisano Defendants cannot be resolved on a motion to dismiss. Further, the court partially denied BWI's motion because plaintiff sufficiently pled that BWI knowingly benefitted from the sex trafficking and that this venture violated the TVPRA.

CHAPTER 6

A.D. v. Cavalier MergerSub LP, No. 2:22-CV-649-JES-NPM, 2023 WL 3073599 (M.D. Fla. Apr. 25, 2023). The court granted the franchisor defendant's ("La Quinta Hotels") motion to dismiss plaintiff's complaint, which alleged that La Quinta Hotels violated the Trafficking Victims Protection Reauthorization Act of 2008 ("TVPRA"), because it benefitted from participating in a sex trafficking venture in which plaintiff was a victim. Although the court found that plaintiff sufficiently pled that La Quinta Hotels knowingly benefitted from participating in the alleged venture and that the venture violated the TVPRA, it held that plaintiff failed to plausibly allege that La Quinta Hotels participated in the venture and that it knew or should have known that the venture violated the TVPRA, elements which are required to prove a TVPRA beneficiary liability claim. Accordingly, the Court dismissed the complaint.

A.D. v. Choice Hotels International, Inc., No. 2:22-CV-647-JES-NPM, 2023 WL 2991041 (M.D. Fla. Apr. 18, 2023). The court granted the franchisor defendant's ("Choice Hotels") motion to dismiss plaintiff's complaint, which alleged that Choice Hotels violated the Trafficking Victims Protection Reauthorization Act of 2008 ("TVPRA"), because it benefitted from participating in a sex trafficking venture in which plaintiff was a victim. Although the court found that plaintiff had not sufficiently pled that Choice Hotels knowingly benefitted from participating in the alleged venture and that the venture violated the TVPRA, plaintiff failed to plausibly allege that Choice Hotels participated in the venture and that it knew or should have known that the venture violated the TVPRA, elements which are required to prove a TVPRA beneficiary liability claim. Accordingly, the Court dismissed the complaint.

A.D. v. Choice Hotels International, Inc., No. 2:22-CV-646, 2023 WL 3004545 (M.D. Fla. Apr. 19, 2023). The court dismissed the complaint against the defendant franchisor Choice Hotels for failure to state a claim under the Trafficking Victims Protection Reauthorization Act. Plaintiff failed to plausibly plead that Choice Hotels participated in a sex trafficking venture by alleging that the hotel "actively participated in this illegal endeavor by knowingly or negligently providing lodging in which to harbor A.D. while he was trafficking her" and "taking no action while A.D. was being trafficked at the hotel." The court determined that plaintiff's allegations that the hotel did not take enough action did amount to participating in a venture, particularly because the Choice Hotel did not have direct contact with the alleged venture partners. Thus, the court granted defendant's motion to dismiss.

A.D. v. Choice Hotels International, Inc., No. 2:22-CV-648-JES-NPM, 2023 WL 3004547 (M.D. Fla. Apr. 19, 2023) The court dismissed plaintiff's claims against the franchisee defendant Tampa Bay Hotels, LLC, in a case in which plaintiff claimed that the franchisee and franchisor violated the Trafficking Victims Protection Reauthorization Act of 2008 ("TVPRA") because they had benefited from participating in a sex trafficking venture in which plaintiff was a victim. The court found that the plaintiff had not sufficiently pled that the franchisee knowingly benefited from the venture, participated in the venture, or knew or should have known that the venture violated the TVPRA.

A.D. v. Marriott International, Inc., No. 2:22-CV-645-JES-NPM, 2023 WL 2991042 (M.D. Fla. Apr. 18, 2023) (The United States District Court for the Middle District of Florida granted the franchisor defendant's ("Marriott") motion to dismiss plaintiff's complaint, which alleged that Marriott violated the Trafficking Victims Protection Reauthorization Act of 2008 ("TVPRA"), because it benefitted from participating in a sex trafficking venture in which plaintiff was a victim. Although the court found that plaintiff sufficiently pled that Marriott knowingly benefitted from participating in the alleged venture and that the venture violated the TVPRA, plaintiff failed to plausibly allege that Marriott participated in the venture and that Marriott knew or should have known that the venture violated the TVPRA, elements which are required to prove a TVPRA beneficiary liability claim. Accordingly, the court dismissed the matter.)

A.D. v. Marriott International, Inc., No. 2:22-cv-644-JES-NPM, 2023 WL 3004549 M.D. Fla. Apr. 19, 2023) (dismissing complaint that failed to allege sufficient facts to support a claim under the Trafficking Victims Protection Reauthorization Act of 2008 ("TVPRA") because the complaint failed to adequately assert that defendant participated in a common undertaking of a sex trafficking venture involving risk or profit and that defendant knew or should have known that the venture violated the TVPRA.)

A.D. v. Wyndham Hotels & Resorts, Inc., No. 2:22-CV-643, 2023 WL 2974171 (M.D. Fla. Apr. 17, 2023). The court dismissed the complaint against the defendant franchisors Wyndham Hotels & Resorts, Inc. ("WHRI") and Quorum Hotels & Resorts ("Quorum") for failure to state a claim under the Trafficking Victims Protection Reauthorization Act. The court determined that Plaintiff failed to plausibly plead either WHRI or Quorum participated in a sex trafficking venture by alleging that the hotels "actively participated in this illegal endeavor by knowingly or negligently providing lodging in which to harbor A.D. while he was trafficking her" and "taking no action while A.D. was being trafficked at the hotel[s]." The court determined that plaintiff's allegations that neither of the hotels took enough action did not amount to participating in a venture, particularly because neither WHRI nor Quorum had direct contact with the alleged venture partners. Thus, the court granted defendants' motion to dismiss.

A.R. v. Wyndham Hotels & Resorts, Inc., No. 2:21-CV-04935, 2022 WL 17741054 (S.D. Ohio Dec. 16, 2022). In this case, Wyndham Hotels & Resorts, Inc. ("Wyndham"), the franchisor, moved to dismiss a complaint filed against them by an alleged sex-trafficking victim pursuant to the Trafficking Victim Protection Reauthorization Act ("TVPRA"). The court denied Wyndham's motion to dismiss, finding that the plaintiff sufficiently pled claims against Wyndham under the TVPRA.

The plaintiff alleged that she had been trafficked for sex and held captive at Super 8 and Hawthorne Suites by Wyndham in Columbus, Ohio. The court analyzed the plaintiff's claims under the "beneficiary theory" of the TVPRA, which requires a showing that a defendant (1) knowingly benefited financially or received anything of value; (2) from participating in the trafficking venture; and (3) that a defendant either knew or should have known that the venture violated the TVPRA.

The court noted that to meet the first prong of "knowingly benefitted," a plaintiff must allege that the defendant received a financial benefit. The allegation that Wyndham received revenue from the room rentals sufficed to show an alleged financial benefit and therefore met the first prong of the test.

The court then analyzed the third prong, "that a defendant either knew or should have known that the venture violated the TVPRA." Wyndham moved to dismiss the plaintiff's claim on the basis that, as a result of its franchisor/franchisee relationship with the subject hotels, its relationship with the hotel staff was too attenuated to show that Wyndham had sufficient knowledge of the alleged trafficking. Wyndham also argued that the plaintiff had to allege that Wyndham, as the franchisor, had knowledge of a specific trafficking venture to be liable under the TVPRA. The court disagreed and found that the plaintiff did not have to show that Wyndham had actual knowledge of the sex trafficking venture. Instead, the court found that allegations of constructive knowledge are sufficient. The court found that the alleged notice of sex trafficking generally at the franchisor's hotels and the failure to take adequate steps to train staff, as well as allegations of signs that should have alerted staff to plaintiff's situation, met the constructive knowledge requirement under the TVPRA.

As to the second prong, "participation in a venture", the court again noted that actual knowledge was not required. Instead, a plaintiff must show a "continuous business relationship between the trafficker and the hotels such that it would appear the trafficker and the hotels have established a pattern of conduct or could be said to have a tacit agreement." The plaintiff alleged that owning, operating, and supervising the subject hotels; Wyndham's licensing of its brand to the franchisee hotels in exchange for royalties; Wyndham's receipt of a percentage of the room revenues from which trafficking occurred; and Wyndham's promulgating the policies and procedures over hiring, training and retention, met the standard. Wyndham relied on the Eleventh Circuit's decision *Doe #1 v. Red Roof Inns, Inc.*, 21 F.4th 714, 724 (11th Cir. 2021) to argue that the "participation in a common venture" should be defined as "an undertaking or enterprise involving risk and potential profit."

The court distinguished *Red Roof Inns*, on the basis that the plaintiff in *Red Roof Inns* argued before the trial court that similar allegations related to the franchisor/franchisee relationship were sufficient to show that Red Roof Inns participated in the sex trafficking ventures, a theory the Eleventh Circuit rejected. In this case, the court found that the plaintiff argued that Wyndham was participating in a commercial business venture under the TVPRA by receiving royalties and through the control of the hotels' policies and operations, not that Wyndham had participated in the trafficking itself. The court found these allegations of participation in a commercial venture, as opposed to participation in the sex trafficking venture, were sufficient to allege "participation in a venture" to establish liability under the TVPRA.

The court then addressed whether imputed liability was sufficient to state a claim under the TVPRA. Wyndham cited cases dismissing vicarious liability claims against hotel franchisors under the TVPRA on the basis that the franchisors lacked the requisite control over the franchised hotels' daily operations. The court analyzed this issue under both federal common law and Ohio common law because the TVPRA is silent as to imputed liability and because no federal circuit court has ruled on whether to apply state or federal common law as to vicarious liability.

The court found that the plaintiff's allegations that Wyndham's control of brand quality standards; use and placement of Wyndham's name; the local hotel's reservation systems, brand loyalty programs, and websites; and employment policies and procedures, established Wyndham's control over the subject hotels and were therefore sufficient to meet the standard of vicarious liability under Ohio common law and federal common law. The court found that the franchisor/franchisee relationship did not bar application of the vicarious liability theory. The court also found that the plaintiff's allegations that Wyndham promulgated policies related to the hiring, retention

CHAPTER 6

and training, including training and policies specific to sex trafficking, were sufficient to show Wyndham also qualified as a joint employer, at the pleading stage.

Lastly, the court rejected Wyndham's argument that the allegations were not sufficiently pled because the allegations failed to tie the particular allegations to any specific hotel. The court found that the allegations were sufficient to meet the standard under Rule 8 of the Federal Rules of Civil Procedure.

B.J. v. G6 Hospitality, LLC, No. 22-CV-03765-MMC, 2023 WL 3569979 (N.D. Cal. May 19, 2023). Plaintiff, who was trafficked for commercial sex at five California hotels, sued the hotel owners (and franchisors of the hotels) under the Trafficking Victims Protection Reauthorization Act for ignoring and profiting off her commercial sex trafficking. The court granted defendants' motion to dismiss. The court reasoned that while the franchisors did knowingly benefit from the sex trafficker (through room rental revenue), the franchisors did not take part in a common undertaking of a sex trafficking venture and they did not know nor should they have known the of the trafficking venture, as required for a statutory claim. Further, the plaintiff's arguments to impose vicarious liability on the franchisors failed because the court found no actual or apparent agency relationship.

C. T. v. Red Roof Inns, Inc., No. 2:22-CV-834-JES-KCD, 2023 WL 3510879 (M.D. Fla. Mar. 11, 2023). Plaintiff C.T. brought suit under the Trafficking Victims Protection Reauthorization Act ("TVPRA") against various defendants in federal court in Ohio. The case was later transferred to the Middle District of Florida, where several defendants were dismissed from the case. C.T. then sought leave to amend the complaint to assert a single TVPRA claim against defendants Best Western International, Inc. ("Best Western") and Red Roof Inns, Inc. ("Red Roof") alleging that Best Western and Red Roof "turned a blind eye to evidence of sex trafficking in their hotels" while enjoying profits from the activity and making no effort to stop the abuse. Best Western opposed the motion on the grounds of futility, arguing that the amended complaint would not survive a motion to dismiss.

The court granted C.T.'s motion to amend the complaint, finding that the proposed amended complaint pled sufficient factual matter to plausibly allege a TVPRA claim against Best Western and survive a motion to dismiss. In particular, the court found that Best Western could be held vicariously liable because C.T. pled that it exercised a level of control over franchisees greater than that of an ordinary franchisor–in terms of profit sharing, standardized rules and procedures, regular inspection, and price fixing–

sufficient to plausibly infer an agency relationship. The court further found that C.T. had plausibly alleged the remaining elements of a TVRP violation, including knowing benefit, existence of a venture, participation in a venture, knowledge, and plausibility. Accordingly, the court granted leave for C.T. to amend the complaint.

J.M. v. Choice Hotels International, Inc., No. 2:22-cv-00672-KJM-JDP, 2023 WL 3456619 (E.D. Cal. May 15, 2023) (denying motion to dismiss where amended complaint sufficiently alleges facts to support a claim for violation of the Trafficking Victims Protection Reauthorization Act, including the defendant's actual knowledge of the alleged abuse and defendant's clear benefit and ability to control booking and payment processing of hotel rooms.)

Lundstrom v. Holiday Hospitality Franchising, LLC, No. 1:22-CV-056, 2023 WL 4424725 (D.N.D. May 22, 2023) (The court dismissed the complaint against Choice Hotels International, Inc., the franchisor, under the Trafficking Victims Protection Reauthorization Act of 2008 because, although the allegations were sufficient to show that the franchisor "knowingly benefitted" from the trafficking, the allegations failed to show that the franchisor knew or should have known that it was participating in a venture engaged in sex trafficking. The court noted that general knowledge of commercial sex activity was not sufficient, the plaintiff had to show the franchisor knew or should have known what happened to this particular plaintiff. For these same reasons, plaintiff's agency theory claims failed. The court also noted that any alleged trafficking that occurred ten years prior to the filing of complaint were barred by the statute of limitations, rejecting the continuing violation doctrine.)

XII. Other

Achieve 24 Fitness Limited Liability Co. v. Alloy Personal Training Solutions, LLC, No. CV 21-12085 (GC), 2023 WL 2264129 (D.N.J. Feb. 28, 2023) (The United States District Court, D. New Jersey, granted in part Alloy Personal Training Solutions, LLC's ("Alloy") motion to dismiss against Achieve 24 Fitness Limited Liability Company's ("Achieve") claims that Alloy violated the New Jersey Franchise Practices Act ("NJFPA") and the New Jersey Consumer Fraud Act ("NJCFA") under its License Agreement with Achieve. The court found that Achieve failed to sufficiently allege its gross sales which is a requirement to bring a NJFPA claim and failed to adequately assert a violation of the NJCFA or common law fraud. This case is also discussed in Chapter 5, Section II.

CHAPTER 6

Brown v. Woodbury Auto Group, LLC, No. 3:21-CV-00955, 2023 WL 2529055 (M.D. Tenn. Feb. 22, 2023) (Plaintiff filed an amended complaint claiming that defendants, a car sales distributor, sold him a damaged car without disclosing the damages. Defendants filed a motion to dismiss the amended complaint and the United States District Court, M.D. Tennessee denied defendants' motion finding that plaintiff properly stated its fraud claims of intentional misrepresentation, fraudulent inducement, negligent misrepresentation and fraudulent concealment against defendants. Additionally, the court also found that plaintiff properly pled its claims under the Magnuson-Moss Warranty Act and the Tennessee Consumer Protection Act.)

Burnett v. National Association of Realtors, No. 4:19-CV-00332-SRB, 2022 WL 17741708 (W.D. Mo. Dec. 16, 2022) (The district court denied defendants' motions for summary judgment, holding that plaintiffs showed genuine disputes of material facts within their claims that defendants breached the Sherman Act, the Missouri Merchandising Practices Act and the Missouri Antitrust law by imposing an anticompetitive restraint that inflated defendants' residential real estate commissions throughout Missouri.)

Doe #21 v. CFR Enterprises, Inc., No. A163543, 2023 WL 4783591 (Cal. Ct. App. June 29, 2023). Several dozen plaintiffs sued franchisor Massage Envy, LLC and several franchisees of Massage Envy, claiming various violations of California state law for alleged sexual assaults that occurred at Massage Envy franchise locations between 2003 and 2014. The trial court dismissed the claims of certain plaintiffs as being time-barred under the applicable statute of limitations. Eighteen of the plaintiffs whose claims had been dismissed appealed, arguing that a recently enacted amendment to the California Code of Civil Procedure revived their claims.

The California Court of Appeal reversed the dismissals, finding that the new law revived some, if not all, of the plaintiffs' claims. The new law provided that certain claims for damages as a result of sexual assault would be revived despite being otherwise barred by the applicable statute of limitations. However, the court did not order that the complaints be revived in their entirety because the parties' briefs were not sufficient on that point. Instead, the court remanded to the trial court for further consideration.

In *Hyundai Construction Equipment Americas, Inc. v. Southern Lift Trucks, LLC*, No. SC-2022-0675, 2023 WL 3402311 (Ala. May 12, 2023), plaintiff, a heavy-equipment dealer filed suit against defendants, a manufacturer and its parent company, alleging defendants breached the parties' dealer agreements and violated the Alabama Heavy Equipment Dealer Act (AHEDA), and seeking to enjoin defendants from terminating the agreements and for declaratory judgment that all of the provisions of the dealer agreements that were inconsistent with the AHEDA were unenforceable. Defendants moved to dismiss the complaint and then moved to compel arbitration. The trial court granted the injunction and denied the motion to compel arbitration.

Defendants appealed and the appellate court found that all of the claims were subject to arbitration except the claim seeking declaratory judgment as to the enforceability of the dealership agreements. The court also found that the parent company could compel arbitration even though it was not a party to the dealer agreements because plaintiff alleged agency and conspiracy liability.

As for the preliminary injunction, the appellate court found that the preliminary injunction was properly issued as to the lift truck agreement, but not as to the construction equipment agreement. The court noted that under Alabama law a trial court has jurisdiction to enter a preliminary injunction to maintain the status quo even where the dispute is subject to arbitration. For the construction equipment agreement, there had been no sales by the heavy equipment dealer. Thus, there was no status quo to maintain and no irreparable harm would result from termination, even if that termination were found to have been wrongful. For the lift truck agreement, the court noted that there had been sales and, in addition to monetary damages, plaintiff alleged that it had also invested substantially in its efforts to serve as a dealer of the lift trucks, and that it stood to suffer harm to its reputation.

Hyundai Subaru of Nashville, Inc. v. Hyundai Motor America, Inc., No. 3:22-CV-00817, 2023 WL 2201015 (M.D. Tenn. Feb. 24, 2023) (The United States District Court, M.D. Tennessee, denied defendants' motion to dismiss the plaintiff's complaint for failure to state a claim under the Automobile Dealer's Day in Court Act ("ADDCA"), holding that the fact that plaintiff's car dealership was open and operating did not prevent it from stating a claim under the ADDCA, and also holding that plaintiff sufficiently alleged that defendants failed to act in good faith by refusing to approve plaintiff's car dealership relocation.)

In re Arcimoto Inc. Securities Litigation, No. 21-CV-2143 (PKC), 2022 WL 17851834 (E.D.N.Y. Dec. 22, 2022) (The United States District Court, E.D.N.Y, granted defendant's motion to dismiss the amended complaint based on plaintiff's failure to state its claim under Rule 12(b)(6) that defendant

CHAPTER 6

violated various federal securities laws including 15 U.S.C. § 78j(b), 15 U.S.C. § 78t(a) and 17 C.F.R. §§ 240.10b-5, by failing to allegedly disclose key information in a press release about its relationship with certain related parties).

In *Louis DeGidio, Inc. v. Industrial Combustion, LLC*, 66 F.4th 707 (8th Cir. 2023) the United States Court of Appeals, Eighth Circuit affirmed the lower court's grant of summary judgment in favor of defendant manufacturer, Industrial Combustion, LLC ("IC") and its parent company, Cleaver-Brooks, Inc. The court held that the distributorship agreement at issue was not a franchise subject to the Minnesota Franchise Act ("MFA") and that IC did not breach a contract when it terminated plaintiff's sales representative without cause.

This dispute arose out of a distributorship agreement between IC and defendant Louis DeGidio Inc. ("LDI"). In September 2019, IC gave LDI notice that it would terminate the distributorship in thirty days. Defendants then filed this action seeking a declaratory judgment that the MFA precludes termination without good cause and damages for violation of the MFA, for breach of contract and promissory estoppel.

The court held that defendant Louis DeGidio Services, Inc.'s ("LDSI"), payments to IC were not a requirement to do business with IC and thus those payments did not constitute a franchise fee. Accordingly, the MFA did not apply to the distributorship agreement. Further, the court held that the oral implied contract between LDSI and IC did not create an enforceable limit on IC's right to terminate business relations. Therefore, LDSI's breach of contract and promissory estoppel claims against IC were properly dismissed.

Moody v. Circle K Stores, Inc., No. 2:18-cv-435-CLM, 2023 WL 404018 (N.D. Ala. Jan. 25, 2023). Plaintiffs' putative class action accusing defendant of violating the Americans with Disabilities Act survived defendant's motion for judgment on the pleadings, with the court finding that plaintiffs had stated a plausible claim for relief by pointing to the standards and specifications Circle K requires its franchisees to comply with in terms of store design, construction, maintenance and repair, and which allegedly resulted in a pattern and practice of discrimination on Circle K's part against individuals with mobility disabilities. This case is discussed in Chapter 7, Section 3.

New Jersey Coalition of Automotive Retailers, Inc. v. Mazda Motor of America, Inc., No. CV1814563ZNQTJB, 2023 WL 2263741 (D.N.J. Feb. 28, 2023) (The United States District Court for the District of New Jersey granted defendant's motion to dismiss plaintiff's complaint which claimed that defendant violated provisions of New Jersey's Franchise Practices Act. The court held that plaintiff lacked statutory standing to bring its claim because plaintiff is not a franchisee within the meaning of the statute. Accordingly, plaintiff's Amended Complaint failed to state a claim.)

Rich Morton's Glen Burnie Lincoln Mercury, LLC v. Williams-Moore, No. 1844, SEPT.TERM 2021, 2023 WL 166277 (Md. Ct. Spec. App. Jan. 12, 2023) (The Appellate Court of Maryland affirmed the Circuit Court's judgment holding that Appellant, a car sales franchise violated the Maryland Consumer Protection Act by making misrepresentations to Appellee about the vehicle she purchased. Appellant was also not entitled to a second opportunity to remedy the condition of the vehicle and therefore violated the vehicle's implied warranty of merchantability.)

Rushing v. McAlister's Franchisor SPV LLC, No. 22-CV-649-SMY, 2023 WL 2163388 (S.D. Ill. Feb. 22, 2023), *reconsideration denied,* 22-CV-649-SMY, 2023 WL 2955315 (S.D. Ill. Apr. 14, 2023) (The United States District Court for the Southern District of Illinois denied the franchisor defendants' motion to dismiss plaintiff's complaint for failure to state a claim under Section 15(b) of the Illinois Biometric Information Privacy Act ("BIPA"). The court found that although defendant was not plaintiff's direct employer, BIPA's plain language does not support limiting liability to employers but instead any entity that collects biometric data may incur liability. Accordingly, plaintiff adequately stated a claim against defendants under Section 15(b) of BIPA.)

Titshaw v. Geer, Nos. A23A0410, A23A0439, 2023 WL 3609488 (Ga. Ct. App. May 24, 2023) (The Court of Appeals of Georgia affirmed the trial court's dismissal of plaintiff franchisees' legal malpractice claim against attorneys who recommended bankruptcy as barred by the statute of limitations. The court reversed the trial court's denial of defendant attorneys' motion to dismiss plaintiffs' breach of contract claim as duplicative of their legal malpractice claim.).

CHAPTER 7

Control-Related Liability of Franchisors

I. Introduction

As discussed in Chapter 5, franchisors go to great lengths to protect their trademarks and brands. They also train and require their franchisees to comply with various standards so that the franchise system as a whole maintains a consistent level of quality and the goods and services customers purchase from one franchisee are the same as what they would be provided by any other franchisee. For example, many franchisors require their franchisees to purchase supplies from certain approved vendors, and franchisors in the quick-serve restaurant industry will require their franchisees to use the same recipes and offer the same menu items.

However, franchisors are also very careful not to become too involved in the franchisee's day-to-day business operations, including, for example, the hiring and firing of employees. This is because doing so could put them at risk of being deemed a joint employer (together with the franchisee) and can expose them to claims and liability to the franchisee's employees, customers, and others, including the franchisee's vendors and other business partners. These cases, including those discussed below, are decided by looking at the facts of the specific case.

The case involving Papa John's, *Kyles v. Hoosier Papa LLC*, No. 1:20-CV-07146, 2023 WL 2711608 (N.D. Ill. Mar. 30, 2023), is interesting in that there, the franchisor required franchisees to use a biometric fingerprint

CHAPTER 7

scanning machine for their workers to clock in. This gave rise to an employee's claim - against both the franchisee *and* Papa John's - for violation of Illinois' Biometric Privacy Act. Papa John's motion to dismiss the claim against it was denied. Similarly, in the Circle K case discussed in this Chapter, ***Moody v. Circle K Stores, Inc.***, No. 2:18-cv-435-CLM, 2023 WL 404018 (N.D. Ala. Jan. 25, 2023), the franchisor was held to be a proper defendant in an Americans with Disabilities Act claim involving the disabled plaintiff's inability to navigate through a Circle K store, because the franchisor had required the franchisees to comply with various design standards and specifications when constructing the store. And in ***Interstate Restoration, LLC v. Marriott International, Inc.***, No. 21-cv-01380-NYW-SKC, 2023 WL 2528779 (D. Col. Mar. 15, 2023), the franchisor subjected itself to claims by the plaintiff, which made various repairs to a Marriott hotel after a mudslide damaged it, by involving itself in the hiring of the contractor to do the repair work. Franchisors therefore, as has always been the case, need to be careful not to get too involved in the franchisee's operations, despite their interest in making sure the franchisee's business is successful and protected.

Related to this question is whether franchisors (or, in one case discussed below, manufacturers and distributors) have classified their franchisees (or in the one case mentioned, their dealers) properly, as independent contractors as opposed to employees. This issue continues to come up in a variety of cases, some of which are brought as class actions.

II. **Franchisor-Franchisee Liability to Franchisee's Employees**

Fuentes v. Jiffy Lube International, Inc., No. CV 18-5174, 2023 WL 2539008 (E.D. Pa. Mar. 16, 2023) (The United States District Court for the Eastern District of Pennsylvania granted Jimenez, a former Jiffy Lube franchise employee, the right to intervene in plaintiff's action against Jiffy Lube, finding that in reaching a proposed settlement with Jiffy Lube, plaintiff was no longer an adequate representative of Jimenez's interest. Further, the court also found that Jimenez met the requirements to intervene under Rule 24(a)(2) of the Federal Rules of Civil Procedure because his application was timely, he demonstrated sufficient interest which may be impaired by the disposition of the action and his interest was not adequately represented by plaintiff.)

Hegazy v. Halal Guys, Inc., No. 22 CIV. 1880 (JHR), 2023 WL 4405804 (S.D.N.Y. July 7, 2023) (court granted in part the plaintiff employees' motion to compel the defendant franchisor and franchisees to produce information pertaining to employee hours and compensation, where the information had been redacted in the defendants' document productions, and the plaintiffs were asserting claims for violations of the Fair Labor Standards Act and New York's Labor Law).

Jackson v. Chick & Seafood, Inc., No. 3:22-CV-1687-N, 2023 WL 2799736 (N.D. Tex. Apr. 4, 2023). Plaintiff Jackson, a former employee of a Henderson's Chicken franchise location, alleged that she suffered both racial and sexual harassment as an African-American female while employed at that location, and that she was ultimately fired as a result of her reporting this conduct to the franchise location's owner. Jackson sued the owner of the franchise location, Chick and Seafood, Inc. ("CSI"), and the franchisor of the Henderson's Chicken franchise system, Linda Henderson ("Henderson"), for claims of discrimination and retaliation under Title VII of the Civil Rights Act of 1964.

CSI and Henderson jointly moved to dismiss Jackson's Title VII claims, arguing that Jackson failed to administratively excuse those claims and that CSI is not an employer for Title VII purposes, as it does not have fifteen or more employees and engage in an industry affecting commerce.

Regarding administrative exhaustion, the court found that although Jackson had not received a "right to sue letter" from the Equal Employment Opportunity Commission ("EEOC"), Jackson sufficiently alleged that she filed an EEOC charge and requested a right to sue letter, and that the EEOC's failure to issue that letter in compliance with its own regulations did not require dismissal of Jackson's complaint, as she had taken reasonable steps to comply with the jurisdictional prerequisites for bringing suit.

With respect to whether CSI should be classified as an employer for Title VII purposes, Jackson argued, and the court agreed, that all employees of Henderson's Chicken franchises (as an integrated enterprise) should count towards the 15-employee requirement of Title VII. Specifically, Jackson alleged that the different franchise locations transferred employees without any new hire paperwork, traded missing ingredients, and shared materials and supplies. Jackson further alleged that Henderson, the franchisor, regularly visited all of the locations and instructed employees in how to perform their job duties, controlled the terms and conditions of employment for all workers, as franchisees could not make changes to employee salaries without her approval, and she treated financial assets of the different restaurants as her own and even often helped herself to cash from the cash register. On the basis of these allegations, the court found that Jackson had alleged sufficient facts demonstrating the interrelated nature of CSI and Henderson's Chicken, such that CSI could be deemed to be an "employer" for Title VII purposes.

CHAPTER 7

The court therefore denied CSI and Henderson's joint motion to dismiss Jackson's complaint.

Kyles v. Hoosier Papa LLC, No. 1:20-CV-07146, 2023 WL 2711608 (N.D. Ill. Mar. 30, 2023). Plaintiff Preston Kyles ("Kyles") brought a putative class action against his former employer, Hoosier Papa LLC ("Hoosier Papa"), and Hoosier Papa's franchisor, Papa John's International ("Papa John's"), for allegedly violating his rights under the Illinois Biometric Information Privacy Act ("BIPA"). Specifically, Kyles alleged that, while he was employed by Hoosier Papa, it used a proprietary point-of-sale system, known as FOCUS, developed and operated by Papa John's, which had a built-in fingerprint scanner. Kyles further alleged that Papa John's required that its franchisees, including Hoosier Papa, to use FOCUS's fingerprint scanner for employees to clock in and out, to authenticate themselves to access the system, and to input delivery routing.

According to the complaint, Papa John's had remote access to FOCUS systems at franchise locations through which it could (and did) download, collect data, and monitor fingerprint-scanner usage. Kyles alleged that despite being required to use FOCUS's fingerprint scanner in connection with his employment, neither Papa John's nor Hoosier Papa sought employees' consent prior to collecting fingerprint templates or fingerprint data through the FOCUS system, nor did they tell employees how they would use the fingerprint data or how long they would store the data, or provide a publicly available retention policy regarding retention and storage of biometric data. The employees also did not consent to the defendants disclosing any fingerprint data collected through FOCUS.

Kyles alleged on behalf of himself and other similarly situated current and former employees who had used the FOCUS fingerprint scanner that defendants' conduct with respect to those scanners violated BIPA. Papa John's moved to dismiss Kyles' claims against it in their entirety, arguing that the claims were time barred, that Papa John's did not "possess" or "actively collect" Kyles' biometric data, that the BIPA claims were preempted by the Illinois Workers' Compensation Act ("IWCA"), and that Kyles had failed to allege the recklessness or intent required for heightened damages under BIPA.

Regarding the timeliness of Kyles' claim, the court noted that, after Papa John's filed its motion to dismiss, the Illinois Supreme Court had issued an opinion in another case wherein it found that Illinois' five-year catchall statute of limitations applied to all BIPA claims, such that Kyles' claims were timely. As for Papa John's argument that it did not "possess" the biometric data in the manner required by BIPA, the court ruled that Papa John's had too narrowly interpreted "possession" in BIPA, and that the complaint more than sufficiently alleged that Papa John's exercised the amount of control over the biometric data sufficient to find that it had "possession" of that data under BIPA.

The court also held that although BIPA requires some active step with respect to biometric data beyond mere possession, it does not necessarily require the sort of "active collection" argued by Papa John's. And based upon a plain reading of BIPA, the court found that the complaint plausibly alleged that Papa John's collected, captured, purchased, or otherwise obtained Kyles' fingerprint data.

The court further found that the IWCA did not preempt Kyles' BIPA claims, and that Kyles was not yet required to allege state-of-mind for his BIPA claims to proceed, as state-of-mind was only relevant to the kind of damages he might recover, not to whether or not he had plausibly alleged BIPA claims. Accordingly, the court denied Papa John's motion to dismiss.

In *Mouanda v. Jani-King International*, 653 S.W.3d 65 (Ky. Aug. 18, 2022), the Supreme Court of Kentucky reversed and remanded the decision by the Kentucky Court of Appeals that found the plaintiff did not have proper standing to bring claims in her personal capacity instead of in the capacity of the limited liability company (the "LLC") plaintiff formed in order to become a franchisee of Cardinal Franchising, Inc. ("Cardinal"), a master franchisee for Jani-King International ("Jani-King").

The plaintiff filed suit against Jani-King and Cardinal alleging (1) fraud, (2) breach of contract, (3) unconscionability, and (4) failure to comply with Kentucky's wage and hour laws under the Kentucky Wage and Hour Act ("KWHA"). Cardinal filed a motion to dismiss, asserting that the plaintiff lacked standing to bring the claims because the Franchise Agreement was between Cardinal and the LLC and that the plaintiff was an independent contractor, not an employee, of the LLC. Jani-King also filed a motion to dismiss asserting that it had no contractual or employment relationship with the plaintiff or the LLC. In response, the plaintiff asserted that discovery would show Cardinal is Jani-King's agent, and that the fraud and wage and hour claims belonged to her individually, since the fraud was perpetrated in part before the LLC was formed, and because she was, individually, a *de facto* employee of Cardinal and Jani-King.

The trial court granted Cardinal and Jani-King's motions to dismiss. The plaintiff appealed and the court of appeals unanimously affirmed the trial court's ruling.

The Supreme Court of Kentucky addressed the plaintiff's wage and hour claims first, noting that in order for the KWHA to apply to the plaintiff, the plaintiff must have an employer-employee relationship with the defendant.

CHAPTER 7

The court recognized that although a 2017 amendment to the KWHA explicitly excludes franchisees and their employees from qualifying as employees of the franchisor, the exclusion did not apply to the plaintiff because the LLC, not the plaintiff, was the franchisee, and the plaintiff was the owner of the LLC, not its employee. The court also distinguished the language in the franchise agreement that described the relationship between the franchisor and the franchisee of that as an independent contractor relationship, because the LLC, not the plaintiff, was the franchisee.

To determine whether the plaintiff is an employee of Cardinal and/or Jani-King, the court turned to an analysis of the distinction between employees and independent contractors under the Fair Labor Standards Act ("FLSA"), since Kentucky's wage and hour laws are the 'analogue' to the FLSA. The court explained that none of the FLSA, other federal law, or case law from the United States Supreme Court provide a substantive framework or test for determining employees from independent contractors. Without this framework, the court noted that many courts have applied different classification tests, one of which is the economic realities test, which the court described as focusing on "the economic interactions between workers and an employer beyond the plain terms of a contract."

The court noted that Kentucky has not addressed the distinction between employees and independent contractors under the KWHA, but that the Sixth Circuit had applied the economic realities test when interpreting the FLSA and that the court's predecessor had applied a variation of the economic realities test when determining whether or not a plaintiff had been discriminated against. The court then discussed case law from other jurisdictions who applied the economic realities test in assessing whether or not a plaintiff was considered an employee or an independent contractor in the context of a multi-tiered franchising relationship for janitorial services.

Following the reasoning of the Supreme Judicial Court of Massachusetts, the court concluded that the lack of a contract between the plaintiff and Cardinal and/or Jani-King does not necessarily shield the defendants from liability for wage and hour claims and that the trial court erred in granting the defendants' motion to dismiss with respect to the wage and hour claims and the fraud claim. The court found that the trial court was correct in dismissing the breach of contract and unconscionability claims, since those should have been brought by the LLC, not the plaintiff. The court remanded the case to the trial court, directing the trial court to apply the economic realities test and examine the "true nature" of the relationship between the plaintiff and the defendants to determine whether the plaintiff was an employee or an independent contractor with respect to the defendants.

Related Liability of Franchisors

Patel v. 7-Eleven, Inc., No. CV 17-11414-NMG, 2022 WL 4540981 (D. Mass. Sept. 28, 2022). Convenience store franchisees brought a putative class action in the Commonwealth of Massachusetts alleging that the 7-Eleven franchisor had misclassified the franchisees as independent contractors instead of employees in violation of the Massachusetts Independent Contractor Law, Mass. Gen. L. c. 149, §148B (the "ICL"). Following removal to federal court, the U.S. District Court for the District of Massachusetts denied franchisees' motion to certify the class and granted summary judgment in favor of franchisor. Franchisees appealed, and the Massachusetts Supreme Judicial Court (the "SJC") answered a certified question submitted by the First Circuit Court of Appeals, wherein the SJC explained that the three-prong test for independent contractor status set forth in the ICL both applies to the franchisor-franchisee relationship and does not conflict the federal franchisor disclosure requirements of the FTC Franchise Rule. The First Circuit Court of Appeals then vacated the district court's decision and remanded the case for further proceedings consistent with the guidance provided by the SJC on the certified question.

On remand, the district court considered the ICL's rebuttable presumption that "an individual performing any service for another is an employee" (Mass. Gen. L. c. 149, §148B(a)), which the purported employer can rebut by proving three conjunctive elements of an independent contractor relationship. The threshold inquiry before reaching that three-prong test, however, is whether the purported employee "perform[s] any service" for the alleged employer.

The district court had initially declined to enter summary judgment in franchisor's favor with respect to this threshold inquiry. But in answering the certified question, the SJC explained that this "threshold is not satisfied merely because a relationship between the parties benefits their mutual economic interests." *Patel v. 7-Eleven, Inc.*, 489 Mass. 356, 411 (2022). Guided by the SJC's explanation, the district court on remand concluded that "7-Eleven does not pay the franchisees for the performance of any alleged obligations. In fact, the opposite is true, because 7-Eleven actually provides the franchisees with services in exchange for franchise fees." The district court reasoned that the franchisor's mutual economic interests with the franchisees' in their stores' sales and revenue are inherent in legitimate franchise relationships, that the ICL does not prohibit such relationships, and the mere fact that the parties share economic interests does not imply that the franchisees perform services for the franchisor.

The district court therefore granted summary judgment in franchisor's favor as to the franchisee's claim that 7-Eleven had misclassified the franchisees as independent contractors.

CHAPTER 7

Pina v. Shaman Botanicals, LLC, No. 21-007772-CV-W-WBG, 2023 WL 1070604 (W.D. Mo. Jan. 27, 2023). Plaintiff began working as a social media coordinator for Defendant American Shaman Franchise, LLC ("Shaman Franchise"), which operates the nationwide franchise system of stores for Defendant Shaman Botanicals, LLC ("Shaman Botanicals"), which manufactures and produces CBD American Shaman products that are sold online and in stores. After her employment was terminated by Shaman Franchise, Pina sued both Defendants, claiming that they racially discriminated against her, created a hostile work environment, and retaliated against her when she complained of race discrimination. Plaintiff further claimed that Shaman Botanicals and Shaman Franchise were either a single employer (or integrated enterprise) or joint employers, therefore both were liable for her claims and alleged damages. However, the court found that the evidence did not demonstrate that Shaman Botanicals employed Plaintiff singly or jointly with Shaman Franchise. To the contrary, the evidence clearly showed that Plaintiff was hired and paid by Shaman Franchise and supervised by a Shaman Franchise employee. Shaman Botanicals did not have any input into Plaintiff's work schedule, conditions or work, or the rate and method of pay. The court therefore granted Shaman Botanicals' motion for summary judgment on all of Plaintiff's claims.

Rodo Inc. v. Guimaraes, No. 22-CV-9736 (VSB), 2023 WL 2734464 (S.D.N.Y. Mar. 30, 2023) (The United States District Court for the Southern District of New York denied plaintiff Rodo, Inc.'s motion for a temporary restraining order ("TRO") as to defendant Ari Cohen and also denied plaintiff's request to reconsider the lower court's denial of plaintiff's TRO against defendant Guimaraes.)

In ***Roman v. Jan-Pro Franchising International, Inc.***, No. C 16-05961 WHA, 2022 WL 3046758 (N.D. Cal. Aug. 2, 2022), three unit-franchisees of master franchisees brought claims against franchisor, Jan-Pro Franchising International, Inc. ("Jan-Pro") alleging Jan-Pro violated California's minimum wage, overtime, expense reimbursement, and unlawful deduction laws, and sought class certification as to these issues. Jan-Pro utilized a three-tiered system whereby it entered into agreements with master franchisees who then entered into agreements with unit franchisees, such as the named plaintiffs. The master franchisees were not parties to the litigation. The unit franchisees sought to certify a class of all unit franchisees who signed franchise agreements in California and who have performed cleaning services for Jan-Pro since December 12, 2004.

Related Liability of Franchisors

The unit franchisees argued that they had been misclassified as independent contractors and that they therefore were entitled to minimum wage for mandatory training, reimbursement for expenses incurred for required uniforms, cleaning supplies and equipment, as well as unlawful deductions of management fees and sales and marketing fees. The court initially granted summary judgment in favor of Jan-Pro on the misclassification claim. The unit franchisees appealed that order. While the appeal was pending, the California Supreme Court adopted the "ABC test" in *Dynamex Operations W. v. Superior Court*, 4 Cal. 5th 903, 955, 416 P.3d 1, 34 (2018), which is discussed below, for determining employee classification under California wage orders. The California Supreme Court also ruled that the ABC test applied retroactively. The Ninth Circuit Court of Appeals vacated the summary judgment order in favor of Jan-Pro, remanded the case and this decision followed.

The court ultimately certified the following issues for class treatment: (1) whether Jan-Pro is liable to unit franchisees for failure to pay for mandatory training; (2) whether Jan-Pro is liable to unit franchisees for failure to reimburse them for required uniforms and necessary cleaning supplies and equipment; and (3) whether Jan-Pro unlawfully deducted from unit franchisees' wages management fees and sales and marketing fees. The court then granted summary judgment in favor of plaintiffs on all of the class-certified claims. The court denied certification as to the remaining claims and issues.

The court noted that under California law, the Industrial Welfare Commission of California publishes wage orders regulating hours, wages, and working conditions. When a wage order encompasses a provision of the California labor code, employee classification is decided under *Dynamex*, 4 Cal. 5th at 955, 416 P.3d at 34, which presumes that workers are employees and can only be classified as independent contractors if all of the following three conditions are satisfied: (1) the worker is free from the control and direction of the hirer in connection with the performance of the work; (2) the worker performs work that is outside the usual course of the hiring entity's business; and (3) the worker is customarily engaged in an independently established trade, occupation, or business of the same nature as that involved in the work performed.

With that backdrop, the court applied Federal Rule of Civil Procedure 23(a)'s four requirements for class certification: (1) that the class is so numerous that joinder of all members is impracticable; (2) that there are questions of law or fact common to the class; (3) that the claims or defenses of the representative parties are typical of the claims or defenses of the class; and (4) that the representative parties will fairly and adequately protect the

CHAPTER 7

interests of the class. The court found that the numerosity requirement was satisfied because one master franchisee had over 100 unit franchisees. Commonality was satisfied because no class member can recover if Jan-Pro's classification of the unit franchisees as independent contractors was proper. Typicality was satisfied because the unit franchisees and the putative class members all alleged that they had been injured by Jan-Pro's failure to provide them with minimum wage, overtime pay, and expense reimbursements, and that Jan-Pro made unlawful deductions. Adequacy was satisfied because the lead counsel submitted evidence to the court of her qualifications and extensive experience in wage-and-hour litigation, including serving as class counsel in numerous wage-and-hour misclassification actions. The unit franchisees also submitted evidence to the court that they understood the duty to consider the best interests of the class over their own, they intended to participate in the litigation, and they had no conflicts with the class members.

The court rejected Jan-Pro's argument that typicality and adequacy were not satisfied because Jan-Pro had only waived the right to arbitrate with the named unit franchisees and had not waived the right to arbitrate with the putative class members and found that Jan-Pro had waived the right to arbitrate with the remaining unit franchisees. The court found that Jan-Pro had defended the merits of the case by making system-wide arguments in favor of classifying the unit franchisees as independent contractors on a system-wide basis. The court reasoned that by defending the practice on a system-wide basis, it could not later seek to arbitrate that same issue with the other putative class members.

The court then analyzed the claims under Federal Rule of Civil Procedure 23(b) to determine whether common questions of law or fact predominated over questions affecting individual members, and whether a class action was superior to other methods to fairly and efficiently adjudicate the controversy. The court found that common questions predominated because Jan-Pro classified all unit franchisees as independent contractors, and it provided a standard master franchise agreement to the master franchisees, who frequently used that agreement as a model for their agreements with the unit franchisees. Specifically, the court found that class certification was warranted for the following claims under the *Dynamex* standard: (1) failure to pay minimum wage for mandatory training; (2) failure to reimburse for expenses incurred for required uniforms, and necessary cleaning supplies and equipment; and (3) unlawful deductions of management fees and sales and marketing fees.

After finding that common questions of law and fact predominated, the court awarded summary judgment to the plaintiffs on the second prong of the ABC test, finding that the work performed was not outside of the usual course of Jan-Pro's business, the unit franchisees performed work that was necessary to Jan-Pro, and the work was continuous. The court also found that Jan-Pro was in the business of cleaning, as opposed to franchising. Therefore, the plaintiffs were entitled to summary judgment as to the misclassification claims under *Dynamex*.

Noting that the remaining non-wage order claims must be decided under the more multifactorial standard set forth in *S. G. Borello & Sons, Inc. v. Dep't of Indus. Relations*, 48 Cal. 3d 341, 769 P.2d 399 (1989), the court denied class certification as to those claims. The court noted that under *Borello*, the court must consider a variety of factors to determine whether an employment relationship existed. Two of the *Borello* factors in particular would require individualized inquiries: (1) whether the unit franchisees engaged in a distinct occupation or business; and (2) whether the unit franchisees subjectively believed they were creating an employer-employee relationship. As a result, the court found that common questions did not predominate and denied class certification to the claims that fell outside of the California wage orders.

The court then considered whether class certification was appropriate for the minimum wage and overtime claims and denied class certification. Jan-Pro did not have a uniform pay policy and the plaintiffs failed to provide any evidence that would allow the court to efficiently determine: (1) the rate of pay for the unit franchisees on a class-wide basis; (2) whether unit franchisees were not paid for reimbursable travel time; or (3) whether they were not paid for overtime. The only issue the court found appropriate for class certification under the minimum wage claims was the failure to pay the unit franchisees for mandatory training because that presented a common question.

The court also certified the class for claims related to Jan-Pro's alleged improper failure to reimburse for cleaning supplies and uniforms. The court found that class certification was proper because the unit franchisees were all required to wear a Jan-Pro uniform and the work required cleaning supplies and equipment.

As to the claims for failure to reimburse for auto insurance and gas, the court denied class certification as to those claims. These claims fell within the more particularized *Borello* test, and the unit franchisees failed to show that common questions predominated.

Plaintiffs also sought class certification that Jan-Pro unlawfully deducted certain management and sales and marketing fees. Under California wage orders, it is unlawful for an employer to shift operational expenses to employees. The court found that these amounts represented such a shift and granted class certification as to these claims.

CHAPTER 7

The court rejected Jan-Pro's arguments that the unit-franchisees were not employees based on the business to business exception, because common evidence showed that the unit franchisees could not set their own rates; rather, those rates were determined by master franchisees. The court also rejected Jan-Pro's argument that, under the joint employer test, the master franchisees were the agents of misclassification because of Jan-Pro's three-tiered system. The court rejected this argument for three reasons: (1) because the appellate court had directed the lower court to apply the ABC test, not the joint employer test; (2) there is no requirement that the actual hirer be the agent of misclassification before the ABC test applies; and (3) Jan-Pro as the top tier agent was the agent of misclassification because, Jan-Pro's master franchisee template designed and implemented the framework under which the unit franchisees were misclassified.

Having certified the foregoing classes, the court then awarded summary judgment to the unit franchisees on all of the following: (1) Jan-Pro's liability to pay minimum wages for mandatory training of unit franchisees, because the training benefited Jan-Pro, not the unit franchisees; (2) Jan-Pro's liability for unpaid expense reimbursements for uniforms and cleaning supplies, because these items were necessary for the unit franchisees to perform their work; and (3) Jan-Pro's unlawful deductions of management fees and sales and marketing fees, because these fees represented Jan-Pro's unlawful shifting of operational costs from Jan-Pro to the unit franchisees.

Salinas v. Cornwell Quality Tools Company, No. 5:19-CV-02275-FLA (SPX), 2022 WL 16735823 (C.D. Cal. Oct. 17, 2022). The court considered whether to certify a plaintiff class of dealers in a class action against the defendant distributor. Plaintiff was a dealer of Cornwell Quality Tools Company's ("Cornwell") products, and alleged that Cornwell improperly classified its dealers as independent contractors rather than employees. Plaintiff filed a class action complaint against Cornwell in California state court, and Cornwell removed the action to federal court.

Plaintiff asserted nine claims against Cornwell, including several claims for violation of different sections of California's Labor Code. Plaintiff moved to certify a class consisting of "[a]ll persons who signed Dealer Agreements in California and personally operated a mobile store at any time within four years preceding the filing of this action" for all but one of his claims. The court certified the class, finding that plaintiff had satisfied the requirements of Federal Rules of Civil Procedure 23(a) and 23(b)(3). The key issue was whether plaintiff's claims satisfied the predominance requirement of 23(b)(3).

Related Liability of Franchisors

In finding that common issues of law or fact predominated over individual issues, the court first ruled that the "ABC Test" established in *Dynamex Operations West, Inc. v. Superior Court*, 416 P.3d 1 (Cal. 2018), rather than the multi-factor test explained in *S. G. Borello & Sons, Inc. v. Dept. of Industrial Relations*, 769 P.2d 399 (Cal. 1989) applied to the threshold issue of whether Cornwell misclassified its dealers as independent contractors. Under the ABC Test, workers are presumptively classified as employees, unless the hiring business satisfies each of three conditions (Prongs A, B, and C). Because "each prong may be dispositive in a plaintiff's favor on the merits . . . the predominance of common issues on a single prong of the ABC test will support class certification." Specifically, the court found that "the amount of control Cornwell retained over its Dealers' hours and/or working conditions under Prong A of the ABC Test . . . predominates over individualized issues" sufficiently to support class certification. The court then concluded that common issues predominated for Plaintiff's other claims, holding that Cornwell's "uniform practices and policies" regarding its dealers predominated over individualized issues with respect to any particular dealer. This case is also discussed in Chapter 6, Section VI and in Chapter 8, Section IX.

Teague v. 7-Eleven, Inc., No. 4:21-cv-04097-SLD-JEH, 2023 WL 4426017 (C.D. Ill. July 10, 2023). Tashimia C. Teague ("Teague"), an employee of a 7-Eleven franchisee, brought claims against the franchisor for employment discrimination under Title VII of the Civil Rights Act of 1964. After its motion to dismiss was denied, 7-Eleven, Inc. ("7-Eleven") filed a motion for summary judgment, which the court granted. The court's analysis began by noting that an employee can have multiple employers for the purpose of Title VII and may bring claims against the employee's direct employer, and also against an indirect employer, as long as the indirect employer meets the criteria established by the Seventh Circuit. The court noted that determining whether an entity is an indirect employer under Title VII is a fact-specific inquiry that hinges on the "economic realities of the employment relationship." The Seventh Circuit uses a five-factor balancing test, evaluating: (1) the extent of the employer's control and supervision over the employee; (2) the kind of occupation and nature of skill required; (3) the employer's responsibility for the costs of operation; (4) the method and form of payment and benefits; and (5) the length of the job commitment. Proof of each of the five factors is not required to establish an employment relationship and the employer's right to control is the most important factor.

7-Eleven provided declarations from two of its employees and a copy of the relevant franchise agreement, all of which pointed out the numerous ways in which 7-Eleven had no control over the franchisee's employees, or over the franchisee's costs of operation, or methods and forms of payments and benefits of the franchisee's employees, and also established that 7-Eleven could find no record of Teague in its employment records. In response, Teague submitted an affidavit stating that to the best of her knowledge, she only worked for 7-Eleven, as "almost everything" presented to her was branded as 7-Eleven, such as employee shift schedules, employee instructions on selling alcohol or tobacco products, proof of name tags bearing the 7-Eleven logo, performance notice forms, and 7-Eleven's cash accountability policy and procedures, among other items. Teague did admit, however, that she knew that her pay stubs were from the franchisee's entity. Based on the affidavits presented, and the terms of the franchise agreement, the court concluded that there was no genuine dispute of material fact that 7-Eleven was not Teague's employer for purposes of Title VII. The court noted that Teague's evidence demonstrating that the 7-Eleven name and logo appeared on her uniform and on various company papers did not show that 7-Eleven exercised control over her, but rather suggested that Teague worked at a 7-Eleven franchise that was conforming to the required 7-Eleven franchise image and that these signs of belonging to a franchise were not, by themselves, sufficient to establish the required level of control to be considered her employer under Title VII.

The court did note that 7-Eleven's providing its cash accountability policy and procedures to the franchisee could be considered a level of control over the franchisee's employee, but that the existence of the policy showed a minimal level of control over the employee's daily tasks.

Whitlach v. Premier Valley, Inc., No. 21-CV-2143 (PKC), 2022 WL 17751550 (Cal. Ct. App. Nov. 18, 2022). Plaintiff was a former real estate agent affiliated with a franchisee of real estate brokerage franchisor. Plaintiff filed a class action complaint against franchisee and franchisor alleging that plaintiff and those similarly situated had been misclassified as independent contractors under California law.

On appeal, the California court affirmed the trial court's ruling that plaintiff was an independent contractor as a matter of law. In doing so, the court held that California's Assembly Bill No. 5 (which codified the ABC test for determining a worker's employment status under California's Labor Code) did not apply to real estate licensees such as plaintiff. To the contrary, a "real estate licensee" was one of the occupational classifications specifically exempted from the ABC test. Therefore, the court applied California's long standing test for real estate salespeople for purposes of the wage and hour provisions of California's Labor Code.

Related Liability of Franchisors

Under this test, the plaintiff was an independent contractor as a matter of law, because he was a licensed real estate agent; was paid by commission; and he entered into a written contract that specified that he was an independent contractor for state tax purposes. The court therefore affirmed the trial court's dismissal of plaintiff's misclassification claims against both the franchisee and the franchisor.

III.   Franchisor-Franchisee Liability to Third Parties

In *Ariza v. Coffee Beanery, Ltd.*, No. 22-61516-CIV, 2022 WL 17333106 (S.D. Fla. Nov. 29, 2022), the court held that a franchisor could be held liable to a disabled customer of its franchisee's restaurant under the Americans with Disabilities Act where a website owned and operated by the franchisor is not accessible to blind and visually impaired individuals and thereby creates intangible barriers to those individuals being able to access the coffee shop, that is, the physical place of public accommodation, owned and operated by defendant's franchisee. This case is discussed in Chapter 6, Section V.

Barrett v. New American Adventures, LLC, No. 2:20-CV-01813-CRE, 2023 WL 4295807 (W.D. Pa. June 30, 2023). A patron of an Urban Air Trampoline and Adventure Park ("Urban Air") in Cranberry Township, Pennsylvania brought a personal injury suit against the franchisee owner of the Urban Air park and the franchisee's landlord, as well as against the franchisor of the Urban Air franchise system, for injuries the patron received while participating on an obstacle course at the park called the Warrior Course. On cross motions for summary judgment the court ruled that the landlord defendant owed no duty to the plaintiff as a landlord out of possession of the premises, and it further found that neither the franchisee defendant nor the franchisor defendant owed a duty to the plaintiff under Pennsylvania's "no-duty" rule, which provides that an owner or operator of a place of amusement has no duty to protect patrons from any hazards that are inherent in the amusement activity. The injuries sustained by the patron plaintiff were the result of falling from an obstacle into a ball pit, which the court found as a matter of law to be injuries arising out of a risk inherent in the Warrior Course attraction, and defendants owed no duty to plaintiff to protect her from that risk. The court therefore granted summary judgment in favor of the defendants as to all of plaintiff's claims.

In ***Caceres v. Toyota Motor North America, Inc.***, No. 2020-08580, 2023 WL 3328701 (N.Y. App. Div. May 10, 2023), the Supreme Court, Appellate Division, Second Department, New York, reversed the lower court's order

CHAPTER 7

finding that it erred in denying the franchisor defendants' (collectively, "Toyota") motion for summary judgment.

This dispute arose out of plaintiff Joan Caceres' lawsuit to recover damages for injuries he sustained when the front driver's side wheel of the vehicle he was operating fell off shortly after it was serviced at franchisee defendant Plaza Toyota, a car dealership and service center. Plaintiff moved for summary judgment on the issue of liability against defendants Plaza Auto Mall, Ltd., and Plaza Automotive Ltd. Toyota cross-moved for summary judgment dismissing the complaint and all cross-claims against them (the "Motion"), on the basis that they should not be held vicariously liable for franchisee's actions. However, the lower court denied Toyota's motion and Toyota appealed.

On appeal, Toyota submitted affidavits showing that they lacked the requisite control over the manner in which franchisee serviced vehicles. The court found that this evidence supported Toyota's claim that they should not be held vicariously liable for franchisee's actions. Further, the court also found that Toyota's failure to submit a dealership agreement with Plaza Toyota did not negate Toyota's entitlement to summary judgment. Accordingly, the court found that the lower court should have granted Toyota's motion for summary judgment dismissing the complaint and all cross-claims insofar as asserted against Toyota.

In *Cawley v. Kenyon*, No. KNL-CV22-6055032-S, 2023 WL 2386114 (Conn. Super. Ct. Mar. 2, 2023) the Superior Court of Connecticut granted franchisor defendant Pillar to Post Home Inspection's motion for summary judgment on plaintiff, John Cawley's complaint, holding that there was no genuine issue of material fact as to whether defendant owed a legal duty to plaintiff because Plaintiff failed to establish any facts showing that defendant had possession or control over the premises where the alleged injury occurred.

This dispute arose out of a franchise agreement between defendant and franchisee, Stephen Bakowicz ("Bakowicz"), granting Bakowicz the right to operate a Pillar to Post franchise. On May 17, 2021, Bakowicz performed a home inspection for Kathleen Kenyon's property (the "Property"). However, on July 29, 2021, plaintiff suffered injuries when a stairway at the Property collapsed. Accordingly, on July 25, 2022, plaintiff filed a complaint against defendant alleging that defendant caused his injuries by failing to adequately inspect the Property.

Defendant moved for summary judgment on the complaint and the court ruled in defendant's favor finding that defendant had no possession or control of Bakowicz's conduct or of the Property, that the franchise agreement clearly provides that no agency relationship exists between defendant and

Related Liability of Franchisors

Bakowicz. Accordingly, no genuine issue of material fact exists as to whether defendant owed a legal duty to plaintiff.

In *Doe v. Massage Envy Franchising, LLC*, 87 Cal. App. 5th 23, 303 Cal. Rptr. 3d 269 (Cal. Ct. App. 2022), the California Court of Appeals held that the defendant franchisor could not compel arbitration of the plaintiff's claims stemming from an alleged sexual assault at one of its franchisees' massage clinics because the plaintiff did not have reasonable notice that she was assenting to arbitration of any claims against the franchisor. This case is discussed in Chapter 8, Section VI.A.

In *Doe #21 v. CFR Enterprises, Inc.*, No. A163543, 2023 WL 4783591 (Cal. Ct. App. June 29, 2023), the court reversed the trial court's dismissal on statute of limitations grounds of eighteen plaintiffs' claims against the franchisor and franchisees of several Massage Envy locations stemming from alleged sexual assaults that occurred at such locations. The court held that a recently-enacted law revived some, if not all, of the plaintiffs' claims notwithstanding the statute of limitations. This case is discussed in Chapter 6, Section XII.

Estate of Myrick v. 7-Eleven Inc., No. 23-829, 2023 WL 4140829 (E.D. Pa. June 22, 2023). In a premises liability case where an individual died at a franchised location as a result of gunfire, 7-Eleven sought to remove the action based on diversity under the theory of fraudulent joinder, and the plaintiffs moved to remand. 7-Eleven asserted that the plaintiff added a 7-Eleven corporate asset manager to destroy diversity, but the court disagreed and remanded the case to state court, explaining that the responsibility of the corporate asset manager at the franchised location was a question of fact. This case is discussed in Chapter 8, Section XVI.

Fernald v. JFE Franchising, Inc., No. 2:22-cv-02761-JTF-cgc, 2023 WL 2938312 (W.D. Tenn. Apr. 13, 2023) (granting defendant-franchisor's motion to dismiss claims for negligence and negligent hiring where the franchisor's franchisee carried out a mass shooting, because the complaint did not establish a basis by which the defendant owed a duty of care to the victims of the shooting that included the anticipation of such an event, and under Tennessee law a franchisee is not deemed an employee of the franchisor for any purpose).

Herrera v. Highgate Hotels, L.P., No. 151096/18E, 2023 WL 1826823 (N.Y. App. Div. Feb. 9, 2023). The court denied plaintiff's motion to amend its complaint as to third-party defendant Subway Real Estate Corp. ("Subway")

CHAPTER 7

after the plaintiff sustained injuries due to a slip. The court determined that the proposed amended complaint was without merit as Subway had already subleased the space to other defendants pursuant to a sublease, assignment, assumption, and franchise agreement. Thus, Subway could not be held liable to plaintiff for the other defendants' failure to maintain their stairs.

In *International Samarkand Hotel Group, LLC v. Wynn*, No. HHD-CV-17-5045384-S, 2023 WL 3000455 (Conn. Super. Apr. 14, 2023), the Superior Court of Connecticut held that defendants, American Hospitality Management 1, LLC, American Hospitality Management 2, LLC and American Hospitality Management, Inc., (collectively, "AHM") were not vicariously liable for the theft committed by their attorney, defendant, James Wynn ("Wynn"), who allegedly stole $250,000 from the franchisee plaintiff, International Samarkand Hotel Group, LLC ("Samarkand").

In 2016, Samarkand purchased property on which it intended to build a hotel based on its franchise agreement with franchisor, International Hotel Group. Samarkand sought management assistance and construction financing for this hotel from AHM. Therefore, Samarkand's attorney entered negotiations with Wynn. Wynn prepared a Good Faith Deposit Escrow Agreement (the "Agreement"), which required Samarkand to pay $250,000 to Wynn which was to be held in escrow. Samarkand's managing partner signed the agreement but AHM's president, Donald Schappacher, decided not to proceed with the deal. However, despite this, Wynn forged Schappacher's signature and Samarkand wired $250,000 to Wynn pursuant to the Agreement.

Accordingly, Samarkand brought this claim arguing that AHM is liable for Wynn's theft of Samarkand's funds because AHM made statements about Wynn that made him an apparent agent of AHM. Nevertheless, the court held otherwise, finding that AHM cannot be held liable because there is no evidence that Wynn's forging of Schappacher's signature was in furtherance of AHM's business. Additionally, the evidence did not show that AHM said or did anything to convey to Samarkand that Wynn had actual or apparent authority to bind AHM. Therefore, Samarkand failed to prove its vicarious liability claim and the Court entered judgment in AHM's favor.

Interstate Restoration, LLC v. Marriott International, Inc., No. 21-cv-01380-NYW-SKC, 2023 WL 2528779 (D. Col. Mar. 15, 2023). In February 2019, a mudslide caused millions of dollars of property damage to the Sheraton Grand Rio Hotel & Resort, Marriott-branded hotel in Rio de Janeiro, Brazil. Marriott is the franchisor of the hotel; the franchisee is a Brazilian entity named Companhia Palmares Hoteis e Turismo S.A. ("Companhia").

Related Liability of Franchisors

Shortly after the mudslide occurred, Marriott's Senior Vice President of Risk Management called plaintiff and requested that it conduct urgent repairs at the hotel. Plaintiff agreed and sent Marriott an Advanced Work Order ("AWO") setting forth the terms of the agreement and the scope of work to be performed. Marriott had the manager of the hotel, who was employed by Companhia, sign the AWO under the term "Owner." The AWO did not define the term "Owner." Over the next few months, Interstate provided and signed four additional agreements named "National Agreement Work Orders" ("NAWOs") for various aspects of the repairs at the hotel, and presented them to the hotel's manager. The NAWOs were between Interstate and "Client/Owner," and did not define the term "Client/Owner." But they did state "Marriott Int'l" with the hotel's address in the "Project Name and Location" section of each NAWO and, for "Company Name," identified "Marriott International."

The hotel was insured by Zurich America and Zurich Brazil (collectively, "Zurich"). Around the time the AWO was executed, Marriott filed an insurance claim with Zurich. After completing its work, Interstate issued invoices to Marriott and/or the hotel that totaled approximately $7.2 million. Zurich retained a building consultant to determine whether the amount of Interstate's invoices were appropriate. That consultant found the invoices to be "far above market value," and valued Interstate's services at a much lower amount.

Interstate was not paid for the amounts it billed for its services. It sued Marriott for breach of contract and unjust enrichment. It also sued Zurich for intentional interference with its contract with Marriott. The defendants moved for summary judgment. Among other things, Marriott argued that it could not have breached the contracts with Interstate, because it was not a party to those contracts, and the contracts were with the hotel's owner and Marriott does not own the hotel. The court denied the motion, finding that genuine factual disputes existed that precluded summary judgment. For one thing, the court found there were genuine issues of material fact as to what constituted the contract underlying Interstate's claims and what precise terms such contract includes. Interstate pointed to not only the AWO and NAWOs but to certain conversations it had with Marriott and others regarding the repair work as constituting the contract, and Marriott disagreed that all of those agreements and communications constituted a single "juggernaut agreement."

The court then noted that Interstate's involvement and work on the hotel began with a conversation between Interstate and a Senior Vice President at Marriott who potentially could bind the corporation. Moreover, the court held that neither the AWO nor the NAWOs defined the terms "Owner" and "Client/Owner," and the faces of those agreements did not

CHAPTER 7

clearly establish that these terms as used in the contracts excluded Marriott (the court noted, among other things, that the agreements could be interpreted to include both Marriott and Companhia as owners of the hotel). Furthermore, the court recognized the importance of the initial conversation between Interstate and Marriott in interpreting who the "owner" of the hotel was, and that the credibility of witnesses' testimony, such as Interstate's principal's belief based on what occurred and prior dealings Interstate had had with Marriott over the years that its contract was with Marriott, was for the jury to decide. With respect to the unjust enrichment claim, the court disputed Marriott's claim that, because it was not the hotel's owner, it did not receive any benefit from Interstate's repairs at the hotel, pointing to the fact that Marriott executives had helped coordinate the repair work. For all of these reasons, the court denied Marriott's motion for summary judgment.

Kelley v. AW Distributing, Inc., No. 20-cv-06942-JSW, 2023 WL 2167391 (N.D. Cal. Feb. 21, 2023). Plaintiffs are relatives of individuals who were struck and killed by drivers that had bought and inhaled spray products manufactured and distributed by the various defendants. The distributor defendant brought a motion to dismiss the claims against it for strict liability and the court granted the motion, finding that the defendant did not design the specific product in question and that its relationship with the manufacturer defendant had ended before the injuries occurred. The court allowed the common law negligence claim against the distributor to go forward, finding that the design did not change from the time the defendant was involved to the time the injury occurred. The manufacturer's cross-claim against the distributor for contribution was denied as violating the settlement agreement in a related underlying claim between the two parties.

Merlino v. Knudson, No. 2020-07327, 214 A.D.3d 642, 184 N.Y.S.3d 280 (2d Dep't March 1, 2023). Plaintiff was a relative of a person using homecare services provided by the defendant's franchisor and franchisee (collectively, the "Home Instead Defendants") and brought a claim for conversion against the Home Instead Defendants, among other parties. The court affirmed the dismissal of the claims as against the Home Instead Defendants, finding that the plaintiff was not an intended third party beneficiary of the contract between the two Home Instead Defendants and further that the claim for conversion was time-barred.

Moody v. Circle K Stores, Inc., No. 2:18-cv-435-CLM, 2023 WL 404018 (N.D. Alabama Jan. 25, 2023). Defendant moved for judgment on the pleadings on the four plaintiffs' (who have mobility disabilities) putative class action complaint, which asserted that defendant's stores violated the Americans with Disabilities Act ("ADA"). Among other things, defendant argued that plaintiffs had failed to state a plausible claim for relief, because they had failed to allege a common discriminatory architectural design or policy applicable to the thousands of Circle K stores across the country. The court disagreed, finding that the plaintiffs had adequately pleaded a violative policy resulting in a pattern and practice of discrimination. It pointed to the plaintiffs' allegations that the vast majority of Circle K stores are operated exclusively by defendant and the limited number of locations that are not are controlled by defendant through franchising agreements. It also noted plaintiffs' allegations that Circle K requires its franchisees to comply with various standards and specifications, including with respect to the exterior and interior design of the stores, and their construction, renovation, maintenance and repair, and that this system allegedly creates a pattern and practice of willfully and systematically denying equal access to individuals with disabilities. Construing these allegations in the light most favorable to plaintiffs, the court concluded that plaintiffs had stated a plausible claim for violation of the ADA, and denied defendant's motion.

Orlando v. Choice Hotels International, Inc., No. 2:22-cv-00404-APG-BNW, 2023 WL 4025886 (D. Nev. June 15, 2023). The court denied the defendant franchisor's motion to dismiss for failure to name the franchisee as a defendant. The plaintiff was injured at a hotel for which the defendant was the franchisor. The court ruled that the franchisee was not an "required party" under FRCP 19 which requires joinder of "required parties," noting that the fact that the franchisee had a contractual obligation to indemnify or defend the franchisor was irrelevant to the question of whether it was a "required party." Regardless, the court then granted the plaintiff's motion to amend the complaint to add the franchisee as a defendant.

Pereda v. Atos Jiu Jitsu LLC, No. B313718, 85 Cal.App.5th 759, 301 Cal. Rptr. 3d 690, 2022 WL 17174558 (Cal. Ct. of App., Nov. 23, 2022). A student at a Jiu-Jitsu studio who was injured during a sparring match brought a negligence action not only against the owners of the studio, but also against a national jiu-jitsu association and its founder, on the basis that the studio's owners were the ostensible agents of the association. The trial court granted summary judgment to the association and its founder, finding the relationship between the studio owners and the association to be very similar to "an ordinary franchise relationship," and holding that such relationship does not give rise to liability on the part of the franchisor for the acts of the franchisee

CHAPTER 7

unless the franchisor is involved in the specific acts that caused the plaintiff's injury.

The plaintiff appealed. The appellate court considered in detail the ostensible agency issue, noting first that whether ostensible agency exists turns on whether the principal intentionally, or by want of ordinary care, causes a third person to believe another to be his agent, even when the third person is not actually an agent. The court further held that the principal cannot be held liable for the acts of its ostensible agent unless the plaintiff, when dealing with the agent, did so with a reasonable belief in the agent's authority, that belief was generated by some act or neglect by the principal, and the plaintiff was not negligent in relying on the agent's apparent authority. In analyzing these issues, the court discussed the relationship between franchisors and franchisees. It first acknowledged that a franchisee may be deemed to be an agent of the franchisor where, for example, the franchisor retains "the right of complete or substantial control over the franchisee" or is reasonably perceived as having that right. However, the court next recognized that a franchisor's controlling the franchisee's use of its mark and business plan or system, alone, cannot establish ostensible agency, as doing so would effectively render franchisees the agents of franchisors in every case, disrupting and "turning on its head" one of the key aspects of the franchise business model, namely, the ability of a franchisor to share its goodwill with its franchisees without assuming all responsibility for how they operate their otherwise independent businesses. The court cautioned that, to avoid this, courts need to be mindful when applying agency theory in the franchise context. The court held that a franchisor can only be liable for the conduct of its franchisee if the franchisor actually exercises control, or is reasonably believed to exercise control, over the means and manner of the franchisee's operation *that caused the plaintiff's alleged injury.*

Determining that question here involved the consideration of whether the association controlled the studio owners' oversight of the sparring that took place in their studio, and which led to plaintiff's injury. Furthermore, because ostensible agency focuses on what a reasonable person knowing what the plaintiff knew at the time of the accident would have believed, the court looked at such information and concluded that such knowledge did not, as a matter of law, give rise to a reasonable belief on the plaintiff's part that the association and its founder had control over the studio owners' supervision of sparring during its classes. The display of an association banner in the studio was found to be insufficient to create such reasonable belief, as were certain statements included on the association's website such as a listing of various "affiliates" of the association, including the studio in question. And in contrast to other cases where ostensible agency was found, in this case, the association did not make any statements that it "stood behind" all of its franchisees or affiliates or that otherwise would have given rise to a reasonable belief that the association was in control of the studio's sparring sessions. The court therefore affirmed the trial court's granting of summary judgment in favor of the association and its founder.

Root v. MaidPro Wilmington, No. N20C-05-156 CLS, 2022 WL 17039161 (Del. Super. Nov. 17, 2022). A MaidPro franchisee in Wilmington, Delaware hired a woman but, 9 days later, after reviewing her background report, terminated her. Four months later, the woman broke into the plaintiffs' home while they were on vacation and stole personal property. Plaintiffs sued the franchisee (MaidPro Wilmington) and franchisor (MaidPro Franchise, LLC) for *Respondeat superior*/vicarious liability, negligent hiring, civil conspiracy and intentional/negligent infliction of emotional distress. The court granted the franchisor's motion to dismiss all of plaintiffs' claims against it, holding, among other things, that the former employee was not acting in the scope of her employment with the defendants when she burglarized plaintiffs' home (the act occurred well after the woman's employment was terminated and the act of breaking into a home and stealing items is not commonly done by a housekeeper), and plaintiffs failed to sufficiently allege that the franchisor's control over the franchisee was actual, participatory and total, therefore the franchisor was not liable to the franchisee's actions.

Sant v. Marriott International, Inc., No. GJH-22-1036, 2023 WL 2213926 (D. Md. Feb. 24, 2023). Plaintiff brought claims in the District of Maryland related to plaintiff's slip and fall at a franchised JW Marriott hotel located in India against the franchisor and the franchisee. Marriott's principal place of business is Maryland. The franchisee was incorporated under the laws of India. The court denied Marriott's motion to dismiss for failure to state a claim, determining that although Marriott had no ownership over the hotel, Marriott may still otherwise maintain control over its franchisees and hotels carrying its brand, which was a fact question entitled to discovery. This case is discussed in Chapter 8, Section III.

Sheriff v. Four Cousins Burgers and Fries of NH, LLC, No. 21-cv-571-PB, 2023 WL 3393394 (D.N.H. May 11, 2023). Plaintiff was making a delivery to a Five Guys restaurant in Tilton, New Hampshire when he was accosted by some individuals doing maintenance work at the restaurant, allegedly causing him post-traumatic stress disorder. He filed a lawsuit for negligence against the franchisee operating the restaurant, its management company ("Gellfam"), a subsidiary of the management company ("Great Bons"), and certain

CHAPTER 7

individuals, including those who were doing the maintenance work there and the manager. The court considered plaintiffs' motion for summary judgment against the franchisee and its management company under a theory of *respondeat superior*. The defendants argued that the responsible individuals were employees of Great Bons (not the franchisee) and, regardless, were acting outside of their scope of their employment. The court disagreed and granted plaintiff's motion for summary judgment as to Gellfam, finding that Gellfam exercised the requisite control over the individuals working there such that they were properly considered employees of Gellfam, noting (quoting the Restatement (Third) of Agency) that "an employee can be entrusted to use 'discretion in performing their work,' so long as the employer 'retains a right of control, however infrequently exercised.'"

The court denied the plaintiff's motion as against franchisee, Four Cousins, finding the evidence inconclusive because the plaintiff relied solely on a provision in the franchise agreement requiring Four Cousins "to maintain a competent, conscientious, properly trained staff."

IV. Other Franchisor Liability

Courser v. Radisson Hotels International, Inc., No. 1:18-cv-1232, 2023 WL 4364066 (W.D. Mich. June 13, 2023). Former Michigan legislator Todd Courser sued franchisor Radisson Hotels. He contended that the franchisor gave employees at a Radisson Hotel where he had an extramarital affair unauthorized access to his room to install surveillance devices and shared his private information to aid in a conspiracy to oust him from office.

The court ruled that the Radisson defendants could not be held vicariously liable for the actions of the franchisee-hotel owner's staff as there was no principal-agent relationship between the franchisor and such staff. The court reviewed the license agreement between the hotel owner franchisee, Block 100, and franchisor Radisson Hotels, that established the franchisor-franchisee relationship. The court determined that no agency relationship existed because Radisson did not control the day-to-day operations of the hotel under the license agreement. Radisson therefore could not be held vicariously liable for any alleged actions of the franchisee hotel's staff. The court granted summary judgment to the hotel defendants and dismissed all of plaintiff's claims, finding Courser failed to provide evidence to support his allegations against the franchisor and to demonstrate any genuine disputes of material fact.

In re McDonald's Corporation Stockholder Derivative Litigation, No. 2021-0324-JTL, 291 A.3d 652, 2023 WL 2293575 (Del. Ch. Ct. Mar. 1, 2023).

Related Liability of Franchisors

McDonald's stockholders asserted a derivative claim against the franchisor, claiming that nine individuals who served on the company's board of directors between 2015 and 2020 had ignored certain "red flags" about a corporate culture that condoned sexual harassment and other misconduct, which led to employee lawsuits, loss of trust of the company among its employees, and harm to McDonald's reputation. In granting the defendants board members' motion to dismiss, the court noted that the plaintiffs were relying on a principle that corporate fiduciaries cannot act loyally and in the best interests of the corporation they serve if they consciously ignore evidence indicating that the corporation is suffering or will suffer harm. To state a claim under this theory, however, the plaintiffs had to allege facts supporting an inference that the directors knew about a problem but consciously ignored it. While the court held that the plaintiffs satisfied the first element, that is, they adequately pleaded facts supporting an inference that the defendants knew about a problem with sexual harassment and misconduct at the company, it held that the allegations in the complaint did not support an inference that the defendants failed to respond. To the contrary, the court noted several ways in which the defendants, during 2019, tried to address the sexual harassment and other problems at the company, such as hiring outside consultants, revising corporate policies and implementing new training programs. Even if these steps did not fully fix the problem, the court held, that is not the test; rather, the board need only make a good faith effort to fix the issues in question. The court also held that the business judgment rule provided protection to the defendants for any good faith errors regarding certain decisions the plaintiffs referenced, and that there no allegations that undermined the presumption that the board acted properly in addressing issues of sexual harassment facing the company.

Olguin v. FCA US LLC, No. 1:21-CV-1789 JLT CDB, 2023 WL 1972223 (E.D. Cal. Feb. 13, 2023). The court denied defendant automobile manufacturer's motion to dismiss plaintiff's fraud in the inducement claim. Plaintiff sufficiently pleaded that Fiat Chrysler Automobiles US, LLC (FCA US) was aware of a stalling defect with the type of vehicle in question based in part on information FCA US received from its dealership, which had received various consumer complaints, plus FCA US had access to warranty and part replacement data compiled by its dealerships.

In ***Whitlach v. Premier Valley, Inc.***, 86 Cal. Ct. App. 5th 673 (2022), *reh'g denied* (Dec. 5, 2022) the California Court of Appeal affirmed the Superior Court's judgment which held that the applicable test for determining whether a real estate salesperson is an employee or independent contractor for

CHAPTER 7

purposes of the Labor Code's wage and hour provisions is the Labor Code section 2778, subdivision (c)(1), (the "Labor Statute").

Plaintiff, a real estate agent, filed a claim against defendants, Premier Valley, LLC ("Franchisee") and Century 21 Real Estate LLC ("Franchisor"), asserting a cause of action under the Labor Code Private Attorney General Act of 2004 ("PAGA") alleging that: 1) defendants misclassified him as an independent contractor as opposed to an employee; 2) the independent contractor agreement he signed with Franchisee was unconscionable and therefore unenforceable, alternatively; 3) if he is considered to be an independent contractor pursuant to the Labor Statute then the Labor Statute is unconstitutional under the California Constitution and; 4) that he is an employee because he entered into a management employee agreement with Franchisee in his capacity as a sales manager for the firm.

The court of appeal applied the Labor Statute and found that plaintiff was an independent contractor because he was a licensed real estate agent, he was paid by commission and entered into an independent contractor agreement. The court found that the independent contractor agreement was valid and not unconscionable pursuant to the Business and Professions Code Section 10032(b) which authorizes the use of independent contractor agreements for real estate agents to determine their relationship. The court also found that the Labor Statute was constitutional because plaintiff failed to show that real estate salespersons are similarly situated as other persons who are not subject to the Labor Statute. Finally, the court found that the management employee agreement did not affect his independent contractor status because it had no relevance to his PAGA claim and was not a novation or modification to his independent contractor agreement. Accordingly, the court of appeals affirmed the Superior Court's judgment in favor of defendants.

CHAPTER 8

Issues Specific to Litigation and Arbitration

I. Introduction

This year was like others in that there were many decisions involving procedural skirmishes before the parties got to the merits of their dispute. For example, there were numerous decisions considering and determining motions to dismiss for lack of personal jurisdiction, although the authors did not review any that made new law. There were also numerous cases in which a party sought to enforce - or, at times, avoid application of - a franchise (or distribution or other) agreement's forum selection clause. In the decisions discussed below, the courts generally enforced such clauses; and, in at least one case, the judge used sarcasm in pointing out how a litigant ignored what the contract provided, including its forum selection clause, commenting that "words mean stuff." Courts also considered whether non-signatories to franchise and other agreements could be held bound by the agreement's forum selection clause.

That same question also arose several times this year in the context of arbitration provisions, and there were several cases determining motions to compel arbitration. Courts in these cases generally enforced arbitration agreements (except in the rare case where an arbitration clause was found to be unconscionable), and narrowly construed any claimed exemptions to them, including under the Federal Arbitration Act. In the remainder of the chapter, a wide variety of other procedural issues were raised and determined, including issues relating to discovery, class actions, removal (and remand), default judgments and settlement agreements and releases.

II. Substantive and Personal Jurisdiction

Bakhtiari v. Doe, No. 22 C 2406, 2022 WL 17593027, (N.D. Ill. Dec. 13, 2022). A Dunkin' Donuts customer brought a discrimination action against an individual Dunkin' store, the owners of the store at issue, individual managers of the store, and Inspire Brands, the indirect parent company of the franchisor, Dunkin Donuts Franchising LLC. Inspire Brands brought a motion to dismiss for lack of personal jurisdiction. The court found that it lacked either general or specific jurisdiction over Inspire Brands, and therefore granted its motion to dismiss. The court quickly disposed of the general jurisdiction issue, because Inspire Brands is not an Illinois company and this was not an exceptional case warranting a consideration that it is "at home" in Illinois. Regarding specific jurisdiction, the court engaged in a more thorough analysis regarding the level of control exercised by the franchisor over the franchisee (despite the fact that Inspire Brands is not actually the franchisor), and ultimately found there was little to no control in this case. The court also analyzed under corporate law when jurisdictional "touch points" of a subsidiary can be imputed to the parent corporation, and found that where the corporate form is recognized and there is no control over the subsidiary, such imputation is unwarranted.

Barnett v. Vapor Maven OK 1, LLC, No. 21-CV-423-TCK-JFJ, 2022 WL 17740971 (N.D. Okla. Dec. 16, 2022). A former employee of a chain of sixteen vape stores sued a number of related individuals and corporate entities as joint employers, alleging they operated the vape store chain as a joint venture or general partnership under the trademark "Vapor Maven." The court denied the out-of-state defendants' motion to dismiss for lack of personal jurisdiction, finding that the "Vapor Maven" enterprise was a family business, run by a husband-and-wife team who owned and controlled a number of companies that indiscriminately shared resources in furtherance of that enterprise, rather than as atomistic corporate entities.

Braman Motors, Inc. v. BMW of North America, LLC, No. 17-23360-CIV, 2023 WL 3509818 (S.D. Fla. Apr. 28, 2023), *report and recommendation adopted*, 1:17-CV-23360, 2023 WL 3496807 (S.D. Fla. May 17, 2023) (The court denied the defendant BMW of North America, LLC's motion to dismiss claims solely for injunctive relief brought by franchisees under the Florida Motor Vehicle Dealer Act after the other claims for monetary relief were

CHAPTER 8

dismissed because diversity jurisdiction that exists at the time of filing is not divested by subsequent events, such as the change in the amount in controversy.) This case is discussed in Chapter 3, Section III.

CAO Lighting, Inc. v. Signify, N.V., No. 2:21-cv-08972-AB-SP, 628 F.Supp.3d 996, 2022 WL 16894500 (C.D. Cal. Sept. 19, 2022) (court granted defendant Signify, N.V.'s motion to dismiss for lack of personal jurisdiction, where defendant was only a holding company that did not design, manufacture market or sell any of the allegedly infringing lighting products, and did not direct or control the product design, development, manufacture, marketing or sales efforts of any of its subsidiaries, including Signify North America Corporation, which was involved in distributing the accused products in the U.S.).

Cutillo v. Cutillo, No. 5:21-CV-02787-JMG, 2023 WL 4306731 (E.D. Pa. June 30, 2023). A minority owner in a franchisor entity sued the franchisor and its majority owner for violating the Computer Fraud and Abuse Act ("CFAA"), along with related state law claims, after her email access was blocked. The court found on summary judgment that the plaintiff had failed to show that she had sustained the statutorily-required $5,000 in aggregate losses during a one-year period, as required to maintain a CFAA claim, and dismissed that claim. The court declined to extend supplemental jurisdiction to the remaining state law claims, which it dismissed without prejudice.

Dana Innovations v. Trends Electronics International Inc., No. 8:22-cv-02155-FWS-ADS, 2023 WL 3335909 (C.D. Cal. Apr. 21, 2023). Defendant sought to dismiss plaintiff's common counts claim under California law for lack of personal jurisdiction. Defendant was to be an exclusive distributor of plaintiff's audio electronics products, and plaintiff asserted the common counts claim, which is a simplified form of pleading to indicate the existence of a debt. While the other claims plaintiff raised were covered under a California forum selection clause in the agreement between the parties, defendant argued that there was a lack of personal jurisdiction over it as to the common counts claim because that was allegedly not covered by the agreement. The court disagreed, and determined that there was substantial overlap between plaintiff's breach of contract claim and the common counts claim. Thus, it held the common counts claim fell within the agreement and its forum selection clause. This case is discussed in Chapter 4, Section II.A.

Energium Health v. Gabali, No. 3:21-CV-2951-S, 2022 WL 16842660 (N.D. Tex. Nov. 9, 2022). Energium Health filed an action against two individuals,

Gabali and Alam, as well as several Michigan business entities associated with them. The parties had a commission agreement whereby Energium agreed to supply Hematology Oncology Global Services ("HOGS") with COVID testing supplies. Gabali would then procure customers and sell them the kits in exchange for a commission. The parties also had a billing contract that allowed one defendant to disburse money to the plaintiff as payment for the kits. Both the commission agreement and billing contract had choice of law and forum selection clauses stating that all claims and disputes were subject to jurisdiction in Texas, that disputes should be settled with the application of Texas law, and that the venue for all disputes should be in Texas. Energium claimed that Gabali and Alam were using their business entities to shield themselves from their obligations under the two agreements while continuing to benefit from them. It also claimed that it relied on false representations from Gabali about major testing contracts and subsequently invested in a testing laboratory, a call center, a warehouse, and equipment. The plaintiff maintained that the funding that Gabali received was transferred to other business entities for Gabali's personal use and gain.

The court held that the defendants were subject to minimum-contacts specific personal jurisdiction in Texas and denied their motion to transfer venue. Energium established personal jurisdiction over Gabali and HOGS because all of the alleged torts occurred in the course of either invoking a right or executing an obligation specified in the commission agreement. Second, the court held that by signing the forum selection clauses in one or both of the agreements, HOGS, Gabali, and another defendant, Diagnostic Hematology, P.C., consented to being subject to personal jurisdiction in Texas. Three other defendants were also found to be subject to personal jurisdiction in Texas because, while they were non-signatories, they were still bound by the clause. In reaching that conclusion, the court analyzed four factors: common ownership between the signatory and non-signatory; benefits obtained from the contract at issue; knowledge of the agreement; and awareness of the forum selection clause. The first three factors weighed in favor of applying the forum selection clauses to these defendants. Regarding the other defendants, the court held that they were also governed by the forum selection clause pursuant to an analysis conducted by the Seventh Circuit, which stated that a non-signatory defendant was closely related enough to invoke a forum selection clause if the defendant's partners' affiliates were signatories to the contract.

Franlink Inc. v. BACE Services., Inc., 50 F.4th 432 (5th Cir. 2022). The Fifth Circuit held that certain non-signatories to a franchise agreement could not be bound by the franchise agreement's forum selection clause, which meant that

CHAPTER 8

the district court did not have personal jurisdiction over those defendants. This case is discussed in Chapter 8, Section III.

Functional HIIT Fitness, LLC v. F45 Training Incorporated, No. 5:22-CV-10168, 2022 WL 17828930 (E.D. Mich. Oct. 26, 2022) (recommending dismissal of certain individual defendants based on lack of personal jurisdiction in the forum state). This case is discussed in Chapter 8, Section IV.

Gaska v. Darcars of Railroad Avenue, Inc., No. 3:22-cv-1201-MPS, 2023 WL 3493820 (D. Conn. May 17, 2023). Plaintiffs, who purchased a car from the defendant dealership, sued, on behalf of themselves and others similarly situated, defendant for violation of the Connecticut Unfair Trade Practices Act. They asserted that defendant had a practice of selling cars for more than their advertised price and also adding onto the sale price a commission or approximately two percent. In plaintiffs' case, this resulted in plaintiffs paying $2,764.23 more for their car. Defendant removed the case to federal court under the Class Action Fairness Act ("CAFA") and submitted a declaration in support of its removal notice. Plaintiffs moved to remand the case to state court, first arguing that defendant could not meet their burden of establishing that the damages in the case would exceed CAFA's $5 million threshold for removal. The court noted, however, that in its declaration, defendant stated that the potential class consisted of 3,862 car buyers and multiplying that by the damages plaintiffs suffered (which were likely on the low side of most buyers' claims) easily exceeded the threshold. Plaintiffs in the alternative argued that remand was required under CAFA's local controversy exception, because more than two-thirds of all class members are citizens of Connecticut. On this point, the court again pointed to the facts set forth in defendant's removal notice, which stated that more than one-half, but less than two-thirds, of the class members were Connecticut residents, and held that the exception did not apply. However, the court, after inviting supplemental briefing on the issue, declined to exercise jurisdiction and remanded the case to state court under CAFA's discretionary exception, which is available when greater than one-third but less than two-thirds of the proposed class and the primary defendant are citizens of the state and remand is in the interests of justice after considering the totality of the circumstances. Referring to it as the "discretionary home state exception," the court noted that the case involved only claims brought under Connecticut law, based on harm that occurred in Connecticut that was allegedly caused by a Connecticut corporation whose operations are in Connecticut, and Connecticut citizens represented the largest group of class members.

Issues Specific to Litigation and Arbitration

Gizmocup L.L.C. doing business as Northeast Pharma and Atlantic Pharm Co, LLC v. Medline Industries Inc., No. 2:21-cv-00213, 2023 WL 3687716 (D. Vt. May 26, 2023). Plaintiffs Gizmocup L.L.C. d/b/a Northeast Pharma and Atlantic Pharma Co LLC (collectively, "Plaintiffs") brought this action against Medline Industries Inc. ("Medline") alleging tortious interference with contractual relations and defamation. Plaintiffs' claims stem from complaints that Medline filed with Amazon.com ("Amazon") alleging that plaintiffs were selling counterfeit goods on Amazon's website. Medline, formed in Delaware and headquartered in Illinois, filed a motion to dismiss challenging personal jurisdiction, as all of its actions took place outside of Vermont, and failure to state a claim.

     Plaintiffs ordered genuine Medline products from an authorized Medline distributor, and Medline directly filled the order. Plaintiffs then began selling the products through its store on the Amazon website. When Medline discovered this, it filed a complaint with Amazon, alleging that the products infringed on its Medline trademark and were counterfeit products. In response, Amazon removed the products from plaintiffs' Amazon store. Plaintiffs then provided Amazon with proof of the authenticity of the products and attempted to do the same with Medline. Amazon then permitted plaintiffs to relist the products on their Amazon store.

Medline then sent a letter to plaintiffs stating that Medline distributors were not permitted to sell Medline products that were intended for resale on the Internet, and that "Unauthorized Resellers who induce Authorized Medline Distributors to sell Medline products to them for resale on the Internet tortiously interfere with the Distributor Agreement." With this letter, Medline knew that plaintiffs' products were authentic Medline products, but that plaintiffs had not been approved as resellers. On receipt of this letter, plaintiffs contacted Medline to begin the process of becoming an authorized reseller. One month later, Medline filed a second complaint with Amazon, alleging that plaintiffs' Medline products were counterfeit. In response, Amazon completely shut down plaintiffs' Amazon store, precluding sales of all of its products, not just the Medline products, and froze its Amazon seller account funds, thereby preventing plaintiff's from paying their vendors and employees. plaintiffs store front was shut down for about two weeks. This litigation followed.

     As to personal jurisdiction in Vermont over the Illinois based Medline, the court noted that its analysis included two parts, the minimum contacts with the forum and the reasonableness of exercising jurisdiction. If the conduct that gives rise to liability occurs entirely outside the forum, courts may employ the "effects test," which permits a court to assert specific

CHAPTER 8

personal jurisdiction over a defendant if the defendant expressly aimed its conduct at the forum. The "effects test" theory of personal jurisdiction is typically invoked where the conduct that forms the basis for the controversy occurs entirely out-of-forum, and the only relevant jurisdictional contacts with the forum are therefore in-forum effects harmful to the plaintiff. By the time of the April Complaint, Medline knew or reasonably should have known that it was shipping its products to an unauthorized distributor in Vermont and that its allegedly false communications to Amazon that plaintiffs were selling counterfeit products arose out of those shipments and pertained to them, and that its allegedly false and defamatory statements affected the reputation of and caused financial harm to a company doing business in Vermont. The court found that Medline thereby created its own contacts with the forum and that plaintiffs had plausibly alleged that Medline was not seeking to safeguard the authenticity of its products; it was seeking to disrupt a Vermont company's ability to re-sell its products on Amazon's website. Plaintiffs plausibly allege that Medline directed its activities at the forum, knowing that a Vermont business would suffer injury in Vermont as a result of its false accusations of counterfeiting to Amazon. These allegations were sufficient to establish the minimum contacts necessary for specific personal jurisdiction over Medline based on the "effects test."

As to the tortious interference claim, the court found that plaintiffs plausibly alleged that by the second complaint, Medline knew plaintiffs had a contractual relationship with Amazon and that Amazon had suspended plaintiffs' Amazon storefront solely because of Medline's improper claim of counterfeiting. Finally, as to the defamation claim, the court noted that statements that falsely accuse a plaintiff of committing a crime (i.e., counterfeiting) are defamatory per se. Medline had alleged that its complaints to Amazon were absolutely privileged because they were pre-litigation statements. The court noted that the privilege is conditional and could be defeated by showing malice in one of two ways: knowledge of the statement's falsity or with reckless disregard of the truth, or conduct manifesting personal ill will, reckless or wanton disregard of plaintiff's rights, or carried out under circumstances evidencing insult or oppression. Plaintiffs had cited Amazon's own definition of counterfeiting and Medline's knowledge of that definition to support their contention that Medline knew its accusations were false. Plaintiffs further alleged that they had notified Medline that its false allegations were harming their business and employees, and Medline refused to rectify that harm, thereby allegedly demonstrating a reckless disregard for plaintiffs' rights. The court found these allegations sufficient and denied Medline's motion to dismiss.

Good Clean Love, Inc. v. Epoch NE Corporation and Lawrence Luo, Civ. No. 6:21-cv-01294-AA, 2023 WL 2709653 (D. Or. Mar. 30, 2023). Epoch NE Corporation ("Epoch") was a former distributor for Good Clean Love, Inc. ("GCL") and had attempted, unsuccessfully, to distribute GCL's feminine products in the Chinese market under a Distribution Agreement with GCL from November 2016 until the Distribution Agreement expired in February 2019. Within months after the expiration of the Distribution Agreement, Epoch filed a U.S. trademark application for "Feminilove", and later for "FeminiCare", for products that were substantially similar to those that Epoch had distributed for GCL. Epoch then began distributing its new products in China and in the U.S. through Amazon, using substantially similar formulas, product packaging and marketing claims, and using the same company that provided packaging services to GCL.

GCL filed suit against Epoch for trademark infringement under the Lanham Act, common law trade dress infringement, conversion, common law unfair competition, common law unfair trade practices, breach of contract, and tortious interference with contract. Defendant Lawrence Luo ("Luo"), an officer of Epoch, alleged that the court did not have specific personal jurisdiction over him, as he had acted only as an officer of Epoch, and not on his own behalf. The court noted that it could exercise specific jurisdiction over him if he had purposefully directed his activities at residents of the forum, and the litigation resulted from alleged injuries that arise out of or relate to those activities. The court used a three-part test to evaluate specific personal jurisdiction: (1) The non-resident defendant must purposefully direct his or her activities or consummate some transaction with the forum or a resident thereof; or perform some act by which he or she purposefully avails himself or herself of the privilege of conducting activities in the forum, thereby invoking the benefits and protections of its laws; (2) The claim must be one that arises out of or relates to the defendant's forum-related activities; and (3) The exercise of jurisdiction must comport with fair play and substantial justice.

With regard to the first part of the test, the court noted that it could meet this test in either of two ways: either the nonresident defendant must purposefully direct his or her activities at the forum state, or the defendant must purposefully avail himself or herself of the privilege of conducting activities in the forum. "Purposeful direction" is only available in claims of intentional tort. GCL based its allegation of personal jurisdiction over Luo using the purposeful direction test and alleged that Luo had engaged in tortious activities, as his actions in acting merely as an officer of Epoch would be insufficient to establish specific personal jurisdiction over him individually. The court agreed with GCL, noting that a corporate officer is,

CHAPTER 8

in general, personally liable for all torts that he authorizes or directs or in which he participates, even if he acted as an agent of the corporation and not on his own behalf. The court found that Luo was the "primary participant" and "central figure" in the alleged torts, even though he acted as an officer of Epoch.

G&S Beshay Trading Co., LLC v. 7-Eleven, Inc., No. 18cv3909 (EP(JRA) 2023 WL 3735959 (D.N.J. May 31, 2023). Following the dismissal of the plaintiff franchisee's claims, the court adopted a report and recommendation that it should exercise supplemental jurisdiction over the only remaining claims in the action, which were defendant's compulsory counterclaims against the plaintiff franchisee. The plaintiff argued against the exercise of supplemental jurisdiction primarily because the amount in controversy was now less than the $75,000 requirement for diversity jurisdiction. The court rejected plaintiff's argument, noting that it had discretion in the exercise of supplemental jurisdiction and briefly evaluated and applied a four-factor test regarding what would best serve the principles of 1) judicial economy; 2) procedural convenience; 3) fairness; and 4) comity. Relying on the case's lengthy procedural history as underscoring the fairness in keeping the case in federal court, the court adopted the report and recommendation regarding its exercising supplemental jurisdiction.

Hyundai Motor America Corp. v. EFN West Palm Motor Sales, LLC, No. CV 20-82102, 2022 WL 604071 (S.D. Fla. Mar. 1, 2022) (EFN West Palm Motor Sales, LLC ("EFN") sued Jose Munoz ("Munoz"), President and Chief Executive Officer of Hyundai Motor America Corporation, for allegedly conspiring to interfere with EFN's contractual relationship with Hyundai. Munoz argued for summary judgment because he stated the court lacked personal jurisdiction over him as a non-resident of Florida without sufficient minimum contacts with Florida. The court granted Munoz's motion for summary judgment).

Luxury Concepts, Inc. v. Bateel International, LLC, No. 22-10793, 2023 WL 360649 (E.D. Mich. May 23, 2023). Plaintiff entered into two franchise agreements with defendants in Michigan and Texas, which granted plaintiff the "sole right to develop retail outlets and e-commerce presence and business for the sale and promotion of products" in those states. Defendants are based in the United Arab Emirates and the agreements contained choice of law provisions applying the laws of the United Arab Emirates. When plaintiff brought a suit for breach of contract against the defendant franchisor and its officers and directors, defendants asserted a lack of personal jurisdiction defense. The court determined that it could not exercise personal jurisdiction over the officers and directors because plaintiff did not adequately plead that they had personal contacts with the state of Michigan. The fact that their company did business in Michigan was not sufficient to support personal jurisdiction over the individual defendants without more specific, individualized accusations. The court, however, determined that there was personal jurisdiction over Bateel International, LLC because the franchise agreement established that the company purposefully availed itself of the privilege of acting in the state of Michigan or causing consequences in the state.

Proximo Spirits, Inc. v. Green Lake Brewing Co., LLC, No. 2:22-cv-02879-SPG-SK, 2022 WL 17224545 (C.D. Cal. Sept. 9, 2022). Plaintiff, a Delaware corporation with its principal place of business in New Jersey, makes and sells various brands of liquor and alcohol, including KRAKEN brand rums. Plaintiff owns several trademarks relevant to its KRAKEN brand. Plaintiff sued Green Lake, a craft brewery based in the state of Washington and which in 2019 began selling SKY KRAKEN Hazy Pale Ale, for trademark infringement and related claims in California, which is the largest and most important market for Plaintiff with respect to the sale of its KRAKEN goods. In denying Green Lake's motion to dismiss for lack of personal jurisdiction, the court focused on, among other things, the fact that Green Lake, while not having many direct contacts with California, had in 2020 and 2022 strategically entered into distributor agreements with two California companies, one that enabled Green Lake's SKY KRAKEN and other products to be sold in various parts of southern California, and one that enabled Green Lake's products to be sold in northern California. The court found this to be evidence that Green Lake had directed its actions to the forum state, satisfying the "purposeful direction" test, and one of the elements for finding specific jurisdiction to exist. The court further found that defendant knew its conduct was likely to cause harm to plaintiff in California, plaintiff's trademark claims arose from defendant's California-related activities, and its exercise of jurisdiction over defendant was reasonable under the circumstances.

Stingray IP Solutions, LLC v. TP-Link Technologies Co., Ltd., Nos. 2:21-CV-00045-JRG, 00046-JRG, 2022 WL 17357774 (E.D. Tex. Oct. 13, 2022). The court granted in part the motion to dismiss for lack of personal jurisdiction filed by defendants, Chinese companies accused of selling networking devices that infringed plaintiff's patent. Plaintiff argued personal jurisdiction was proper due to Defendants having a distribution agreement with an independent, non-party entity in California whose "entire function is . . . to

CHAPTER 8

sell products in the United States" and that imported defendants' products into the U.S., placed them into the stream of commerce in the U.S., and sold them to various customers, including a small number in Texas. The court held that the Plaintiff had failed to show that the defendants did anything more than "simply place their products into the stream of commerce - in Asia - and thereafter through a non-party U.S. distributor." Under these facts, the court held that the exercise of personal jurisdiction over defendants in Texas would be unreasonable.

III. Venue and Choice of Forum

Aerial Adventure Technologies, LLC v. C3 Manufacturing, LLC, No. 523CV00018KDBDSC, 2023 WL 3267750 (W.D.N.C. Apr. 14, 2023), *report and recommendation adopted*, No. 523CV00018KDBSCR, 2023 WL 3562978 (W.D.N.C. May 19, 2023) (enforcing forum selection clause in distributor agreement and remanding case back to state court).

AFC Franchising, LLC v. Purugganan, No. 2:20-CV-00456-JHE, 2023 WL 373873 (N.D. Ala. Jan. 24, 2023). Plaintiff AFC Franchising, LLC ("AFC") commenced an action against Danilo Purugganan ("Purugganan") in the Circuit Court of Shelby County, Alabama, asserting two counts for declaratory judgment concerning provisions of a Master Development Agreement and one count for attorneys' fees and costs. Purugganan then removed the action to the U.S. District Court for the Northern District of Alabama. Following a lengthy procedural battle, the court ruled that AFC's declaratory judgment action was an improper anticipatory action and that the applicable discretionary factors weighed against the court hearing it. The court therefore transferred the case to the United States District Court for the District of Connecticut—where the parties were also litigating the same dispute.

In August 2009, Purugganan executed a Master Developer Agreement ("MDA") with franchisor Doctors Express Franchising, LLC ("DEF") wherein Purugganan obtained the rights to develop and manage DEF urgent care centers. After a series of acquisitions, AFC took assignment of DEF's interest in the MDA. The parties succeeded to the terms of the MDA, including a "floating" forum selection that required the litigation to commence in the state in which AFC had its "principal place of business at the time the action is commenced." A dispute then arose between AFC and Purugganan over the interpretation of certain provisions in the MDA, and the parties engaged in negotiations. Purugganan threatened to file suit in venues other than Alabama, which AFC regarded as a breach of the MDA's forum selection clause.

Due to Purugganan's alleged threat, AFC filed its declaratory judgment action against Purugganan in the Circuit Court of Shelby County, Alabama, in March 2020. AFC's primary claim was for a declaratory judgment that the MDA's forum selection clause requires the parties to litigate any contract disputes in Alabama. Shortly thereafter, Purugganan filed suit against AFC in the United States District Court for the District of Connecticut. In the Connecticut complaint, Purugganan asserted thirteen claims against AFC related to the MDA. Purugganan asserted that he sued in the District of Connecticut because, among other reasons, all franchise businesses that he developed and managed pursuant to the MDA were in Connecticut and New York. Purugganan also removed the Shelby County action to the Northern District of Alabama based on diversity jurisdiction. He then moved to dismiss the Shelby County action for lack of personal jurisdiction and improper venue or, alternatively, to transfer this action to the District of Connecticut.

AFC countered that the forum selection clause in the MDA defeated Purugganan's attempt to dismiss the Shelby County action or transfer it to Connecticut. AFC argued that the forum selection clause unequivocally required Purugganan to litigate any disputes in Alabama because that is where AFC's principal place of business was located. AFC asserted that the forum selection clause was enforceable and required litigation in Alabama even though DEF had its principal place of business in Maryland at the time the MDA was executed and later assigned its interest in the MDA to AFC. AFC thus moved to remand the action back to the Circuit Court for Shelby County, Alabama, based on the forum selection clause.

In September 2020, the court denied AFC's motion to remand and granted Purugganan's motion to dismiss. The court granted Purugganan's motion to dismiss for lack of personal jurisdiction, reasoning that Purugganan did not have sufficient contacts with Alabama and the forum selection clause did not subject him to suit in Alabama.

AFC appealed that dismissal for lack of personal jurisdiction and the Eleventh Circuit reversed. First, the Eleventh Circuit concluded that the forum-selection clause was applicable to the suit in the Northern District of Alabama, where AFC had its principal place of business. The Eleventh Circuit described the forum selection clause as "floating" because it tied the chosen forum to a mutable fact—here, the franchisor's principal place of business. Next, the Eleventh Circuit determined that the forum selection clause was enforceable. Because the forum selection clause would otherwise apply, Purugganan had "the burden of demonstrating—by a strong showing—that enforcement would be 'unfair or unreasonable under the circumstances.'" The

CHAPTER 8

Eleventh Circuit held that Purugganan did not satisfy this burden. The Eleventh Circuit concluded that Purugganan knew generally that the litigation forum could change over the 15-year life of the contract, the bargained-for forum would depend on the location of the franchisor's principal place of business at the time the action was commenced, and the franchisor could assign its rights and obligations under the agreement to a third party without restriction.

The Eleventh Circuit further concluded that Purugganan voluntarily agreed to an applicable and enforceable floating forum-selection clause, and therefore waived his right to contest personal jurisdiction and venue in this case. Accordingly, the Eleventh Circuit reversed the Northern District of Alabama's dismissal for lack of personal jurisdiction.

On remand, the Northern District of Alabama nevertheless declined to hear AFC's complaint for a declaratory judgment regarding the forum-selection clause. In doing so, the court explained that the federal Declaratory Judgment Act does not require a court to accept jurisdiction over a declaratory judgment claim. Instead, a district court has discretion in deciding whether to entertain an action under the Act. The court also found that, although there is a strong presumption that favors the forum of the first-filed suit under the "first-filed rule," an exception may apply where the first-filed action is in anticipation of the other pending proceeding."

In conducting its analysis, the court noted that before AFC filed this action, Purugganan's attorney sent AFC a notice demanding mediation after Purugganan learned that AFC intended to purchase franchises for itself in the territory covered by the MDA. Purugganan's attorney requested a response from AFC concerning mediation within ten business days. That same day, Purugganan's attorney sent a separate letter to AFC indicating that Purugganan was prepared to file suit in Connecticut or New York if AFC did not respond to the mediation demand.

These letters reflect that, absent an attempt at mediation, Purugganan intended to file a coercive lawsuit and that AFC was aware of that intention when it decided to file the action in Shelby County, Alabama, one week later and before the 10-day response period in the mediation demand expired. The day after AFC filed its complaint, AFC's attorney sent an email to Purugganan's attorney stating that AFC would not participate in mediation. In the court's view, AFC had thus walked away from discussions and an opportunity to mediate in order to file suit in its preferred forum.

Although the majority opinion in the Eleventh Circuit Court of Appeal's decision determined that Purugganan's personal jurisdiction and venue defenses lacked merit, the majority did not address the impact of an improper anticipatory filing on the exercise of the court's discretion under the

Declaratory Judgment Act. As noted by the court, this discretionary issue is separate and distinct from the personal jurisdiction and venue questions.

The court thus ruled that AFC could not rely on the deference typically given to a plaintiff's choice of forum, because AFC had filed an improper anticipatory action. The court therefore ruled that AFC's anticipatory filing was a compelling circumstance that warranted an exception to the first-filed rule. The court thus held that trial efficiency and the interests of justice, based on the totality of the circumstances, weighed in favor of transferring the entire action to the District of Connecticut. For these reasons, the court declined to exercise jurisdiction over AFC's claims for declaratory judgment and transferred the case.

Ecovirux LLC v. Biopledge LLC, 357 So.3d 182 (Fla. Dist. Ct. App. 2022), reh'g denied (Feb. 15, 2023) (Affirming dismissal for improper venue in an action brought by a distributor against a supplier and supplier's owners, alleging breach of contract, fraud, conspiracy to commit fraud, negligent misrepresentation, and violation of Florida Deceptive and Unfair Trade Practices Act. On appeal, the court affirmed enforcement of the mandatory forum selection clause where the provision referenced "the exclusive venue," and the supplier company's owners named as defendants were also entitled to enforce the venue selection provision as non-signatories because all claims stemmed directly from the contract.)

Energium Health v. Gabali, No. 3:21-CV-2951-S, 2022 WL 16842660 (N.D. Tex. Nov. 9, 2022). The court held that transfer of venue was not proper, because the signatory defendants were bound by forum selection clauses in the agreements at issue requiring all disputes to be brought in Texas, and the non-signatory defendants were closely related to the signatory defendants. The court also concluded that for reasons of judicial economy, all of the claims should be determined within a single lawsuit. This case is discussed in Chapter 8, Section II.

In ***Flick v. Sterling***, No. 3:22-CV-00039, 2022 WL 4593097 (W.D. Va. Sept. 29, 2022), the court granted Defendant's motion to transfer a libel claim to the Northern District of Illinois, where litigation involving breach of the parties' franchise agreement was already pending. The court found that the similar factual allegations and potential witnesses who had relevant knowledge regarding the libel and breach of the franchise agreement claims justified the transfer and that it was in the interests of justice, since both claims arose from and related to the breakdown in the parties' franchise relationship.

CHAPTER 8

Fogle Enterprises Inc. v. Cici Enterprises, L.P., No. 6:22-cv-03134-MDH, 2022 WL 5246446 (W.D. Mo., October 6, 2022). Plaintiff franchisee filed a complaint in the Western District of Missouri against the franchisor seeking declaratory judgment, injunctive relief and damages based on the franchisee's allegations that the franchisor wrongfully terminated the franchise agreement. The franchisor moved to dismiss the complaint on the basis that the franchise agreement contained a mandatory forum selection provision requiring litigation to be brought in Texas. In opposing the motion to dismiss, the franchisee argued that the forum selection provision in the franchise agreement was unenforceable because it was "unjust, unreasonable, or invalid for reasons such as fraud and overreaching". In support of its argument, the franchisee cited to Missouri statute Section 407.405 which is "designed to regulate the marketplace to the advantage of those traditionally thought to have unequal bargaining power as well as those who may fall victim to unfair business practices." The court rejected the franchisee's argument on the basis that the franchisee and franchisor negotiated the terms of the franchise agreement, and the complaint did not include any allegations of fraud, coercion or that the franchise agreement was otherwise unjust or unreasonable. The court further reasoned that the franchisee's claims did not involve "allegations concerning the protection of those traditionally thought to have unequal bargaining power or those who may fall victim to unfair business practices." As a result, the court granted the franchisor's motion to dismiss.

Franlink Inc. v. BACE Services, Inc., 50 F.4th 432 (5th Cir. 2022). A franchisor ("Link") brought suit in the U.S. District Court for the Southern District of Texas based on the forum-selection clause in its franchise agreement, naming as defendants the signatories to the franchise agreement and three non-signatories. Link's claims were based on the covenant not to compete and the non-solicitation provisions in the franchise agreement.

The dispute arose when the franchisee ("BACE") purported to terminate the franchise agreement, and the franchisee's principals ("the Wells'") began to operate a competitive company ("PayDay") while also diverting and soliciting customers of Link. When Link learned of these activities, it formally terminated the franchise agreement. Separately, the Wells' son ("Morton"), who had been a manager at BACE, became a branch manager of a separate competitive business ("JTL"), which was operating in the same territory as the BACE franchise. Link thus filed suit in the Southern District of Texas against the signatories to the franchise agreement (BACE and the Wells'), and the non-signatories PayDay, Morton, and JTL.

Issues Specific to Litigation and Arbitration

The non-signatory defendants (PayDay, Morton, and JTL) filed a motion to dismiss for lack of personal jurisdiction, arguing that the forum selection clause in the franchise agreement did not apply to them. The district court denied the motion, and in doing so held that the forum selection clause applied to the non-signatories because they were "so closely related" to the signatories that it was "foreseeable" that they would be bound by it. After a four-day bench trial, the district court granted each of Link's claims against all defendants. As a remedy, the district court issued injunctive relief to enforce the non-compete and non-solicitation provisions and awarded Link $378,562.22 in damages, $731,295.30 in attorney's fees, and $113,484.04 in costs.

On appeal to the U.S. Court of Appeals for the Fifth Circuit, the court first formally adopted the "closely related doctrine" as an equitable doctrine that permits a party to enforce a forum selection clause against non-signatories to a franchise agreement under certain circumstances. As set out by the Fifth Circuit, those circumstances may be found where a non-signatory enjoys a sufficiently close nexus to the dispute or to another signatory to the franchise agreement such that the non-signatory should have foreseen that they would be bound by the forum selection clause.

After formally recognizing the doctrine, the Fifth Circuit then reversed the trial court's entry of judgment against Morton and JTL on the basis that they were not sufficiently close to the signatories of the franchise agreement such that Morton and JTL could properly be bound by the "closely related doctrine." This in turn meant that the trial court lacked personal jurisdiction over Morton and JTL, because the forum selection clause was determinative on the issue of personal jurisdiction.

First, the Fifth Circuit held that Morton could not be bound by the forum selection clause under the closely-related doctrine. In doing so, the court noted that Morton was not an owner of BACE, but rather only an employee. Morton also did not receive a direct benefit from the franchise agreement itself, and no evidence was presented that Morton was aware of the franchise agreement's forum selection clause. Second, the Fifth Circuit held that JTL could not be bound by the forum selection clause in the franchise agreement. JTL was fully owned by a non-party to the litigation and had not received any direct benefit from the franchise agreement. JTL was also not aware of the forum selection clause in the franchise agreement.

The Fifth Circuit nevertheless affirmed the trial court's ruling that PayDay could be bound by the forum selection clause in the franchise agreement. As to PayDay, the Fifth Circuit noted that PayDay was fully owned by the Wells' and thus received a direct benefit from the franchise

CHAPTER 8

agreement. And through the Wells', PayDay was also aware of the forum selection clause.

The court then reversed and remanded on the issue of the amount of damages awarded by the district court against BACE and PayDay (the Wells' had filed for individual bankruptcy and were dismissed from the appeal). First, the Fifth Circuit held that the district court erred in awarding the full amount of Link's requested damages, because the franchise agreement entitled Link to only a percentage of the BACE's receivables. Second, the court reversed and vacated the district court's award of future damages in the amount of $147,900 based on claims for breach of a covenant not to compete, because the district court had awarded Link a permanent injunction, which did not allow for a separate award of future damages. Finally, the court reversed and remanded the issue of the proper amount of attorney's fees to be awarded to Link in light of the holdings by the Fifth Circuit, which significantly altered the results achieved by Link's attorneys.

Hofbräuhaus of America, LLC. v. Oak Tree Management Services, Inc., No. 2:22-cv-000421, 2023 WL 24179 (D. Nev. Jan. 3, 2023). The court ultimately concluded that venue should be transferred to the Southern District of Illinois because the material events took place in Illinois and the franchise at issue was located in Illinois, holding that in trademark infringement cases, the place where the infringing activity occurs is generally the correct venue. This case is discussed in Chapter 5, Section VI.

Jackson Hewitt Inc. v. Active Personal Taxes, Inc., No. 22-CV-02354, 2022 WL 17490540 (D.N.J. Dec. 6, 2022). Plaintiff franchisor sued terminated franchisee and its guarantors in the District of New Jersey for liquidated damages and other damages allegedly owed under the parties' franchise agreement. Defendants moved to dismiss the case for improper venue or to transfer the case to the U.S. District Court for the Northern District of Illinois, where defendants and their terminated franchise were located. The court dismissed the defendants' motion, as it could not conclude that the events that had occurred in New Jersey, where plaintiff franchisor has its headquarters, were insubstantial or tangential to plaintiff's claims.

Jackson Hewitt Inc. v. New Age Taxes, Inc., No. 22-cv-2352, 2022 WL 17069801 (D.N.J. Nov. 17, 2022). Plaintiff and franchisor Jackson Hewitt, which is based in New Jersey, sued its former franchisee which operated two Jackson Hewitt tax preparation franchises in Illinois, for breach of contract, for allegedly failing to perform several post-termination obligations.. The franchisee moved to dismiss for improper venue or, in the alternative, to transfer the case to Illinois. Defendants contended that the relevant events and conduct (giving rise to the terminations) occurred in Illinois, where the franchises operated. Jackson Hewitt argued in response that a substantial part of the relevant events occurred in New Jersey, where it claimed it rendered services under the parties' franchise agreements, including training and support, where Jackson Hewitt executed the agreements and performed its obligations under them, where defendants called and emailed plaintiff, and from where Jackson Hewitt directed and conducted a post-termination audit. The court did not find such conduct to be tangential to plaintiff's claims, and concluded that Defendants had not met their burden of demonstrating that New Jersey was an improper venue.

Jackson Hewitt Inc. v. O & W Taxes, Inc., No. 22-cv-02350, 2022 WL 17466428 (D.N.J. Dec. 5, 2022). This matter arose from franchise agreements between plaintiff, franchisor Jackson Hewitt Inc. ("JHI"), and defendant, franchisee O&W Taxes, Inc. ("OWTI") and various individual defendants, (collectively, "defendants"). Plaintiff alleged breach of contract, misappropriation of trade secrets, and breach of guaranty in connection with two franchise agreements. JHI and OWTI were the parties to the franchise agreements, and each individual defendant was a guarantor of OWTI's obligations to Jackson Hewitt. The franchise agreements authorized OWTI to operate a Jackson Hewitt income tax preparation business in two separate Illinois territories, included a general right for JHI to inspect and audit the books and records of OWTI, and further provided that defendants would bear the costs of the audit if the defendants failed to comply with their obligations under the agreements. In 2020, Jackson Hewitt learned of potential wrongdoing by the defendants and exercised its rights under the franchise agreements to inspect and audit OWTI's books and records. JHI alleged that the audit substantiated the alleged misconduct. JHI then terminated the agreements effective July 16, 2022.

An addendum to the franchise agreements had been executed by the parties in 2019, and deleted a section of the agreements and substituted a new clause with respect to venue and jurisdiction. More specifically, the relevant clause of the addendum provided that defendants consented to venue and personal jurisdiction in all litigation brought by JHI in: the appropriate federal or state court in Illinois; the state or county court of any city or county where defendants have their principal place of business (which was Morris County, NJ); and the U.S. District Court nearest to defendant's principal place of business (which was the District of NJ, Newark Division). The addendum further provided that "all litigation brought against" JHI and arising out of the

CHAPTER 8

parties' franchise relationship "shall be brought and venue shall be proper only in the[se] [] courts and no others."

Defendants moved to transfer this case to the U.S. District Court for the Northern District of Illinois pursuant to 28 U.S.C. § 1404(a), which governs changes of venue "for the convenience of the parties," and argued that the terms of the addendum required such transfer. The court therefore analyzed whether the addendum mandated that actions arising out of the franchise agreements had to be brought in Illinois and whether Illinois is a permissive or mandatory forum under the contract. Focusing on the agreements' plain language, the court found that the addendum provided that defendants "consent to venue and personal jurisdiction in all litigation brought by JHI" and arising out of the franchise agreements "in the following courts," which included both the appropriate federal or state court in Illinois *and* the District of New Jersey. Thus, the clause did not obligate JHI to bring any litigation in Illinois. Under the relevant clause, the defendants also waived any objections to venue or personal jurisdiction in the listed courts.

The district court ultimately denied the motion and cited several of the private and public factors courts consider in determining whether transfer of venue is appropriate under § 1404(a). For instance, the defendants made several "conclusory statements" in support of their motion, such as the fact that the convenience of the parties and witnesses would be met if defendants and defendants' witnesses would not have to travel "half[-]way across the country" to litigate in the plaintiff's home forum and that all of the facts forming the basis of plaintiff's complaint occurred in Illinois. As such, the court held that the defendants failed to meet their burden of demonstrating that Illinois is a more convenient forum.

JTH Tax, LLC v. Leggat, No. 2:22-CV-41 (RCY), 2022 WL 3970197 (E.D. Va. Aug. 31, 2022) (despite franchise agreement's choice of law provision stating that Virginia law applies, the court held that California law would be applied to a dispute between plaintiff franchisor and defendant, plaintiff's former franchisee, because of a California Addendum to the agreement that said if there was a conflict with the agreement and California law, California law would take precedence over the contract's choice of law provision). This case is discussed more fully in Section III of this Chapter.

JTH Tax, LLC, d/b/a Liberty Tax Service v. Lowensky Cortorreal, No. 4:23-cv-0173-P, 2023 WL 4673278 (N.D. Tex. Fort Worth Division July 20, 2023. The court in this case made short work of Lowensky Cortorreal's ("Cortorreal") motion to transfer venue. JTH Tax, LLC ("Liberty Tax") filed suit in Texas against Cortorreal, a former franchisee, seeking to prevent

Cortorreal from violating the post-termination provisions of the franchise agreement. In granting Cortorreal's motion to transfer the case to Virginia, the court colorfully explained: "Each franchise agreement at issue in this case 'unequivocally chooses' the state law of Virginia as its governing law and the state or federal courts of Virginia as their jurisdiction and venue of choice. And as is regular practice, this court will honor the choice of law and venue provisions of a voluntarily executed contract. It is truly perplexing to this court how such a collection of agreements from Norfolk sailed their way to the Trinity River of North Texas. This court would refer plaintiff's counsel to the most fundamental canon of contractual construction: 'words mean stuff.' Applying this, they may then find that-even in 2023-contracts still bind a party, agreements still carry weight, and proofreading is still a good idea."

JTH Tax, LLC v. Younan, No. 2:22cv383 2023 WL 3069767 (E.D. Va. Mar. 1, 2023). The court denied the defendant's motion to dismiss for improper venue or in the alternative to transfer forum, finding that the requisite "substantial part of the events" which gave rise to the claim occurred in its district. The court further noted that federal law rather than state law governs the venue analysis and venue may be proper in multiple judicial districts. The franchise agreement included a forum selection clause and the court upheld it, noting the party challenging its application bears a "heavy burden of proof."

Kava Culture Franchise Grp. Corp. v. Dar-Jkta Enterprises LLC, No. 2:23-CV-278-JLB-KCD, 2023 WL 3568598, at *1 (M.D. Fla. May 18, 2023) (The Federal District Court for the Middle District of Florida dismissed the franchisor's complaint against the parties to the franchise agreement on the basis that the franchise's agreements forum selection clause was mandatory and required that all litigation between the parties be brought in "the Lee County, Fort Myers, Florida;" thus, forum did not include a federal court in Lee County Florida.)

LG2, LLC v. American Dairy Queen Corporation, No. 22-cv-1044 (WMW/JFD), 2023 WL 171792 (D. Minn. Jan. 12, 2023), the franchisee brought an action against the franchisor in the district where the franchisor was located, and after weighing the four transfer factors applied by 28 U.S.C. § 1404(a), the court denied the franchisor's motion to transfer to the venue where the franchisee restaurant was located. This case is discussed in Chapter 2, Section II.

Luxury Concepts, Inc. v. Bateel International, LLC, No. 22-10793, 2023 WL 360649 (E.D. Mich. May 23, 2023). Plaintiff entered into two franchise

CHAPTER 8

agreements with defendants in Michigan and Texas that contained choice of law provisions applying the laws of the United Arab Emirates ("UAE"). The court determined that because the applicable law was that of the UAE, Michigan's interests were not fundamental, and courts of the UAE would be far more experienced in applying the laws of the UAE. The court therefore dismissed the action for forum non conveniens. This case is discussed in Chapter 8, Section II.

Marina Group LLC v. Shirley May International US Inc., No. 2:21-cv-18733 (BRM) (MAH), 2022 WL 17622679 (D.N.J. Dec. 13, 2022). Plaintiff contended it had an exclusive distributor agreement with defendant Swiss Arabian, a manufacturer of perfumes based in the United Arab Emirates. Plaintiff imported substantial amounts of Swiss Arabian's products, spent a considerable amount in marketing the products in the United States, and sold the products through its website and Amazon. In 2021, plaintiff placed an order with Swiss Arabian for perfumes and related products, and paid a portion of the price for them in advance. Swiss Arabian then requested that plaintiff pay the remaining amount owed, which it did. However, at some point thereafter, while the order was in transit, the consignee of the shipment was changed from plaintiff to another entity, and plaintiff never received the goods. It was also unable to obtain replacement products in time for the important holiday season. Plaintiff sued Swiss Arabian and other entities involved in the shipping of the products in question for conversion, breach of contract and other claims. Defendants moved to dismiss, arguing that the terms and conditions that were part of the bill of lading for the shipment at issue contained a forum selection clause providing that any claims arising from the bill of lading had to be determined exclusively in the courts of Hamburg, Germany. While the plaintiff was the original consignee on the bill of lading, it was not a party to the bill, rather the bill was between the shipper and the carrier.

The court first held that while federal law controls the question of whether to enforce a forum selection clause, state law determines the scope of the clause, including the question of whether the clause applies to a non-signatory as an intended beneficiary or a closely related party. But whether plaintiff was an intended beneficiary of the bill of lading or not, the court agreed with plaintiff that it was not suing on the bill of lading, rather it was suing under and to enforce the distributorship agreement between plaintiff and Swiss Arabian. Given that and the fact that plaintiff was not a signatory to the bill of lading, the court held that the forum selection clause in the bill did not apply to mandate a transfer of the case to the Hamburg courts.

Metro Chrysler Plymouth, Inc. v. FCA US LLC, No. 22-CV-05646 (HG), 2022 WL 16834572 (E.D.N.Y. Nov. 9, 2022). Metro Chrysler Plymouth, Inc. ("M-C"), a car dealership based in Queens, New York, sued vehicle manufacturer FCA US LLC ("FCA") in New York State court, alleging that FCA violated the New York Franchised Motor Vehicle Dealer Act ("Dealer Act") by planning on allowing another dealership, South Shore Autoplex LLC ("South Shore") to relocate into M-C's market area. M-C joined South Shore as an indispensable party to the action. FCA then removed the case to the United States District Court for the Eastern District of New York on the basis of diversity of citizenship. M-C filed a motion to remand on the basis that both M-C and South Shore are citizens of New York, and South Shore was an indispensable party. FCA countered that South Shore had been fraudulently joined for the sole purpose of defeating federal diversity jurisdiction.

The District Court granted M-C's motion for remand, concluding that South Shore was in fact an indispensable party, and therefore there was no diversity of citizenship. The court reasoned that because South Shore was in the process of relocating into M-C's market area, South Shore was therefore critical to M-C's claims for violation of the Dealer Act. Further, the court noted that South Shore could be inequitably affected by an injunction or other judgment in the case. Accordingly, the court held that South Shore was properly joined as a defendant and remanding the case to the state court was appropriate.

Proximo Spirits, Inc. v. Green Lake Brewing Co., LLC, No. 2:22-cv-02879-SPG-SK, 2022 WL 17224545 (C.D. Cal. Sept. 9, 2022). After denying Defendant's motion to dismiss for lack of personal jurisdiction (see discussion of this case above in Section II of this Chapter), the court denied Defendant's alternative motion to transfer venue. The court, in determining whether transfer (to Washington, where Defendant's business was located) was in the interests of justice, held that the facts demonstrated that Defendant had partnered with two California-based distributors for the sole purpose of distributing its craft beers across that state and that, as a result of those distributor agreements, Defendant's products (including its allegedly infringing product) were sold at hundreds of California retailers.

Salsarita's Franchising LLC v. Gibson Family Enterprises LLC, No. 3:22-CV-00206, 2022 WL 15046281 (W.D.N.C. Oct 25, 2022). The court denied the defendant franchisee's motion to transfer venue in the plaintiff franchisor's action alleging breach of the franchise agreement. The court relied on the forum selection clause in the franchise agreement and found that the defendant, as the party opposing enforcement of the forum selection clause, failed to meet its burden of establishing that the clause should not be upheld. The court noted that a forum selection clause represents the parties' agreement as to the proper forum, protects their legitimate expectations, and furthers the vital interests of the justice system. The court held that "[a] valid forum-selection clause should be given controlling weight in all but the most exceptional cases," and it is the party opposing application of the forum selection clause that bears the burden of establishing that enforcement of the clause is unwarranted.

Sant v. Marriott International, Inc., No. GJH-22-1036, 2023 WL 2213926 (D. Md. Feb. 24, 2023). Plaintiff brought claims in the District of Maryland related to plaintiff's slip and fall at a franchised JW Marriott hotel located in India against the franchisor and the franchisee. Marriott's principal place of business is Maryland. The franchisee was incorporated under the laws of India. The court denied Marriott's motion to dismiss for failure to state a claim, determining that although Marriott had no ownership over the hotel, Marriott may still otherwise maintain control over its franchisees and hotels carrying its brand, which was a fact question entitled to discovery. The court granted the franchisee's motion to dismiss for lack of personal jurisdiction, finding that the franchise agreement with Marriott with its principal place of business in Maryland was insufficient to show that the franchisee had sufficient contacts with Maryland, particularly, when the claims fail to establish an affiliation between the forum and the underlying controversy.

Stingray IP Solutions, LLC v. TP-Link Technologies Co., Ltd., Nos. 2:21-CV-00045-JRG, 00046-JRG, 2022 WL 17357774 (E.D. Tex. Oct. 13, 2022). Court granted motion to transfer patent infringement to the Central District of California, which is where defendants' U.S. distributor had its principal place of business and where that entity could be properly joined as a defendant, and where the witnesses and evidence related to the importation and sale of the accused products were located. This case is also discussed in Section II of this Chapter.

IV. Choice of Law

Cipercen, LLC v. Morningside Texas Holdings, LLC, No. N19C-12-074 EMD CCLD, 2022 WL 4243687 (Super. Ct. Del. Sept. 14, 2022) The court dismissed both the franchisee's claim that franchisor tortiously interfered with a prospective economic advantage and franchisor's counterclaim for breach of contract, based on franchisee's failure to pay franchise fees, as time-barred. The court held that both the tortious interference and breach of contract claims were subject to a three-year statute of limitations under North Carolina law, which governed pursuant to the franchise agreement's choice-of-law provision. This case is discussed in Chapter 4, Section II.D.

Functional HIIT Fitness, LLC v. F45 Training Incorporated, No. 5:22-CV-10168, 2022 WL 17828930 (E.D. Mich. Oct. 26, 2022). A former franchisee ("Functional Fitness") that had entered into three franchise agreements to operate training studios in Michigan brough ten claims against the franchisor ("F45 Training") and five of F45 Training's officers and employees. Those claims included claims for fraud and negligent misrepresentation based on allegedly false information in F45 Training's Franchise Disclosure Document, claims for breach of contract and the implied covenant of good faith and fair dealing, and claims under the Michigan Franchise Investment Law ("MFIL"), the California Franchise Investment Law ("CFIL"), and the Delaware Uniform Deceptive Trade Practices Act.

As support for its claims, Functional Fitness alleged that it had received and relied on an outdated Franchise Disclosure Document when entering into the first two agreements and that it did not receive any Franchise Disclosure Document before entering into the third agreement. Functional Fitness also alleged that all of the named individual defendants helped create or issue the multiple Franchise Disclosure Documents. Functional Fitness further alleged that it had received a number of financial performance representations from the defendants that were false or misleading. These financial representations were allegedly made in financial modeling spreadsheets and by email. Functional Fitness also alleged that F45 Training charged fees that were not set forth in the franchise agreements.

In response, the defendants filed a motion to dismiss based on failure to state a claim, lack of personal jurisdiction over the individual defendants, and issues of choice of law. The magistrate court began its analysis by evaluating whether Functional Fitness had met its burden of establishing personal jurisdiction over the individual defendants. At the conclusion of that analysis, the magistrate court recommended dismissal of four of the individual defendants based on a lack of personal jurisdiction. For each of those four individual defendants, the magistrate ruled that the defendants' emails with Functional Fitness were insufficient to establish that the individual defendants had "purposefully availed" themselves of the state of Michigan. The magistrate court also ruled that the mere fact that an individual defendant had signed a franchise agreement at issue was likewise insufficient to subject the individual defendant to the court's jurisdiction. The magistrate court also noted that the mere fact that a corporation did business in Michigan was

CHAPTER 8

insufficient to assert personal jurisdiction over the corporation's officers and directors.

The magistrate court nevertheless ruled that personal jurisdiction was proper as to F45 Training's President of U.S. Expansion ("Marano"). In doing so, the court noted that Marano had extensive contacts with Functional Fitness regarding opening franchise locations in Michigan, and Functional Fitness's claims arose from Marano's communications with Functional Fitness in Michigan. The magistrate court also concluded that the exercise of personal jurisdiction over Marano was fair and comported with due process.

As to the substance of Functional Fitness's claims, the magistrate court first recommended dismissal of Functional Fitness's claims under the MFIL and the CFIL. In doing so, the magistrate court first noted that the franchise agreements at issue were governed by a choice-of-law provision that applied Delaware law. Because the federal magistrate court was located in Michigan, the magistrate court thus applied Michigan's choice-of-law rules to determine whether this choice-of-law provision was enforceable. In doing so, the magistrate court ruled that, under Michigan's choice-of-law rules, the choice of law provision calling for the application of Delaware law was enforceable. The magistrate court thus recommended that the district court enforce the choice-of-law provision in the franchise agreement and dismiss the franchisee's claims under the Michigan Franchise Investment Law and the California Franchise Investment Law. The magistrate court also explicitly rejected the franchisee's unsupported attempt to pick and choose statutes from across the country and apply them all to the same dispute.

The magistrate court also recommended dismissal of Functional Fitness's claim for breach of the implied covenant of good faith and fair dealing on the basis that this claim was barred by the *force majeure* provision in the franchise agreement. Specifically, Functional Fitness had argued that F45 Training had breached the implied covenant of good faith by charging for royalties despite the effects of the COVID-19 pandemic. The magistrate court, however, recommended the dismissal of this claim, because Functional Fitness had failed to avail itself of the governing *force majeure* provision in the franchise agreement.

As to the fraud and negligent misrepresentation claims, the magistrate court recommended that the district court deny the franchisor's motion to dismiss. The magistrate court ruled that those claims were properly based on information provided to Functional Fitness by F45 Training in its Franchise Disclosure Document, in statements made by Marano, and in a spreadsheet related to financial modeling. The magistrate court thus ruled that Functional Fitness had sufficiently identified the information that it relied on and the information that it now believed to be false.

Lastly, the magistrate court also recommended the dismissal of Functional Fitness's claims under the Delaware Uniform Deceptive Trade Practices Act. Under this Act, a plaintiff must have a "horizontal relationship" with the defendant such that the two parties are direct competitors. As a franchisee, Functional Fitness's relationship with F45 Training was "vertical" in nature, and therefore, the magistrate court recommended that this claim also be dismissed.

JTH Tax LLC v. Irving, No. RDB-21-3000, 2023 WL 1472021 (D. Md. Feb. 1, 2023) (holding that Maryland choice of law provision applied and mandated a three-year statute of limitations for contractual claims).

JTH Tax, LLC v. Leggat, No. 2:22-CV-41 (RCY), 2022 WL 3970197 (E.D. Va. Aug. 31, 2022). The plaintiff, franchisor, brought this suit in the Eastern District of Virginia after the expiration of the franchise agreement alleging that the defendant, franchisee, was wrongfully continuing to use the physical location and phone number of the former franchise. The franchise agreement contained a choice of law provision stating that Virginia law would apply; but the agreement also had a separate California Addendum provision disclaiming that where in conflict with California law, California law would apply over the choice of law clause in the contract. The court reviewed whether the California Addendum constituted a separate choice of law provision and ultimately found the agreements wording to be ambiguous and applied rules of contract interpretation to resolve the ambiguity in favor of the defendants. Specifically, the court held that the California Addendum is not a choice of law clause but that it does alter the existing Virginia choice of law clause in that where there is conflict between Virginia law and California Business and Professions Code Sections 20000 through 20043, the California rule would apply.

The court next evaluated the defendant's motion to transfer venue to the Southern District of California. The court noted the two step analysis consisting of: 1) whether venue would be proper in the transferee forum; and 2) the balance of interest of justice and convenience of the parties and witnesses. The balance of interest question included a four part analysis consisting of: 1) the plaintiff's initial choice of venue (weight afforded to this varies depending on the amount of contacts with the forum); 2) Witness convenience and access to sources of proof; 3) convenience of the parties; and 4) the interest of justice. It was the fourth prong - the interest of justice - that heavily weighed into the court's decision to rule for the defendant and grant the transfer of venue to the Southern District of California.

CHAPTER 8

Lockard Aircraft Sales Co. v. Dumont Aircraft Sales, LLC, No. 23-CV-1004-JWB, 2023 WL 4198596 (D. Kan. June 27, 2023) (A broker's commission agreement was found to be subject to interpretation under Oklahoma law, as Oklahoma was the place where the majority of the contractual duties were to be carried out).

Luxury Concepts, Inc. v. Bateel International, LLC, No. 22-10793, 2023 WL 360649 (E.D. Mich. May 23, 2023). Plaintiff entered into two franchise agreements with defendants in Michigan and Texas that contained choice of law provisions applying the laws of the United Arab Emirates. The choice of law provision was a key part of the court's determination that Michigan was not the proper venue for the action, and the court granted defendants' motion to transfer for forum non conveniens. This case is discussed in Chapter 8, Section II.

Peterson Motorcars, LLC v. BMW of North America, LLC, No. 3:19-cv-277-DJH-RSE, 2022 WL 4125102 (W.D. Ky. Sept. 9, 2022). In a lawsuit brought by a Kentucky MINI vehicle dealer against the defendant franchisor, claiming that the franchisor had failed to adequately support its dealers, including plaintiff, by failing to advertise its products sufficiently and failing to introduce new models of its cars, the court held that Kentucky law governed the dispute, despite the franchise agreement's New Jersey choice of law provision. The court explained that under Kentucky's choice of law rules, which the court was bound to apply, provide that a court must apply Kentucky law if Kentucky has "the most significant relationship" to the contract and the parties, which the court found it did here. This case is discussed in Section XVI of this Chapter and in Chapter 4, Section II.A.

Sea Tow Services International, Inc. v. Tampa Bay Marine, No. 20-CV-2877(JS)(SIL), 2022 WL 5122728 (E.D.N.Y. Sept. 30, 2022). The court denied the franchisor's motion to dismiss claims for violation of the Florida Business Opportunities Act on the basis that the Florida state law claims were prohibited by the franchise agreement's New York choice of law provision. The court ruled that the choice of law provision did not preclude claims under other states' statutes. This case is discussed in Chapter 2, Section III.

V. Amendment of Pleadings and Joinder of Claims and Parties

CBD Franchising, Inc. v. Dres, No. 8:22-cv-00313-FWS-JDE, 2023 WL 4155419, (C.D. Cal. May 19, 2023). The court granted the defendant's motion for leave to file a cross-complaint against the plaintiff and a third party. The plaintiff's initial complaint alleged that the defendant breached a franchise agreement and guarantor agreement. The court found that the defendant met the requirements of F.R.C.P 15(a)(2) that 1) there was no prejudice to the opposing party; 2) the amendment was not sought in bad faith; 3) the amendment would not cause undue delay; and 4) the amendment would not add a futile claim.

In *C. T. v. Red Roof Inns, Inc.*, No. 2:22-CV-834-JES-KCD, 2023 WL 3510879 (M.D. Fla. Mar. 11, 2023), the district court granted the plaintiff's motion for leave to amend the complaint to include a single claim against the defendant hotel franchisors under the Trafficking Victims Protection Reauthorization Act. This case is discussed in Chapter 6, Section XI.

DMO Norwood LLC v. Kia America, Inc., No. 22-cv-10470-ADB, 2023 WL 2021321 (D. Mass. Feb. 15, 2023). This case involved a motion to amend an answer to add counterclaims and counterclaim defendants arising out of a decision to terminate a dealer agreement following an audit of sales records. Plaintiff DMO Norwood LLC d/b/a Dan O'Brien Kia Norwood ("DMO Norwood") filed an eight-count complaint against Kia America, Inc. ("Kia") alleging that Kia's audit of DMO Norwood and termination of the parties' Dealer Sales and Services Agreement ("Dealer Agreement") violated various provisions of Massachusetts General Laws Chapter 93B and breached the Dealer Agreement. Plaintiff sought preliminary and permanent injunctive relief.

DMO Norwood operated as an authorized Kia Dealer pursuant to the Dealer Agreement. DMO Norwood's sole owner, Dan O'Brien, also owns other Kia Dealerships as well as three non-Kia dealerships in Massachusetts and New Hampshire. DMO Norwood submitted sales records to Kia pursuant to a sales policy that provides incentives to drive specific sales, and the purpose of the audit was to confirm compliance with that policy. In January 2022, Kia communicated the final results of the audit, stating that roughly 20 sales were subject to chargeback since DMO Norwood had submitted fraudulent sales records to Kia to receive incentive payments to which the dealership was not entitled.

As a result, Kia sent DMO Norwood a termination notice of the Dealer Agreement. The notice cited several reasons, including but not limited to the fact that DMO Norwood failed to furnish accurate sales information and data to Kia in response to Kia's audit procedure. More specifically, Kia contended the audits it conducted revealed that the dealership had perpetrated a fraud on Kia through the submission of false sales information. DMO Norwood argued that the termination grounds were "pretextual" and that the

CHAPTER 8

termination and audits were done in retribution for DMO Norwood's owner's decision to stop contributing funds to a voluntary marketing program run by Kia.

During the course of discovery, Kia learned that DMO Norwood's owner had attempted to cover up its improper conduct from Kia's auditor and of additional fraudulent sales reports. When the complaint was filed, Kia answered DMO Norwood's Complaint but did not raise any counterclaims at the time. A month before the close of discovery, however, Kia moved for leave to amend its answer to add seven counterclaims and three counterclaim defendants: DMO Concord, DMO North Hampton, and O'Brien (as sole owner of the defendants). The proposed counterclaims alleged additional violations, including fraud and civil conspiracy.

The court held that Kia's proposed amendment, if allowed in its entirety, would significantly expand the case and trial, putting at issue a broad alleged practice of fraudulent activity by numerous entities and entirely new theories of liability, including complex RICO and other conspiracy claims. DMO Norwood's claim, on the other hand, was narrowly focused on Kia's audit of DMO Norwood and its subsequent effort to terminate the Dealer Agreement. Thus, the court found that granting Kia's motion – filed only three months before the original trial date – would unduly prejudice DMO Norwood. However, the court permitted Kia to amend its answer to add the breach of contract claim against DMO Norwood since the Dealer Agreement and the alleged fraudulent activity were "all squarely at issue in DMO Norwood's claims."

Foremost Groups Inc. v. Tangshan Ayers Bath Equipment Co. Ltd., No. 2:14-cv-00188-SVW-RZ, 2023 WL 4203476 (C.D. Cal. May 3, 2023). Plaintiff had an agreement with defendant, a Chinese manufacturer of ceramic bathroom products, to be the exclusive distributor of defendant's products in the United States and Canada. In 2011, plaintiff sued another company, Ayers Bath USA, after learning that Ayers Bath was offering to sell defendant's products to various plumbing and wholesale distributors for lower prices than plaintiff was selling them for. Plaintiff initially sued Ayers Bath in 2011, and obtained a preliminary injunction. Ayers Bath then filed for bankruptcy. Plaintiff filed a proof of claim and ultimately received a very small distribution from the bankruptcy estate. In 2014, plaintiff sued defendant, based on Ayers Bath's conduct, but seeking to hold defendant liable under an alter ego theory of liability. The court dismissed Plaintiff's original and amended complaints for different reasons. After plaintiff filed a second amended complaint, the court stayed the case and asked the bankruptcy court to determine the issue of whether Ayers Bath was defendant's alter ego. It took approximately five years for the bankruptcy court to issue its report and recommendation after resolution of objections to the report. The report recommended rejecting plaintiff's attempt to amend its judgment from the bankruptcy court.

Plaintiff sought leave to again amend its complaint against defendant. Defendant argued such amendment would be futile, because plaintiff's claims were outside the statute of limitations and they would be subject to mandatory arbitration. The court disagreed, finding that plaintiff's claims related back to its original complaint and were never abandoned by plaintiff, and defendant had and remained on notice of such claims. The court also held that it could not compel arbitration since there was no motion to compel arbitration pending, it was still possible defendant could waive arbitration, and there were questions regarding whether plaintiff was required to arbitrate its claims in the first place. The court further found defendant would not be prejudiced by the amendment.

Herrera v. Highgate Hotels, L.P., No. 151096/18E, 2023 WL 1826823 (N.Y. App. Div. Feb. 9, 2023). The court denied plaintiff's motion to amend its complaint as to third-party defendant Subway Real Estate Corp. ("Subway") after plaintiff sustained injuries due to a slip. The court determined that the proposed amended complaint was without merit as Subway had already subleased the space to other defendants pursuant to a sublease, assignment, assumption, and franchise agreement. Thus, Subway could not be held liable to plaintiff for the other defendants' failure to maintain their stairs.

O'Neal v. American Shaman Franchise System, LLC, No. 8:20-CV-936-KKM-AAS, 2023 WL 1105209 (M.D. Fla. Jan. 30, 2023). Plaintiff O'Neal agreed to manage multiple company-owned retail establishments selling hemp-derived CBD products in the Florida market. Following the termination of his employment, O'Neal filed suit against the franchisor for breach of contract and for violations of the Fair Labor Standards Act. O'Neal settled with the franchisor and obtained a default judgment against certain individual defendants.

After the default judgment was entered, O'Neal sought leave to file a supplemental complaint. In the proposed supplemental complaint, O'Neal sought to rescind his settlement agreement with the franchisor and add additional causes of action. The court denied O'Neal's request to supplement his complaint on the basis that O'Neal failed to adequately allege a claim for rescission of the prior settlement agreement. In particular, the court ruled that because O'Neal had failed to return the benefits of the settlement agreement, he could not state a claim for rescission of the agreement. The court also ruled

CHAPTER 8

that O'Neal's substantially delayed attempt to supplement his complaint to add new causes of action suggested bad faith and a dilatory motive. The court therefore denied the motion for leave to supplement the complaint under Federal Rule of Civil Procedure 15(a).

Orlando v. Choice Hotels International, Inc., No. 2:22-cv-00404-APG-BNW, 2023 WL 4025886 (D. Nev. June 15, 2023). The court denied the defendant franchisor's motion to dismiss for failure to name the franchisee as a defendant. The plaintiff was injured at a hotel for which the defendant was the franchisor. The court ruled that the franchisee was not an "required party" under FRCP 19, which requires joinder of "required parties," noting that the fact that the franchisee had a contractual obligation to indemnify or defend was irrelevant to the question of whether it was a "required party." Regardless, the court then granted the plaintiff's motion to amend the complaint to add the franchisee as a defendant. This case is also discussed in Chapter 7, Section III.

Roy v. Fedex Ground Package Systems, Inc., No. 3:17-cv-30116-KAR, 2023 WL 4186291 (D. Mass. June 26, 2023). Fedex Ground Package Systems, Inc.'s ("FedEx") motion to redact documents included in plaintiffs' motion to compel was denied because FedEx had itself made the purportedly confidential documents public by attaching copies of the documents to its own motion without first requesting redaction of the purportedly sensitive documents. The court found that FedEx waived its claim for sealing by failing to move to redact the allegedly objectionable portions of plaintiffs' motion when plaintiffs' motion was filed, and waiting for about a month to request redactions to that motion. When FedEx finally moved to redact portions of plaintiffs' motion, FedEx included the portions of plaintiffs' motion that it sought to seal in its own publicly filed motion.

VI. Arbitration

A. ENFORCEABILITY

Lunt v. Frost Shades Franchising, LLC, No. 3:22-cv-00775, 2023 WL 3484202 (M.D. Tenn May 16, 2023). The court granted the franchisor's motion to compel arbitration related to claims for damages, but retained jurisdiction over the claims for injunctive relief. This case is discussed in Chapter 2, Section 2.

B&P Glass and Mirror, LLC v. Clozetivity Franchising, LLC, No. 3:22-cv-00772 (M.D. Tenn. May 16, 2023) (The United States District Court for the

Issues Specific to Litigation and Arbitration

Middle District of Tennessee granted defendant franchisor's motion to compel arbitration, finding that although Tennessee law historically barred arbitration of fraudulent inducement claims, the Federal Arbitration Act displaces any conflicting state law prohibiting arbitration of particular types of claims. The court further found that nothing in the parties' franchise agreement reflected a meeting of the minds on intent to exclude fraudulent inducement claims from the franchise agreement's arbitration clause.).

Butler Brothers Supply Division, LLC v. HN Precision Co., No. 220418-U, 2022 WL 17094960 (Ill. App. Ct. 2d Nov. 21, 2022). Plaintiff Butler Brothers Supply Division, LLC ("Butler Brothers") sued defendants HN Precision Company ("HN"), Scott Narrol, Jeanne Perron, and Premier Industrial Group, LLC d/b/a HN Precision ("Premier") for an allegedly fraudulent scheme involving an integrated supply agreement. The alleged fraudulent scheme claim involved the failure of HN to pay for orders and HN's later sale of the ordered products to Premier, among other bases. Following oral argument, the trial court dismissed the complaint without prejudice and referred the matter to arbitration pursuant to the arbitration clause in a related contract between plaintiff and HN. The appellate court affirmed the dismissal, because the integrated supply agreement included an "in connection with" arbitration clause—that is, any claim arising "in connection with" the supply agreement and its purchase orders was to be referred to arbitration—and the court found Butler Brothers' claim against HN regarding the alleged fraudulent scheme to clearly be "in connection with" the supply agreement.

Canales v. CK Sales Co., LLC, 67 F.4th 38 (1st Cir. 2023). Lepage Bakeries Park Street, LLC ("Lepage") is a Maine-based bakery. Lepage delivers its products directly to stores through its subsidiary CK Sales Co., LLC ("CK") which sells distribution rights to "independent distributors." The independent distributors purchase the rights to distribute Lepage's baked goods along particular routes by executing distributor agreements with CK. A group of CK's distributors brought suit against CK and Lepage, alleging that the defendants misclassified them as independent contractors rather than employees. The defendants moved to compel arbitration pursuant to provisions in the distributor agreements. The plaintiffs countered that they qualified as transportation workers engaged in interstate commerce, who are exempt from the Federal Arbitration Act. The district court denied the motion, finding that the plaintiffs were exempt from the Federal Arbitration Act.

The First Circuit affirmed, agreeing with the district court that the distributors qualified as transportation workers engaged in interstate commerce, and rejecting the defendants' arguments on appeal. First, the court

CHAPTER 8

rejected the defendants' arguments that the plaintiffs were not "engaged in" interstate commerce and that the plaintiffs did not have "contracts of employment" because the defendants failed to make those arguments before the district court and therefore waived them on appeal. Second, the court rejected the argument that the plaintiffs were not "transportation workers" because the plaintiffs' job duties mainly consisted of transporting goods. Finally, the court denied the defendants' argument that plaintiffs' responsibilities were those of a business owner rather than a transportation worker because each plaintiff spent at least fifty hours per week delivering products. Accordingly, the court affirmed the denial of the motion to compel arbitration because the plaintiffs were exempt from the Federal Arbitration Act.

Carmona Mendoza v. Domino's Pizza, LLC, No. 21-55009, 2023 WL 4673469 (9th Cir. July 21, 2023). Three truck drivers brought a putative class action against Domino's Pizza, LLC ("Dominos"), alleging various labor law violations. Domino's moved to compel arbitration pursuant to an arbitration agreement in the drivers' employment agreements. The district court denied Domino's motion, holding that the drivers were exempt from the Federal Arbitration Act as transportation workers engaged in interstate commerce. On appeal, the Ninth Circuit affirmed, agreeing with the district court that the drivers were engaged in the stream of interstate commerce. The United States Supreme Court then vacated the Ninth Circuit's decision and remanded for reconsideration in light of *Southwest Airlines Co. v. Saxon*, 142 S. Ct. 1783 (2022). In *Saxon*, the Supreme Court held that the critical question in evaluating this exemption is whether the workers are actively "engaged in transportation" of goods in interstate commerce and play a "direct and necessary role in the free flow of goods across borders." *Id.* at 1790.

On remand, the Ninth Circuit again affirmed the district court's denial of Domino's motion to compel arbitration. Specifically, the court found that *Saxon* did not alter its initial analysis–and that *Saxon* was not "inconsistent, let alone irreconcilable," with its prior reasoning in concluding that the drivers were engaged in interstate commerce.

Choice Hotels International, Inc. v. C & O Developers, L.L.C., 199 N.E.3d 1 (Ohio Ct. App. Sept. 15, 2022). Assignee of franchise agreement which had an arbitration provision entered into and then subsequently defaulted on separate loan documents with the franchisor. The appellate court affirmed the lower court's denial of defendant's motion to compel arbitration, finding the loan documents, which provided for litigation of any disputes, were for a separate transaction than the franchise agreement. This case is discussed further in Chapter 4, Section II.A.

In *Choice Hotels International v. Seven Star Hotels Group, LLC*, No. 8:22-CV-748-AAQ, 2023 WL 1928016 (D. Md. Feb. 10, 2023), Plaintiff's motion for default judgment was granted by the court, enforcing the arbitration award, including damages, procured by the plaintiff against the defendants, after the court found that a valid arbitration agreement existed between the parties, the defendants were nonresponsive to both a summons and application, and there was no basis for vacating the award.

CTA Hot Bread, Inc. v. Flowers Baking Company of Oxford, Inc., No. 21-cv-6488 (E.D.N.Y. Mar. 10, 2023). The Magistrate Court recommended granting the motion to compel arbitration filed by defendant, a distributor franchisor for Flowers Foods, in an action brought by its franchisee for wrongful termination, notwithstanding the franchisee asserting that a prior class action settlement terminated the arbitration agreement.

Doctor's Associates, LLC v. Reino, No. 3:22-cv-00786, 2023 WL 2687529 (D. Conn. Mar. 28, 2023). Subway's real estate affiliate, SRE, brought a state court collections action against a franchisee for past due rent at a closed location under the sublease between the parties. The franchisee counterclaimed, asserting a fraudulent inducement claim related to the franchise agreement and sublease. Franchisor Doctor's Associates, LLC's (DAL) then petitioned the district court to compel arbitration based on the arbitration provision in the franchise agreement. The district court ordered the franchisee to submit to arbitration to determine whether the claims the franchisee raised or could have raised as to DAL are arbitrable.

Doe v. Massage Envy Franchising, LLC, 87 Cal. App. 5th 23, 303 Cal. Rptr. 3d 269 (Cal. Ct. App. 2022). The California Court of Appeals considered whether the defendant franchisor could compel arbitration of the plaintiff's claims for damages stemming from a sexual assault that allegedly occurred at a franchisee's massage clinic. Plaintiff Jane Doe ("Doe") alleged that she was sexually assaulted by a massage therapist at a Massage Envy franchise in San Rafael, California. The franchise was independently owned and operated by a franchisee, who licensed the "Massage Envy" name from the defendant franchisor Massage Envy Franchising, LLC ("MEF"). Doe sued both the franchisee and MEF for sexual battery and fraud, among other claims. MEF moved to compel arbitration, but the trial court denied the motion on the bases that no agreement to arbitrate existed as between Doe and MEF, or in the

CHAPTER 8

alternative, that Doe's claims were outside the scope of the arbitration agreement. On appeal, the California Court of Appeals affirmed, holding that the arbitration agreement between Doe and MEF was not enforceable.

Sometime before the alleged assault, Doe entered into a "Wellness Agreement" with the franchise location at issue. In exchange for a monthly fee, Doe was entitled to one free massage per month and discounts on any additional massages. The Wellness Agreement did not include an arbitration provision.

Years later, on August 7, 2021, Doe arrived at the franchise location for a massage appointment. However, on this visit, unlike previous visits, a staff member handed her an electronic tablet and instructed her to use the tablet to check in for her appointment. The tablet was running an "In-Store Application" that MEF had recently developed for its franchisees to use during check-ins. No one informed Doe that using the "In-Store Application" would bind her to a contract with MEF. Nonetheless, the check-in process required Doe to fill out various questionnaires and health history forms, as well as agree to a "General Consent" with the franchisee and "Terms of Use Agreement" with MEF. While the Application required Doe to scroll through the General Consent form before signing, it did not require Doe to scroll through the Terms of Use before agreeing to the massage, and Doe never read or was even aware of the Terms of Use. The Terms of Use consisted of ten pages of single-spaced text, and contained the sole mention of the binding arbitration provision at issue.

The Court of Appeals affirmed the trial court's denial of the motion to compel arbitration, holding that Doe did not have reasonable notice that she was entering into any sort of agreement with MEF, much less notice of the binding arbitration provision. The court noted that the strong public policy favoring arbitration of disputes and enforcing arbitration provisions cannot apply to parties who did not in fact agree to arbitrate their disputes. Applying California contract law, the court concluded that Doe did not agree to arbitrate any disputes with MEF for several reasons. First, Doe did not have reason to believe that the check-in process or her massage would involve MEF, an entity with which she had no prior relationship, because the check-in application only identified the franchisee. Second, Doe had no reason to believe that she was agreeing to the Terms of Use Agreement containing the arbitration provision because the placement of the check-box and other context of the application suggested that she was merely agreeing to the General Consent form she was required to scroll through (and which did not contain an arbitration provision).

Ultimately, the court concluded that the arbitration provision was not presented to Doe in such a way as to make it apparent that she was agreeing to that provision when she completed the check-in application. Accordingly, Doe did not enter into any contract, much less an arbitration agreement, with MEF, and the court affirmed the denial of the motion to compel arbitration.

In *Dow v. Keller Williams Realty, Inc.*, No. 4:21-CV-1209-P, 2022 WL 4009047 (N.D. Tex. Sept. 2, 2022), the franchisee brought sexual harassment and related claims against franchisor, its founder and CEO, and several men associated with franchisor. The court compelled arbitration as to the claims franchisee brought against the franchisor and its founder, but it found that the franchisee's claims against the other defendants, who had not signed arbitration agreements, were not subject to arbitration, though the court stayed litigation as to those claims pending disposition of the arbitration.

Fujitsu Semiconductor Ltd. v. Cypress Semiconductor Corp., No. 22-MC-80313-VKD, 2023 WL 3852701 (N.D. Cal. June 5, 2023). Fujitsu Semiconductor Ltd. ("FSL") entered into a Foundry Agreement to manufacture microchip wafers for Cypress Semiconductor Corp.'s ("Cypress") predecessor in interest. Then, in 2015, Cypress entered into a distributor agreement with a subsidiary of FSL. In 2018, FSL sold the subsidiary to Kaga Electronics Co., Ltd. ("Kaga"), after which Cypress terminated the distributor agreement. Kaga then sued Cypress for breach of contract, and Cypress filed a cross-complaint naming FSL as a cross-defendant. FSL moved to compel arbitration of Cypress's claims against it pursuant to the United Nations Convention on the Recognition and Enforcement of Foreign Arbitral Awards as well as the Federal Arbitration Act.

The court granted FSL's petition to compel arbitration. First, the court found that a valid agreement to arbitrate existed between FSL and Cypress in the Foundry Agreement executed between FSL and Cypress's predecessor in interest. It did not matter that the subsequent distributor agreement did not contain an arbitration clause, because FSL was not a party to that agreement. Second, the court found that Cypress's claims against FSL were within the scope of the agreement, and therefore entered an order compelling the parties to arbitrate.

In ***Goergen v. Black Rock Coffee Bar, LLC***, 2023 WL142911 (D. Or. Jan. 10, 2023), the United States District Court, District of Oregon found that it was the duty of the court, not the arbitrator, to determine whether the plaintiffs had a valid agreement for arbitration with the defendant as the threshold issue. Further, the court found that it was appropriate for the court to determine whether the defendant could enforce the arbitration provisions within the geographic territory agreement and the related franchise agreements against the plaintiffs, if the court indeed found that a valid arbitration agreement existed between the defendant and the plaintiffs. The court put the defendant and plaintiffs on notice that it would rule on these two issues and would allow the parties to submit one final brief before its decision on the issues at hand.

Goergen v. Black Rock Coffee Bar, LLC, No. 3:22-CV-1258-SI, 2023 WL 1777980 (D. Or. Feb. 6, 2023). The court held that the guarantor plaintiffs were not signatories to the franchise agreement between the franchisees and defendant franchisor and were therefore not subject to the arbitration clause within the franchise agreement. Accordingly, plaintiffs were not responsible for the arbitrator's damage award, which awarded tens of millions of dollars in damages, plus attorney's fees in favor of defendant.

This dispute arose out of defendant's amended petition to compel arbitration against Plaintiffs pursuant to the arbitration clause in the franchise agreement. Defendant argued that although plaintiffs were nonsignatories to the franchise agreement, plaintiffs were still bound by its arbitration clause as "Controlling Principals" of franchisees and as third-party beneficiaries of the franchise agreement under principles of estoppel. Additionally, defendant claimed that plaintiffs were bound by the arbitration clause under the alter ego doctrine and also bound by the guarantees plaintiffs signed which allegedly incorporated the arbitration clause by reference.

The court held in favor of plaintiffs, finding that plaintiffs were not "controlling principals" and were not third-party beneficiaries, that the guarantees did not incorporate the arbitration clause and that defendant did not timely raise its alter ego claim. Accordingly, Plaintiffs as nonsignatories to the franchise agreement were not bound by the arbitration clause within this agreement. Therefore, defendant was enjoined from directly enforcing any portion of the arbitration award against plaintiffs.

Gray v. Schmidt Baking Company, Inc., No. 22-CV-00463-LKG, 2023 WL 2185778 (D. Md. Feb. 23, 2023) (court granted defendant's motion to compel arbitration of claims brought by certain distributors of defendant's products, finding that the parties' distribution agreements continued valid arbitration agreements and a valid delegation clause requiring the threshold issue of arbitrability to be decided by the arbitrator).

Holmes v. Diza Tacos Streeterville, LLC, No. 22 C 3378, 2023 WL 1777463 (N.D. Ill. Feb. 6, 2023) (rejecting unconscionability arguments and compelling arbitration of employee's overtime claims against franchisee).

Issues Specific to Litigation and Arbitration

In *Hyundai Construction Equipment Americas, Inc. v. Southern Lift Trucks, LLC*, No. SC-2022-0675, 2023 WL 3402311 (Ala. May 12, 2023), a heavy-equipment dealer filed suit against the manufacturer and its parent company, alleging that the manufacturer and its parent company breached the parties' dealer agreements and violated the Alabama Heavy Equipment Dealer Act (AHEDA). The heavy equipment dealer sought to enjoin the manufacturer from terminating the subject dealer agreements. The heavy equipment dealer also brought a claim for declaratory judgment that all of the provisions of the dealer agreements that were inconsistent with the AHEDA were unenforceable.

The manufacturer and its parent company moved to dismiss the complaint and then moved to compel arbitration. The trial court denied the motion to compel arbitration. The manufacturer and parent company appealed.

The appellate court found that all of the claims were subject to arbitration except the claim seeking declaratory judgment as to the enforceability of the dealership agreements. This case is discussed in Chapter 6, Section XI and in Chapter 8, Section VI.B.

Mayorga v. Ridgmar Urban Air, LLC, No. FBT-CV22-6113435 S 2023 WL 1246280 (Super. Ct. Conn. Jan. 23, 2023). The court granted the defendants' motion to enforce an arbitration agreement. Defendants were the franchisee and franchisor of an outdoor adventure park and entrants to the park signed a waiver which contained the arbitration provision in question. The court noted that Connecticut public policy favors resolving disputes through arbitration and that the arbitration agreement must be clearly stated, then reviewed the term in the contract, and found that it was clear and unambiguous, and thus enforceable.

Moore v. Bob Howard German Imports, LLC, No. 120,124, 2023 WL 3579057 (Okla. Civ. App. May 19, 2023) (The Court of Civil Appeals of Oklahoma affirmed an order compelling arbitration, holding that a defendant car dealership had no duty to explain arbitration provisions to buyers and any question as to which of two signed arbitration provisions applied was for the arbitrator in the first instance. The plaintiff car buyer had claimed he was fraudulently induced into signing the arbitration agreements when the dealer breached a duty to clear false impressions, but the court found that failing to affirmatively explain a contract provision is not equivalent to creating a false impression.).

CHAPTER 8

O'Bryant v. Flowers Foods, Inc., No. 2:21-cv-3501-BHH, 2022 WL 4368237 (D.S.C. Sept. 21, 2022). Plaintiff had two distributor agreements with Derst Baking Company, a wholly-owned subsidiary of Flowers Foods. The agreements gave plaintiff the right to deliver defendants' bakery products in certain geographic territories. The agreements were amended and the amendments included an agreement to submit any disputes to mandatory and binding arbitration. Plaintiff received consideration for the amendment, including additional money and other favorable terms. Plaintiff later sold his distributor franchises.

Plaintiff subsequently filed a putative class and collective action against defendants, asserting that he (and other regional distributors like him) was misclassified as an independent contractor, rather than an employee, under the Fair Labor Standards Act, and defendants had failed to properly pay him under that Act and South Carolina's Payment of Wages Act. The court granted defendants' motion to dismiss the action in favor of arbitration. The court found that the arbitration agreement was validly entered into, its terms were fair, the agreement explicitly covered claims challenging plaintiff's status as an independent contractor, and it also contained a class and collective action waiver that was prominently disclosed. Plaintiff argued that the lawsuit was exempted from arbitration pursuant to Section 1 of the Federal Arbitration Act, which excludes coverage for, among other things, contracts of employment of workers engaged in interstate commerce. The court disagreed, first noting that the Supreme Court has held that this exemption "should be narrowly construed." It further held that plaintiff could not establish that he worked in the transportation industry, because defendants were bakeries and not "carriers such as a railroad, a maritime shipping company, or a trucking company." In addition, plaintiff's deliveries were purely *intrastate*, therefore he was not engaged in interstate commerce.

Passion for Restaurants, Inc. v. Villa Pizza, LLC, No. CV 20-15790 (KSH) (CLW), 2022 WL 18024209 (D. N.J. Dec. 30, 2022) (granting defendant-franchisee's motion to dismiss where the arbitrator dismissed franchisor Villa Pizza, LLC's claims due to franchisee's failure to pay its share of arbitrator's fees, where the parties' agreement compelled arbitration under the United Nations Commission on International Trade Law ('UNCITAL") and the UNCITAL Rules permitted the arbitrator to require each party to deposit an equal amount of fees).

Rivas v. Coverall North America, Inc., No. SACV181007JGBKKX, 2022 WL 17960776 (C.D. Cal. Nov. 28, 2022). Defendant Coverall North America, Inc. ("Coverall") renewed a motion seeking to compel Carlos Rivas ("Rivas") to arbitrate his claim under the California Private Attorney General Act on an individual basis. The court granted Coverall's motion because Rivas did not make a showing that he was unable to vindicate his rights in arbitration.

Roleo Beverage Corp. v. Pepsi-Cola Bottling Co. of New York, Inc., No. 1:22-CV-6921 (MKV), 2022 WL 3974465 (S.D.N.Y. Sept. 1, 2022). The court held that the parties' dispute was covered by an arbitration clause in their distributor agreement, which was enforceable under the Federal Arbitration Act. This case is discussed in Chapter 4, Section VI.

Sanders v. Savannah Highway Automotive Company, No. 2021-000137, 2023 WL 4752347 (S.C. July 26, 2023). In August 2012, Sanders purchased a vehicle from the Rick Hendrick Dodge automotive dealership ("Rick Hendrick"), pursuant to which he executed a retail installment sales contract ("RISC") containing a binding arbitration clause. Rick Hendrick subsequently assigned the RISC to Santander Consumer USA Holdings, Inc. ("Santander"), though Sanders alleged that in doing so Rick Hendrick misrepresented Sanders' income, ultimately resulting in monthly car payments constituting 37% of his true pretax monthly income. Sanders' vehicle was then repossessed when he failed to make those car payments.

Sanders sued Rick Hendrick and Santander, among others (collectively, the "Petitioners"), in circuit court in South Carolina, to which Petitioners responded by moving to compel arbitration under the RISC. Sanders argued that the Petitioners could not rely upon the arbitration provision in the RISC because Rick Hendrick had fully assigned the RISC and its rights thereunder to Santander. Petitioners acknowledged the assignment, but they argued that it was the arbitrator, and not the circuit court, that should decide the gateway question of whether the arbitration provision was enforceable. The circuit court disagreed with Petitioners, ruling that it had jurisdiction to rule on the gateway question of enforceability, and it ruled on the merits that petitioners' right to compel arbitration was extinguished with Rick Hendrick's assignment of the RISC to Santander.
The court of appeals affirmed and the Supreme Court of South Carolina then granted Petitioners' writ of certiorari to review the court of appeals' decision.

The only question posed to the Supreme Court on appeal by Petitioners was whether the Federal Arbitration Act ("FAA") required the arbitrator, and not the circuit court, to decide the gateway question of whether the assignment extinguished Petitioners' right to arbitration.

The Supreme Court stated the baseline rule that the FAA requires courts to separate the validity of an arbitration clause from the validity of the contract in which it is embedded, with the former to be decided by courts and

CHAPTER 8

the latter to be decided by the arbitrator. The court recognized, however, that it is often the case that the application of this baseline rule to a given set of facts is not so simple, as was the case with the case at bar.

Ultimately, however, the court reasoned that because Sanders' challenge to arbitration was not directed to the arbitration provision specifically, but rather to Petitioners' ability to enforce the RISC as a whole, the gateway issue of the enforceability of the arbitration provision was one for the arbitrator to decide. The court therefore reversed the court of appeals' decision and vacated the circuit court's order.

Streedharan v. Stanley Industrial & Automotive, LLC, No. 5:22-cv-0322-MEMF (KSx), 630 F.Supp.3d 1244 (C.D. Cal. Sept. 27, 2022). Defendant moved to compel arbitration of its distributor's claims pursuant to the terms of the parties' franchise agreement. The court denied the motion, agreeing with the plaintiff franchisee that the arbitration provision was permeated with unconscionability such that it could not be applied nor severed from the unconscionable portions to save its applicability. Specifically, the court found procedural unconscionability existed in that the franchise agreement was a contract of adhesion that was offered to the plaintiff on a "take it or leave it" basis and there was great disparity in the parties' bargaining power. The court further found that the arbitration provision contained a statute of limitations that only applied to the plaintiff, whereas the defendant could bring any claims at any time, without any restriction. The court also considered the substantive limitations on the remedies afforded to plaintiff under the arbitration clause in concluding that the provision was unconscionable and could not be applied, and it was so permeated with unconscionability that its unconscionable portions could not be severed to save its application. This case is also discussed in Chapter 6, Section VI.

B. BINDING NON-SIGNATORIES

Coons v. Yum! Brands, Inc., No. 21-CV-45-SPM, 2023 WL 3320149 (S.D. Ill. May 9, 2023). The court granted Yum! Brands, Inc.'s ("Yum!") motion to compel arbitration pursuant to the arbitration provision in the employment agreement Yum!'s franchisee had with Coons, the franchisee's former employee. The court determined the arbitration provision was valid and binding, even on non-signatory Yum!, whose Taco Bell franchisee entered into the employment agreement with Coons, because of the agency relationship between Yum! and its franchisee.

Issues Specific to Litigation and Arbitration

Escobar v. National Maintenance Contractors, LLC, No. 21-35765, 2022 WL 17830001 (9th Cir. Dec. 21, 2022) (in case involving individual plaintiffs' claim that they were employees and not franchisees under the parties' agreement, the court found the agreement's arbitration provision to be unconscionable and therefore unenforceable given the individual plaintiffs' financial situation and the agreement's cost sharing provision).

Hagenbaugh v. Nissan North America, No. CV 3:20-1838, 2023 WL 361786 (M.D. Pa. Jan. 23, 2023). Six plaintiffs brought a putative class action against Hyundai North America ("Hyundai"), Kia Motors America ("Kia"), Nissan North America ("Nissan"), three automobile dealerships, and two automobile dealership owners. The plaintiffs alleged that the three defendant dealerships, with the manufacturers' and owners' approval, advertised a "Set for Life Program" representing that vehicle purchasers would receive certain benefits free for the duration of their ownership. The three defendant dealerships subsequently went out of business, and thereafter the defendant manufacturers and owners refused to honor the plaintiffs' requests for benefits under the Set for Life Programs. Hyundai and Nissan moved to compel arbitration of the plaintiffs' claims against them, arguing that the plaintiffs had signed binding arbitration provisions with the dealerships when they purchased the vehicles. The plaintiffs opposed, arguing that Hyundai and Nissan were not signatories to the arbitration agreements.

The court granted the motion to compel arbitration of the claims against Hyundai and Nissan. First, the court noted that the arbitration agreements between the plaintiffs and the dealerships were enforceable under the Federal Arbitration Act because they were valid under Pennsylvania contract law, and because the dispute fell within the scope of the agreements' terms. Second, the court concluded that the arbitration agreements applied to the non-signatories Hyundai and Nissan under the doctrine of equitable estoppel, which provides that a non-signatory to a contract may bind a signatory to a contract where a close relationship exists between the entities involved and the claims against the non-signatory are intimately founded in and intertwined with the underlying contractual obligations. Because the plaintiffs' claims against Hyundai and Nissan were intertwined with the plaintiffs' sale contracts with the dealerships, equitable estoppel applied to bind the plaintiffs to the arbitration agreements.

In ***Hyundai Construction Equipment Americas, Inc. v. Southern Lift Trucks, LLC***, No. SC-2022-0675, 2023 WL 3402311 (Ala. May 12, 2023) a heavy-equipment dealer filed suit against the manufacturer and its parent company, alleging that the manufacturer and its parent company breached the

CHAPTER 8

parties' dealer agreements and violated the Alabama Heavy Equipment Dealer Act (AHEDA). The manufacturer and its parent company moved to dismiss the complaint and then moved to compel arbitration. The trial court denied the motion to compel arbitration. The manufacturer and parent company appealed.

The court found that the parent company could compel arbitration even though it was not a party to the dealer agreements because the heavy equipment dealer alleged agency and conspiracy liability; therefore, the claims against the parent company were subject to arbitration. This case is discussed in Chapter 6, Section XI and in Chapter 8, Section VI.A.

Montemayor v. Ford Motor Co., No. B320477, 2023 WL 4181909 (Cal. Ct. App. June 26, 2023). Ford Motor Company ("Ford") could not enforce an arbitration provision against a purchaser in a sales contract entered into between the purchaser and a dealership, to which Ford was not a signatory. The purchaser's claims against Ford were founded on Ford's express warranty for the purchased vehicle, not on any obligation imposed on Ford by the sales contract, and thus, the purchaser's claims against Ford were not inextricably intertwined with any obligations under the sales contract, such that Ford could compel arbitration as to the express warranty claim.

Ochoa v. Ford Motor Company (Ford Motor Warranty Cases), Nos. B312261, JCCP 4856, 2023 WL 2768484, 89 Cal.App.5th 1324 (Cal. Ct. App. April 4, 2023). Defendant car manufacturer Ford Motor Company ("FMC") appealed an order denying its motion to compel arbitration of plaintiffs' claims arising from a manufacturer warranty against vehicle defects. The arbitration clause at issue appeared in retail sale contracts between Plaintiffs (the buyers) and vehicle dealers, but FMC was not a signatory to the sale contracts. FMC argued that agency allegations in plaintiffs' complaints entitled it to enforce the provision as an undisclosed principal; that it was an intended third-party beneficiary of the provision; and that plaintiffs were equitably estopped from avoiding the obligation to arbitrate in the sale contracts when suing on warranties acquired upon purchase of their vehicles. The court rejected each of FMC's arguments.

The court held that equitable estoppel did not apply to compel arbitration because plaintiffs' claims against FMC were not founded in or intertwined with the sales contract. Under California law, manufacturer warranty claims are not based on car sale contracts themselves but are obligations of the manufacturer independent of the sale contracts' terms, and plaintiffs never alleged that FMC violated the sales contracts. The court also found that FMC was not a third-party beneficiary of the sales contracts because nothing in the sales contracts offered a benefit to FMC and dealers were not acting as agents of FMC in executing the sales contracts.

C. CLASS/COLLECTIVE ARBITRATION

Peacock v. First Order Pizza, LLC, No. 22-CV-02315, 2022 WL 17475791 (W.D. Tenn. Dec. 6, 2022). (Plaintiff Peacock, who worked as a delivery driver for a franchisee of Domino's Pizza, brought putative class claims against the defendants for failure to pay minimum wage and failure to pay overtime wages under the Fair Labor Standards Act. The defendants moved to dismiss the case and compel arbitration pursuant to an arbitration agreement. The court granted the order to compel arbitration.)

D. AWARD CONFIRMATION

Choice Hotels International, Inc. v. Patel, No. CV TDC-22-2310, 2023 WL 3276487 (D. Md. May 5, 2023). Plaintiff Choice Hotels International, Inc. ("Choice Hotels") filed an application to confirm an arbitration award against defendant Nick Patel ("Patel"). The underlying facts involved an alleged breach of the franchise agreement by Patel, who failed to initiate hotel construction by a stipulated deadline.

Choice Hotels and Patel had entered into a franchise agreement for Patel to manage a hotel, which contained an arbitration clause. Patel allegedly breached the agreement by failing to commence hotel construction by the deadline, leading Choice Hotels to initiate arbitration against Patel per the agreement. Patel did not participate in the arbitration process, resulting in the arbitrator awarding Choice Hotels damages totaling $156,755 for Patel's breach.

Choice Hotels filed an application in federal court to confirm the arbitration award. Patel did not respond to the application or subsequent motion for default judgment. The court established that it had diversity jurisdiction over the case under 28 U.S.C. § 1332. The Federal Arbitration Act ("FAA") allowed the court to confirm the arbitration award made pursuant to the valid arbitration agreement.

Patel failed to provide any grounds under the FAA to vacate the award. The court granted a default judgment in favor of Choice Hotels, as Patel failed to participate or respond, confirming the $156,755 arbitration award plus $400 in costs. The court confirmed the arbitrator's award after determining the arbitration and award were proper under the terms of the parties' franchise agreement.

CHAPTER 8

HayDay Farms, Inc. v. FeeDx Holdings, Inc., 55 F.4th 1232 (9th Cir. 2022) (confirming $21 million arbitration award entered against defendant because courts "may vacate an arbitration award only 'where the arbitrators exceeded their powers, or so imperfectly executed them that a mutual, final, and definite award upon the subject matter was not made.'").

Next Level Ventures, LLC v. Avid Holdings, Ltd., No. C22-1083-JCC, 2023 WL 3382539 (W.D. Wash. May 11, 2023) (manufacturer moved to vacate arbitration award in favor of its distributor, but court denied the motion on the grounds that it was untimely, as it was filed seven months after the award was sent to the parties, and the manufacturer did not offer any evidence to support its argument that equitable tolling should apply).

NuVasive, Inc. v. Absolute Medical, LLC, 71 F.4th 861 (11th Cir. 2023). In a dispute in which a manufacturer accused its exclusive distributor of breaching distribution and noncompetition agreements, the appellate court affirmed the district court's vacatur of a final arbitration award based on a finding of fraud in the arbitration. The appellate court held that the Federal Arbitration Act's three-month vacatur motion deadline is subject to equitable tolling and is not jurisdictional.

Strickland v. Foulke Management Corp., No. A-0455-21, 475 N.J. Super. 27, 290 A.3d 1259 (Mar. 3, 2023). Plaintiffs, purchasers of a used car from defendant, which was repossessed after plaintiffs failed to make payments, filed a motion for an order to show cause to vacate an arbitration award that dismissed plaintiffs' claims against the defendant. While the parties' arbitration agreement expressly stated the agreement was governed by the Federal Arbitration Act ("FAA"), plaintiff cited a clause in the agreement allowing a court to review an arbitrator's award for errors of New Jersey law. The court affirmed the award, finding the clause plaintiff contended permitted the court to review the award under the New Jersey Arbitration Act to be unenforceable, because it expanded the court's jurisdiction to review the award beyond the very limited and specific list of instances in which a court may vacate an arbitration award as set forth in the FAA, which the parties had expressly agreed governed their arbitration agreement. The court held that the FAA does not allow parties to contractually agree to expand the basis or review of an arbitration award governed by the FAA. While the clause allowing review for errors of New Jersey law was found to be unenforceable, the court held that that provision could be severed from the arbitration agreement and the remaining provisions could be enforced, in large part because the parties' agreement provided that if any term of the agreement was found to be unenforceable, the remaining terms "are severable and enforceable to the fullest extent of the law."

E. WAIVER

The authors' review of cases decided during the reporting period did not reveal any significant decisions addressing this topic.

VII. Mediation

CJ Consultants, LLC v. Window World, Inc., No. 22-CV-3, 2022 WL 4354265 (W.D. Mich. Sept. 20, 2022). Franchisor, Window World, prevailed on its motion to dismiss as to all claims brought by franchisee, CJ Consultants. Window World asserted that CJ Consultants had failed to comply with the pre-litigation mediation provision in the franchise agreement and, as such, could not adequately state a claim. The district court determined that the mediation provision in the franchise agreement was enforceable. The mediation provision required the franchisee to provide notice of the claims and a good faith attempt to mediate before filing suit against the franchisor. In enforcing the pre-litigation mediation requirement in the franchise agreement, the court rejected CJ Consultants' unconscionability arguments. The district court also rejected CJ Consultants's request to stay the proceeding while it complied with the mediation requirement. The full summary for this case is in Chapter 4, Section II.F.

VIII. Statutes of Limitations

Doe (L.G.) v. Hand & Stone Franchise Corp., No. 862 EDA 2022, 2022 WL 17661068 (Pa. Super. Ct. Dec. 14, 2022). Appellant Jane Doe alleged she was sexually assaulted by an employee at a franchise location of Hand and Stone Franchise Corp ("Hand & Stone"). Two years after the assault, Appellant informed Hand & Stone of the 2016 assault. In November 2021, Hand & Stone filed a motion for summary judgment, and in February 2022, the court granted the motion and dismissed appellant's complaint as time barred. Appellant's appeal hinged on four issues related to whether the statute of limitations barred her claim. The court agreed with the trial court that appellant's action was time barred, because the record showed appellant had actual knowledge of the assault in April 2016 and had two years to commence an action against Hand & Stone and the employee, and had failed to do so.

CHAPTER 8

In *Doe #21 v. CFR Enterprises, Inc.*, No. A163543, 2023 WL 4783591 (Cal. Ct. App. June 29, 2023), the court reversed the trial court's dismissal on statute of limitations grounds of eighteen plaintiffs' claims against the franchisor and several franchisees stemming from alleged sexual assaults that occurred at certain Massage Envy franchises. The court held that a recently-enacted law revived some, if not all, of the plaintiffs' claims notwithstanding the statute of limitations. This case is discussed in Chapter 6, Section XII.

Poe v. FCA US LLC, No. 2:21-CV-11668-TGB-CI, 2022 WL 4491055 (E.D. Mich. Sept. 27, 2022) (court dismissed plaintiff's claims against defendant, franchisor of two Texas auto dealerships, for breach of contract, conspiracy, tortious interference and other torts, finding that all of the claims were barred by the applicable statutes of limitations).

IX. Collateral Estoppel/*Res Judicata*

Sungyou Enterprise Co. v. Ghirardelli Chocolate Co., No. 22-CV-05306-TSH, 2023 WL 3134207 (N.D. Cal. Apr. 26, 2023) (dismissing exclusive distributor's claims on the basis of claim preclusion).

X. Class Actions

Fikes Wholesale, Inc. v. HSBC Bank USA, N.A., 62 F.4th 704 (2d Cir. 2023). A putative class of over 12 million merchants brought an antitrust action against Visa, Inc. ("Visa") and MasterCard International, Inc. ("MasterCard") alleging that Visa and Mastercard unlawfully adopted and enforced rules that allowed them to charge supracompetitive interchange fees on each payment card transaction a merchant accepted. After 15 years of litigation, the United States District Court for the Eastern District of New York approved a $5.6 billion settlement. However, a dispute over the interpretation of the settlement class broke out between franchisor integrated oil companies and their franchisee branded service station owners. The district court appointed a special master to ascertain whether the franchisors or the franchisees should receive settlement funds. Nonetheless, certain franchisors appealed the district court's approval of the settlement class.

On appeal, the Second Circuit affirmed the district court's approval of the settlement. The appellant franchisees' first objection was that the class was not ascertainable, because it was defined as all merchants that "accepted" Visa or MasterCard within a certain timeframe and it was unclear who "accepted" payment as between the franchisors and franchisees. The court rejected this argument, noting that the district court made clear that the class only included entities that were direct payors of the interchange fees, which could be objectively determined during settlement administration.

Second, the franchisees objected that they did not receive adequate representation during negotiation of the settlement because no class representative had the same interest as the franchisees in their dispute with the franchisors. However, the court found this argument unavailing because the dispute between the franchisors and franchisees was a dispute over class membership rather than a dispute between members.

Third, the franchisees claimed that a special master should not be used to resolve the franchisor-franchisee dispute because a class should be defined so all members have standing, and that the special master process would be unfair and too complicated. The court disagreed, finding that there is nothing unusual about a special master determining whether an entity is a class member.

Lastly, the appellants claimed that certain franchisees lacked adequate notice of the settlement before its approval. The court likewise rejected this argument, finding that the notice was reasonable and sufficient.

Foley v. Wildcat Investments, LLC, No. 2:21-cv-5234, 2023 WL 4485571 (S.D. Ohio July 12, 2023) (The United States District Court for the Southern District of Ohio denied plaintiff franchise delivery driver's motion to send court-approved notice to potential class members in his FLSA minimum wage and overtime action for failure to demonstrate a strong likelihood that there was a class of similarly situated delivery drivers where plaintiff relied only on hearsay and lacked actual knowledge about how employees at other locations were paid).

In ***Haitayan v. 7-Eleven, Inc.***, No. 21-56144, 2022 WL 17547805 (9th Cir. Dec. 9, 2022), the appellate court affirmed the district court's dismissal of plaintiff-franchisees' claim that the franchisees should be classified as employees rather than independent contractors under California law. The appellate court found that the district court erred by refusing to analyze plaintiffs' claims that accrued after 2020 with the 2018-adopted "ABC" test for California wage order violations. However, the appellate court found that this was a harmless error since the three prongs of the ABC test were already part of and considered in the "Borello" factors that the district court used.

McLaren v. UPS Store, Inc., No. 21-14424 (MAS) (DEA), 2023 WL 3182842 (D.N.J. Apr. 29, 2023). Plaintiff brought a class action lawsuit in state court against The UPS Store and "all persons and business entities of

CHAPTER 8

every kind who owned and/or operated a UPS Store in the State of New Jersey that provides and provided notary services to the public at such facility." Plaintiff alleged that defendants charged consumers in excess of the statutory maximum amount permitted under New Jersey law. Defendants removed the lawsuit to federal court pursuant to the Class Action Fairness Act of 2005 (CAFA). Plaintiff then attempted to remand the case to state court by arguing that the case fell under the local controversy exception to CAFA.

The court determined that the case did not fall under the local controversy exception because the only evidence plaintiff relied on was documentation from a single UPS Store location. The court refused to make an inference that the documentation from a single store showing that over two-thirds of its customers seeking notary services were New Jersey citizens meant that over two-thirds of customers in every UPS Store in New Jersey were New Jersey citizens. Furthermore, the court rejected plaintiff's arguments that a single local store was the more significant defendant over The UPS Store itself. For those reasons, the court denied plaintiff's arguments and ruled that the case was properly removed under CAFA.

Moehrl v. National Association of Realtors, No. 19-cv-01610, 2023 WL 2683199 (N.D. Ill. Mar. 29, 2023). This case involved individuals who sold their home using a local database of properties for sale known as a Multiple Listing Service ("MLS"), and as a condition of listing their homes on an MLS, each plaintiff's listing had to include, then subsequently pay, a set offer of compensation to any broker who found a buyer for the home. Plaintiffs argued that the rules governing the commission requirements for an MLS listing were anticompetitive and caused them to pay artificially inflated, supracompetitive commission rates. Plaintiffs brought an antitrust action against defendant National Association of Realtors ("NAR"), along with defendants Realogy Holdings Corp, HomeServices of America, Inc., HSF Affiliates, LLC, The Long & Foster Companies, Inc., BHH Affiliates, LLC, RE/MAX LLC, and Keller Williams Realty, Inc., who are all franchisors or owners of residential real estate brokerage firms. This opinion addressed plaintiffs' motion to certify two classes of similarly situated home sellers who sold their homes on NAR-affiliated MLSs across the United States, and defendants' motion to exclude the opinion of two expert witnesses plaintiff relied upon in seeking class certification.

The court determined that defendants' attack on the methodologies used by plaintiffs' first expert effectively amounted to accusations that the defendants' expert's analysis was stronger and attacks on the plaintiffs' expert's conclusions. The court determined that both arguments were inappropriate for the current stage of litigation and denied defendant's efforts to exclude plaintiffs' first expert. Regarding plaintiffs' second expert, defendants similarly attacked the expert's methodologies with accusations that they were unreliable. The court, however, determined that the plaintiffs' second expert sufficiently explained the basis for his conclusions and pointed out that defendants had only pointed to weaknesses in the expert's analysis. The court noted that "[w]hether an expert might have done a better job is not the test for admissibility of his testimony."

The court then considered plaintiffs' motion for class certification under FRCP Rule 23(a). Defendants only challenged plaintiffs' ability to satisfy the commonality and typicality requirements. The court determined that there was a common question underlying the claims of all class members, namely, whether defendants conspired to artificially inflate the buyer-broker commissions paid by the class by adopting common NAR rules underpinning plaintiffs' allegations. Thus, plaintiffs satisfied the commonality requirement. The court also determined that the class satisfied the typicality requirement, even though defendants alleged that the named class members only used five of the fifteen covered MLSs. This was because the class members as a whole used all of the identified MLSs and all the covered MLSs implemented the same rules at issue. Thus, all of plaintiffs' claims shared the same essential characteristics as the rest of the class, satisfying typicality.

The court then turned to an in-depth analysis of whether a common question predominated across the class pursuant to FRCP Rule 23(b)(3). Ultimately, the court determined that defendants failed to show that individual questions predominated over the common issues capable of common proof identified by the plaintiffs. Thus, the court found that plaintiffs had satisfied that aspect of the predominance requirement. The court also determined that defendants' attacks on plaintiffs' damages model went to the merits of the case, but did not undermine plaintiffs' showing of common question, and thus could not prevent class certification. Last, considering the large number of potential class members, the court determined that a class action was a superior format for litigation. The court therefore granted plaintiffs' motion to certify a Rule 23(b)(3) damages class.

Plaintiffs also sought certification as an injunctive relief class under FRCP Rule 23(b)(2). Since plaintiffs only sought a single injunction that applied generally to the class, and there were plaintiffs with standing to represent the class, the court found that that certification was proper under Rule 23(b)(2).

Park 80 Hotels, LLC v. Holiday Hospitality Franchising, LLC, No. 1:21-CV-04650-ELR, 2023 WL 2445437 (N.D. Ga. Feb. 16, 2023). Operators of Holiday Inn Express, Holiday Inn Express & Suites, and Staybridge Suites

CHAPTER 8

hotel franchises brought a consolidated class action against the franchisor of those hotel concepts, asserting various claims for breach of contract and breach of the duty of good faith and fair dealing, deceptive trade practices in violation of the Georgia Uniform Deceptive Trade Practices Act, declaratory judgment, and Sherman Act violations, as well as various claims for remedies in the nature of an accounting, attorneys' fees, and punitive damages. The franchisor moved to dismiss the plaintiffs' complaint, which the court granted in part and denied in part.

Regarding the plaintiffs' breach of contract claims, the plaintiffs alleged that the franchisor breached twelve "express and implied duties" under the parties' franchise agreement, and that franchisor had routinely violated its duty of good faith and fair dealing in eight ways. The court found that all but one of the plaintiffs' claims based on the parties' franchise agreement were foreclosed as a matter of law by that agreement's plain terms, and that the plaintiffs' breach of contract claims that were based either on pre-contractual representations or on the relevant franchise disclosure document were not enforceable as a result of the franchise agreement's "Entire Agreement" provision.

As for the one breach of contract claim that survived dismissal, that claim concerned the manner in which the franchisor managed the relevant franchise owners' association. Considering that the franchise agreement did not specify how that association's board was to be elected, the court ruled it was appropriate to read into the franchise agreement a requirement that the franchisor exercise "good faith" in its management of the owners' association, which the plaintiffs alleged the franchisor had failed to do. Thus, that single breach of contract claim survived dismissal.

The plaintiffs' deceptive trade practices claim also survived dismissal, as the court concluded that the plaintiffs' allegations that the franchisor had misrepresented various benefits and features of the franchise system, taken together, could state a plausible claim for deceptive trade practices.

As for the plaintiffs' other claims, the court found that they had not alleged facts sufficient for a declaratory judgment that the franchise agreement was unconscionable, and the court found plaintiffs failed to adequately allege either a relevant product or geographic market sufficient to support their Sherman Act claim.

The court did not permit the plaintiffs leave to amend their consolidated complaint, reasoning among other things that the pleading deficiencies could not be cured through more careful pleading.

Issues Specific to Litigation and Arbitration

Pender v. Wings, No. 2:21-CV-4292, 2023 WL 2472035 (S.D. Ohio Mar. 13, 2023). Former bartender employee brought putative Fair Labor Standards Act ("FLSA") collective action against employer defendant entities doing business as Buffalo Wild Wings, alleging violations of FLSA wage laws. The defending parties were owners and operators of the franchises located in Ohio and West Virginia. The court certified the plaintiff's class, finding that the burden was met to show other individuals were similarly situated under the same ownership and larger franchise system.

Salinas v. Cornwell Quality Tools Co., No. 5:19-CV-02275-FLA (SPX), 2022 WL 16735823 (C.D. Cal. Oct. 17, 2022). Plaintiff, a former dealer of defendant, distributor Cornwell Quality Tools ("Cornwell"), filed a class action against Cornwell, alleging misclassification of Cornwell's dealers as independent contractors rather than employees and violations of certain California labor laws. The proposed class consisted of dealers who signed Dealer Franchise Agreements with defendant in California within the past four years and operated a mobile store. The court granted plaintiff's motion for class certification under Federal Rules of Civil Procedure 23(a) and (b)(3), determining that common issues of misclassification and Cornwell's control were dominant over individual issues. The court's analysis of the provisions of Cornwell's standard Dealer Franchise Agreements was integral to the court's focus on the degree of control retained by Cornwell over the putative class. The court found the Agreements were also consistent among the various dealers in the proposed class, therefore the typicality and adequacy requirements were also met. This case is also discussed in Chapter 7, Section II.

In ***Spencer v. JRN, Inc.***, No. 3:22-CV-00024-GFVT, 2023 WL 2278644 (E.D. Ky. Feb. 28, 2023), defendant, JRN, Incorporated, moved to dismiss plaintiff's claim concerning violations of the Americans with Disabilities Act ("ADA") at all of the Kentucky Fried Chicken restaurants owned by defendant that the plaintiff had not personally visited, based on a lack of subject matter jurisdiction. Defendant further moved to strike plaintiff's class allegations based on a failure to plead a viable class under Federal Rule of Civil Procedure 23(a). The court denied the defendant's motion to dismiss in its entirety.

Concerning the defendant's assertion that the plaintiff lacked subject matter jurisdiction to bring the complaint with respect to restaurants the plaintiff had not personally visited, the court noted that the Sixth Circuit had not made a determination on whether individual standing could confer class standing. The court further noted that even courts that hold individual standing does not confer class standing require the "alleged discrimination to arise from

CHAPTER 8

a common architectural design or policy." Applying the same logic, the court found that the plaintiff sufficiently pled a "common design or policy" because the restaurants share "similar violations and [the plaintiff] alleges that the violations stem from a centralized facility maintenance policy."

Finally, the court determined that dismissing the plaintiff's class claim before there was an opportunity for discovery to be complete would be premature and that it would wait until the plaintiff submitted a motion for class certification.

Tripicchio v. The UPS Store, Inc., No. CV2114512MASDEA, 2023 WL 3182915 (D.N.J. Apr. 30, 2023) (granting in part and denying in part franchisor and franchisee's motion to dismiss putative class action related to alleged excessive notarial service fees in violation of New Jersey state law).

Williams v. D'Argent Franchising, L.L.C., No. 1:20-CV-01501, 2023 WL 3059192 (W.D. La. Apr. 24, 2023). Plaintiffs, former employees of the defendants, brought a putative collection action for violations of the Fair Labor Standards Act ("FLSA") against the defendants, alleging that the defendants operated as an integrated single enterprise that had a common policy and practice of not paying employees for any hours worked over 40 hours in one week. Those defendants were D'Argent Franchising, L.L.C., a franchisee entity that owned and operated a Huddle House franchise and a CC's Coffee House franchise, D'Argent Construction, L.L.C., a construction services company, and D'Argent Companies, L.L.C., alleged to be the parent company of D'Argent Franchising and D'Argent Construction. Plaintiffs also sued the individual owners of the D'Argent businesses.

Plaintiffs moved to certify their collective action and to define the class for that action as all employees who had been employed by any of the three D'Argent businesses at any time from three years prior to the date of the filing of the complaint through the present, who had worked over 40 hours in at least one workweek and had been subject to the pay practices of the D'Argent defendants during that time. Plaintiffs argued that their proposed class definition was appropriate, notwithstanding the fact that it included employees of three different businesses, because all employees of those businesses who had been denied overtime pay by those businesses were "similarly situated" because they had all been subjected to the defendants' unlawful pay practices, which were applicable to all D'Argent businesses.

In response, defendants argued that their businesses constituted three separate entities, and not a single enterprise, because they each had their own timekeeping systems, payroll providers, management structures and managers, locations, schedules, handbooks, job titles, job descriptions and employment policies, and each business performed entirely different business services in different industries.

The court, however, concluded that its focus must be on whether the employees of the putative class were impacted by common employment policies, which the court found to be the case with respect to the three D'Argent businesses. Accordingly, the court determined that the putative class members were similarly situated and it granted the plaintiffs' motion to certify a collective action.

XI. Discovery Issues

ASA Enterprise, Inc. v. Stan Boyett & Son, Inc., No. 1:21-cv-00915-BAK, 2022 WL 4182188 (E.D. Cal. Sept. 13, 2022). Plaintiffs are the owners and operators of a gas station and convenience store and entered into a franchise agreement with defendant by which plaintiffs agreed the gas station would be branded "76". Defendant Boyett had a separate agreement with Phillips 66 Company ("P66"), the owner of the 76 mark and brand. Boyett terminated plaintiffs' franchise after plaintiffs failed two consecutive "mystery shop" inspections, because they failed to maintain their 76-branded gas station according to minimum imaging standards set by P66, and failed to cure by achieving a passing score on the third mystery shop inspection.

Plaintiffs sought in discovery (1) the Trademark License Agreement between Boyett and P66 and any related documents, and (2) the identities of any other franchisees of Boyett who received similar notices of default or termination for failed image standards. They contended that nowhere in the franchise agreement did it specify that three (or any other number of) failed mystery shop inspections would be the basis for terminating the agreement. Boyett argued that its Agreement with P66 was proprietary, confidential and a trade secret and that it was the franchise agreement that was relevant and at issue in the case, not the License between Boyett and P66. On issue 1, the court applied the following balancing test regarding the P66 License Agreement: first, Boyett had to show that the information is a trade secret or other confidential research, development or commercial information, and disclosure would be harmful; the burden then shifted to plaintiffs to show the information is relevant and necessary to prepare for trial; and if relevance and necessity are established, the court had to weigh the injury that disclosure might cause against the plaintiffs' need for the information. The court found Boyett established the Agreement is a trade secret and that disclosure would be harmful. The court did not find that the plaintiffs demonstrated the discovery is relevant or necessary to the claims and defenses in the action, rather it held that certain provisions of the franchise agreement, discovery

CHAPTER 8

concerning the mystery shop program and imaging standards, communications regarding the decision to terminate that had been produced, and other available sources of information provided a sufficient basis to adjudicate the claims and defenses in the case. The court further held that, even if the plaintiffs had established the Agreement was relevant and necessary for trial, the injury its disclosure might cause outweighed the need for the information.

Regarding the identities of other Boyett franchisees who were sent notices of default and/or termination for not earning passing scores on mystery shop inspections, the court agreed with Boyett that such information was not directly relevant to the claims and defenses in the action. Even if the information were relevant, the court held that it would be outweighed by other considerations under Rule 26(b)(1), namely the requested discovery was not proportional to the needs of the case considering the various factors set forth in the Rule. The trier of fact had other ample evidence by which to consider the claims and defenses, including the franchise agreement terms, the alleged instances of non-compliance by plaintiffs with the imaging standards, and communications and documentation regarding the mystery shop inspections and decision to terminate.

Eddie's Truck Center, Inc v. Daimler Vans USA LLC, No. 5:21-CV-05081-VLD, 2023 WL 4624888 (D.S.D. July 19, 2023). Plaintiff Eddie's Truck Center sued defendants Daimler Vans USA LLC and Mercedes-Benz USA, LLC after defendants allegedly ended the distribution and production of Freightliner Sprinter vehicles, which, according to plaintiff, was made without "good cause" in violation of an applicable statute. The court granted in part and denied in part plaintiff's motion to compel and defendants' motion for a protective order. The court determined that plaintiff (i) was not entitled to be given access to information related to non-Freightliner Sprinter vehicles, because that information was irrelevant to its claims and would be a burden for defendants to gather and produce, and (ii) could have access to documents after the date of termination of its franchise, because documents showing subsequent transactions involving the sale of Freightliner Sprinter dealerships by defendants was relevant and proportionate to the needs of plaintiff's case, and how much a willing buyer has paid for such a dealership is not speculative and would be relevant for determining profits (or losses) to plaintiff's franchise if its franchise had not been terminated. This case is also discussed in Chapter 4, Section II.

Hernandez v. Syncrasy, No. 21-CV-09212, 2023 WL 2600452 (N.D. Cal. Mar. 21, 2023). Defendant sought a protective order for its leasing documents by stating, in part, that the documents reflect proprietary business terms relating to gross sales from its third-party franchise agreement. The court determined that disclosure of such information would harm defendant's competitive standing, and granted the protective order as to that category of information.

Housemaster SPV LLC v. Burke, No. CV 21-13411 (MAS), 2022 WL 17904254 (D.N.J. Dec. 23, 2022). Plaintiff-franchisor HouseMaster SPV LLC ("HouseMaster") sells home and building inspection business franchises, and entered into a franchise agreement with defendant-franchisee John Burke ("Burke"). Burke agreed to several restrictive covenants in the franchise agreement, including to refrain from operating a competing business within 25 miles from his approved territory. HouseMaster subsequently sued Burke, alleging that Burke violated these covenants by forming a new home inspection company within the restricted geographic area.

Burke allegedly hired and used the same team in his new company as he did with HouseMaster, including the company's Director of Marketing, Michelle Burke ("Michelle"). During discovery, HouseMaster filed a motion to compel and for sanctions after it received what it believed to be an incomplete production of documents from Michelle. Michelle had produced some documents and represented under oath that she had conducted a reasonable search for all relevant documents. The court denied the motions to compel and for sanctions, noting that Michelle as a non-party must be afforded greater protection from discovery than an actual party.

Howard P. Fairfield LLC v. Cives Corp., No. X07HHDCV196160194S, 2022 WL 17438467 (Conn. Super. Ct. Nov. 30, 2022). (Cives Corporation d/b/a Viking Cives ("Viking") brought a motion to compel Howard P. Fairfield ("HPF") to respond to discovery requests. HPF resisted because of the breadth of discovery. In HPF's complaint, HPR sought damages from Viking for the termination of a dealer agreement in violation of General Statutes §45-345, which states how a dealer agreement between a "dealer" of a farm and a "supplier" of farm inventory may be terminated. The court overruled and sustained a number of HPR's objections related to the series of items to be compelled.)

Jani-King of Miami, Inc. v. Leicht, No. 3:23-CV-0389-B, 2023 WL 2825689 (N.D. Tex. Mar. 17, 2023). Jani-King of Miami, Inc. served several discovery requests related to its non-competition claim against its former franchisee. The court granted in part and denied in part Jani-King's motion to compel responses to the discovery requests, considering, among other things, the

CHAPTER 8

considerable volume of documentation requested (including business communications and depositions) and the short period of time to produce and review it.

Jose Santiago Inc. v. Smithfield Foods, Inc., No. 22-1239(SCC/BJM), 2023 WL 4420257 (D.P.R. July 10, 2023) (distributor's motion to compel discovery from a manufacturer covering the entire 28-year relationship was denied as too broad where the most relevant time period was much shorter and the marginal relevance of older documentation would not outweigh the burden of collection).

MD Auto Group, LLC d/b/a I-90 Nissan v. Nissan North America, Inc., No. 1:21-cv-01584-CEF, 2023 WL 41812595 (N.D. Ohio, Eastern Division June 26, 2023. MD Auto Group, LLC d/b/a I-90 Nissan ("I-90") filed a motion requesting an *in camera* review of documents that Nissan North America, Inc. ("NNN") had redacted in its discovery responses on the grounds of attorney-client privilege or attorney work product. NNN indicated that virtually all of the withheld or redacted documents consisted of communications or PowerPoint presentations involving non-lawyers that reflected or conveyed the advice of NNN's counsel. I-90 disputed that the documents were properly subject to the attorney-client privilege or the attorney work product doctrine. To succeed on its motion, I-90 needed to make a factual showing adequate to support a good faith belief that the review would uncover unprivileged documents. In determining whether an *in camera* review is appropriate, the court noted a list of non-exhaustive factors that the court should consider, including: (1) the facts and circumstances of the particular case; (2) the volume of materials the moving party has asked the court to review; (3) the relative importance of the alleged privileged information to the case; and (4) the likelihood that review will reveal the documents are not shielded by the privilege. The court also noted that in a diversity case, the court applies federal law to resolve work product claims and state law to resolve attorney-client privilege claims.

As to the attorney client privilege claims, Ohio law provides eight criteria under which privilege can be asserted: (1) where legal advice of any kind is sought (2) from a professional legal adviser in his or her capacity as such, (3) the communications relating to that purpose, (4) made in confidence (5) by the client, (6) are at his or her instance permanently protected (7) from disclosure by himself, herself or by the legal adviser, (8) unless the protection is waived. I-90 claimed that its cursory review of NNN's redacted documents indicated that no legal advice was requested and none given that would rise to the level of an attorney-client communication, particularly because most of the disputed documents involved communications between non-lawyers or PowerPoint presentations that primarily address business concerns. However, the court noted that the privilege can apply to communications between non-lawyers if the communications were made for purposes of securing legal advice from counsel and in relaying that legal advice.

I-90 also alleged that the disputed documents could not be privileged as a claim of privilege required that the primary purpose of the communication must be the solicitation of legal advice, rather than business advice. In response, the court noted that the fact that business considerations were weighed in the providing of the legal advice would not destroy the attorney-client privilege. The court ultimately decided that I-90 had not sufficiently demonstrated that it had a good faith belief that an *in camera* inspection would uncover privileged documents, and therefore denied I-90's motion.

O'Neal v. American Shaman Franchise System, LLC, No. 8:20-CV-936-KKM-AAS, 2023 WL 2164211 (M.D. Fla. Feb. 22, 2023) The United States District Court, M.D. Florida, denied plaintiff's motion for an order that the crime-fraud exception applied to Defendants' attorney-client and attorney work-product privileges. The court found that the crime-fraud exception did not apply because plaintiff failed to tie his request to a specific document or testimony that would further criminal or fraudulent activity. Additionally, Plaintiff failed to establish a prima-facie case for granting the crime-fraud exception to Defendants' attorney-client privilege in this matter.

OYO Hotels Inc. v. Om Chamunda LLC, No. 3:20-CV-3433-N, 2023 WL 3491742 (N.D. Tex. May 16, 2023) (The United States District Court for the Northern District of Texas, Dallas Division denied franchisees' motion to compel the franchisor to organize its document production and produce a privilege log, finding that the franchisor already satisfied its Rule 34 discovery obligations.)

Pac-West Distributing NV LLC v. AFAB Industrial Services, Inc. et al., Civil Action No. 19-3584, 2023 WL 3952347 (E. D. Pa. June 12, 2023). This case involves a Rule 37 motion to exclude unidentified witnesses. Pac-West Distributing NV LLC ("Pac-West") sued AFAB Industrial Services, Inc. ("AFAB") for trademark and trade dress infringement and breach of a previous settlement agreement. During discovery, AFAB disclosed only one witness for trial. Then, just days before a final pretrial conference was to be held, AFAB identified three new witnesses for the first time. Pac-West moved to exclude these witnesses on the grounds that they had not been disclosed in AFAB's initial disclosures and that allowing the witnesses to testify would

CHAPTER 8

prejudice Pac-West by requiring them to reopen discovery and seek new testimony from witnesses who had already been subpoenaed and deposed.

The court noted that under Rule 26, a party has an ongoing obligation to supplement or correct its disclosures when it learns that in some material respect the disclosure or response is incomplete or incorrect, unless that information is otherwise made known during discovery. Under the "otherwise made known" requirement, the information must be clear and unambiguous, and not merely the mention of an individual's name. Reference to a witness in discovery documents, interrogatories, or depositions or even knowledge that someone has relevant information is insufficient to provide the required notice that the person might be called as a witness. The court determined that the attenuated references to the witnesses were insufficient to put Pac-West on notice that they might be potential witnesses. In evaluating whether the failure was harmless, the court determined that allowing these witnesses to testify would significantly prejudice Pac-West, as it would have to reopen fact and expert discovery, recall witnesses who had already been deposed, respond to all of the new issues that AFAB raised, and amend its pleadings and arguments accordingly. Finding this to be harmful to Pac-West, the court excluded these witnesses from testifying at trial.

Roadbuilders Machinery and Supply Co., Inc. v. Sandvik Mining and Construction USA, LLC, No. 2:22-cv-2331-HLT-TJJ, 2023 WL 3790691 (D. Kan. June 2, 2023). In this dealer termination case, during discovery, Roadbuilders Machinery and Supply Co., Inc. ("Roadbuilders") served notice to take the depositions of multiple individuals, one of which was Sandvik Mining and Construction USA, LLC's ("Sandvik") in-house counsel. Sandvik moved to quash this deposition, citing attorney-client privilege. The court noted that attorneys with knowledge of discoverable facts, not protected by attorney-client privilege or work product, are not exempt from being a source for discovery by virtue of their license to practice law or their employment by a party to represent them in litigation. However, in order to depose an in-house attorney, the party requesting the discovery must establish that (1) no other means exist to obtain the information except to depose opposing counsel; (2) the information sought is relevant and non-privileged; and (3) the information is crucial to the preparation of the case. These criteria are known as the *Shelton/Simmons* criteria.

The first issue addressed was whether the in-house counsel qualified as an opposing counsel. If not, the above *Shelton/Simmons* criteria would not apply. The court considered the nature of the in-house counsel's position, duties, and involvement in the litigation, and the underlying events giving rise to the litigation, whether the attorney to be deposed was listed as a potential witness in the party's Rule 26(a)(1) initial disclosures or as a Rule 30(b)(6) deposition witness, and the likely delay and disruption of the case, harassment, unnecessary distractions into collateral matters, and/or potential for abuse. Based on its analysis, the court determined that the *Shelton/Simmons* criteria should be applied to the in-house counsel.

Under the first prong of the test, the court determined that there were three other witnesses that could provide the same information as the in-house counsel. As to the second prong, Roadbuilders argued that Sandvik had waived attorney-client privilege by asserting its affirmative defenses, which prompted the court to analyze the requirements for it to find a waiver. The court noted that there were generally three approaches to determining whether a party had waived the attorney-client privilege by placing protected information at issue. The first approach is the "automatic waiver" rule, which provides that a litigant automatically waives the privilege on assertion of a claim or affirmative defense that raises as an issue a matter to which otherwise privileged material is relevant. The second approach provides that the privilege is waived only when the material to be discovered is both relevant to the issues raised in the case and either vital or necessary to the opposing party's defense of the case. The third approach holds that a litigant waives the attorney-client privilege if the litigant directly puts the attorney's advice at issue in the litigation. The court noted that while the Tenth Circuit had not adopted any of these approaches, Kansas had adopted a form of the second approach, under what is known as the *Hearn* approach. The *Hearn* approach required: (1) assertion of the privilege was the result of some affirmative act, such as filing suit, by the asserting party; (2) through this affirmative act, the asserting party put the protected information at issue by making it relevant to the case; and (3) application of the privilege would have denied the opposing party access to information vital to its defense. Under the facts of this case, the court determined that Sandvik had not waived attorney-client privilege. The court also found that the third prong of the *Shelton/Simmons* criteria had not been met, and so granted Sandvik's motion to quash.

In ***Window World of Baton Rouge, LLC v. Window World, Inc.***, No. 15 CVS 1, 2022 WL 17177467 (N.C. Super. Ct. Nov. 10, 2022), the plaintiffs, franchisees and franchisee owners, sought to compel the production of billing records and communications and documents between the franchisor-defendants and their counsel, on the basis that these documents and communications would show that the franchisor-defendants knew they were operating a franchise when they induced the plaintiffs to sign licensing agreements disclaiming a franchise relationship.

CHAPTER 8

The franchisor-defendants agreed to produce the billing records, but moved the court to allow the total redaction of all billing descriptions in the billing records. The franchisor-defendants also asked the court to allow the *in camera* and *ex parte* testimony of an attorney who assisted the franchisor-defendants with franchise law matters beginning on June 20, 2011 in deciding whether to grant the plaintiffs' motion to compel pursuant to the crime-fraud exception.

The court denied both of the franchisor-defendants' requests. The court ordered that the billing records only be redacted for privilege and that they be produced with a privilege log detailing the basis of the privilege claims. The court noted that there is little precedent for such *in camera* and *ex parte* testimony, and that the request was untimely. The court also denied, however, the request to compel the communications based on the crime fraud exception. The court noted that the plaintiffs, as the party seeking production, had not met their burden to show that there was a close relationship between the communications and any scheme on the part of the franchisor-defendants to commit a crime or fraud. The court conducted an *in camera* review as to the remaining documents that the plaintiffs claimed were improperly withheld or improperly redacted and found that all but two of the challenged documents were privileged and properly withheld.

The court did, however, sanction the franchisor-defendants finding that the franchisor-defendants' in-house counsel falsely testified in a deposition that she had not provided legal advice or any work on franchise disclosure documents prior June 2011. The court found that the testimony could not be reconciled with the documents produced in the case, which showed that the in-house counsel had prepared several draft franchise disclosure documents.

XII. Default Judgment

Americinn International, LLC v. Patel, No. 21-20068 (ES)(AME), 2022 WL 17176935 (D.N.J. Nov. 23, 2022). The district court granted default judgment in favor of plaintiff-franchisor, Americinn International, LLC, a subsidiary of Wyndham Hotels & Resorts, Inc. The judgment arose from a dispute between plaintiff and the defendant-franchisee related to the termination of a franchise agreement between the two for the construction and operation of a new guest lodging facility. The franchise agreement provided for liquidated damages in the event defendant terminated the agreement, plus any interest accrued at a rate of 1.5% between the due date and date of payment. Defendant informed plaintiff of his intent to terminate the agreement, and plaintiff filed suit to recover unpaid liquidated damages. The district court granted default judgment against the defendants, both the franchisee himself and his guarantor on the franchise agreement, and found them liable for the liquidated damages. In doing so, the court pointed to the fact that the "Defendants ha[d] not participated in the litigation despite being served with the Complaint nearly one year [earlier]." However, because plaintiff requested what appeared to the court to be an inappropriate amount of liquidated damages under the terms of the franchise agreement, the district court reserved decision on the amount of liquidated damages to be awarded pending a motion by plaintiff.

Choice Hotels International, Inc. v. Patel, No. CV TDC-22-2310, 2023 WL 3276487 (D. Md. May 5, 2023). The court affirmed an arbitration award, pursuant to an arbitration provision in a franchise agreement, because the franchisee failed to participate in the arbitration proceeding and, subsequently, failed to respond to the court action and provide grounds to vacate the award, resulting in a default judgment for the award. This case is discussed in Chapter 8, Section VI.D.

In ***Choice Hotels International v. Seven Star Hotels Group, LLC***, No. 8:22-CV-748-AAQ, 2023 WL 1928016 (D. Md. Feb. 10, 2023), plaintiff's motion for default judgment was granted by the court, enforcing the arbitration award, including damages, procured by the plaintiff against the defendants, after the court found that a valid arbitration agreement existed between the parties, the defendants were unresponsive to both a summons and application, and there was no basis for vacating the award.

Cynthia Gratton LLC v. Original Green Acres Café LLC, No. 2:20-cv-02085-MHH, 2023 WL 1070606 (N.D. Ala. Jan. 27, 2023). This is a case involving allegations of trademark infringement under the Lanham Act, trademark dilution, and false designation of origin, which allegedly caused customer confusion, damaged Green Acres's goodwill, and damaged the value of the marks and brand. This decision involved Green Acres Café's motion for a default judgment against Original Green Acres Café, which had not appeared in the action.

The court held that Green Acres was entitled to default judgment on its claim of trademark infringement under the Lanham Act by analyzing seven factors under a totality of the circumstances test to assess the likelihood of confusion. Under this analysis, the court held that the registered trademark was a strong mark and the two parties' marks were identical in spelling, among other reasons.

The court further issued a permanent injunction to prevent violations of trademark law by applying the traditional four-factor framework that

CHAPTER 8

governs the award of injunctive relief (as set forth in *eBay Inc. v. MercExchange, LLC*, 547 U.S. 388, 394 (2006)). Since defendants admitted that Green Acres experienced harm to its goodwill and reputation due to the trademark infringement and given that Green Acres's interest in controlling its mark outweighed any harm to Original Green Acres Café, the court held that an injunction would not disserve the public.

Additionally, the court awarded damages to compensate Green Acres for unpaid royalties and franchise fees, for incidental expenses Acres may have incurred because of the infringement, and for income Green Acres could have generated had it invested the franchise fees and royalties that defendants should have paid. Under this analysis, a court may award actual damages by calculating the amount of royalty payments a plaintiff would have received during the period that the defendants were diluting or using a colorable imitation of the plaintiff's trademark "had the defendants been a genuine franchise."

Last, the court awarded attorney's fees and deemed this to be an "exceptional case" because the court inferred from the defendant's failure to respond to Green Acres's request to stop using the Green Acres trade name and marks that the defendants' conduct was intentional. As a result, the court granted the default judgment and in a separate order, permanently enjoined the defendants from infringing on the Green Acres trademark.

Hicks v. Colorado Hamburger Company, Inc., No. 22CA0968, 2022 WL 17982947 (Colo. App. Ct. Dec. 29, 2022). The Colorado Court of Appeals heard an interlocutory appeal of the trial court's denial of the plaintiff's motion to certify a class of fast-food workers. Plaintiff was employed by Colorado Hamburger, owner of a McDonald's franchise. Plaintiff claimed that defendant had violated certain Colorado regulations designed to protect hourly wage earners, in particular requirements that employees be provided with meal and rest breaks. These regulations provide employees with a private right of action if they are paid "less than the full wages or other compensation owed" by their employers.

The meal break regulation requires employers to provide employees with "an uncompensated, uninterrupted, and 'duty-free meal period'" of at least 30 minutes when a shift exceeds five consecutive hours. There is an exception, however, if providing a 30-minute uninterrupted meal period is impractical. In that case, employees can instead consume an on-duty meal and be fully compensated for their time. The rest break regulation requires employers to provide employees with "a compensated 10-minute rest period for each 4 hours of work, or major fractions thereof." If the employer fails to do so, it has effectively failed to pay the employee ten minutes of wages.

After some discovery was completed, the district court determined that, while the putative class met certain of the requirements for certification (such as numerosity and adequacy of the class representative), there was no common question that predominated over individual ones. On appeal, the court considered whether plaintiff had offered sufficient evidence to support an inference that there was a predominant question of law or fact among the members of the class. More specifically, the court considered whether Colorado Hamburger's employee handbook, timesheets, and seventy affidavits that were submitted (and that uniformly stated that the employees always clocked in and out for rest breaks, however their timesheets did not reflect that they took rest breaks) supported an inference that Colorado Hamburger did not authorize and permit breaks in violation of the above-cited regulations, or whether the evidence established that employees may have waived their breaks or failed to record them. Regarding meal breaks, the court determined that individual questions predominated over common issues due to the exception in the regulation allowing for on-the-clock meals. To prove liability and damages on this point, plaintiffs would have to individually show that their managers failed to provide them with an option to have an on-the-clock meal for every missed meal break on their timesheets. Since the individualized inquiries predominated over common issues, the court affirmed the trial court's decision that Plaintiff had failed to meet his burden for certifying a class on the meal break issue.

With respect to rest breaks, however, the court rejected the district court's finding that a class-wide inference was impermissible because the franchise's employees could have waived or failed to record their rest breaks, and found there was sufficient circumstantial evidence to support the possibility of a class-wide inference. The court also pointed to Colorado's policy favoring maintenance of a class action, and held that a jury could reasonably conclude that defendant's managers were unable or unwilling to authorize rest breaks because of staffing issues. In addition, after the lawsuit was filed, the franchise's employees "effectively ceased 'waiving' their breaks," which further supported an inference that they had not waived them in the first place. The court therefore determined that plaintiff satisfied the requirements for class certification with respect to the rest break regulation and claim.

JTH Tax LLC v. Caswell, No. 2:21-cv-339, 2022 WL 3580747 (E.D. Va. Aug. 19, 2022). The court entered a default judgment in favor of the plaintiff franchisor, which franchises Liberty Tax Service businesses, owns the federally-registered Liberty Tax Service® trademarks, and is one of the largest tax preparation businesses in the U.S. The case arose from a dispute between the plaintiff defendant, plaintiff's former franchisee. Plaintiff terminated the parties' franchise agreements due to defendant's abandonment of the business. It subsequently filed a lawsuit asserting several breach of contract claims against defendant. When defendant failed to respond, plaintiff moved for a default judgment and submitted documentary and other evidence to establish its damages. In its judgment, the court held defendant liable for, and awarded to plaintiff, damages, attorney's fees, and post-judgement interest.

Kraze Burger, Inc. v. Kraze International, Inc., No. 1:19cv0717 (CMH/JFA), 2023 WL 4357251 (E.D. Va. May 19, 2023). In 2010, plaintiff and Kraze International entered into a master franchise agreement ("MFA") for plaintiff to become the master franchisee in the United States for the Kraze Burger chain. Kraze International was the master franchisor and was based in South Korea. Defendant Il Seon Noh ("Noh") was a director and President of Kraze International. Plaintiff claimed that it invested millions of dollars and otherwise used its best efforts to establish a successful Kraze Burger franchise system and operation in the United States. But it accused defendants of breaching their agreements to provide various forms of support to plaintiff (including training, product information, recipes and advisory assistance), eventually causing Kraze Burger to fail as a burger restaurant franchise in the U.S. In 2014, plaintiff sued Kraze International in state court in Virginia for breach of contract. In 2016, Kraze International filed for bankruptcy protection in Korea. The company then filed a petition for recognition of foreign bankruptcy in the Bankruptcy Court for the Eastern District of Virginia. Noh signed the U.S. bankruptcy petition as the authorized representative of Kraze International and also completed a form designating him as an individual with authority to act on behalf of the company. The Virginia state court action (which was against Kraze International only, and not Noh) was stayed pending the outcome of the Korean bankruptcy proceeding. The Korean bankruptcy proceeding was dismissed in September 2016, however neither Kraze International nor Noh advised plaintiff or the Virginia bankruptcy court of this until Kraze International filed a motion to dismiss the state court case in June 2018. In 2017, Kraze International had transferred and/or sold significant corporate assets worth about $4 million to third parties.

After the stay was lifted, in February 2019, the jury in the Virginia state court case found that Kraze International breached its contract with plaintiff and awarded plaintiff $750,000 in damages. In June 2019, plaintiff filed a complaint for fraud and fraudulent conveyance against Kraze International and Noh in the Eastern District of Virginia. Neither defendant responded and plaintiff moved for entry of a default and, subsequently, for a final default judgment against Noh only. The magistrate judge issued his proposed findings of fact and recommendations, including a finding that Noh was liable for fraud, and recommended a default judgment be entered in plaintiff's favor against Noh for $750,000 plus post-judgment interest, costs and attorney's fees.

Little Caesar Enterprises, Inc. v. Walters Investments, Inc., No. 2:21-CV-12829-TGB, 2023 WL 373869 (E.D. Mich. Jan. 24, 2023). The court granted plaintiff franchisor's motion for a default judgment against its franchisee based on the franchisee's violations of the parties' franchise agreement. Among other things, the court noted that the franchisee had failed to pay Little Caesar required payments under the agreement and had also stopped operating the franchise for three or more consecutive days. The court enforced the agreement's liquidated damages provision for such a default, and awarded Little Caesar a lump sum payment as damages for the franchisee's breach and for Little Caesar's lost future revenues. The court held that liquidated damages provisions are enforceable under Michigan law, especially where damages arising from the breach are uncertain and difficult to determine. The court also awarded Little Caesar its attorney's fees.

Super 8 Worldwide Inc. v. Nirgam Enterprises, LLC, No. 2:11-CV-06447 (WJM), 2023 WL 1360135 (D.N.J. Jan. 30, 2023). Plaintiff franchisor obtained default judgment in the amount of $687,097.86 against its franchisee for violation of the franchise agreement, in addition to attorneys' fees and costs. Plaintiff assigned the judgment to Poser Investments, which moved for an order to turnover funds, following which defendants filed a notice of appearance for the first time since the case had been filed eleven years earlier, for the purpose of opposing Poser's motion and to move to vacate the default judgment. The court granted plaintiff's motion to turnover funds and denied defendants' motion to vacate, finding that three of the reasons a court may vacate a judgment under Fed. R. Civ. P. 60(b) were time barred, and that as to the remaining three reasons the defendants had failed to make arguments in support of those reasons "within a reasonable time," as required under Rule 60(b).

Udenze v. Monique Johnston, Director, Motor Vehicle Division Texas DMV, No. 03-22-00084-CV, 2023 WL 4110854 (Tex. App. June 22, 2023). Plaintiffs Anthony Udenze and Fidel Udenze ("the Udenzes") filed this appeal of the DMV's revocation of their vehicle dealer license and imposition of an $8,000 civil penalty for various violations of the dealer license laws. The

CHAPTER 8

Udenzes received a Notice of Departmental Decision ("NODD") from the Motor Vehicle Division Texas DMV ("DMV") that notified them that they could appeal the decision by making a written request for an administrative hearing. The Udenzes failed to make this request but undertook informal settlement discussions with a DMV attorney. In the absence of a written request for hearing, the DMV issued a final order adopting the NODD. The Udenzes filed a Motion for Rehearing, which was denied. This appeal followed. On appeal, the Udenzes made three claims: (1) the DMV should have interpreted their initial emailed settlement discussions as a written request for a hearing, (2) under what is known as a *Craddock* defense, the default order against them should be vacated because (a) their default was unintentional and not the result of conscious indifference, (b) they had a meritorious defense to the allegations, and (c) setting aside the default will not delay or otherwise injure the DMV, and (3) the DMV's action denied them due process. As to the first claim, the court found that none of the Udenzes' actions could be interpreted as a hearing request. On the second claim, while acknowledging that a *Craddock* defense can be applied in administrative proceedings, the court noted that to meet the first prong, the Udenzes would have had to provide an excuse for originally failing to request a hearing, with verified factual allegations or an affidavit authenticating documents supporting their claim, neither of which was present. The court also found no merit to the third claim.

XIII. Settlements and Releases

Hillstone Restaurant Group Inc. v. Houston's Hot Chicken Inc., No. CV-22-02004-PHX-MTL, 2023 WL 110926 (D. Ariz. Jan. 4, 2023) (court found defendant had breached a settlement agreement it entered into with plaintiff, which owns the mark Houston's and operates several Houston's restaurants, and pursuant to which defendant agreed to cease using the mark Houston's Hot Chicken in connection with its restaurants, several of which are operated by franchisees, and therefore granted in part plaintiff's motion for preliminary injunction and required defendant to notify its franchisees of the terms of the settlement and to cease the use of paper products in its restaurants that have the Houston's Hot Chicken mark on them). This case is also discussed in Chapter 5, Section II.

In *O'Neal v. American Shaman Franchise System, LLC*, No. 8:20-CV-936-KKM-AAS, 2023 WL 2455627 (M.D. Fla. Jan. 30, 2023), report and recommendation adopted sub nom. O'Neal v. American Shaman Franchise System, 8:20-CV-936-KKM-AAS, 2023 WL 2071911 (M.D. Fla. Feb. 17,

2023), the plaintiff, who was hired to manage one or more company-owned franchise locations, sued the franchisor and related parties for breach of contract and violations of the Fair Labor Standards Act. The plaintiff also sued two franchise owners for tortious interference with contract. The plaintiff settled with the franchisor and its related parties. The plaintiff then obtained a judgment by default against the owners of the other franchise. Post-judgment, the plaintiff obtained leave to file a supplemental complaint. The franchisor and related party defendants counterclaimed to the supplemental complaint on the basis that filing the supplemental complaint violated the settlement agreement between those parties and the franchisor defendants also sought attorneys' fees as part of the counterclaim.

The court had previously granted the franchisor-defendants' motion for judgment on the pleadings and dismissed the supplemental complaint. The plaintiff then moved for summary judgment on the counterclaims, arguing that Florida's litigation privilege gave him immunity from suit for filing the supplemental complaint, and arguing further that the supplemental complaint did not violate the terms of those parties' settlement agreement. Lastly, the plaintiff argued that no statute or contract afforded the franchisor-defendants attorneys' fees. The court denied summary judgment, finding that the plaintiff had violated the terms of the settlement agreement, which barred him from reasserting the claims against the franchisor-defendants. The court also found that the litigation privilege is inapplicable to the filing of a lawsuit where the filing violates a contract. The court also denied summary judgment on the request for attorneys' fees, noting that there was evidence to suggest that the plaintiff and/or his counsel may have acted in bad faith in bringing the supplemental complaint.

XIV. Enforcement and Collection

Tropical Paradise Resorts, LLC v. JBSHBM, LLC, No. 18-CV-60912, 2023 WL 1927298 (S.D. Fla. Feb. 10, 2023) Choice Hotels International Inc. ("Choice"), the franchisor, obtained a judgment against Point Conversions LLC ("PC"). Thereafter, Choice filed a supplemental pleading in aid of judgment in which Choice named the attorney who had represented PC in the underlying litigation that resulted in the judgment and in more than forty-five other cases PC brought against Choice's franchisees, along with other defendants. The claims against PC's attorney were based on allegations of alter-ego and veil piercing. PC's attorney defaulted by failing to answer the supplemental proceeding. The court denied his motion to vacate the default, finding that the failure to answer was willful because the defendant knew the supplemental proceeding was filed against him, he actively filed papers with

CHAPTER 8

the court on behalf of PC after being served with the supplemental complaint, but failed to respond or to request an extension to respond by the February 3, 2022 response deadline or by the court-ordered deadline of February 15, 2022. The court then entered judgment by default against the defendant in the amount of $106,696.25, which was the balance outstanding on the underlying judgment.

XV. Withdrawal/Disqualification of Counsel

The authors' review of cases decided during the reporting period did not reveal any significant decisions addressing this topic.

XVI. Other Issues

Braman Motors, Inc. v. BMW of North America, LLC, No. 17-23360-CIV, 2022 WL 17583440 (S.D. Fla. Nov. 18, 2022). Plaintiffs Braman Motors, Inc. and Palm Beach Imports, Inc., brought claims for injunctive relief (not damages) against defendant BMW of North America, LLC for violation of the Florida Dealer Act. Defendant moved in limine to preclude plaintiffs from offering evidence of nominal damages and to exclude such expert testimony because damages were not at issue. The magistrate judge recommended that plaintiffs be allowed to present expert testimony as to harm, but not as to damages.

Brar v. Sourdough & Co., No. C095424, 2023 WL 3219706 (Cal. Ct. App. May 3, 2023). This case discussed the applicability of an exception to California's Anti-SLAPP statute for commercial speech. The licensor tried to sustain a fraud and deceit claim against a licensee, citing language the licensee raised in its complaint that contradicted a purported agreement between the licensor and the licensee. The court determined that language in a complaint is not commercial speech and sustained the lower court's application of the anti-SLAPP statute to the licensor's claim.

Contour-Sierra Inc. v. AEBI Schmidt International, AG, No. 2:22-CV-00414-JAM-JDP, 2022 WL17670009 (E.D. Cal. Dec. 14, 2022). In an action for breach of a dealership agreement, the Swiss defendant moved to dismiss the action under Fed. R. Civ. P. 12(b)(5) for insufficient service of process, asserting that it was not served with the incorporated exhibits as required Fed. R. Civ. P. 10(c) and the exhibits were not translated, as required by the Hague convention. The district court agreed that plaintiff's failure to serve the incorporated exhibits – the exclusive dealership agreement and notice of termination – amounted to insufficient service of process. The court converted plaintiff's motion to a motion to quash service rather than dismissing the action and provided plaintiff an opportunity to cure the service defect.

Craig Alan Herremans v. Randy Fedo, Adversary Proceeding No. 17-80086, 2023 WL 4611429 (Bankr. W.D. Mich. July 18, 2023). In this adversary shareholder oppression proceeding in the bankruptcy court, the court determined that requiring one shareholder to buy out the other shareholder was the appropriate remedy after finding shareholder oppression. The court then made a determination of the "fair value" of the oppressed shareholder's stock. Valuation testimony established that the Ponderosa franchise system was in decline, such that the value of the business was in the real estate it owned and the assets on the books with no value attributed to going concern or goodwill. The court then determined the fair value using an asset based approach.

Dana Innovations v. Trends Electronics International Inc., No. 8:22-cv-02155-FWS-ADS, 2023 WL 3335909 (C.D. Cal. Apr. 21, 2023). Defendants filed a motion to stay proceedings while a parallel proceeding was litigated in Canada. The court determined that the interests in the case did not warrant a stay of the action under the *Colorado River* analysis, and that the "'pendency of an action in [a] [foreign] court is no bar to proceedings concerning the same matter in the [f]ederal court having jurisdiction' by itself." This case is discussed in Chapter 4, Section II.A.

Dauntless Enterprises, Inc. v. City Wide Franchise Co., Inc., No. 23-2273-JAR-TJJ, 2023 WL 4264118 (D. Kan. June 29, 2023) (denying party's request to bar franchise expert from testifying due to expedited discovery schedule and notice of expert requirements).

District of Columbia v. JTH Tax, LLC, No. C.A. 22-3165(CKK), 2023 WL 130736 (D.C. Jan. 9, 2023) (remanding case after finding the parties lacked diversity because the District of Columbia, which sued the defendant franchisor for alleged deceptive business practices employed by its franchisees, was a real party in interest and not merely a nominal party on behalf of the citizens of its jurisdiction).

Estate of Myrick v. 7-Eleven Inc., No. 23-829, 2023 WL 4140829 (E.D. Pa. June 22, 2023). In a premises liability case where an individual died at a franchised location as a result of gunfire, 7-Eleven sought to remove the action

CHAPTER 8

based on diversity under the theory of fraudulent joinder, and the plaintiffs moved to remand. 7-Eleven asserted that the plaintiff added a 7-Eleven corporate asset manager to destroy diversity, but the court disagreed and remanded the case to state court, explaining that the responsibility of the corporate asset manager at the franchised location was a question of fact. As such, the court determined that the plaintiffs had asserted a colorable claim as to the asset manager, so 7-Eleven failed to meet the high standard to prevail on its fraudulent joinder theory and removal was improper.

Eskimo Hut Worldwide, Ltd. v. South Plains Sno, Inc., No. 07-22-00259-CV, 2023 WL 177684 (Tex. Ct. App. Jan. 9, 2023) (court granted Eskimo Hut's petition and allowed a permissive, interlocutory appeal of the lower court's order granting partial summary judgment, in a dispute regarding whether certain requirements of the parties' franchise agreement (such as a prohibition on the defendant franchisee's mixing and selling frozen alcoholic beverages which do not include flavoring mixes specified by plaintiff, conflicted with the Texas Alcoholic Beverage Code, since the order involved controlling questions of law to which there was a substantial ground for difference of opinion, and immediate appeal may materially advance the ultimate termination of the litigation).

Franlink Inc. v. BACE Services, Inc., 50 F.4th 432 (5th Cir. 2022). The Fifth Circuit held that the district court miscalculated the amount of damages owed to a franchisor under the franchise agreement and that the district court improperly awarded future damages in addition to a permanent injunction. This case is discussed in Chapter 8, Section III.

Gonzalez v. Coverall North America, Inc., No. EDCV1602287JGBKKX, 2022 WL 17903078 (C.D. Cal. Dec. 8, 2022). In 2016, plaintiff Sergio Gonzalez ("Gonzalez") filed a class action against defendant Coverall North America, Inc. ("Coverall"), alleging that he, along with others similarly situated, were misclassified as independent contractors instead of employees. In response, Coverall moved to compel arbitration based on the parties' janitorial franchise agreement.

In April of 2017, Gonzalez moved to dismiss the case without prejudice so he could appeal the arbitration order. The court granted the motion to dismiss. In June of 2017, Gonzalez appealed the arbitration order to the Ninth Circuit. The Ninth Circuit dismissed his appeal, holding that Gonzalez lacked jurisdiction. Specifically, the Ninth Circuit held that Gonzalez's voluntary dismissal without prejudice was not a final judgment upon which he could appeal. In March of 2019, Gonzalez filed a renewed motion to reopen the case pursuant to Rule 60(b)(6), and in April of 2019, the court denied his motion. In May of 2019, Gonzalez appealed the court's reconsideration order to the Ninth Circuit. While the appeal was pending, the Ninth Circuit decided *Henson v. Fidelity National Financial, Inc.*, 943 F.3d 434 (9th Cir. 2019). In October 2020, the Ninth Circuit remanded the case to allow this court to consider whether *Henson* factors applied to the case at hand.

Henson outlined several factors for a district court's consideration when evaluating a Rule 60(b)(6) motion seeking relief from a dismissal of a lawsuit on the grounds of an intervening change of law. The court ultimately decided that the case at hand was different from *Henson* because Gonzalez was not blindsided by an unfavorable change in the law; in fact, when Gonzalez moved to voluntarily dismiss his claims, the Ninth Circuit relied on long-standing precedent in their decision to deny such a motion. According to the court, given pre-existing case law, Gonzalez knew or should have known the risk in his litigation strategy.

In sum, the court denied Gonzalez's motion because he asked for the court to undo a dismissal he himself requested, over Coverall's objections, under pre-existing law that disfavored his litigation strategy, and instead of seeking other options that were available.

Peterson Motorcars, LLC v. BMW of North America, LLC, No. 3:19-cv-277-DJH-RSE, 2022 WL 4125102 (W.D. Ky. Sept. 9, 2022). In case involving MINI dealer's claim that the defendant franchisor did not adequately support the efforts of its dealer franchisees, primarily by failing to conduct sufficient advertising regarding MINI vehicles and also failing to introduce new models of the car that customers would want to purchase, the court granted defendant's motion to exclude plaintiff's expert who opined on these issues. The court held that the expert had not conducted any independent market analysis to support his opinion, made certain unfounded assumptions, and failed to take into account various important factors that would affect his analysis and opinions. The court found that plaintiff's expert's "reliance on unsupported speculation and improper extrapolation and the absence of any independent analysis render[ed] his opinions unreliable." The court therefore granted BMW's motion to exclude the expert's opinions. This case is discussed in Chapter 4, Section II.A.

Reinvestment Fund, Inc. v. Rauh, No. A-3184-21, 2022 WL 17587863 (N.J. Super. Ct. App. Div. Dec. 13, 2022). Plaintiff-lender sued multiple defendants alleging a default of the licensing agreements for the acquisition of Save-a-Lot stores. Some defendants were parties to the licensing agreements, while other defendants were not. The district court compelled arbitration for claims against defendants who were parties to the licensing agreements and severed and then stayed claims against defendants who were not parties to the licensing agreements.

The appellate court vacated the stay and remanded because the district court judge did not provide any rationale for staying the non-arbitrable claims. The appellate court also noted that the decision to stay proceedings on only some of the claims was not clear considering the overlap of discovery in both the arbitrable and non-arbitrable claims.

Wheelmaxx, Inc. v. Mahul, No. 1:22-CV-01506-ADA-SKO, 2023 WL 3224161 (E.D. Cal. May 3, 2023) (court denied franchisor's motion for permission to serve franchisee by publication, finding that the franchisor, which was suing the franchisee for breaches of the parties' franchise agreement, had not demonstrated reasonable diligence in its efforts to serve the defendant, but providing plaintiff with an additional 60 days to effectuate service).

CHAPTER 9

International Developments

I. Introduction

This international chapter reports on cases, laws and developments affecting franchising in eight countries. A recurring theme across the countries is the increased focus on data privacy and cybersecurity. This chapter also reports on developments related to competition law and antitrust matters. While more countries are adding franchise specific laws, it is worth noting that many still do not have franchise specific laws. In those instances, general commercial law should be consulted.

II. Australia

By Iain Irvine and Riley Tully, VARDONS

Iain Irvine is a commercial lawyer and provides specialized advice in relation to franchising, licensing, distribution and intellectual property.

Riley Tully is a commercial litigator and assists with preparation of commercial lease agreements and landlord enforcement actions.

CHAPTER 9

A. LEGISLATIVE UPDATE

1. Franchise Disclosure Register

A mandatory online register of franchises (franchisedisclosure.gov.au), administered by the Australian Government's Department of the Treasury, commenced November 15, 2022. Franchisors who previously made a disclosure under the *Franchising Code of Conduct* on or before October 31, 2022 were required to register on or before November 14, 2022. However, a master franchisor in a master franchise system, was only required to register if it had two (2) or more subfranchisors.

Franchisors proposing to grant a franchise in Australia must register at least fourteen (14) days before entering into a franchise agreement. The registration requirement will not apply if franchising is limited to a single master franchise grant.

The requirement to register is a civil penalty provision of the Code. Franchisors must enter the following information on the register:

(a) The franchisor's name.
(b) The name under which the franchisor carries on business in Australia relevant to the franchise.
(c) If the franchisor has an ABN—the franchisor's ABN.
(d) The address, or addresses, of the franchisor's registered office and principal place of business in Australia.
(e) The business telephone number and email address of the franchisor.
(f) The Australian and New Zealand Standard Industrial Classification (ANZSIC) division and subdivision codes for the industry in which the business operated under the franchise operates.
(g) Any other information required by the Secretary and which is required to be included in a disclosure document excluding:
  (i) personal information that relates to an individual other than the franchisor; or
  (ii) information that relates to a particular franchisee or a particular site being occupied by a franchisee.

Immediately prior to commencement of the register the Secretary made the *Competition and Consumer (Industry Codes—Franchising) (Additional Information Required by the Secretary) Determination 2022* requiring the following additional information to be included on the register:

International Developments

(a) The number of years that the franchise or franchise system has operated in Australia.
(b) The number of existing franchised businesses and franchisees, and businesses owned or operated by the franchisor or an associate of the franchisor in Australia that are substantially the same as the franchised business.
(c) Each State or Territory in which a franchisor owned unit or franchisee operates.g
(d) In relation to a franchisor's requirements for the supply of goods or services to a franchisee—whether there are restrictions on the acquisition of goods or services by the franchisee from other sources.
(e) If the franchisor requires payment before a franchise agreement is entered into—why the money is required, how the money is to be applied, who will hold the money, and the conditions under which a payment will be refunded.
(f) Details of the costs payable by a franchisee to start operating the franchised business. Details of costs may include upper and lower limits of potential costs, a description of potential costs or both.
(g) Details of payments payable by a franchisee to the franchisor, or an associate of the franchisor, during the term of the franchise agreement. Details of payments may include upper and lower limits of potential payments, a description of potential payments or both.
(h) Details of payments payable by a franchisee to a person other than the franchisor or an associate of the franchisor. Details of payments may include upper and lower limits of potential payments, a description of potential payments or both.
(i) Whether the franchise agreement may be varied, unilaterally, by the franchisor.
(j) The term of the franchise agreement.
(k) Whether a franchisee has an option to renew the franchise agreement.
(l) Whether a franchisee has any rights relating to any goodwill generated by the franchisee.
(n) Whether the franchise agreement includes a restraint of trade or similar clause.

For existing franchisors, this additional information was not required if the franchisor had entered into only one franchise agreement and did not intend to enter into further agreements.

CHAPTER 9

Franchisors are permitted, on a voluntarily basis, to upload copies of their disclosure document, Key Facts Sheet, standard form franchise agreement and trademark. Any personal information relating to an individual, information relating to a particular franchisee or information relating to a particular franchised site must be redacted and any commercially sensitive information may be redacted.

Registrations must be updated annually on or before the 14th day of the fifth month following the end of the franchisor's financial year.

Section 53J of the Code provides for review of the new Part 5A of the Franchising Code (which addresses the register) between November 15, 2023 and June 30, 2024. The review must include an opportunity for franchise industry stakeholders to make written submissions.

2. Unfair Terms in Standard Form Small Business Contracts

Section 23 of the *Australian Consumer Law* provides that unfair terms in standard form small business contracts are void. On November 9, 2023 amendments to these laws will commence pursuant to the *Treasury Laws Amendment (More Competition, Better Prices) Act 2022*. The amendments introduce a civil penalty regime prohibiting the use and reliance on unfair contract terms in standard form small business contracts, expand the class of contracts covered by the unfair contract terms provisions and make clarifying amendments in relation to the meaning of standard form. These laws will apply to many franchise and distribution agreements. The changes include:

(a) A prohibition on a person making a standard form small business contract containing an unfair term the person proposed.

(b) A prohibition on a person applying or relying on or purporting to apply or rely on an unfair term in a standard form small business contract.

(c) The maximum applicable penalty is:
  (i) for a company, the greater of:
    - AU$50 million;
    - if the court can determine the value of the benefit obtained from the contravention—three (3) times the value of that benefit;
    - if the court cannot determine the value of that benefit—30% of the body corporate's adjusted turnover during the breach turnover period;

International Developments

(ii) for a natural person, AU$2.5 million.

Adjusted turnover includes the revenues of the body corporate as well as its related bodies corporate but excludes the value of any supplies that are not connected with the indirect tax zone.

Breach turnover period means the longer of: a period of 12 months ending at the end of the month in which the contravention ceased or proceedings commenced (whichever is earlier); or a period commencing at the beginning of the month in which the contravention occurred or began and ending at the end of the month in which the contravention ceased or proceedings commenced (whichever is earlier).

(d) Actions by persons affected by a contravention or by the regulator seeking injunctions and compensation or damages can also be brought.

(e) In determining whether a contract is standard form a court must take account whether a party has made substantially similar contracts prepared by it and, if so, how many such contracts it has made.

(f) A contract may be determined to be standard form despite the existence of one or more of the following:
  (i) An opportunity for a party to negotiate changes to terms of the contract, that are minor or insubstantial in effect.
  (ii) An opportunity for a party to select a term from a range of options provided by another party.
  (iii) An opportunity for a party to another contract to negotiate terms of the other contract.

(g) A contract is a small business contract if the contract is for a supply of goods or services, or a sale or grant of an interest in land and at least one party to the contract satisfies either or both of the following conditions:
  (i) The party employs fewer than 100 persons.
  (ii) The party's turnover for the party's last income year is less than AU$10 million.

The current test is much more limited, requiring one party to employ fewer than 20 persons and the upfront price payable under the contract to be below certain thresholds.

These changes apply to contracts made, renewed, or varied on or after November 9, 2023.

CHAPTER 9

B. CASE LAW DEVELOPMENTS

Narellan Franchise Pty Ltd v RBME Pty Ltd (No 2) [2022] NSWSC 1590. The franchisor of a fiberglass swimming pool sale and installation system sought to enforce restraints of trade following ending of two franchise agreements. The term of one of the written agreements expired and the franchise agreement provided for a monthly license on the terms set out in the franchise agreement, as appropriate. The restraints were expressed to run from expiration or termination and the franchisee argued the formal expiration date of the agreement was the relevant date. The court disagreed finding that on a commercial construction of the terms the end of the license period was the relevant date. The court determined that the restraint against operating a competing business was unreasonable as the franchises did not benefit from repeat customers and work was obtained by the franchisor (e.g. by means of a centralized customer enquiry system) as the result of its brand and system marketing. The length of the restraint was also found to be unreasonable as it extended beyond the necessary period to train a replacement franchisee which could receive the franchisor's work referrals. The restraint sought against completing customer contracts entered into prior to expiry was also found to be unreasonable on the basis that this would not protect a legitimate interest of the franchisor and would be more likely to harm the Narellan brand. Further, the franchisor was in a good position to acquire these contracts in the absence of the restraint (as the former franchisee could not complete the contracts using the ordered product) if it chose to do so.

III. Cambodia

By Jay Cohen, Chanraksmey Sokun and Teo Pastor, TILLEKE & GIBBINS

Jay Cohen is a partner and director of the firm and leads the Phnom office's commercial and intellectual property practice. He has over fifteen years of

International Developments

experience assisting clients in inbound transactions, and his practice covers a broad spectrum of investment processes.

Chanraksmey Sokun is an associate and assists clients in trademarks, patents and other intellectual property matters, including registration, enforcement, anti-counterfeiting strategies and commercialization.

Teo Pastor is an associate in the corporate and commercial practice and has broad experience in various transactional practice areas, such as capital markets, corporate finance, banking and corporate/M&A.

A. NEW COMPETITION REGULATION SETTING PENALTY FOR VERTICAL AGREEMENTS

In March 2023, Cambodia issued three administrative regulations to strengthen its competition law framework. One of such regulations, Inter-Ministerial Prakas No. 168 on Penalties for Persons Violating the Law on Competition ("Prakas 168"), March 28, 2023, complements the Law on Competition by setting penalties for anti-competitive activities, such as entering into vertical agreements. Pursuant to the 2021 Law on Competition and Prakas 168, vertical agreements involve:

(i) requiring buyers to resell goods or services in limited geographic locations;
(ii) requiring buyers to resell goods or services to specific customers or specific types of customers;
(iii) requiring buyers to purchase goods or services from one seller only;
(iv) preventing sellers from selling goods or service to other buyers; or
(v) requiring buyers to buy additional goods or services that are not related to the goods or services being sold.

The penalty for entering into a vertical agreement is a fine of three percent (3%) to ten percent (10%) of the infringer's total turnover during the period of violation, limited to a period of three years.

The Law on Competition and Prakas 168 does not include any specific carve-outs or thresholds for franchise agreements that limit distribution to a certain geographic area or contain other limitations common in franchise operations. This legal gap risks deeming franchise agreements in Cambodia as vertical agreements, which are prohibited, as outlined above.

Thus, parties to franchise agreements in Cambodia may wish to submit a request for an exemption to the Cambodia Competition Commission

CHAPTER 9

as provided in the Law on Competition. The parties must provide documentary evidence that the franchise agreement fulfills all the following criteria:

(i) there are significant identifiable technological, economic or social benefits;
(ii) such benefits would not exist without the agreement or activities;
(iii) the benefits significantly outweigh the anti-competitive effects; and
(iv) the agreement does not eliminate competition in relevant goods or services.

B. NEW LAW ON TAXATION AND ITS IMPACTS ON FRANCHISES

On May 16, 2023, Cambodia introduced a new Law on Taxation that replaced the previous law from 1997, as amended in 2003.

The new Law on Taxation sets forth a straight-line method of depreciation that is applicable when calculating depreciation of intangible property with a limited lifespan, including franchises. However, if the lifespan of the intangible property is undeterminable, the straight-line method is applied to calculate the annual depreciation for a period of ten (10) years.

In respect of withholding tax, the new law maintains the previous law's provisions mandating that payments of royalties, when made between resident taxpayers, are subject to a 15% withholding tax, and that payments of royalties made to non-resident taxpayers are subject to a 14% withholding tax.

International Developments

IV. India

By Srijoy Das, Disha Mohanty, and Shivalik Chandan

Srijoy Das is a partner and has been practicing for twenty-five years. He leads the firm's commercial intellectual team as well as its franchising and licensing team.

Disha Mohanty is a partner and heads the labor and employment practice. She has extensive experience advising clients on a broad spectrum of employment law matters.

Shivalik Chandan is an associate with the franchise and licensing team.

A. LEGISLATIVE UPDATE

1. Amendments to India's Antitrust Legislation

In April 2023, the Indian Parliament passed an amendment to India's antitrust statute, the Competition Act, 2002. The amendment is aimed at enabling the law to deal with new sectors, including digital markets, and introduces new enforcement mechanisms for offences under the Act. Some of the major changes brought about by the amendment are as follows:

a) In order to cover killer acquisitions, a deal value threshold has been introduced, whereby the antitrust regulator's (Competition Commission of India or CCI) approval is required for transactions where the value exceeds INR 20,000,000,000 (approximately USD 241,340,800) and where the entity being acquired, taken control of, merged, or amalgamated has "substantial business operations" in India. What constitutes "substantial business operations" is to be determined by regulations, which have not been issued yet.

b) The time limit for the CCI to form its opinion on a combination approval has been reduced – the maximum timeframe has been reduced from 210 days from date of issue of notice to the CCI to 150 days from date of issue of notice.

c) The maximum penalty for furnishing false information in cases of combinations has been increased from INR 10,000,000 (approximately USD 120,700) to INR 50,000,000 (approximately USD 603,000).

CHAPTER 9

d) The amendment introduces mechanisms for settlements and commitments of disputes. Entities which are being investigated by the CCI for contravention of the Competition Act, 2002 may make applications for settling the case or offering a commitment regarding the contravention.

While several of the above provisions will need to be notified in order to come into effect, the increase in the maximum penalty for furnishing false information was effective on 18 May 2023.

2. Draft Bill on Protection of Personal Data

In November 2022, the Ministry of Electronics and Information Technology (MEITY) published the draft Digital Personal Data Protection Bill, 2022 (DPDPB). The DPDPB is the latest in a series of draft legislations published by the Indian Government regarding a comprehensive data protection and processing regime. The key definitions under the DPDPB are as follows:

a) Personal Data defined as any data about an individual who is identifiable "by or in relation to" such data.
b) Data Fiduciary, defined as any person who determines the purpose and means of processing the Personal Data (either alone or in conjunction with others). This is similar to the concept of "data controller" under the EU's General Data Protection Regulation.
c) Data Processor defined as any person who processes Personal Data on behalf of the Data Fiduciary.
d) Processing defined as automated operations on Personal Data, including collection, recording, organization, storage, adaptation, use, sharing, dissemination, restriction, or destruction.

Certain key features of the DPDPB have been expanded upon below:

a) The DPDPB will be applicable to the processing of personal data within India, and processing of personal data outside India when such processing is in connection with the profiling of Data Principals within the territory of India or any activity of offering goods or services to such Data Principals.
b) Personal Data may only be processed for a purpose for which the Data Principal has given consent, or when such consent has been deemed to have been given as per the DPDPB.
c) While seeking consent from a Data Principal, the Data Fiduciary must provide an "itemised notice in clear and plain language,"

containing the description of Personal Data to be collected and the purpose of the processing of data. Once consent has been given, the Data Fiduciary must provide an "itemised notice in clear and plain language," with a description of the Personal Data collected and the purpose of the processing. These notices must be provided in English, or any language notified in the Eighth Schedule of the Indian Constitution, on the option of the Data Principal.

d) Any consent given by the Data Principal for the purposes of the DPDPB must be freely given, specific, informed, and unambiguous. The Data Principal may withdraw their consent for processing their Personal Data at any time, and the consequences of such withdrawal are to be borne by the Data Principal. In the event of any proceedings where a question arises as to the consent given by the Data Principal for processing of Personal Data, the Data Fiduciary shall have to prove that a notice was given to the Data Principal, and consent was obtained from the Data Principal for the processing of the Personal Data.

e) Significant Data Fiduciaries are those Data Fiduciaries which may be notified as Significant Data Fiduciaries by the Indian Government, based on an assessment of relevant factors such as the volume and sensitivity of Personal Data processed, risk of harm to the Data Principal, and potential impact on India's sovereignty and integrity. Such Significant Data Fiduciaries will be subject to some enhanced obligations, such as the requirement of appointing a Data Protection Officer and undertaking a Data Protection Impact Assessment as per the DPDPB.

f) The DPDPB provides for the Central Government to notify a list of countries to which a Data Fiduciary may transfer Personal Data, in accordance with any terms and conditions which may be prescribed.

g) Penalties for non-compliance of the provisions of the DPDPB may be imposed, and such penalties may extend up to INR 5,000,000,000 (approximately USD 60,000,000).

A host of obligations have been prescribed for all Data Fiduciaries, some of which are:

a) Notifying the Data Protection Board of India, and affected Data Principals in the event of a data breach, in a manner that is yet to be prescribed. Specific monetary penalties have been prescribed for non-compliance, including a failure to take reasonable

security safeguards to prevent personal data breaches, and failures to notify the aforementioned Board and affected Data Principals of such breaches. These penalties are in the order of INR 2,500,000,000 (approximately USD 30,200,000) and INR 2,000,000,000 (approximately USD 24,200,000) respectively.
b) A Data Fiduciary is required to make reasonable efforts to ensure that personal data processed by it, or on its behalf, is accurate and complete if such data is being used for decision making that might affect the Data Principal, or is likely to be disclosed to another Data Fiduciary.
c) Significant Data Fiduciaries will be required to appoint a Data Protection Officer based in India, and where applicable, publish the contact information of such Data Protection Officer to answer Data Principal's questions about the processing of their Personal Data.

These provisions were published for public feedback as part of a public consultation exercise, and are yet to be tabled in the Indian Parliament. The Central Government has stated that the DPDPB is ready to be tabled in the Monsoon Session of the Parliament, which generally begins in July. It is possible that the version of the DPDPB tabled in Parliament may differ from the draft version made available to the public.

The DPDPB, if and when passed into law, will likely have a significant impact on the operation of franchising in India with regard to data protection. Depending on the nature of the franchising agreement, franchisors may be considered Data Fiduciaries and as such, the obligations regarding data protection may be imposed upon franchisors.

B. CASE LAW UPDATE

N.N. Global Mercantile Pvt. Ltd. v. Indo Unique Flame Ltd., Civil Appeal Nos. 3802-3803 of 2020. In April 2023, the Supreme Court of India held that when a document on which stamp duty is to be paid as per the Indian Stamp Act contains an arbitration clause and stamp duty has not been paid on such document, it cannot be deemed to be an enforceable contract and the arbitration clause will stand unenforceable as well.

This judgement was passed in furtherance of a referral by a three-judge bench of the Supreme Court to a Constitution bench (a five-judge bench). The three-judge bench asked that a Constitution bench authoritatively answer the question of whether a document being unstamped would render an arbitration clause contained in it unenforceable. In the Order issued by the Constitution bench, the Supreme Court held (by a 3:2 majority) that if a contract which is to be stamped as per applicable law has not been stamped, any arbitration agreement or clause which is a part of that contract will not be enforceable. Such a contract (and the corresponding arbitration agreement) will only be enforceable once the stamp duty and requisite penalty for delay in stamping is paid on the underlying contract.

The minority dissenting opinion in this judgement pointed out the adverse effect this would have on the intent of the Indian Arbitration and Conciliation Act, which was passed with a view to streamline the arbitration process in India. An appeal has also been made to the Indian legislature in the dissenting opinion to pass appropriate amendments to the provisions of the Indian Stamp Act with regard to their applicability on the Indian Arbitration and Conciliation Act. However, until such time as such amendments are made (or the present judgement is overruled), care must be taken to ensure that all agreements enforceable in Indian courts which contain arbitration clauses are adequately stamped at their execution.

Gujarat State Civil Supplies Corpn. Ltd. v. Mahakali Foods (P) Ltd., AIR 2022 SC 5545. The Supreme Court of India has held that if an entity defined as a Micro or Small enterprise under the Micro, Small and Medium Enterprises Development Act, 2006 (MSME Act) is entitled to recover an amount due to it from the buyer for the supply of goods or services, such entity may refer the dispute to the Facilitation Council as provided under the MSME Act, even in the presence of an arbitration agreement between the parties which states that any disputes would be referred to arbitration.

The MSME Act grants "suppliers" the right to recover any unpaid amounts from a "buyer" along with interest at a rate of three times the bank rate prescribed by the Reserve Bank of India (India's central bank). The supplier may also refer the dispute to the Facilitation Council set up under the MSME Act for conciliation, and failing a resolution through conciliation, arbitration.

The Supreme Court of India held that as the MSME Act is a special legislation, its provisions override those of the Arbitration and Conciliation Act, 1996 (which the Supreme Court interpreted as a general legislation). Additionally, the Supreme Court observed that the rights given to suppliers under the MSME Act are, by the letter of the law, effective notwithstanding any other inconsistent provision in any other applicable law in India, and as such, these rights would have an overriding effect on any other rights prescribed by Indian law.

In the event that a franchising agreement is entered into with a Micro or Small enterprise, or in the event that sub-franchisees under such an agreement are Micro or Small enterprises, a dispute under such an agreement

CHAPTER 9

regarding unpaid dues for the provision of goods or services may be referred to conciliation and subsequent arbitration (if required) by the Facilitation Council. As held by the Supreme Court in this decision, such reference to the Facilitation Council may be made even if there is a specific and enforceable arbitration agreement between the parties as a part of the franchise (or sub-franchise) agreement.

***Patil Automation Private Limited v. Rakheja Engineers Private Limited.*, AIR 2022 SC 3848.** The Supreme Court reaffirmed that the pre-institution mediation process as outlined in the Commercial Courts Act, 2015 (CC Act) is mandatory, and any suit instituted in a court violating this mandate must be visited with a rejection of the complaint.

The CC Act has set up Commercial Courts in India, whose jurisdiction lies over "commercial disputes" (which specifically include disputes arising from franchise agreements) with a value of INR 300,000 (approximately USD 3,600) or more. The CC Act provides that prior to instituting any suit in a Commercial Court (as long as the suit does not require any urgent interim relief under the CC Act), the plaintiff must exhaust the remedy of mediation in accordance with the rules prescribed for this purpose.

The Supreme Court has held that this requirement is mandatory, keeping in mind the legislative intent behind this provision and the fact that Indian courts are suffering from a very high case load.

Additionally, the Supreme Court set out some requirements which, in its view, are essential for the effective functioning of the CC Act, and specifically the provision regarding mediation:

a) Existence of adequate infrastructural facilities and trained mediators. As such, State Governments and all relevant authorities must focus their attentions towards providing the required facilities and training.

b) Knowledge of the law for the mediators, and the required regular and frequent training by experts, keeping in mind the dearth of trained mediators.

International Developments

V. MALTA

By Philip Formosa and Andrea Grima, Ganado Advocates

Philip Formosa is a senior associate in the intellectual property group. He also regularly assists client with data protection matters.

Andrea Grima is an advocate with the shipping team. He assists companies with corporate and liquidation matters.

A. NO FRANCHISE SPECIFICATION LAW – GENERAL LAW GOVERNS

Franchise arrangements are not specifically regulated under Maltese law, and in fact the terms "franchisor" and "franchisee" find no specific legal definition in Malta. At present, there are thus no mandatory rules or elements prescribed by Maltese law relating to the form or content of a franchise agreement, thereby giving the parties some flexibility as to their mode of contracting and on the contractual terms they may wish to include. In view of this, franchises, much like distribution agreements, are regulated under Maltese law by our general rules and principles on contract. Other legal areas such as real estate, intellectual property, data protection (depending on the extent of any data sharing involved) and competition laws are generally also relevant matters to address in any franchise. There is no legal requirement or specific system *per se* under Maltese law for the registration of a franchise.

B. LEGISLATIVE UPDATE

The main legislative development to have taken place over the past year arguably relates to competition, with the European Union ("EU") having adopted a new Vertical Block Exemption Regulation ("VBER"), which entered into force on June 1, 2022 following the expiry of its predecessor. Retaining generally the same approach and substance as its predecessor, the new VBER provides a safe harbour exemption for vertical agreements, such as franchise agreements, that may in principle fall within the scope of article 101 of the Treaty on the Functioning of the European Union ("TFEU"), but are otherwise deemed to be largely unproblematic on the ground that they meet certain defined conditions (namely, if neither of the party's market share exceeds thirty percent (30%) on the relevant sales and purchasing markets and provided that the terms of the relevant agreement do not contain any so-called "*hardcore restrictions*", such as price resale maintenance). Agreements which do not necessarily meet all such conditions could still be deemed compatible

CHAPTER 9

with article 101, TFEU and thus not anti-competitive, but this would require an individual assessment pursuant to article 101(3), TFEU.

These retained rules are then supplemented by certain novelties that have been introduced by the new VBER, with the main key revisions or changes relating to dual distribution, exclusive and selective distribution networks, parity and most favoured nation clauses, and online sales restrictions. The new VBER is comprised in Commission Regulation (EU) 2022/720 and is supported by revised Vertical Guidelines. It applies to agreements concluded after May 31, 2022 and is valid for a period of twelve (12) years. A one-year transition which was given to allow existing agreements to align with the new VBER and Vertical Guidelines recently expired on May 31, 2023.

Being a Member State, the new VBER is directly applicable in Malta. Therefore, new and existing franchise agreements which are either governed by Maltese law, or which otherwise relate to or are likely to have an effect on competition on the Maltese market and which may affect trade between Malta and any EU Member State, will need to respect and be aligned with such rules in order to benefit from these block exemptions.

As mentioned, this requirement also extends to franchise agreements which are already in effect in view of the expiry of the transition period. Both the VBER and its related guidelines (and their predecessors) have traditionally been relied upon by the competent authority for competition matters in Malta, that is the Office for Competition within the Malta Competition and Consumer Affairs Authority ("MCCAA"), in its assessment on potentially anti-competitive agreements in terms of article 5 of the Maltese Competition Act, Chapter 379 of the laws of Malta, which is the domestic provision in Maltese law mirroring article 101, TFEU, both for agreements having an effect on trade between Member States and for agreements having solely a national dimension.

C. CASE LAW DEVELOPMENTS

In the absence of specific legislation, questions relating to franchising agreements, such as their performance, are thus typically determined based on general rules and principles of contract, as delineated in the Maltese Civil Code, Chapter 16 of the laws of Malta, and in turn further developed through local jurisprudence. Central to this are the principles of "good faith" (requiring contracts to be carried out in good faith) and that of "pacta sunt servanda" (requiring the terms of an agreement to be honoured), both of which have been codified into Maltese law under article 992 and article 933 of the Maltese Civil Code, respectively.

International Developments

Against this background, a wide body of case-law, developed and accumulated by the Maltese Civil Courts, provides further clarity and guidance on the interpretation and application of Maltese contract law to franchise and distribution agreements. Although the larger part of this case-law deals with distribution agreements as their subject matter, the principles espoused in them are generally analogous and relevant to franchising relationships as well.

Turning attention to recent cases, in **Michele Peresso Limited (C-6469) and Michele Peresso Fashion Limited (C-45807) v Upim S.r.l. a foreign company registered in Milan, Italy Cod. Fiscale 05034590967 and Gruppo Coin S.p.A a foreign company registered in Mestre (VE), via Terraglio n.17, 30174, Italy**[1] (Application Number 208/2013 FDP) decided by the First Hall of the Civil Court on the 29th of September 2022, the court found and confirmed that the defendant's (the franchisor) conduct vis-à-vis the plaintiff (the franchisee), both in the negotiations prior to them entering into the respective franchise agreement and also during its operation, demonstrated a lack of loyalty and bad faith which gave rise to extra-contractual damages due to the plaintiff which fell outside of the framework of that franchise agreement and thus not subject to or limited by its contractual provisions.

The case involved a clothing distributor (the plaintiff) who had entered into a 10-year franchise agreement for Malta with the Italian brand "UPIM" in 2008. The franchise was proposed by UPIM, who purposely approached the plaintiff about this, stating that they wanted to expand their brand outside of Italy and into other countries. However, as a negotiating condition to granting the franchise, UPIM insisted that the plaintiff would need to immediately open four dedicated outlets in prominent parts of Malta and the neighbouring island of Gozo. The plaintiff elected to accept this, and the parties set out about identifying potential sites and also proceeded to sign and finalise the franchise agreement. However, shortly after signing the agreement, the plaintiff (as the franchisee) started to experience material delays and errors with the merchandise ordered from the defendant UPIM, to the extent that it even had to open with limited items and stock. Furthermore, later that year, to its surprise, the plaintiff discovered that UPIM was sold in its entirety to the other defendant, Gruppo Coin S.p.A ("COIN"), who announced that it had also assumed all of its debts and planned on reorganising the whole operations of UPIM, including by closing a number of its outlets and revising its product line.

---

[1] The successful franchisee in this case was represented by Ganado Advocates.

CHAPTER 9

From the evidence produced, it transpired that negotiations for the sale of UPIM to COIN had commenced months prior to this franchise agreement and that this information, which was found to be material and would have influenced the plaintiff's decision, had not actually been disclosed. Moreover, the plaintiff had entered into obligations and incurred significant costs based on expectations and demands set up by UPIM, even though the latter was concurrently negotiating its sale to COIN and in circumstances where both UPIM and COIN, as argued by the plaintiff, would not be able to, and knew that they would not manage, to fulfill the contractual obligations assumed to the plaintiff.

As the plaintiff's action was characterised as being based on tortious liability arising from conduct by the defendants of an extra-contractual nature, it was thus deemed to subsist outside of the framework of the parties' franchise agreement and thus, not constrained by its clauses on governing law and jurisdiction (which had provided for Italian law and the Courts of Milan as the venue for contractual disputes). Applying this, the Maltese court determined itself competent to hear the dispute and eventually ruled in favour of the plaintiff, holding itself persuaded that UPIM was aware that, had it informed the plaintiff that it was in the process of being acquired by another company (that is, COIN), the plaintiff would not have entered into a commercial commitment for a period of 10 years, especially in view of the significant costs and investments which this necessitated, ultimately even causing it serious financial difficulties.

The court established that the defendants' decision not to inform the plaintiff of the pending acquisition evidenced both a lack of good faith and malicious intent on their part, thus rendering them liable for the damages suffered by the plaintiff (as liquidated by the court). The case, which has since been appealed by the defendants, highlights that a party's conduct to another, particularly at pre-contractual stage, will not always necessarily be captured by their contractual framework and could thus escape the application of contractual provisions intended to establish a favourable governing law and venue for disputes and even liability limitations.

In *Jane Chircop (I.D. 46644M) vs. Davor Puncuh (Slovenian I.D. 002646115) and Emina Puncuh, joined as a party to these proceedings through a decree on the 14th of March 2019* (Application Number 337/2017 TA) decided by the First Hall, Civil Court on 3rd of March 2022, provided a further assessment into the notion of good faith within the context of a franchise agreement. The plaintiff (being the franchisor) was the owner of a real estate company who entered into a franchise agreement with the defendants (the franchisee), whereby it gave them the right to use and sublicense certain brands, specifically "Sapphire Real Estate Services" and "Only Made in Malta a concept by Sapphire Real Estate", subject to certain terms and conditions.

The plaintiff contended that, despite the defendants having terminated the agreement, they were in default of a number of post-termination obligations included within the contract, had also retained certain proprietary items which they were obliged to return to the plaintiff and furthermore, had continued to use these brands without an existing contract and thus in the absence of the plaintiff's authorisation.

The defendants countered these claims, holding that it was misleading to characterise the agreement as a genuine franchise agreement and that it was null and without effect on the ground that the plaintiff had falsely misrepresented these brands and painted a picture which was divorced from reality in order to, as claimed by the defendants, induce and deceive them into investing in the business. The defendants thus exercised the general remedy for rescission under the Maltese Civil Code, requesting that the agreement be rescinded and dissolved on the ground that their consent had been vitiated by fraud.

The court established that the plaintiff had not presented sufficient evidence proving that it operated a real estate agency business, as had been represented by it in the franchise agreement. It further concluded that there was no brand intellectual property to truly licence in the circumstances and that, in practice, there was no difference between the franchise agreement signed by the defendants and a normal real estate agency agreement. Indirectly, this would imply that, whilst there are no specific elements prescribed by Maltese law that must be included in a franchise agreement, parties still cannot just term or refer to an agreement as a franchise agreement when, as a matter of industry practice, that agreement more closely resembles something else (such as a real estate agency in this case). The court further held that the plaintiff failed to prove that it had actually suffered damages due to the defendants' alleged contractual defaults. It also found that the defendants had a justifiable excuse for such defaults, observing that their failure to perform the obligations asserted by the plaintiff was a direct consequence of the plaintiff's own breach. The court ruled in favour of the defendants and held that the plaintiff had acted fraudulently and in bad faith with the object of inducing them to enter into the agreement. In addition to ordering the rescission of the contract, the court held the plaintiff responsible for damages.

CHAPTER 9

VI. New Zealand

By Stewart Germann, STEWART GERMANN LAW OFFICES

Stewart Germann is a barrister and has over forty years of experience in franchise law. He provides counsel for both franchisors and franchisees doing business in New Zealand.

New Zealand is one of the most deregulated countries in the world to conduct small to medium-sized business. There is no specific legislation controlling the operation of franchising in New Zealand and other countries like New Zealand include Singapore and the United Kingdom.

Prospective franchisees who are looking at buying into a franchise must tread carefully and do their homework. New Zealand is an exciting and fast developing market which contains at least 590 franchise systems. The Franchising New Zealand 2021 Survey results showed that the sales turnover for business format franchises was estimated at $36.8 billion, and the sales turnover for the entire franchising sector was estimated at $58.5 billion.

- There is an estimated total of 32,300 units operating in business format franchises.
- More than 156,820 are employed directly in business format franchises.
- 70% of franchise brands originated in New Zealand.
- Online sales grew tremendously with now almost 80% of brands engaging in online sales.
- More than 20% of franchisors have entered international markets.
- 90% of franchise brands return profits back into the community.
- Almost two-thirds of franchisors identified environmental sustainability and ethical supply chain examples, with the principal examples being enforced recycling of materials, waste minimization programs and hybrid car use.
- Only 18.5% of franchisors were involved in a substantial dispute (with one or more franchisees) in the past 12 months.
- COVID-19 brought considerable disruptions to trading, greater stress and mental health considerations, adjusted hours of operation, supply chain interruptions, significant sales reductions, and many other issues.

International Developments

A. NO FRANCHISE SPECIFIC LAW

Although there are no specific franchising laws, there are existing laws which protect franchisees; and the three main laws which provide such protection are the Fair Trading Act 1986, the Commerce Act 1986 and the Contract and Commercial Law Act 2017. Those Acts focus in particular on misrepresentations and restrictive trade practices which include anti-competitive behavior.

B. CODE OF PRATICE – FRANCHISEASSOCIATION OF NEW ZEALAND

Once a franchisee has chosen a particular brand and franchise system and wishes to progress further with enquiries, the first question to ask is whether the franchisor belongs to the Franchise Association of New Zealand (FANZ). The FANZ was formed in 1996 and publishes the Code of Practice and the Code of Ethics which all members must comply with. Many franchisors belong to the FANZ but some have chosen not to join yet still comply with the Codes. Others may choose not to join and do not comply with the Codes.

The Code of Practice has four main aims which are as follows:
- To encourage best practice throughout franchising.
- To provide reassurance to those entering franchising that any member displaying the logo of the FANZ is serious and has undertaken to practice in a fair and reasonable manner.
- To provide the basis of self-regulation for franchising.
- To demonstrate to everyone the positive will within franchising to regulate itself.

The Code applies to all members including franchisors, franchisees, or affiliates such as accountants, lawyers and consultants and all prospective new members of the FANZ must agree to be bound by the Code before they can be considered for membership.

What does the Code cover?

1. Compliance - all members must certify that they will comply with the Code and members must renew their certificate of compliance on an annual basis.
2. Disclosure - a disclosure document must be provided to all prospective franchisees at least fourteen (14) days prior to signing a franchise agreement. This disclosure document must be updated at least annually, and it must provide information including a company profile, details of the officers of the company, an outline of the franchise, full disclosure of any payment or commission made by a

CHAPTER 9

franchisor to any adviser or consultant in connection with a sale, listing of all components making up the franchise purchase, references and projections of turnover and possible profitability of the business.

3. Certification - the Code requires franchisors to give franchisees a copy of the Code and the franchisee must then certify that he or she has had legal advice before signing the franchise agreement.
4. Cooling Off Period - all franchise agreements must contain a minimum seven (7) day period from the date of the agreement during which a franchisee may change its mind and terminate the purchase. This is very important and the cooling off period does not apply to renewals of term or re-sales by franchisees.
5. Dispute Resolution - the Code sets out a dispute resolution procedure which can be used by both franchisor and franchisee to seek a more amicable and cost-effective solution. The Code requires all members to try to settle disputes by mutual negotiation in the first instance. However, this process does not affect the legal rights of both parties to resort to litigation.
6. Advisers - all advisers must provide clients with written details of their relevant qualifications and experience and they must respect confidentiality of all information received.
7. Code of Ethics - all members must subscribe to the Code of Ethics which sets out the spirit in which the Code of Practice will be interpreted.

All franchisor members of the FANZ must have a franchise agreement which contains a dispute resolution clause and a cooling-off provision. In order to resolve disputes, mediation is the favoured method and it has a high success rate in relation to franchising disputes. However, if mediation does not work then there is always litigation which is certainly at the divorce stage of the relationship.

Prospective franchisees must be given a disclosure document and franchise agreement by the franchisor. The disclosure document must provide certain information including the following:

- Details of the franchisor and its directors including experience and a viability statement with key financial information of the franchisor;
- Details of any bankruptcies, receiverships, liquidations or materially relevant debt recovery;
- Criminal, civil or administrative proceedings within the past five years;
- A summary of the main particulars and features of the franchise;
- A list of components making up the franchise purchase;

- Details of any financial requirements by the franchisor of the franchisee; and
- Other information as listed in the Code.

Franchising in New Zealand covers goods and services in many areas including general retail, leisure and education, business and commercial, food and beverage, health and fitness, computer and technology, home and building services.

C. FORCE MAJEURE PROVISIONS IN NEW ZEALAND

All franchise agreements in New Zealand should contain a robust force majeure clause. The author would go so far to say that if any franchise agreement does not contain a force majeure clause then the drafter of the document may be negligent. An example of a force majeure clause is as follows:

> Neither party shall be liable to the other and neither party shall be deemed to be in default for any failure or delay to observe or perform any of the terms and conditions applicable to the party under this Agreement (other than the payment of money) caused or arising out of any act beyond the control of that party including (but not limited to) fire, flood, lightning, storm and tempest, earthquake, strikes, lock-outs or other industrial disputes, acts of war, acts of terrorism, riots, civil commotion, explosion, malicious damage, government restriction, unavailability of equipment or product, disease and/or virus of epidemic or pandemic proportions or other causes whether the kind enumerated above or otherwise which are beyond the control of that party and where such failure or delay is caused by one of the events above then all times provided for in this Agreement shall be extended for a period commensurate with the period of the delay.

The purpose of the above clause is to ensure that neither party will be liable to the other for any events outside their control. Common events are listed in the clause like fire, flood, lightning, storm and tempest and, of particular relevance to current events, the phrase "*disease and/or virus of epidemic or pandemic proportions.*"

No one can predict the future and all parties, especially a franchisor and a franchisee, should be afforded the protection of a well-drafted force majeure clause. COVID-19 is merely a symptom of the greater problem of unexpected or unanticipated events, be they in the form of the next pandemic or some other future disaster. Uncertainty will always pose a risk to interference with contractual relations, and a well-drafted force majeure clause is a necessary component of mitigating contractual risk.

CHAPTER 9

D. COMPETITION LAW

The Commerce (Cartels and Other Matters) Amendment Act 2017 changed the Commerce Act 1986 by replacing the previous prohibition on price-fixing between competitors with an expanded prohibition on cartel provisions, which extends to market allocations and output restrictions, as well as to price-fixing, by competitors. The New Zealand cartel prohibition is very wide and will have quite an impact on franchise networks. Some additional clauses must be inserted into franchise agreements and there must be explanations, in plain language, as to why certain clauses are necessary. Consideration must be given to cartel clauses in franchise agreements; for example, clauses that set or influence prices, restrict output or allocate markets will be caught. The possibility that alternative arrangements might achieve the same or a similar commercial outcome as a cartel clause should also be considered. Another consideration is whether the collaborative activity exemption or the vertical activity exemption would apply. Expert legal advice should be obtained in relation to this Act.

There will not be a cartel arrangement in place where parties are not in competition with each other. In most franchise systems the franchisor will not be in competition with its own franchisees but that is not always the case. For example, a franchisor that owns its own outlet might be found to be in competition with franchisees. Similarly, where a franchisor sells online direct to the end consumer, yet at the same time has franchisees who sell to those consumers, it may also be in competition with its franchisees. There may also be instances where the franchisees are in competition with each other. Where a franchisor is in competition with a franchisee or where franchisees are found to be in competition with each other, there will be a competitive relationship, so the franchisor needs to be cognisant that there may be provisions in its franchise agreements that amount to cartel provisions.

The Commerce (Criminalisation of Cartels) Amendment Act 2019 introduced a new criminal offence for cartel conduct and the criminal sanctions reflect the covert nature of cartels and the harm they cause to consumers and the economy. The Commerce Act 1986 provides a number of statutory exceptions that would not constitute a cartel arrangement and may be pro-competitive. These exceptions relate to collaborative activities (for example, joint ventures or franchise arrangements), joint buying, vertical supply contracts and specified liner shipping arrangements as stated earlier in this paper. There are no defences for mistakes of fact relating to the elements of joint buying and promotion and vertical supply contracts. Therefore, it would be possible in the future for a director of a franchisor company to be criminally liable under the Act for a cartel offence. For an individual who commits an offence the penalty on conviction could be imprisonment for a term not exceeding 7 years or a fine not exceeding $500,000, or both. For a company which commits an offence the penalty could be up to $10 million so great care must be taken.

E. RESTRICTIVE COVENANTS

The New Zealand courts have recognized that it is reasonable for a person in the position of a franchisor to impose a contractual restraint upon competitive conduct by a franchisee or an ex-franchisee, but such restraints must not exceed the boundaries of the court's notion of reasonableness. The first principle is that it is reasonable for a person to stipulate that if he or she is willing to disclose all secrets of how to establish a particular business enterprise, then the recipient of the information cannot immediately terminate the contract and set up a competitive business using the information received during the course of the relationship. If the courts did not provide protection to franchisors against conduct like this, there would be no incentive for the owners of established businesses to share their secrets with others and enhance their business skills. The second principle is that it is important for the well-being of the community that every individual should, in general, be free to advance his or her skills and earning capacity.

The Contract and Commercial Law Act 2017 in New Zealand gives the courts authority to rewrite a restrictive covenant and to allow an excessive covenant to be enforced at a lesser level. Section 83 of the Act states as follows:

"83 *Restraints of trade*

(1) *The court may, if a provision of a contract constitutes an unreasonable restraint of trade –*

(a) *delete the provision and give effect to the contract as so amended; or*

(b) *modify the provision so that, at the time the contract was entered into, the provision as modified would have been reasonable, and give effect to the contract as so modified; or*

(c) *decline to enforce the contract if the deletion or modification of the provision would so alter the bargain between the parties that it would be unreasonable to allow the contract to stand.*

(2) *The court may modify a provision even if the modification cannot be effected by deleting words from the provision.*"

CHAPTER 9

The ability of the courts to modify excessive restraints is constrained by the principle that terms that could never have been considered reasonable will not be modified, as to do so would be contrary to the public interest. This is the doctrine of restraints that are *in terrorem,* which translates into 'contracts that terrorise a contracting party'. If a franchisor could only ever have reasonably sought a two-year restraint within a 5-kilometre radius of the business in which the person established goodwill, then a nationwide restraint for 10 years could never be regarded as reasonable; and in that case the courts would refuse to rewrite the clause to determine that the period of 10 years should be two years and the area of the restraint should be 5 kilometres rather than the entire country. What then is a reasonable restraint? There are two factors – area and time. So the message is clear in New Zealand – for a restraint to be enforceable, it must be reasonable.

F. UNFAIR CONTRACT TERMS

In relation to distribution, franchising and agency matters in New Zealand, please note that the Fair Trading Amendment Act 2021 ("Amendment Act") extends the existing prohibition on unfair contract terms in consumer contracts to standard form small trade contracts worth under $250,000 (including GST). The Amendment Act also introduced a new prohibition on unconscionable conduct.

The changes came into force on 16 August 2022 and affect standard form small trade contracts. A contract is a standard form small trade contract if it falls within the following definition:

- Each party is engaged in trade (ie two businesses);
- It is not a contract between a business and a consumer; and
- The relationship between the two parties in trade in relation to the goods, services or interest in land provided does not exceed the annual value threshold of $250,000 (including GST) per annum for goods, services or an interest in land when the relationship first arises (i.e. when you first sign the contract).

Any contract signed prior to 16 August 2022 will not be subject to the new amendments. However, if the contract is varied, amended or renewed and it falls within the definition of a standard form small trade contract above then the new regime applies to the varied, amended or renewed contract.

The unfair contract terms previously only applied to contracts between a consumer and a business, for instance gym membership agreement. The new amendments will ensure that small businesses also receive protection against any unfair contract terms.

The following is taken into consideration when assessing whether a term is unfair:
- Whether the term would cause a significant imbalance in the parties' rights and obligations arising under the contract;
- Whether the term is reasonably necessary in order to protect the legitimate interests of the party who would be advantaged by the term; and
- Whether the term would cause detriment (whether financial or otherwise) to a party if it were applied, enforced or relied on.

The new amendments will not apply to the following contractual terms:
- Definition of the main subject matter of the contract.
- Setting the upfront price payable under the contract, so long as the price term is clear and unambiguous.
- Any terms that are required or expressly permitted by any legislation.

The extent to which the term is clear and the context of the contract as a whole will also be taken into account. However, the new amendments will not disadvantage a business that has a legitimate business interest and the term is necessary to protect that interest. At this stage the Commerce Commission has not updated its guidance regarding unfair contract terms but we assume this will be issued soon to assist businesses.

The Commerce Commission can apply to a court for a declaration that a term in a contract is unfair. If it is found to be unfair by a Court then that business must not include a term (or is amended with the Court's approval) or attempt to enforce or rely on the term. A business may also face:
- In the case of an individual fines not exceeding $200,000 and a company a fine not exceeding $600,000.
- Court orders stopping that business from applying or enforcing that term and or orders directing a refund or payment of damages.

G. UNCONSCIONABLE CONDUCT

The unconscionable conduct in trade provisions are much broader as it applies to all conduct not just contractual terms. The term unconscionable conduct is not defined but the Amendment Act states that a Court can take the following into consideration:
- The relative bargaining power of the parties;
- The extent to which the parties acted in good faith;
- Whether the affected person was reasonably able to protect their interests; and
- Whether unfair pressure or tactics were used.

CHAPTER 9

It may be that New Zealand will take guidance from Australian cases but at this stage no guidance or comment has been provided by the Commerce Commission.

The Commerce Commission can seek penalties and fines as above. The Commerce Commission could also could bring civil proceedings; for example seeking a declaration from the Court in relation to unfair contract terms. The remedies include damages, injunctions and other Court orders.

Whether the new amendments apply to any contract will depend on whether it falls within the definition of a standard form small trade contract. When looking at the annual value threshold this is assessed when the relationship first arises.

The unconscionable conduct provisions are much broader so beware of the changes which now apply to New Zealand contracts.

H. DATA PROTECTION AND DATA PRIVACY

It is very important for franchise parties to prevent data privacy violations. Both Franchisors and Franchisees will collect information pertaining to their employees, customers and suppliers. Franchisees must evaluate the information and how to protect it and they should conduct data mapping which is an internal audit process which allows the franchisee to determine what types of personal data it is receiving, where it is being stored, why it is being collected, and how long the franchisee intends on keeping the data. All of these processes must be set out in a privacy policy issued to customers and employees. The modern threat to this is the increased collection and use of personal information which is essential to the operation of all Government and other agencies. Furthermore, with the advent of AI processing tools such as Chat GPT, franchisees must be very careful of personal information being disseminated without that person's consent.

In New Zealand the right to privacy is a fundamental human right and is governed by the Privacy Act 2020. The Act endeavours to control by statute the four ethical issues involved, being privacy, accuracy, property and accessibility. The essence of the Privacy Act is the identification of 13 information privacy principles which were established by the Organisation for Economic Cooperation and Development in Paris as follows:

- Principle 1: Purpose of Collection of Personal Information.
- Principle 2: Source of Personal Information.
- Principle 3: Collection of Information from an Individual.
- Principle 4: Manner of Collection of Information.
- Principle 5: Storage and Security of Personal Information.
- Principle 6: Access to Personal Information.
- Principle 7: Correction of Personal Information.
- Principle 8: Accuracy of Personal Information to be checked before use.
- Principle 9: Agency not to use Personal Information for longer than necessary.
- Principle 10: Limits on use of Personal Information.
- Principle 11: Limits on Disclosure of Personal Information.
- Principle 12: Disclosure of Personal Information outside New Zealand.
- Principle 13: Unique Identifiers.

Franchisors must take an active role in the protection of stored data and compliance with regulations. In the unfortunate event of a data breach or public violation of data privacy regulations, there will be a direct harm to the brand regardless of who is responsible for the violation. Accordingly, franchisors must remain cautious of potentially non-compliant activities by franchisees. They must ensure that all franchisees conduct their businesses to high standards to ensure compliance with the laws. Franchisors can require written confirmation from franchisees that they have complied with any changes to data collection and data privacy laws and require that any changes will replace a current data protection plan.

I. POSITIVITY IN 2023

New Zealand is a very attractive market for franchising and many overseas systems have entered from Australia, USA, Canada and the United Kingdom in particular. International franchising was thriving worldwide until the global pandemic of 2020. Thanks to people getting vaccinated, most countries have recovered in a positive way and international franchising seems to be thriving again.

The FANZ has been very successful in promoting self-regulation and high standards in franchising, and its Code of Practice is widely understood and accepted by franchisors in New Zealand. Franchisees and master franchisees must make the decision whether or not to proceed with the purchase of a franchise or master franchise. Just like in Australia, people like

CHAPTER 9

to own their own businesses and to work hard to make those businesses successful. Most franchisors have an entrepreneurial spirit, so franchising is certain to increase in both countries during the year. However, careful due diligence must always be undertaken so that both parties are fully informed.

VII. Thailand

By Sher Hann Chua & Alan Adcock, TILLEKE & GIBBONS

Sher Hann Chua is a consultant in the firm's Bangkok and Yangon offices and consults on such matters as trademark registration, trademark enforcement and trademark license strategies.

Alan Adcock is a partner specializing in intellectual property and regulatory affairs. He serves on the Emerging Issues Committee of the International Trademark Association.

A. APPLICATION OF THE NOTIFICATION ON THE GUIDELINES FOR THE CONSIDERATION OF UNFAIR TRADE PRACTICES IN FRANCHISE BUSINESSES

The Trade Competition Commission of Thailand (the "TCC") issued a notification on the Guidelines for the Consideration of Unfair Trade Practices in Franchise Businesses (No. 3) on July 13, 2021, which amended the initial Guidelines for the Consideration of Unfair Trade Practices in Franchise Businesses (the "Guidelines") first issued in 2019 and its subsequent amendment in 2020 (collectively the "Franchise Guidelines"). The Franchise Guidelines were issued by the TCC pursuant to powers conferred upon it via Section 17(3) of the Trade Competition Act B.E. 2560 (2017) (the "TCA 2017"), and are aimed at preventing franchisors from adopting overly restrictive and unfair contractual conditions that may cause damage to franchisees.

Since the implementation of the Franchise Guidelines, the Trade Competition Board of the TCC (the "Board") has issued a number of decisions related to franchise disputes, which considered the interpretation and application of the Franchise Guidelines. One of the main changes introduced under the Franchise Guidelines relates to geographical restrictions, which is summarized as follows:

1. When a franchisor decides to open a new outlet, whether by itself or by another franchisee or person, the franchisor must notify the existing franchisee located in the closest proximity

International Developments

          to the intended location and provide such existing franchisee with a right of first refusal for a period of 30 days.
2. A franchisor is exempted from the obligation to provide such franchisee with a right of first refusal if the franchisee's existing performance does not meet the franchisor's criteria as specified and communicated to the franchisee in advance.
3. In considering what constitutes "closest proximity," consideration is given to the demand of the goods and services, the geographical area, and the condition of the market competition.
4. Where a franchisor is not able to grant the rights to operate the new outlet to an existing franchisee due to existing area development rights or other contractual obligations, the franchisor shall consider granting the right to open such new outlet to other suitable franchisees based on reasonable commercial reasons. Clause 2, Guidelines for the Consideration of Unfair Trade Practices in Franchise Businesses (No. 3).

In a case before the Board in 2023 regarding a Thai street food franchise, the franchisor owned two competing franchise businesses selling the same food products under two different names. The franchisor granted two franchisees the rights to the competing businesses, and the second franchisee set up a stall approximately 30 meters away from the first franchisee's stall. This substantially affected the business of the first franchisee. When the case was heard by the Board, the second franchisee had relocated its stall; therefore, the Board held that there was no ongoing act that would deem the franchisor as having acted unfairly towards the first franchisee. Nevertheless, the Board stated that if the second franchisee had not relocated, the franchisor would be deemed to have acted contrary to the TCA 2017 and the Franchise Guidelines.

The Franchise Guidelines also prohibit franchisors from engaging in the following trade practices, which are deemed capable of causing damage to the franchisees under Section 57 of the TCA 2017:
1. Setting restrictive conditions for the franchisees without justifiable reasons, such as requiring the franchisees to purchase products or services that are irrelevant to the operation of the franchise business, exclusively from the franchisors or from sources designated by the franchisors, or requiring the franchisees to purchase more products or raw materials than actually necessary and refusing to accept the return of excess purchases;

CHAPTER 9

2. Setting additional conditions for the franchisees to comply with, after the franchise agreements have been executed, such as requiring the franchisees to perform actions not stated in the franchise agreements. Exceptions may apply if there is a justifiable reason, or if such conditions are necessary in order to maintain the reputation, quality, and standards of the franchise business. In such cases, all additional conditions must be made in writing.
3. Imposing product tying or purchasing restrictions on the franchisees without justifiable reasons, such as restricting the franchisees from purchasing products from other sources that offer products with comparable quality but at a lower price;
4. Restricting the franchisees from offering discounts on perishable goods or products close to their expiration, without justifiable reasons;
5. Stipulating discriminatory conditions among franchisees, without justifiable reasons; and
6. Setting any inappropriate conditions for purposes other than to maintain the reputation, quality, and standards of the franchisors in accordance with the franchise agreement. Clause 5, Guidelines for the Consideration of Unfair Trade Practices in Franchise Businesses.

Notwithstanding the above, recent decisions of the Board have suggested the adoption of a pro-franchisor stance. In a separate case heard by the Board in 2023 relating to a parcel delivery franchise business, the Board decided that the franchisor's act of unilaterally changing the terms and conditions related to the calculation of fines and damages, citing reasons of backlog and insured packages, did not constitute an unfair act under the TCA 2017. Specifically, the Board took the view that such act constituted a normal way of operating the business with reasonable justification.

In another case relating to a milk tea franchise business heard by the Board in 2023, the franchisor had terminated a franchise agreement as the franchisee purchased raw materials from a third party supplier instead of from the franchisor. The terminated franchisee filed a complaint with the TCC, alleging that the franchisor was unfairly obstructing its business operations contrary to the TCA 2017 and the Franchise Guidelines. However, the Board took the view that as parties had mutually agreed in the franchise agreement that the franchisee was required to purchase such raw materials from the franchisor, the franchisee had indeed breached the franchise agreement by buying the products from a third party. Therefore, the franchisor's termination of the agreement was not contrary to the TCA 2017 and the Franchise Guidelines.

Although the Franchise Guidelines do not apply directly to foreign franchisors who do not have a physical presence in Thailand, local master franchisees in Thailand appointed by such foreign franchisors will need to comply with all such requirements prescribed under the TCA 2017 and the Guidelines. Non-compliance with the TCA 2017 and the Franchise Guidelines may subject a business operator to administrative penalties, such as a fine not exceeding 10% of the turnover in the year of the offence, capped at THB one million (approximately USD 30,010), if the violation was committed in the first year of such party's business operations. Section 82, Trade Competition Act 2017. Therefore, it is prudent for foreign franchisors to ensure that the franchise agreement templates and disclosure documents to be used by their local master franchisees when appointing sub-franchisees in Thailand are consistent with the requirements under the TCA 2017 and the Franchise Guidelines.

B. PERSONAL DATA PROTECTION ACT

Thailand's Personal Data Protection Act B.E. 2562 (2019) ("PDPA") which was published in the Government Gazette on May 27, 2019, entered into force in full on June 1, 2022 after a second postponement announced on May 9, 2021 due to the COVID-19 pandemic. The PDPA defines "personal data" as "any data pertaining to a person, which enables the identification of such person, whether directly or indirectly, but not including data of the deceased specifically." Section 6, Personal Data Protection Act B.E. 2562 (2019). Foreign franchisors should be aware of the extra-territorial application of the PDPA. Specifically, the PDPA applies to entities domiciled outside of Thailand that collect, use, or disclose personal data of data subjects in Thailand, under the following situations:

1. Where the activities of collection, use, and disclosure are related to the offering of goods or services to the data subjects who are in Thailand, irrespective of whether the payment is made by the data subject; or
2. Where the activities of collection, use, and disclosure are related to the monitoring of the data subject's behavior in Thailand. Section 5, Personal Data Protection Act B.E. 2562 (2019).

In certain franchising relationships, a foreign franchisor may receive personal data of end consumers, such as names, email addresses, phone numbers, payment information and other shopping preferences, either directly

CHAPTER 9

or from a local franchisee. In circumstances where a foreign franchisor has the power and duties to make decisions regarding the collection, use, or disclosure of such personal data, it will be deemed a data controller under the PDPA. Section 6, Personal Data Protection Act B.E. 2562 (2019). As a data controller, such foreign franchisor must ensure that it obtains the informed consent of data subjects prior to or during the collection of personal data. Franchisors operating in the children's franchise market, such as early childhood education and enrichment programs, should also note that consent related to collection of personal data of a minor must be obtained from the person exercising parental powers over such minor. Section 20(2), Personal Data Protection Act B.E. 2562 (2019).

The PDPA also requires data controllers outside of Thailand to appoint an authorized representative within the jurisdiction, to act on behalf of such data controllers with respect to the collection, use or disclosure of the personal data. Section 37(5), Personal Data Protection Act B.E. 2562 (2019). When collecting personal data, data controllers must inform data subjects of the following matters:

1. The purpose of the collection to use or disclose personal data, including the circumstances in which a data controller is granted statutory powers under the PDPA to collect any personal data without the data subject's consent;
2. Circumstances where the data subject is required to provide personal data for compliance with the law or contractual obligations, and the implications of not providing such personal data;
3. The type of personal data collection and period of retention;
4. The types of persons or agencies to whom the collected personal data may be disclosed;
5. Information of the data controller, contact address, and contact method, or such information of a personal data protection officer or agent, where applicable; and
6. The data subject's rights under the PDPA. Section 23, Personal Data Protection Act B.E. 2562 (2019).

Additionally, a foreign franchisor who receives personal data of end consumers, whether directly or indirectly, should also take note of the restrictions on the transfer of personal data outside of Thailand imposed by the PDPA. When personal data is transferred overseas, the PDPA requires the relevant destination country or organization that receives such personal data to have sufficient personal data protection standards, and for such transfer to be performed in accordance with any rules that may be prescribed by the

Personal Data Protection Committee established under the law. Section 28, Personal Data Protection Act B.E. 2562 (2019).

Non-compliance with the PDPA will subject data controllers to administrative fines of up to THB five million (approximately USD 150,050), as well as criminal fines of up to THB one million (approximately USD 30,010). Chapter VII, Personal Data Protection Act B.E. 2562 (2019). Further, Thai courts may also award punitive damages, as well as impose imprisonment for up to one year. Therefore, it is imperative for foreign franchisors to be fully aware of the potential new obligations imposed upon them under the PDPA.

VIII. Ukraine

By Anzhela Makhinova, SAYENKO KHARENKO

Anzhela Makhinova is a partner and specializes in international trade. She also has extensive experience representing clients before all the relevant bodies in Ukraine and globally and advising on all aspects of international trade including cross-border trade transactions and contracts, agency and distribution, franchising, consumer rights protection, market access, customs and trade compliance issues, as well as legislation shaping and other matters.

A. GENERAL LEGAL FRAMEWORK

Franchising relations have been specifically regulated in Ukraine since January 1, 2004, when the Civil Code of Ukraine dated January 16, 2003 No. 435-IV and the Commercial Code of Ukraine dated January 16, 2003 No. 436-IV were adopted.

It is noteworthy that neither the Civil Code nor the Commercial Code operates with the well-known and internationally acceptable terms, such as "franchising," "franchise agreement," "franchisor," and "franchisee," but with the terms "commercial concession," "commercial concession agreement," "titleholder" and "user" accordingly. However, considering the legal nature of a commercial concession as regulated by both Codes, the latter may be regarded as equal to what is internationally accepted as franchising.

Both Codes regulate franchising relations in a very general manner. For instance, Ukrainian law does not stipulate detailed requirements applicable to pre-contractual disclosure, mandatory testing the franchise before granting it, indemnities to be paid after the agreement termination etc.

Besides, while concluding franchise agreements, the parties shall take into account provisions of competition legislation, legislation regarding

CHAPTER 9

quality, safety of goods and consumers' rights protection, legislation in the sphere of intellectual property and advertising, as well as other mandatory provisions stipulated in the Ukrainian legislation.

The last amendments, specifically relating to franchising, were introduced by both Codes in 2015 when mandatory state registration of the franchise agreements was abolished. However, after the commencement of the war, Ukraine adopted many different regulations that considerably influenced the practical operation of franchise agreements. Our aim in this article is to analyze recent legislative developments.

B. DEVELOPMENTS RELATED TO THE WAR

1. Restrictions of Payments in Foreign Currency

To ensure economic stability during the war period, Ukraine has adopted several restrictions. The Cabinet of Ministers of Ukraine (the Government) has adopted Resolution No.153 dated February 24, 2022 "On List of Critical Import Goods." According to Resolution No.153, the companies were allowed to buy foreign currency to make payments only to import the products included in the List of Critical Imports Goods. In the very beginning, the said List included only up to 10 types of products and no services/works/royalties. Only several months after adoption the list of the products were widen and were works/services then included therein. This influenced ability of the Ukrainian companies to import many products (actually almost all imports were stopped) and pay for works/services (e.g. payments of royalties etc.). Now Resolution No.153 allows importation of all products and also covers an expansive list of services and works. However, in any case, if any new services are rendered, it is crucial to check whether the Ukrainian franchisees will be able to pay for them.

Resolution of the Board of the National Bank of Ukraine (the NBU) "On the operation of the banking system during the introduction of the martial law" dated February 24, 2022 No.18 (Resolution No. 18) stipulates that for operations on export and import of goods carried out from April 5, 2022, the payment deadlines have been reduced from 365 calendar days to 90 calendar days. In practice, this means that if a Ukrainian franchisee has made a pre-payment, importation of the products shall be made during the said 90-day period. If services/works are pre-paid, they shall be rendered during this 90-day period as well and the Ukrainian franchisee shall have the relevant confirmation (usually, an acceptance act executed by both parties). Residents' violation of the payment deadline entails a penalty for each day of delay in the amount of 0.3 % of the amount of uncollected funds under the contract.

International Developments

The NBU revises the said terms from time to time. Now it constitutes 180 days. Hence, the parties to the franchise agreements shall scrutinize payment terms.

By its Resolution No.18, the NBU has also forbidden any payments with the involvement of the Russian/Belarusian companies and/or Russian/Belarusian currency. There have been also other restrictions applicable to foreign currency payments to be made by Ukrainian companies.

2. Sanctions and Other Restrictions Applied by Ukraine Against Russia and/or For Activities Related To Russia

a. Ban on import/export of products from/to Russia

By its Resolution No.426 dated April 9, 2022 "On Application of Ban on Imports of Products from Russian Federation", the Government has forbidden importation of all products from the Russian territory. Moreover, on 27 September 2022, the Government also implemented Resolution No. 1076 "On Ban of Export of Products from Ukraine to the Customs Territory of the Russian Federation". The said Resolution has prohibited any export from the territory of Ukraine to the Russian Federation.

b. Sanctions applied against Russia and/or Russian related Companies/Individuals

According to the War & Sanctions data base, Ukraine has started more actively applying different types of sanctions against Russian companies and individuals after the commencement of the war. The War & Sanctions database can be accessed via following link https://sanctions.nazk.gov.ua/en/. Particularly, as of May 2023, sanctions are applied to more than 9000 individuals and 5900 legal entities. Moreover, the said database contains list of individuals (more than 16600) and legal entities (about 6000) that are not subject to sanctions yet, but who are recommended for application of sanctions. It is worth emphasizing that very different types of sanctions are applied to the said individuals/legal entities, to name but a few: (a) blocking all assets owned by them; (b) ban on all trading operations; (c) ban on all financial and economic operations; (d) ban on participation in privatization; (e) ban on participation in public procurement procedures etc. Moreover, to many of the said individuals/legal entities Ukraine has already applied the strictest sanction possible, namely: the seizure of their assets in the favour of Ukraine.

Additionally, the War & Sanctions database contains lists of companies (26 as of May 2023) and individuals (99 as of May 2023) that are

CHAPTER 9

recognized as International War Sponsors. The list of International War Sponsors can be accessed via following link https://sanctions.nazk.gov.ua/en/boycott/. The following famous companies are already included in the said list: Leroy Merlin, Bonduelle, P&G (Procter & Gamble), Auchan, Metro, Raiffeisen Bank International, Yves Rocher, Xiaomi Corporation etc. From the legal viewpoint, including an individual or a legal entity in the database will not automatically result in the application of sanctions to them. However, the information regarding such companies is forwarded to the LSEG and is included in the World-Check database. The given database is the world's largest database for checking counterparties for links to terrorist organizations, fraud, etc. Thus, although today there are no legal consequences for companies indicated as international sponsors of war, in practice such companies may face difficulties in future, as the banks and insurance companies around the globe use the World-Check database to evaluate the risks. Moreover, we could not exclude that information on such companies will also be forwarded to the relevant authorities for the application of real sanctions in Ukraine.

Notably, one of the main reasons for the inclusion of individuals/legal entities into the War and Sanctions database is the payment of taxes in Russia. Particularly, the following activities shall result in application of sanctions: (a) payment of taxes, and fees to the state budget of the aggressor state, if the total amount of such payments (except customs) for the last four consecutive tax (reporting) quarters exceeds the equivalent of 40 million hryvnias (approximately 1 mln EUR); (b) making donations, charitable, sponsorship assistance, other free transfer of funds or other property for the benefit of state authorities or military administration of the aggressor state, or carry out financing of such activities, if the total amount of such funds or the value of the property during the year is at least 750 thousand hryvnias (approximately 20000 EUR); (c) investing in government bonds of the aggressor state, if the total investment amount during the year is at least 3 million hryvnias (approximately 80000 EUR).

c. Forcible seizure the Russian Federation's and its residents' property in Ukraine

On March 3, 2022, Ukraine adopted the Law "On the Basic Principles of Forcible Seizure of Objects of Property Rights of the Russian Federation and its Residents in Ukraine" No. 2116-IX (the Law). The said Law stipulates forcible seizure of the Russian Federation's and its residents' property in Ukraine. As of today, the residents are clarified quite narrowly. However, there have been several draft laws that have suggested to amend the definition

International Developments

of "residents of the Russian Federation" that could cover in the future also companies continuing their work in Russia.

d. Other restrictions

It is worth emphasizing that Ukraine tries to force companies to leave Russia. Therefore, the Parliament of Ukraine has adopted several initiatives in this respect. For instance, the Parliament of Ukraine has already considered the draft law stipulating higher tax rates (it is suggested to apply an increased coefficient of 1.5) for taxpayers directly or indirectly linked by economic activities with Russia. Particularly, the said tax rates will apply to corporate profit tax (except for withholding tax), environmental tax, rent, and property tax.

Given all the above, now it is crucial to revise trading schemes if they somehow relate to Russia (e.g. if the franchise is operated both in Ukraine and Russia). Otherwise, there are risks of application of sanctions and/or other restrictions to both franchisors and franchisees.

2. Changes to Labour Laws

On March 15, 2022, Ukraine adopted the Law "On the organization of labour relations under martial law." The said Law stipulates (a) a possibility to suspend labour relations for the period of martial law; (b) the employer has a right to limit the duration of the principal annual vacation during martial law to 24 calendar days; (c) unpaid vacation was introduced for an employee who left Ukraine or is an internally displaced person; (d) specified requirements for increased normal and reduced working hours during martial law; (e) the right of the employer and the employee during the martial law to agree on alternative ways of creating, sending and storing the employer's orders and other documents related to labour relations and on other available methods of electronic communication; (f) during the period of martial law, the Law cancels the application of fines for violations of labour legislation if employers properly comply with orders to eliminate violations revealed during unscheduled inspections.

These amendments are important because after the commencement of the war many foreign franchisors suspended their activities in Ukraine and thus, the regulation of labour relations was important.

3. Intellectual Property Deadlines During the Martial Law in Ukraine

On April 1, 2022, the Parliament adopted the Law "On Protection of Persons in the Field of Intellectual Property during Martial Law in connection with

CHAPTER 9

Military Aggression of the Russian Federation against Ukraine" No. 2174-IX (the Law).

The Law has a retroactive effect and applies since February 24, 2022. It stipulates that all deadlines for acquisition and protection of IP rights to trademarks, designs, inventions, utility models, geographical indications, semiconductor technology, copyright, and plant varieties are suspended for the whole period of the martial law in Ukraine. The suspended deadlines include, without limitation, the deadlines concerning:

- Oppositions against Ukrainian trademark applications and Madrid System registrations.
- Challenging decisions of the IP Office in court and the Appeal Board of the IP Office.
- administrative invalidation procedures for patented inventions.
- renewals and reinstatement of IP rights.

IP deadlines will be resumed on the next day after the martial law is cancelled, taking into account the period elapsed before February 24, 2022.

In case annuity/renewal fees are due during martial law, such fees can be paid within 90 days after the martial law is cancelled. According to our reading of the Law, the 90-day Rule also applies to those cases when the IP rights fully expire during martial law.

4. Other Limitations

Ukraine has already applied numerous restrictions to counteract the dissemination of pro-Kremlin propaganda. For instance, on May 22, 2022, the Parliament adopted the Law "On Prohibition of the Propaganda of Russian Nazi Totalitarian Regime, Armed Aggression of the Russian Federation as Aggressor State against Ukraine and the Symbols Associated with Russia's military invasion of Ukraine" No. 2265-IX (the Law). The Law provides the following two groups of prohibited symbols, including letters and words, which are associated with the Russian invasion:

- Usage of "Z" and "V" Latin letters (without a legitimate context or in the context of justifying armed aggression against Ukraine or other military actions) either as standalone symbols or by replacing "З," "С," "В," or "Ф" Cyrillic or other letters in words with "Z" or "V" Latin letters with a visual focus on "Z" or "V" Latin letters.
- Official and unofficial symbols (emblems, logos) of Russia's armed forces, including its ground, aerospace, navy, strategic missile forces, airborne troops, special operations forces, other armed formations and/or bodies of the aggressor state.

International Developments

The Law outlines the "usage" of the prohibited symbols rather broadly concerning which one can argue that it covers all types of their use including in trademarks in the public space.

It is worth emphasizing that Ukrainian regulations are contentiously being revised. For instance, there was a period when import almost of all products has been made without payment of any customs duties. However, all duties have been re-introduced. Therefore, it is crucial to constantly monitor any legislative developments and adapt franchising activities to them.

C. DEVELOPMENTS RELATED TO THE POTENTIAL UKRAINE'S ACCESSION TO THE EU

In June 2022, the EU granted Ukraine the status of the candidate. According to the news from the Government, it is expected that the negotiations on accession could start by the end of 2023. Taking into account that Ukraine would like to join the EU within as short a period as possible, now Ukraine either adopts or amends laws and by-laws to make them fully in compliance with the EU acquis. For instance, Ukraine has adopted new technical regulations, the draft laws in the field of product liability and consumers' rights protection, personal data protection etc. All these amendments shall be monitored and taken into account in franchising activities.

IX. Vietnam

By Tu Ngoc Trinh, Waewpen Piemwichai & Linh Thi Mai Nguyen, TILLEKE & GIBBINS

Trinh Ngoc Tu is a senior associate in the corporate and commercial group. She is an integral part of the firm's franchise team and handles cases related to competition and consumer protection laws.

Waewpen Piemwichai is a senior associate in the corporate and commercial group. She regularly advises companies on data privacy and cybersecurity matters.

Linh Thi Mai Nguyen is a partner in the trademark group and has more than a decade of experience advising companies owning famous brands to assist with protecting all intellectual property rights.

CHAPTER 9

A. PERSONAL DATA PROTECTION DECREE

As a necessary part of operating a franchise business in today's digital age, franchisees and franchisors collect personal information, information on purchasing/consumption behavior, and other customer data to develop the business activities for the franchise system. However, collecting, using, processing, or storing personal data in a franchise business in Vietnam must comply with Vietnamese regulations on personal data protection.

On April 17, 2023, after a protracted period of deliberation, the Vietnamese government ultimately passed the country's first ever Personal Data Protection Decree, as Decree No. 13/2023/ND-CP ("PDPD" or "Decree 13"). The PDPD is a landmark legal instrument that governs the collection and processing of personal data in Vietnam. However, in addition to the data processing requirements under the PDPD, there are also data processing requirements set out under sector-specific laws and regulations, such as requirements for e-commerce services, financial services, healthcare services, etc. The PDPD took effect on July 1, 2023, and it applies to both domestic and foreign entities that directly engage in or relate to personal data processing activities in Vietnam.

The PDPD confines its scope of application to four types of entities, including:

1. Vietnamese organizations and individuals;
2. Vietnamese organizations and individuals operating overseas;
3. Foreign organizations and individuals based in or residing in Vietnam; and
4. Foreign organizations and individuals directly participating in or related to personal data processing activities in Vietnam.

Despite no explicit provisions, the PDPD can be construed as reaching both personal data of Vietnamese people, irrespective of their place of residence, and personal data of foreign people residing in Vietnam fall under the scope of application of the PDPD.

The PDPD introduces eight principles for the processing of personal data: (i) any processing must be in accordance with the law (lawfulness); (ii) the data subjects must be informed of every activity involving the processing (transparency); (iii) personal data must only be processed for the purposes registered and announced in relation to the processing (purpose limitation); (iv) the personal data collected must be relevant and confined to the extent and purposes of the processing (data minimization); (v) personal data must be updated and supplemented in accordance with the purposes of the processing (accuracy); (vi) personal data must be subject to protection and security measures during the processing (integrity, confidentiality and security); (vii) personal data must only be kept for a term appropriate with the purpose of the processing (storage limitation); and (viii) the Controller and Controller-Processor (as defined below) must comply with the above principles and demonstrate their compliance (accountability). Article 3 of the PDPD.

The above principles are extremely important to keep in mind, as they will play a key role in guiding businesses' compliance procedures.

Personal data is broadly defined under the PDPD as information on an electronic medium in the form of symbols, letters, numbers, photos, sounds, or the like that is associated with or helps to identify a specific individual. Article 3 of the PDPD. Information that helps to identify a specific individual is further clarified as information generated from an individual's activities that, when combined with other data and stored information, can identify a particular person. Article 2.2 of the PDPD.

Under the PDPD, personal data is split into two different categories—basic personal data and sensitive personal data. Article 2.3 of the PDPD.

1. Basic personal data includes name, date of birth, gender, nationality, personal photos, phone number, identification number, marriage status, history of one's cyberspace activities, and so on.
2. Sensitive personal data, on the other hand, is more private and, if violated, will jeopardize a person's legitimate rights and interests. Accordingly, sensitive personal data comprises, among other things, political and religious views, health status and private life information as recorded in medical records, racial or ethnic origin, sexual orientation, criminal records, customer information of credit institutions/foreign bank branches/payment intermediary service providers, or location data.

The PDPD divides the persons involved with data processing activities into four categories:

1. Personal data controller ("Controller"); The Controller is an entity or individual that determines the purposes and means of personal data processing (i.e., the "why" and "how" of the processing). Article 2.9 of the PDPD.
2. Personal data processor ("Processor"); The Processor is an entity or individual that conducts the

CHAPTER 9

       processing of personal data on behalf of the Controller via an agreement. Article 2.10 of the PDPD.
3.   Personal data controller-processor ("Controller-Processor"); A Controller-Processor is an individual or entity that performs both the Controller and Processor roles concurrently. Article 2.11 of the PDPD.
4.   Third party is any organization or individual other than the data subject, Controller, Processor, or Controller-Processor that is permitted to process personal data will fall under this category. Article 2.12 of the PDPD.

In general, the PDPD imposes different obligations toward each of the regulated parties. For instance, if the activities of data collection and/or processing are located in Vietnam, the PDPD imposes onerous requirements upon the Controllers and Processors, regardless of whether they are located in Vietnam or overseas, notably including the requirements on:

1.   Preparation and submission of a Data Protection Impact Assessment Profile ("DPIA Profile") to be eligible to process personal data in Vietnam;
2.   Preparation and submission of a Cross-Border Transfer of Personal Data dossier (aka Transfer Impact Assessment dossier) ("TIA Dossier") to be eligible to transfer personal data outside of Vietnam;
3.   Appointing a Data Protection Officer ("DPO") and an internal personal data protection department ("DPD") and notifying the authority of such appointment if the company also needs to process sensitive personal data; and
4.   Data Processing Agreements (for engaging a Data Processor), and Data Transfer Agreements (for cross-border transfer of data outside of Vietnam).

Moreover, there are other requirements with which companies may need to ensure that their privacy and data protection policies are in alignment, such as the requirements on the formality to obtain consent, consent language, content of the privacy notice, rights of the data subjects (with 72-hour timeframe for responding to requests of the data subjects), age verification mechanism for data subject being children, etc.

Violators of the PDPD's regulations, depending on the severity of their violations, may be disciplined, or face administrative penalties or criminal prosecution. Article 4 of the PDPD. The Vietnamese authority is developing a draft decree on administrative penalties in the field of cybersecurity ("Draft Administrative Penalties Decree") that also covers violations against provisions under the PDPD. According to the latest Draft

International Developments

Administrative Penalties Decree, for severe violations, a fine of up to 5% of the enterprise's turnover in the Vietnamese market may be imposed. Further, additional penalties might include the suspension of the processing of personal data, the suspension of service provision, the deprivation of the right to use the business license in the Vietnamese market, etc. The Draft Administrative Penalties Decree is expected to be promulgated soon, possibly within 2023.

In the franchising relationship, it is critical that franchisors and franchisees understand and correctly identify their roles in compliance with data protection policies to minimize potential liability for both parties. In franchising activities, a foreign franchisor may collect, process and/or transfer basic or sensitive personal data of end consumers, either directly or as received from a local franchisee. On the other hand, in addition to franchisees collecting data by themselves, it is very common for franchisees to collect data per the franchisor's instruction for the franchisor's use. Depending on the nature of the transactions, the franchisors or the franchisees could be identified as either Controllers, Processors or Controller-Processors. Thus, it is important for the franchisor and the franchisee to understand their role in a particular data processing activity, as the regulatory requirements applicable to the Controller and the Processor are different. If categorized as a personal data Controller-Processor, the franchisor/franchisee is liable for all responsibilities specified for a Controller and Processor as described above.

In order to comply with personal data protection requirements relating to franchise activities in Vietnam, it is recommended that franchisors and franchisees conduct the following:

1. Thoroughly review franchise agreements, franchise disclosure documents and other agreements relating to franchise activities with the third party that contain provisions relating to personal data processing and ensure that the terms and the roles and responsibilities of the franchisor and franchisee in each data processing activity comply with the requirements and conditions specified in the PDPD.
2. Thoroughly review all operated data flow both within and outside of Vietnam's borders and make sure it aligns with, among other things, the requirements under the PDPD, notably including the requirements on consent format, consent statement, privacy notice, responses to requests relating to data subjects' rights, processing of children's data, data incident notification, etc. In addition, throughout the data flow, a system to protect the safety and

CHAPTER 9

confidentiality of the personal data must be set up according to the principles under the PDPD.
3. Ensure that it prepares and operates sufficient mechanisms to duly obtain affirmative, opt-in consent from data subjects according to the format set out under the PDPD;
4. Deploy necessary measures to protect collected personal data, honor the rights of data subjects as well as implement their requests.
5. Establish internal compliance processes for the franchise system based on the requirements of the PDPD.
6. Comply with the requirements of the PDPD, including but not limited to preparing, maintaining and submitting a copy to the data protection authority of the DPIA Profile, TIA Dossier, or appointment of the DPO/DPD, or preparing a Data Processing Agreement and a Data Transfer Agreement in the applicable case.

TABLE OF CASES

Page(s)

Cases

***360 Painting, LLC v. Misiph*,**
No. 3:22-CV-00056, 2023 WL 4533932 (W.D. Vir. July 13, 2023) 36

***A. D. v. Best Western International, Inc.*,**
No. 2:22-CV-650-JES-NPM, 2023 WL 2955711 (M.D. Fla. Apr. 14, 2023) 146

***A.B. Corp. v. Dunkin' Donuts Franchising, LLC*,**
No. 3:22-CV-1474 (SVN), 2022 WL 17337756 (D. Conn. Nov. 30, 2022) 32

***A.D. v. Best Western International, Inc.*,**
No. 2:22-CV-651-JES-NPM, 2023 WL 2955712 (M.D. Fla. Apr. 14, 2023) 147

***A.D. v. Best Western International, Inc.*,**
No. 2:22-CV-652-JES-NPM, 2023 WL 2955832 (M.D. Fla. Apr. 14, 2023) 148

***A.D. v. Cavalier MergerSub LP*,**
No. 2:22-CV-649-JES-NPM, 2023 WL 3073599 (M.D. Fla. Apr. 25, 2023) 149

TABLE OF CASES

A.D. v. Choice Hotels International, Inc.,
No. 2:22-CV-646, 2023 WL 3004545 (M.D. Fla. Apr. 19, 2023)..................................149

A.D. v. Choice Hotels International, Inc.,
No. 2:22-CV-647-JES-NPM, 2023 WL 2991041 (M.D. Fla. Apr. 18, 2023)..................................149

A.D. v. Choice Hotels International, Inc.,
No. 2:22-CV-648-JES-NPM, 2023 WL 3004547 (M.D. Fla. Apr. 19, 2023)..................................150

A.D. v. Marriott International, Inc.,
No. 2:22-cv-644-JES-NPM, 2023 WL 3004549 150

A.D. v. Marriott International, Inc.,
No. 2:22-CV-645-JES-NPM, 2023 WL 2991042 (M.D. Fla. Apr. 18, 2023)..................................150

A.D. v. Wyndham Hotels & Resorts, Inc.,
No. 2:22-CV-643, 2023 WL 2974171 (M.D. Fla. Apr. 17, 2023)..................................150

A.R. v. Wyndham Hotels & Resorts, Inc.,
No. 2:21-CV-04935, 2022 WL 17741054 (S.D. Ohio Dec. 16, 2022)..................................13, 151

A.W. v. Red Roof Inns, Inc.,
No. 2:21-CV-4934, 2022 WL 17585249 (S.D. Ohio Dec. 12, 2022)..................................142, 152

Absolute USA, Inc. v. Harman Professional, Inc.,
No. 221CV06410MEMFMAAX, 2023 WL 2064048 (C.D. Cal. Feb. 14, 2023)..................................1

TABLE OF CASES

Achieve 24 Fitness Limited Liability Co. v. Alloy Personal Training Solutions, LLC,
No. CV 21-12085 (GC), 2023 WL 2264129
(D.N.J. Feb. 28, 2023) 104, 154

Acuff v. Dy N Fly, LLC,
No. 22-cv-12329, 2023 WL 3293278 (E.D. Mich. May 5, 2023) 134

Advantage Payroll Services, Inc. v. Rode,
No. 2:21-CV-00020-NT, 2022 WL 17737878
(D. Me. Dec. 16, 2022) 72

Aerial Adventure Technologies, LLC v. C3 Manufacturing, LLC,
No. 523CV00018KDBDSC, 2023 WL 3267750
(W.D.N.C. Apr. 14, 2023) 195

AFC Franchising, LLC v. Purugganan,
No. 2:20-CV-00456-JHE, 2023 WL 373873
(N.D. Ala. Jan. 24, 2023) 195

Amaro Oilfield Automation, LLC v. Lithis CM, Inc.,
661 S.W.3d 477, No. 08-21-00013-CV (Tex. App. Jan. 23, 2023) 37, 57, 60

Americinn International, LLC v. Patel,
No. 21-20068 (ES)(AME), 2022 WL 17176935
(D.N.J. Nov. 23, 2022) 245

In re Arcimoto Inc. Securities Litigation,
No. 21-CV-2143 (PKC), 2022 WL 17851834
(E.D.N.Y. Dec. 22, 2022) 156

TABLE OF CASES

Ariza v. Coffee Beanery, Ltd.,
  No. 22-61516-CIV, 2022 WL 17333106 (S.D.
  Fla. Nov. 29, 2022) 123, 133, 173

Armstrong Ford, Inc. v. Ford Motor Co.,
  No. 5:23-CV-167-D, 2023 WL 4585904
  (E.D.N.C. July 18, 2023) 19

Arnone v. Burke,
  211 A.D.3d 998, 181 N.Y.S.3d 311 (2022) 55

Arnone v. Burke,
  211 A.D3d 998 (N.Y. App. Div. Dec. 28, 2022) 82

Arrington v. Burger King Worldwide, Inc.,
  47 F.4th 1247 (11th Cir. Aug. 31, 2022) 13, 123

as Northeast Pharma and Atlantic Pharm Co,
  LLC v. Medline Industries Inc.,
  No. 2:21-cv-00213, 2023 WL 3687716 (D. Vt.
  May 26, 2023) 190

ASA Enterprise, Inc. v. Stan Boyett & Son, Inc.,
  No. 1:21-cv-00915-BAK, 2022 WL 4182188
  (E.D. CA Sept. 13, 2022) 15, 238

B&P Glass and Mirror, LLC v. Clozetivity
  Franchising, LLC,
  No. 3:22-cv-00772 (M.D. Tenn. May 16, 2023) 215

B.J. v. G6 Hospitality, LLC,
  No. 22-CV-03765-MMC, 2023 WL 3569979
  (N.D. Cal. May 19, 2023) 153

Bacardi U.S.A., Inc. v. Major Brands, Inc.,
  2014 WL 2200042 (S.D. Fla. Mar. 20, 2014) 6

TABLE OF CASES

Bahia Bowls Franchising LLC v. DJS LLC,
  No. 2:23-CV-94-JLB-NPM, 2023 WL 2303048
  (M.D. Fla. Mar. 1, 2023)..104

Baim v. Dukart,
  No. CV 21-1696, 2023 WL 2330410 (E.D. Pa.
  Mar. 2, 2023)..37

Bakhtiari v. Doe,
  No. 22 C 2406, 2022 WL 17593027 (N.D. Ill.
  Dec. 13, 2022)..186

Barber Group, Inc. v. New Motor Vehicle Board,
  No. C095058, 2023 WL 4699885 (Cal.App.3d
  July 24, 2023)..20

Barnett v. Vapor Maven OK 1, LLC,
  No. 21-CV-423-TCK-JFJ, 2022 WL 17740971
  (N.D. Okla. Dec. 16, 2022)...186

Barrett v. New American Adventures, LLC,
  No. 2:20-CV-01813-CRE, 2023 WL 4295807
  (W.D. Pa. June 30, 2023)..173

BASF Corp. v. Stoutenger,
  No. 5:22-CV-00281 (MAD/ML), 2023 WL
  3624680 (N.D.N.Y. May 24, 2023)......................................58

Block v. Canepa,
  No. 22-385, 2023 WL 4540523 (6th Cir. July
  14, 2023) 30, 144

*Boca Gas Co. Holdings 2, LLC v. First Coast
Energy, LLP*,
  No. 3:23-CV-366-BJD-PDB, 2023 WL 3563460
  (M.D. Fla. Apr. 26, 2023)..15

TABLE OF CASES

Bowen v. Carlsbad Ins. & Real Estate, Inc.,
724 P.2d 223 (N.M. 1986) 79

BP Products North America Inc., v. Blue Hills Fuels, LLC,
2022 WL 16540804 (S.D.N.Y. Oct. 28, 2022) 15

Braman Motors, Inc. v. BMW of North America, LLC,
No. 17-23360-CIV, 2022 WL 17583440 (S.D. Fla. Nov. 18, 2022) 253

Braman Motors, Inc. v. BMW of North America, LLC,
No. 17-23360-CV, 2023 WL 3509818 (S.D. Fla. Apr. 28, 2023) 21, 186

Branco v. Hull Storey Retail Group, LLC,
No. 2021-000233, 2023 WL 3614244 (S.C. May 24, 2023) 56

Brar v. Sourdough & Co.,
No. C095424, 2023 WL 3219706 (Cal. Ct. App. May 3, 2023) 253

Brow Art Management, LLC v. Idol Eyes Franchise, LLC,
No. CV 23-11434, 2023 WL 4665357 (E.D. Mich. July 20, 2023) 73, 82

Brown v. Woodbury Auto Group, LLC,
No. 3:21-CV-00955, 2023 WL 2529055 (M.D. Tenn. Feb. 22, 2023) 155

TABLE OF CASES

Bruce-Terminix Company v. Terminix
International Company Limited Partnership,
No. 1:20-CV-962, 2023 WL 2974080
(M.D.N.C. Apr. 17, 2023)..82

In re Buck,
No. 19-34052-SWE-7, 2023 WL 3394938
(Bankr. N.D. Tex. May 11, 2023)...128

Burnett v. National Association of Realtors,
No. 4:19-CV-00332-SRB, 2022 WL 17741708
(W.D. Mo. Dec. 16, 2022) 155

Butler Brothers Supply Division, LLC v. HN
Precision Co.,
No. 220418-U, 2022 WL 17094960 (Ill. App.
Ct. 2d Nov. 21, 2022)..216

C. T. v. Red Roof Inns, Inc.,
No. 2:22-CV-834-JES-KCD, 2023 WL 3510879
(M.D. Fla. Mar. 11, 2023)..153, 212

Caceres v. Toyota Motor North America, Inc.,
No. 2020-08580, 2023 WL 3328701 (N.Y. App.
Div. May 10, 2023)..173

Cajunland Pizza, LLC v. Marco's Franchising,
LLC,
2022 WL 4353345 (N.D. Ohio Sept. 20, 2022)................................38, 94

CajunLand Pizza, LLC v. Marco's Franchising,
LLC,
No. 3:20-cv-536-JGC, 2022 WL 3960574 (N.D.
Ohio Aug. 31, 2022) 60, 97

TABLE OF CASES

Calabasas Luxury Motorcars, Inc. v. BMW North America, LLC,
No. CV 21-8825-DMG (ASX), 2022 WL 17350921 (C.D. Cal. Sept. 19, 2022) 61, 123

Canales v. CK Sales Co., LLC,
67 F.4th 38 (1st Cir. 2023) 134, 216

CAO Lighting, Inc. v. Signify, N.V.,
No. 2:21-cv-08972-AB-SP, 628 F.Supp.3d 996, 2022 WL 16894500 (C.D. Cal. Sept. 19, 2022) 187

Carmona Mendoza v. Domino's Pizza, LLC,
No. 21-55009, 2023 WL 4673469 (9th Cir. July 21, 2023) 217

Carpenter v. Pepperidge Farm, Inc.,
No. 20-CV-3881-GJP, 2023 WL 4552291 (E.D. Pa. July 14, 2023) 134

Carts v. Wings Over Happy Valley MDF, LLC,
No. 4:17-CV-00915, 2023 WL 373175 (M.D. Pa., Jan. 24, 2023) 135

Cavalier Distributing Company, Inc. v. Lime Ventures, Inc.,
No. 1:22-cv-121, 2023 WL 2384440 (S.D. Ohio Mar. 7, 2023) 30

Cawley v. Kenyon,
No. KNL-CV22-6055032-S, 2023 WL 2386114 (Conn. Super. Ct. Mar. 2, 2023) 174

CBD Franchising, Inc. v. Dres,
No. 8:22-cv-00313-FWS-JDE, 2023 WL 4155419 (C.D. Cal. May 19, 2023) 211

TABLE OF CASES

Central Jersey Construction Equipment Sales, LLC v. LBX Co., LLC,
No. 22-5581, 2023 WL 3093575 (6th Cir. Apr. 26, 2023) 62

Chilli Associates Limited Partnership v. Denti Restaurants Inc. d/b/a/ Max & Erma's,
No. 22CA30, 2023 WL 4004578 (Ohio Ct. App. June 13, 2023) 94

Choice Hotels International, Inc. v. C & O Developers, L.L.C.,
199 N.E.3d 1 (Oh. App. Sept. 15, 2022) 38, 79, 217

Choice Hotels International, Inc. v. Patel,
No. CV TDC-22-2310, 2023 WL 3276487 (D. Md. May 5, 2023) 228, 246

Choice Hotels International v. Seven Star Hotels Group, LLC,
No. 8:22-CV-748-AAQ, 2023 WL 1928016 (D. Md. Feb. 10, 2023) 218, 246

CiCi Enterprises, LP v. Fogel Enterprises, Inc.,
No. 3:22-CV-1202-E, 2023 WL 2731048 (N.D. Tex. Mar. 30, 2023) 84

Cici Enterprises, LP v. TLT Holdings, LLC,
No. 3:21-CV-02121-S-BT, 2022 WL 17657576 (N.D. Tex. Nov. 18, 2022) 39, 105

Cipercen, LLC v. Morningside Texas Holdings, LLC,
No. N19C-12-074 EMD CCLD, 2022 WL 4243687 (Super. Ct. Del. Sept. 14, 2022) 58, 207

TABLE OF CASES

City Beverages, LLC, dba Olympic Eagle Distributing v. Crown Imports, LLC dba Constellation Brands Beer Division, No. 23-359 (9th Cir. July 20, 2023) 84

City Beverages LLC v. Crown Imports LLC, 2022 WL 17582370 (W.D.Wash, December 12, 2022) 62

CJ Consultants, LLC v. Window World, Inc., No. 22-CV-3, 2022 WL 4354265 (W.D. Mich. Sept. 20, 2022) 64, 230

Coldwell Banker Real Estate LLC v. Bellmarc Group, LLC, No. 21-2862, 2022 WL 3644183 (3d Cir. Aug. 24, 2022) 39

In re Conte, No. 21-13189, 2022 WL 17096645 (Bankr. N.D. Ohio Nov. 21, 2022) 128

Continental Imports, Inc. v. Mercedes-Benz USA, LLC, No. 03-21-00377-CV, 2023 WL 114876 (Tex. App. Jan. 6, 2023) 21

Contour-Sierra Inc. v. AEBI Schmidt International, AG, No. 2:22-CV-00414-JAM-JDP, 2022 WL17670009 (E.D. Cal. Dec. 14, 2022) 253

Coons v. Yum! Brands, Inc., No. 21-CV-45-SPM, 2023 WL 3320149 (S.D. Ill. May 9, 2023) 225

TABLE OF CASES

Corvallis Hospitality, LLC. v. Wilmington Trust,
No. 2017-LC26, 6:22-CV-00024-MC, 2023 WL
3170438 (D. Or. Apr. 28, 2023) 56

Courser v. Radisson Hotels International, Inc.,
No. 1:18-cv-1232, 2023 WL 4364066 (W.D.
Mich. June 13, 2023) 182

Craig Alan Herremans v. Randy Fedo,
No. 17-80086, 2023 WL 4611429 (Bankr. W.D.
Mich. July 18, 2023) 254

CTA Hot Bread, Inc. v. Flowers Baking Company of Oxford, Inc.,
No. 21-cv-6488 (E.D.N.Y. Mar. 10, 2023) 218

Cutillo v. Cutillo,
No. 5:21-CV-02787-JMG, 2023 WL 4306731
(E.D. Pa. June 30, 2023) 187

Cynthia Gratton LLC v. Original Green Acres Café LLC,
No. 2:20-cv-02085-MHH, 2023 WL 1070606
(N.D. Ala. Jan. 27, 2023) 118, 246

D.Q.S.A. LLC v. American Dairy Queen Corporation,
No. CV-22-00335-TUC-JGZ, 2023 WL
4365332 (D. Ariz. July 6, 2023) 85

D3 International, Inc. v. AGGF Cosmetic Group S.p.A.,
No. 21-cv-06409 (S.D.N.Y. March 7, 2023) 40

TABLE OF CASES

Dana Innovations v. Trends Electronics International Inc.,
No. 8:22-cv-02155-FWS-ADS, 2023 WL 3335909 (C.D. Cal. Apr. 21, 2023)..........................40, 187, 254

Dauntless Enterprises, Inc. v. City Wide Franchise Co., Inc.,
No. 23-2273-JAR-TJJ, 2023 WL 4264118 (D. Kan. June 29, 2023),..254

DeCozen Chrysler Jeep Corp. v. Fiat Chrysler Automobiles, LLC,
No. 22-0068, 2022 WL 17094778 (D.N.J. Nov. 21, 2022) 22

Dexon Computer, Inc. v. Cisco Systems, Inc.,
No. 5:22-cv-53-RWS-JBB, 2023 WL 2941414 (E.D. Tex. Feb. 7, 2023) 124

District of Columbia v. JTH Tax, LLC,
No. C.A. 22-3165(CKK), 2023 WL 130736 (D.C. Jan. 9, 2023) 254

DMO Norwood LLC v. Kia America, Inc.,
No. 22-cv-10470-ADB, 2023 WL 2021321 (D. Mass. Feb. 15, 2023)..212

Doan Family Corp. v. Arnberger,
522 P.3d 364 (Kan. Ct. App. 2022) 73

Doctor's Associates LLC v. Khononov,
C.A. No. 22-cv-7637, 2023 WL 184389 (E.D.N.Y. Jan. 13, 2023) 85

Doctor's Associates, LLC v. Reino,
No. 3:22-cv-00786, 2023 WL 2687529 (D. Conn. Mar. 28, 2023)..218

TABLE OF CASES

Doe #1 v. Red Roof Inns, Inc.,
21 F.4th 714 (11th Cir. 2021) 152

Doe #21 v. CFR Enterprises, Inc.,
No. A163543, 2023 WL 4783591 (Cal. Ct. App.
June 29, 2023)..155, 175, 231

Doe (L.G.) v. Hand & Stone Franchise Corp.,
No. 862 EDA 2022, 2022 WL 17661068 (Pa.
Super. Ct. Dec. 14, 2022)...230

Doe v. Golden Krust Caribbean Bakery & Grill, Inc.,
No. 18-cv-05734, 2023 WL 2652264 (E.D.N.Y.
Mar. 27, 2023)...135

Doe v. Massage Envy Franchising, LLC,
87 Cal. App. 5th 23, 303 Cal. Rptr. 3d 269 (Cal.
Ct. App. 2022)...175, 218

Dow v. Keller Williams Realty, Inc.,
No. 4:21-CV-1209-P, 2022 WL 4009047 (N.D.
Tex. Sept. 2, 2022)...220

Dynamex Operations W. v. Superior Court,
4 Cal. 5th 903, 416 P.3d 1 (2018) .... *passim*

E. Moran, Inc. v. Tomgal, LLC
(D.P.R. May 2, 2023)..87

eBay Inc. v. MercExchange, LLC,
547 U.S. 388 (2006)..247

Ecovirux LLC v. Biopledge LLC,
357 So.3d 182 (Fla. Dist. Ct. App. 2022), reh'g
denied (Feb. 15, 2023) 198

TABLE OF CASES

Eddie's Truck Center, Inc. v. Daimler Vans USA LLC,
No. 5:21-CV-05081-VLD, 2023 WL 3388503 (D.S.D. May 11, 2023) 41

Eddie's Truck Center, Inc v. Daimler Vans USA LLC,
No. 5:21-CV-05081-VLD, 2023 WL 4624888 (D.S.D. July 19, 2023) 239

EFN West Palm Beach Motor Sales, LLC v. Hyundai Motor America Corp.,
No. 21-80348-CIV-CANNON/Matthewman, 2023 WL 2825920 (S.D. Fla. March 7, 2023) 42, 65

In re EllDan Corp.,
No. 22-31870, 2023 WL 3394917 (Bankr. D. Minn. May 11, 2023) 75

In re EllDan Corp.,
No. BR 22-31870-KLT, 2023 WL 175195 (Bankr. D. Minn. Jan. 12, 2023) 129

Energium Health v. Gabali,
No. 3:21-CV-2951-S, 2022 WL 16842660 (N.D. Tex. Nov. 9, 2022) 132, 187, 198

Escobar v. National Maintenance Contractors, LLC,
No. 21-35765, 2022 WL 17830001 (9th Cir. Dec. 21, 2022) 226

Eskimo Hut Worldwide, Ltd. v. South Plains Sno, Inc.,
No. 07-22-00259-CV, 2023 WL 177684 (Tex. App. Jan. 9, 2023) 32, 255

317

TABLE OF CASES

Exel Industries SA v. Sprayfish, Inc.,
No. 2:22-CV-00691-RAJ, 2022 WL 17141201
(W.D. Wash. Nov. 22, 2022) 105

F45 Training Pty Ltd. v. Body Fit Training USA Inc.,
No. 20-1194-WCB, 2022 WL 17177621 (D. Del. Nov. 17, 2022) 113

Fenix Group LLC v. GPM Investments, LLC,
No. CV-18-6043242-S, 2023 WL 369986
(Conn. Super. Ct. Jan. 17, 2023) 2

Fernald v. JFE Franchising, Inc.,
No. 2:22-cv-02761-JTF-cgc, 2023 WL 2938312
(W.D. Tenn. Apr. 13, 2023) 175

Fikes Wholesale, Inc. v. HSBC Bank USA, N.A.,
62 F.4th 704 (2d Cir. 2023) 231

FIMIC, S.r.L. v. ADG Solutions, Inc.,
No. 1:19-CV-05636-SDG, 2022 WL 4715685
(N.D. Ga. Sept. 30, 2022) 106, 114

Flawless Style LLC v. Saadia Group LLC,
No. 23 Civ. 2354 (JHR), 2023 WL 3687782
(S.D.N.Y. May 26, 2023) 44, 106

Flick v. Sterling,
No. 3:22-CV-00039, 2022 WL 4593097 (W.D. Va. Sept. 29, 2022) 198

Fluid Power Engineering Co., Inc. v. Cognex Corp.,
No. 22 CV 2707, 2022 WL 16856395 (N.D. Ill. Nov. 10, 2022) 3

TABLE OF CASES

Flynn v. Anytime Fitness, LLC,
No. C.A. 2022-0742, 2022 WL 17982922 (La.
Ct. App. 1st Cir. Dec. 29, 2022) 70

Fogle Enterprises Inc. v. Cici Enterprises, L.P.,
No. 6:22-cv-03134-MDH, 2022 WL 5246446
(W.D. Mo., October 6, 2022) 199

Foley v. Wildcat Investments, LLC,
No. 2:21-cv-5234, 2023 WL 4485571 (S.D.
Ohio July 12, 2023) 232

Foremost Groups Inc. v. Tangshan Ayers Bath Equipment Co. Ltd.,
No. 2:14-cv-00188-SVW-RZ, 2023 WL
4203476 (C.D. Cal. May 3, 2023) 213

Foundation Building Materials, LLC v. Conking & Calabrese, Co., Inc.,
No. 23 CVS 9285, 2023 WL 4561583 (N.C.
Super. Ct. July 7, 2023) 115

Franchise Management Unlimited, Inc. v. America's Favorite Chicken,
561 N.W.2d 123 (Mich. Ct. App. 1997) 64

Francois v. Victory Auto Group LLC,
No. 22-cv-04447 (JSR), 2023 WL 4534375
(S.D.N.Y. July 13, 2023) 32

Franlink Inc. v. BACE Services., Inc.,
50 F.4th 432 (5th Cir. 2022) 188, 199, 255

Fuentes v. Jiffy Lube International, Inc.,
No. CV 18-5174, 2023 WL 2539008 (E.D. Pa.
Mar. 16, 2023) 160

TABLE OF CASES

Fujitsu Semiconductor Ltd. v. Cypress Semiconductor Corp.,
No. 22-MC-80313-VKD, 2023 WL 3852701
(N.D. Cal. June 5, 2023) 220

Functional HIIT Fitness, LLC v. F45 Training Incorporated,
No. 5:22-CV-10168, 2022 WL 17828930 (E.D. Mich. Oct. 26, 2022) 13, 189, 208

G&S Beshay Trading Co., LLC v. 7-Eleven, Inc.,
No. 18cv3909 (EP(JRA) 2023 WL 3735959
(D.N.J. May 31, 2023) 193

G.F.B. Enterprises, LLC v. Toyota Motor Sales U.S.A, Inc.,
No. 23-CV-20392-RAR, 2023 WL 2631467
(S.D. Fla. Mar. 24, 2023) 33

Gaska v. Darcars of Railroad Avenue, Inc.,
No. 3:22-cv-1201-MPS, 2023 WL 3493820 (D. Conn. May 17, 2023) 189

Geib v. Amoco Oil Co,
29 F.3d 1050 (6th Cir. 1994) 64

Gimex Properties Corp., Inc. v. Reed,
205 N.E.3d 1 (Ohio App. Dec. 29, 2022) 74, 115

Goergen v. Black Rock Coffee Bar, LLC,
2023 WL142911 (D. Or. Jan. 10, 2023) 220

Goergen v. Black Rock Coffee Bar, LLC,
No. 3:22-CV-1258-SI, 2023 WL 1777980 (D. Or. Feb. 6, 2023) 221

TABLE OF CASES

Golden Fortune Import & Export Corporation v. Mei-Xin Limited,
No. 22-1710, 2022 WL 3536494 (3d Cir. Aug. 5, 2022) 65

In re Golden Seahorse LLC,
No. 22-11582 (PB), 2023 WL 2472970 (Bankr. S.D.N.Y. Mar. 10, 2023)..................129

Gonzalez v. Coverall North America, Inc.,
No. EDCV1602287JGBKKX, 2022 WL 17903078 (C.D. Cal. Dec. 8, 2022) 255

Good Clean Love, Inc. v. Epoch NE Corporation,
Civ. No. 6:21-cv-01294-AA, 2023 WL 2709653 (D. Or. March 30, 2023) 56, 118, 192

Good Times Restaurants, LLC v. Shindig Hospitality Group, LLC,
No. 21-CV-07688-AGT, 2022 WL 16856106 (N.D. Cal. Nov. 10, 2022)..................4, 5

Got Docs, LLC v. Kingsbridge Holdings, LLC,
No. 19 C 6155, 2023 WL 2078450 (N.D. Ill. Feb. 17, 2023) 74, 113, 115

Gray v. Schmidt Baking Company, Inc.,
No. 22-CV-00463-LKG, 2023 WL 2185778 (D. Md. Feb. 23, 2023)..................221

Greenspire Global, Inc. v. Sarasota Green Group, LLC,
No. 2D22-2653, 2023 WL 4139142 (Fla. 2nd DCA June 23, 2023) 95

TABLE OF CASES

Greentree Hospitality Group Inc. v. Mullinix,
No. CV-22-00088-PHX-DJH, 2022 WL
17832782 (D. Ariz. Dec. 21, 2022) 44

*Gujarat State Civil Supplies Corpn. Ltd. v.
Mahakali Foods (P) Ltd.*,
AIR 2022 SC 5545 270

H-1 Auto Care, LLC v. Lasher,
No. 21-18110 (ZNQ) (TJB), 2022 WL
13003468 (D.N.J. Oct. 21, 2022) 75, 87

*H.H. Franchising System, Inc. v. CareSmart
Solutions, Inc.*,
No. 1:21-CV-575, 2022 WL 4274278 (S.D.
Ohio Sept. 15, 2022) 75

Hagenbaugh v. Nissan North America,
No. CV 3:20-1838, 2023 WL 361786 (M.D. Pa.
Jan. 23, 2023) 226

Haitayan v. 7-Eleven, Inc.,
No. 21-56144, 2022 WL 17547805 (9th Cir.
Dec. 9, 2022) 232

Happy Tax Franchising LLC v. Hill,
No. 19-24539-CIV-MORENO/Louis, 2023 WL
2664261 (S.D. Fla. Jan. 25, 2023) 72

United States ex rel. Hart v. McKesson Corp.,
No. 15-CV-0903 (RA), 2023 WL 2663528
(S.D.N.Y. Mar. 28, 2023) 34

Havtech, LLC v. AAON Inc.,
No. CV SAG-22-00453, 2023 WL 200117 (D.
Md. Jan. 17, 2023) 61

TABLE OF CASES

HayDay Farms, Inc. v. FeeDx Holdings, Inc.,
55 F.4th 1232 (9th Cir. 2022) 229

Hegazy v. Halal Guys, Inc.,
No. 22 CIV. 1880 (JHR), 2023 WL 4405804
(S.D.N.Y. July 7, 2023) 160

Henson v. Fidelity National Financial, Inc.,
943 F.3d 434 (9th Cir. 2019) 256

Hernandez v. Syncrasy,
No. 21-CV-09212, 2023 WL 2600452 (N.D.
Cal. Mar. 21, 2023) 239

Herrera v. Highgate Hotels, L.P.,
No. 151096/18E, 2023 WL 1826823 (N.Y. App.
Div. Feb. 9, 2023) 175, 214

*Hickory Hills Foodmart, Inc. v. Equilon
Enterprises, LLC*,
No. 22 C 5393, 2023 WL 4273664 (N.D. Ill.
June 29, 2023) 44

Hicks v. Colorado Hamburger Company, Inc.,
No. 22-CA-0968, 2022 WL 17982947 (Col. Ct.
App. Dec. 29, 2022) 135, 247

*Hillstone Restaurant Group Inc. v. Houston's Hot
Chicken Inc.*,
No. CV-22-02004-PHX-MTL, 2023 WL
110926 (D. Ariz. Jan. 4, 2023) 107, 251

*Hofbräuhaus of America, LLC. v. Oak Tree
Management Services, Inc.*,
No. 2:22-cv-000421, 2023 WL 24179 (D. Nev.
Jan. 3, 2023) 118, 201

TABLE OF CASES

Holmes v. Diza Tacos Streeterville, LLC,
No. 22 C 3378, 2023 WL 1777463 (N.D. Ill.
Feb. 6, 2023) 221

Home-Grown Industries of Georgia, Inc. v.
Mellow Mushroom of Tom's River, LLC,
No. 1:22-CV-04919-SCJ, 2023 WL 2179474
(N.D. Ga. Jan. 3, 2023) 105

Hopp v. Leistad Systems, Inc.,
No. 22-0056, 2023 WL 383002 (Iowa Ct. App.
Jan. 25, 2023) 44

Housemaster SPV LLC v. Burke,
No. CV 21-13411 (MAS), 2022 WL 17904254
(D.N.J. Dec. 23, 2022) 240

Howard Johnson International, Inc. v. Kunwar,
No. 21-19287, 2023 WL 3199174 (D.N.J. May
1, 2023) 44

Howard P. Fairfield LLC v. Cives Corp.,
No. X07HHDCV196160194S, 2022 WL
17438467 (Conn. Super. Ct. Nov. 30, 2022) 240

Hyundai Construction Equipment Americas, Inc.
v. Southern Lift Trucks, LLC,
No. SC-2022-0675, 2023 WL 3402311 (Ala.
May 12, 2023) 155, 222, 226

Hyundai Motor America Corp. v. EFN West Palm
Motor Sales, LLC,
343 F.R.D. 230 (S.D. Fla. 2022) 58

TABLE OF CASES

Hyundai Motor America Corp. v. Efn West Palm Motor Sales, LLC,
No. 20-82102-CV, 2022 WL 16968426 (S.D. Fla. Nov. 16, 2022) 24, 132

Hyundai Motor America Corp. v. EFN West Palm Motor Sales, LLC,
No. CV 20-82102, 2022 WL 604071 (S.D. Fla. Mar. 1, 2022) 193

Hyundai Subaru of Nashville, Inc. v. Hyundai Motor America, Inc.,
No. 3:22-CV-00817, 2023 WL 2201015 (M.D. Tenn. Feb. 24, 2023) 156

iMotorsports, Inc. v. Vanderhall Motor Works, Inc.,
No. 2-21-0785, 2022 IL App. (2d) 210785 (Ill. App. Dec. 1, 2022) 24

iMotorsports, Inc. v. Vanderhall Motor Works, Inc.,
No. 2-21-0785, 2022 WL 210785 (Ill. App. Ct. Dec. 1, 2022) 45

Innovare, Ltd. v. Sciteck Diagnostics, Inc.,
No. 21-CVS-2180, 2023 WL 325141 (N.C. Super. Ct. Jan. 19, 2023) 45

Innovative Solutions & Technology, LLC v. Pro Spot International, Inc.,
No. CV 21-17302, 2023 WL 3260031 (D. N.J. May 4, 2023) 72

Innovative Sports Management, Inc. v. Gutierrez,
No. 22-CV-05793-BLF, 2023 WL 4157627 (N.D. Cal. June 23, 2023) 33

TABLE OF CASES

Integrity Real Estate Consultants v. Re/Max of New York, Inc.,
213 A.D. 815, No. 2019-06925, 2019-07405, 2019-07406, 2019-09360, 8794/07 (N.Y. App. Div. Feb. 15, 2023) 97

Integrity Real Estate Consultants v. Re/Max of NewYork, Inc.,
213 A.D.3d 815 (2023) 45

International Samarkand Hotel Group, LLC v. Wynn,
No. HHD-CV-17-5045384-S, 2023 WL 3000455 (Conn. Super. Apr. 14, 2023) 176

Interstate Restoration, LLC v. Marriott International, Inc.,
No. 21-cv-01380-NYW-SKC, 2023 WL 2528779 (D. Col. Mar. 15, 2023) 160, 176

J.M. v. Choice Hotels International, Inc.,
No. 2:22-cv-00672-KJM-JDP, 2023 WL 3456619 (E.D. Cal. May 15, 2023) 154

Jackson Hewitt Inc. v. Active Personal Taxes, Inc.,
No. 22-CV-02354, 2022 WL 17490540 (D.N.J. Dec. 6, 2022) 201

Jackson Hewitt Inc. v. New Age Taxes, Inc.,
No. 22-cv-2352, 2022 WL 17069801 (D.N.J. Nov. 17, 2022) 201

Jackson Hewitt Inc. v. O & W Taxes, Inc.,
No. 22-cv-02350, 2022 WL 17466428 (D.N.J. Dec. 5, 2022) 202

TABLE OF CASES

Jackson v. Chick & Seafood, Inc.,
   No. 3:22-CV-1687-N, 2023 WL 2799736 (N.D.
   Tex. Apr. 4, 2023) 161

Jani-King of Miami, Inc. v. Leicht,
   No. 3:23-CV-0389-B, 2023 WL 2335658 (N.D.
   Tex. Mar. 2, 2023) 88

Jani-King of Miami, Inc. v. Leicht,
   No. 3:23-CV-0389-B, 2023 WL 2825689 (N.D.
   Tex. Mar. 17, 2023) 240

Jani-King of New York, Inc. v. Commissioner of Labor,
   214 A.D.3d 1088, 184 N.Y.S.3d 473 (N.Y. App.
   Div. 2023) 12, 137, 142

JB Brothers, Inc v. Poke Bar GA Johns Creek I, LLC,
   No. 2:21-cv-01405-CBM-MRWx 2022 WL
   17080158 (C.D. Cal. Sept. 29, 2022) 66

Jone v. Deeter,
   913 P.2d 1272 (Nev. 1996) 79

Jones v. Embassy Suites, Inc.,
   No. 2:21-CV-5, 2023 WL 113056 (S.D. Ga. Jan.
   5, 2023) 145

Jose Santiago Inc. v. Smithfield Foods, Inc.,
   No. 22-1239(SCC/BJM), 2023 WL 4420257
   (D.P.R. July 10, 2023) 241

José Santiago, Inc. v. Smithfield Packaged Meats Corp.,
   66 F.4th 329 (1st Cir. 2023) 54

TABLE OF CASES

Joseph v. TGI Friday's, Inc.,
No. 21-CV-1340, 2022 WL 17251277 (N.D. Ill.
Nov. 28, 2022) 119

*JTH Tax, LLC, d/b/a Liberty Tax Service v.
Lowensky Cortorreal*,
No. 4:23-cv-0173-P, 2023 WL 4673278 203

JTH Tax, LLC v. Agnant,
No. 22-1229-cv, 62 F.4th 658, 2023 WL
2467363 (2d Cir. Mar. 13, 2023) 76, 88

JTH Tax LLC v. Anderson,
No. CV-23-00209-PHX-DJH, 2023 WL
2072496 (D. Ariz. Feb. 17, 2023) 76

JTH Tax LLC v. Anderson,
No. CV-23-00209-PHX-DJH, 2023 WL
3499645 (D. Ariz. Apr. 18, 2023) 56, 116

JTH Tax LLC v. Caswell,
No. 2:21-cv-339, 2022 WL 3580747 (E.D. Va.
Aug. 19, 2022) 248

JTH Tax LLC v. Gause,
No. 3:21-CV-00543-FDW-DCK, 2023 WL
3081300 (W.D.N.C. Apr. 25, 2023) 76

JTH Tax LLC v. Irving,
No. CV RDB-21-3000, 2023 WL 1472021 (D.
Md. Feb. 1, 2023) 46, 210

JTH Tax, LLC v. Leggat,
No. 2:22-CV-41 (RCY), 2022 WL 3970197
(E.D. Va. Aug. 31, 2022) 203, 210

TABLE OF CASES

JTH Tax LLC v. Pierce,
  No. 1:22-CV-1237-SEG, 2022 WL 4122215
  (N.D. Ga. Sept. 8, 2022) 76

JTH Tax, LLC v. Shahabuddin,
  No. 21-2031, 2023 WL 3002736 (4th Cir. Apr.
  19, 2023) 46

JTH Tax, LLC v. Shahzad,
  199 N.E.3d 1257 (E.D. Wis. Jan. 23, 2023) 77

JTH Tax, LLC v. Younan,
  No. 2:22cv383 2023 WL 3069767 (E.D. Va.
  Mar. 1, 2023)..204

Jumping Jack Retail II, Inc. v. 7-Eleven, Inc.,
  No. 23-CV-60460, 2023 WL 2987666 (S.D. Fla.
  Apr. 18, 2023) 46

*Just Between Friends Franchise Systems, Inc. v.
Samone Gibson Enterprises, LLC*,
  No. 23-CV-098-JFH-JFJ, 2023 WL 2496584
  (N.D. Okla. Mar. 14, 2023)...89

K.C. Company, Inc. v. Pella Corp.,
  No. DKC 20-0227, 2022 WL 3716537 (D. Md.
  Aug. 29, 2022) 79

K.C. v. Choice Hotels International, Inc.,
  No. 22-CV-2683, 2023 WL 2265214 (S.D. Ohio
  Feb. 28, 2023) 142

*KAM Development, LLC v. Marco's Franchising,
LLC*,
  No. 3:20-CV-2024, 2023 WL 3251216 (N.D.
  Ohio May 4, 2023)..46

TABLE OF CASES

Kava Culture Franchise Group Corp. v. Dar-Jkta Enterprises LLC,
No. 2:23-cv-278-JLB-KCD, 2023 WL 3121893 (M.D. Fla. April 27, 2023) 78, 108

Kava Culture Franchise Grp. Corp. v. Dar-Jkta Enterprises LLC,
No. 2:23-CV-278-JLB-KCD, 2023 WL 3568598 (M.D. Fla. May 18, 2023) 204

Kelley v. AW Distributing, Inc.,
No. 20-cv-06942-JSW, 2023 WL 2167391 (N.D. Cal. Feb. 21, 2023) 178

Kentucky Peerless Distilling Co. v. Fetzer Vineyards Corp.,
No. 3:22-CV-037-CHB, 2023 WL 2160851 (W.D. Ky. Feb. 22, 2023) 98

Keshav Convenience Store, LLC v. G & G Oil, Inc.,
573 MDA 2022, 2023 WL 142551 (Pa. Sup. Ct. Jan. 10, 2023) 47, 55

Kia America, Inc. v. Rally Auto Group, Inc.,
No. 822CV00109JVSJDE, 2022 WL 17185011 (C.D. Cal. Oct. 20, 2022) 89

Kraze Burger, Inc. v. Kraze International, Inc.,
No. 1:19cv0717, 2023 WL 4357251 (E.D. Va. May 19, 2023) 249

Kyles v. Hoosier Papa LLC,
No. 1:20-CV-07146, 2023 WL 2711608 (N.D. Ill. Mar. 30, 2023) 159, 162

TABLE OF CASES

In re Lager,
 No. 22-30072-MVL-11, 2023 WL 4676067
 (Bankr. N.D. Tex. July 20, 2023) 136

Le Fort Enterprises, Inc. v. Lantern 18, LLC,
 491 Mass. 144 (2023) 47

Legendary Strikes Mobile Bowling, LLC v. Luxury Strike, LLC,
 No. 1:22-cv-05065-ELR, 2023 WL 4401541
 (N.D. Ga. May 15, 2023) 118

LG2, LLC v. American Dairy Queen Corporation,
 No. 22-cv-1044, 2023 WL 171792 (D. Minn.
 Jan. 12, 2023) 7, 204

Liberty Ford Lincoln Mercury, Inc. v. Ford Motor Co.,
 No. 1:21-CV-02085, 2022 WL 17417258 (N.D.
 Ohio Dec. 5, 2022) 25

Lirette v. Sonic Drive-In Corp.,
 No. CV 22-3594 DIV. (2), 2023 WL 3092984
 (E.D. La. Apr. 26, 2023) 137

Little Caesar Enterprises, Inc. v. Walters Investments, Inc.,
 No. 2:21-CV-12829-TGB, 2023 WL 373869
 (E.D. Mich. Jan. 24, 2023) 250

Lockard Aircraft Sales Co. v. Dumont Aircraft Sales, LLC,
 No. 23-CV-1004-JWB, 2023 WL 4198596 (D.
 Kan. June 27, 2023) 211

TABLE OF CASES

Louis DeGidio, Inc. v. Industrial Combustion, LLC,
 66 F.4th 707 (8th Cir. 2023) 157

Lundstrom v. Holiday Hospitality Franchising, LLC,
 No. 1:22-CV-056, 2023 WL 4424725 (D.N.D. May 22, 2023) 154

Lunt v. Frost Shades Franchising, LLC,
 No. 3:22-cv-00775, 2023 WL 3484202 (M.D. Tenn May 16, 2023)...8, 57, 215

Luxottica of America, Inc. v. Brave Optical, Inc.,
 No. 4:22-CV-244, 2023 WL 4589222 (E.D. Tex. July 18, 2023) 78, 108

Luxury Concepts, Inc. v. Bateel International, LLC.,
 No. 22-10793, 2023 WL 360649 (E.D. Mich. May 23, 2023)...193, 204, 211

LVDV Holdings, LLC v. Shelton,
 No. CV 22-5921-RSWL-PD X, 2023 WL 3258437 (C.D. Cal. May 2, 2023) 119

Mac's Shell Serv., Inc. v. Shell Oil Prods. Co.,
 559 U.S. 175 (2010)..18

Madison Auto Center, LLC v. Lallas,
 No. 2022AP1376, 2023 WL 3880300 (Wis. Ct. App. June 8, 2023)..78

Major Brands, Inc. v. Mast-Jägermeister US, Inc.,
 No. 18-CV-423-HEA, 2022 WL 3585605 (E.D. Mo. Aug. 22, 2022) 5

TABLE OF CASES

Makina Ve Kimya Endustrisi v. Kaya,
  No. 3:20-cv-00072 (W.D. Va. Feb 17, 2023) 110

Marina Group LLC v. Shirley May International US Inc.,
  No. 2:21-cv-18733 (BRM) (MAH), 2022 WL 17622679 (D.N.J. Dec. 13, 2022) 205

Marina Group LLC v. Shirley May International US Inc.,
  No. 2:21-cv-19951, 2022 WL 17622066 (D.N.J. Dec. 13. 2022) 120

Mason Investment Group, LLC v. General Motors, LLC,
  No. CV 3:22-1940-MGL, 2023 WL 1451915 (D.S.C. Feb. 1, 2023) 26

Mayorga v. Ridgmar Urban Air, LLC,
  No. FBT-CV22-6113435 S 2023 WL 1246280 (Super. Ct. Conn. Jan. 23, 2023) 222

In re McDonald's Corporation Stockholder Derivative Litigation,
  No. 2021-0324-JTL, 291 A.3d 652, 2023 WL 2293575 (Del. Ch. Ct. Mar. 1, 2023) 182

McKinney Dodge Chrysler Jeep, Inc. v. Mazda Motor of America, Inc.,
  No. 8:22-CV-00496-HMH, 2022 WL 3053766 (D.S.C. Aug. 3, 2022) 26

McLaren v. UPS Store, Inc.,
  No. 21-14424 (MAS) (DEA), 2023 WL 3182842 (D.N.J. Apr. 29, 2023) 232

TABLE OF CASES

MD Auto Group, LLC d/b/a I-90 Nissan v. Nissan North America, Inc.,
No. 1:21-cv-01584-CEF, 2023 WL 41812595 241

ME SPE Franchising LLC v. NCW Holdings LLC,
No. CV-21-00458, 2023 WL 269162 (D. Ariz. Mar. 29, 2023)..98

Merlino v. Knudson,
No. 2020-07327, 214 A.D.3d 642, 184 N.Y.S.3d 280 (2d Dep't March 1, 2023) 178

Metro Chrysler Plymouth, Inc. v. FCA US LLC,
No. 22-CV-05646 (HG), 2022 WL 16834572 (E.D.N.Y. Nov. 9, 2022)..206

Moehrl v. National Association of Realtors,
No. 19-cv-01610, 2023 WL 2683199 (N.D. Ill. Mar. 29, 2023)..233

Montemayor v. Ford Motor Co.,
No. B320477, 2023 WL 4181909 (Cal. Ct. App. June 26, 2023)..227

Moody v. Circle K Stores, Inc.,
No. 2:18-cv-435-CLM, 2023 WL 404018 (N.D. Ala. Jan. 25, 2023) 157, 160, 178

Moore v. Bob Howard German Imports, LLC,
No. 120,124, 2023 WL 3579057 (Okla. Civ. App. May 19, 2023)..222

Mouanda v. Jani-King International,
653 S.W.3d 65 (Ky. Aug. 18, 2022) 163

TABLE OF CASES

Estate of Myrick v. 7-Eleven Inc.,
No. 23-829, 2023 WL 4140829 (E.D. Pa. June
22, 2023) 175, 254

N.N. Global Mercantile Pvt. Ltd. v. Indo Unique Flame Ltd.,
Civil Appeal Nos. 3802-3803 269

Nakava LLC v. The South Pacific Elixir Company,
No. 22-13567, 2023 WL 4364502 (11th Cir.
July 6, 2023)..111

Nasreen v. Capitol Petroleum Group, LLC,
No. 20-1867(TJK), 2023 WL 2734210 (D. D.C.
March 31, 2023)..16, 47

Neff Group Distributors, Inc. v. Cognex Corp.,
No. CV 22-11270-NMG, 2022 WL 17156025
(D. Mass. Nov. 22, 2022)..4, 67

New Jersey Coalition of Automotive Retailers, Inc. v. Mazda Motor of America, Inc.,
No. CV1814563ZNQTJB, 2023 WL 2263741
(D.N.J. Feb. 28, 2023) 157

New World Car Nissan, Inc. v. Hyundai Motor America,
658 S.W.3d 754 (Tex. App. 2022)..27

Next Level Ventures, LLC v. Avid Holdings, Ltd.,
No. C22-1083-JCC, 2023 WL 3382539 (W.D.
Wash. May 11, 2023)..229

NFVT Motors, LLC v. Jupiter Chevrolet, L.P.,
No. 05-21-01031-CV, 2022 WL 16959260
(Tex. App. Nov. 16, 2022) 98

TABLE OF CASES

North American Specialty Flooring, Inc. v. Humane Manufacturing Company, LLC,
No. 22-CV-244-JDP, 2023 WL 4762592 (W.D. Wis. July 26, 2023) 100

NuVasive, Inc. v. Absolute Medical, LLC,
71 F.4th 861 (11th Cir. 2023) 229

O'Bryant v. Flowers Foods, Inc.,
No. 2:21-cv-3501-BHH, 2022 WL 4368237 (D.S.C. Sept. 21, 2022) 223

O'Neal v. American Shaman Franchise System, LLC,
No. 8:20-CV-936-KKM-AAS, 2023 WL 1105209 (M.D. Fla. Jan. 30, 2023) 214

O'Neal v. American Shaman Franchise System, LLC,
No. 8:20-CV-936-KKM-AAS, 2023 WL 2164211 (M.D. Fla. Feb. 22, 2023) 242

O'Neal v. American Shaman Franchise System, LLC,
No. 8:20-CV-936-KKM-AAS, 2023 WL 2455627 (M.D. Fla. Jan. 30, 2023), report and recommendation adopted sub nom. 251

Ochoa v. Ford Motor Company (Ford Motor Warranty Cases),
Nos. B312261, JCCP 4856, 2023 WL 2768484, 89 Cal.App.5th 1324 (Cal. Ct. App. April 4, 2023) 227

Olguin v. FCA US LLC,
No. 1:21-CV-1789 JLT CDB, 2023 WL 1972223 (E.D. Cal. Feb. 13, 2023) 183

TABLE OF CASES

Orlando v. Choice Hotels International, Inc.,
No. 2:22-cv-00404-APG-BNW, 2023 WL
4025886 (D. Nev. June 15, 2023) 179, 215

OYO Hotels Inc. v. Om Chamunda LLC,
No. 3:20-CV-3433-N, 2023 WL 3491742 (N.D.
Tex. May 16, 2023) 242

Pac-West Distributing NV LLC v. AFAB
Industrial Services, Inc. et al.,
Civil Action No. 19-3584, 2023 WL 3952347
(E. D. Pa. June 12, 2023) 242

Park 80 Hotels, LLC v. Holiday Hospitality
Franchising, LLC,
No. 1:21-CV-04650-ELR, 2023 WL 2445437
(N.D. Ga. Feb. 16, 2023) 234

Parker Powersports Inc. v. Textron Specialized
Vehicles Inc.,
No. cv 122-054, 2023 WL 2695103 (S.D. Ga.
Mar. 29, 2023) 27, 144

Passion for Restaurants, Inc. v. Villa Pizza, LLC,
No. CV 20-15790 (KSH) (CLW), 2022 WL
18024209 (D. N.J. Dec. 30, 2022) 223

Patel v. 7-Eleven, Inc.,
489 Mass. 356, 183 N.E.3d 398 (Mar. 24, 2022) 33, 165

Patel v. 7-Eleven, Inc.,
No. CV 17-11414-NMG, 2022 WL 4540981 (D.
Mass. Sept. 28, 2022) 138, 165

Patel v. 7-Eleven, Inc.,
No. CV 17-11414-NMG, 2023 WL 35357 (D.
Mass. Jan. 4, 2023) 98

TABLE OF CASES

Patil Automation Private Limited v. Rakheja Engineers Private Limited.,
AIR 2022 SC 3848 .... 146, 271

Paul Hobbs Imports Inc. v. Verity Wines LLC,
21 CIV. 10597 (JPC), 2023 WL 374120
(S.D.N.Y. Jan. 24, 2023) 133

Peacock v. First Order Pizza, LLC,
No. 22-CV-02315, 2022 WL 17475791 (W.D. Tenn. Dec. 6, 2022) 228

Pender v. Wings,
No. 2:21-CV-4292, 2023 WL 2472035 (S.D. Ohio Mar. 13, 2023) 236

Pereda v. Atos Jiu Jitsu LLC,
No. B313718, 85 Cal.App.5th 759, 301 Cal. Rptr. 3d 690, 2022 WL 17174558 (Cal. Ct. of App., Nov. 23, 2022) 179

Peterbrooke Franchising of America, LLC v. Miami Chocolates, LLC,
No. 21-10242, 2022 WL 6635136 (11th Cir. Oct. 11, 2022) 48

Peterson Motorcars, LLC v. BMW of North America, LLC,
No. 3:19-cv-277-DJH-RSE, 2022 WL 4125102
(W.D. Ky. Sept. 9, 2022) 48, 211, 256

Philadelphia Indemnity Insurance Co. v. Markel Insurance Co.,
No. 1:20-cv-00669-JRR, 2023 WL 113748 (D. Md. Jan. 5, 2023) 48, 143

TABLE OF CASES

Pina v. Shaman Botanicals, LLC,
  No. 21-007772-CV-W-WBG, 2023 WL
  1070604 (W.D. Mo. Jan. 27, 2023) 166

*Pinnacle Foods of California, LLC v. Popeyes
Louisiana Kitchen, Inc.*,
  No. 21-21555-CIV, 2022 WL 17736190 (S.D.
  Fla., Dec. 16, 2022) 49, 55

Pizza Hut, LLC v. Ronak Foods, LLC,
  No. 5:21-CV-00089-RWS, 2022 WL 18456981
  (E.D. Tex. Dec. 22, 2022) 99

Pizza Inn, Inc. v. Allen's Dynamic Food, Inc.,
  No. CIV-23-00164-PRW, 2023 WL 3015297
  (W.D. Okla. Apr. 19, 2023) 90, 112

Pizza Inn, Inc. v. Odetallah,
  2022 WL 17475784 (W.D. Okla. Dec. 6, 2022) 96

Pizza Inn, Inc. v. Odetallah,
  No. CIV-21-00322-PRW, 2022 WL 4473621
  (W.D. Okla. Sept. 26, 2022) 49, 95

*Planet Fitness International Franchise v. JEG-
United, LLC*,
  No. 20-cv-693-LM, 2022 WL 4484477 (D.N.H.
  Sept. 27, 2022) 57, 96

Poe v. FCA US LLC,
  No. 2:21-CV-11668-TGB-CI, 2022 WL
  4491055 (E.D. Mich. Sept. 27, 2022) 231

Powerlift Door Consultants, Inc. v. Shepard,
  No. 21-CV-1316, 2023 WL 2976031 (D. Minn.
  Apr. 17, 2023) 78, 112

TABLE OF CASES

Powerlift Door Consultants, Inc. v. Shepard,
No. 21-CV-1316, 2023 WL 3012037 (D. Minn. Apr. 18, 2023) 112

Proximo Spirits, Inc. v. Green Lake Brewing Co., LLC,
No. 2:22-cv-02879-SPG-SK, 2022 WL 17224545 (C.D. Cal. Sept. 9, 2022) 194, 206

Qdoba Restaurant Corp. v. Zurich American Insurance Co.,
No. 120CV03575DDDNRN, 2023 WL 2725875 (D. Colo. Mar. 30, 2023) 50

Queen v. Wineinger,
No. 21-cv-378-wmc, 2022 WL 3017004 (W.D. Wis. Aug. 1, 2022) 61, 81

Quiroz v. DCT Enterprises of New Mexico, LLC,
No. 221CV01197MISKRS, 2023 WL 1765383 (D.N.M. Feb. 3, 2023) 138

R Journey, LLC v. Kampgrounds of America, Inc.,
No. CV 22-48-BLG-SPW, 2023 WL 2373352 (D. Mont. Mar. 6, 2023) 120

Ramos v. Willert Home Products, Inc.,
No. 22-1247 (RAM), 2023 WL 234758 (D.P.R. Jan. 18, 2023) 68

Reinvestment Fund, Inc. v. Rauh,
No. A-3184-21, 2022 WL 17587863 (N.J. Super. Ct. App. Div. Dec. 13, 2022) 256

TABLE OF CASES

Reno Dealership Group, LLC v. General Motors, LLC,
No. 21-55609, 2023 WL 234786 (9th Cir. Jan. 18, 2023) 28, 50, 71

Rich Morton's Glen Burnie Lincoln Mercury, LLC v. Williams-Moore,
No. 1844, SEPT.TERM 2021, 2023 WL 166277 (Md. Ct. Spec. App. Jan. 12, 2023) 158

Rivas v. Coverall North America, Inc.,
No. SACV181007JGBKKX, 2022 WL 17960776 (C.D. Cal. Nov. 28, 2022)....................223

RJS Distributors, LLC v. Pepperidge Farm, Inc.,
No. 21 C 2125, 2022 WL 16836383 (N.D. Ill. Nov. 9, 2022) 101

Road King Development, Inc. v. JTH Tax, LLC,
No. 2:21-cv-55, 2023 WL 2090280 (E.D. Va. Feb. 17, 2023) 50

Roadbuilders Machinery and Supply Co., Inc. v. Sandvik Mining and Construction USA, LLC,
No. 2:22-cv-2331-HLT-TJJ, 2023 WL 3790691 (D. Kan. June 2, 2023)..243

Rodo Inc. v. Guimaraes,
No. 22-CV-9736 (VSB), 2023 WL 2734464 (S.D.N.Y. Mar. 30, 2023) 166

Roleo Beverage Corp. v. Pepsi-Cola Bottling,
No. 1:22-CV-6921 (MKV), 2022 WL 3974465 (S.D.N.Y. Sept. 1, 2022)..................................91, 224

TABLE OF CASES

Roman v. Jan-Pro Franchising International, Inc.,
No. C 16-05961 WHA, 2022 WL 3046758
(N.D. Cal. Aug. 2, 2022) 12, 166

Root v. MaidPro Wilmington,
No. N20C-05-156 CLS, 2022 WL 17039161
(Del. Super. Nov. 17, 2022) 181

Roy v. Fedex Ground Package Systems, Inc.,
No. 3:17-cv-30116-KAR, 2023 WL 4186291
(D. Mass. June 26, 2023) 215

Rushing v. McAlister's Franchisor SPV LLC,
No. 22-CV-649-SMY, 2023 WL 2163388 (S.D. Ill. Feb. 22, 2023) 158

S. G. Borello & Sons, Inc. v. Dept. of Industrial Relations,
769 P.2d 399 (Cal. 1989) 138, 169, 171

Sai Nath, LLC v. Patel,
660 S.W.3d 474 (Mo. Ct. App. 2023) 71

Salinas v. Cornwell Quality Tools Co.,
No. 5:19-CV-02275-FLA (SPX), 2022 WL 16735359 (C.D. Cal. Oct. 17, 2022) 138

Salinas v. Cornwell Quality Tools Company,
No. 5:19-CV-02275-FLA (SPX), 2022 WL 16735823 (C.D. Cal. Oct. 17, 2022) 170, 236

Salsarita's Franchising LLC v. Gibson Family Enterprises LLC,
No. 3:22-CV-00206, 2022 WL 15046281
(W.D.N.C. Oct 25, 2022) 206

TABLE OF CASES

San Juan Products, Inc. v. River Pools & Spas, Inc.,
No. 8:21-CV-2469-TPB-JSS, 2023 WL 1994087 (M.D. Fla. Feb. 14, 2023) 120

Sanders v. Savannah Highway Automotive Company,
No. 2021-000137, 2023 WL 4752347 (S.C. July 26, 2023) 224

Sant v. Marriott International, Inc.,
No. GJH-22-1036, 2023 WL 2213926 (D. Md. Feb. 24, 2023) 181, 207

Sasoro 13, LLC v. 7-Eleven, Inc.,
No. 3:18-CV-03274-N, 2023 WL 2290788 (N.D. Tex. Feb. 27, 2023) 17

SBFO Operator No. 3, LLC v. Onex Corp.,
No. 4:19-CV-0321-JAR, 2023 WL 2631521 (E.D. Mo. Mar. 23, 2023) 58

SC America, LLC v. Marco's Franchising, LLC,
No. 3:22-cv-919, 2023 WL 2229654 (N.D. Ohio Feb. 23, 2023) 51

Sea Tow Services International, Inc. v. Tampa Bay Marine,
No. 20-CV-2877(JS)(SIL), 2022 WL 5122728 (E.D.N.Y. Sept. 30, 2022) 9, 113, 211

Shandong Luxi Pharmaceutical Co., Ltd. v. Camphor Technologies, Inc.,
No. 8:21-CV-942-CEH-AEP, 2023 WL 2499157 (M.D. Fla. Mar. 14, 2023) 57

TABLE OF CASES

Sheriff v. Four Cousins Burgers and Fries of NH, LLC,
No. 21-cv-571-PB, 2023 WL 3393394 (D.N.H. May 11, 2023) 181

Singh v. Wireless Vision, LLC,
No. 2:22-CV-01018-JDP, 2023 WL 275284 (E.D. Cal. Mar. 31, 2023) 81

Smash Franchise Partners, LLC v. Kanda Holdings, Inc.,
No. 2020-0302-JTL, 2023 WL 4560984 (Del. Ch. July 14, 2023) 116

SoClean, Inc. vs. Sunset Healthcare Solutions, Inc., No. 2021-2311, 2022 WL 16826171, 52 F. 4th 1363 (Fed. Cir. Nov. 9, 2022) 121

Soderholm Sales & Leasing, Inc. v. BYD Motors, Inc.,
No. 21-16778, 2022 WL 16847543 (9th Cir. Nov. 10, 2022) 97

Sonate Corp. v. Dunkin' Brands Group, Inc.,
No. 6:22-CV-812-WWB-EJK, 2023 WL 2624756 (M.D. Fla. Mar. 24, 2023) 82

Sonic Industries, LLC v. Olympia Cascade Drive Ins LLC,
No. CIV-22-449-PRW, 2022 WL 3654748 (W.D. Okla. Aug. 24, 2022) 91

South Shore D'Lites LLC v. First Class Products Group, LLC,
215 A.D.3d 412, 187 N.Y.S.3d 185 (2023) 34

TABLE OF CASES

Southwest Airlines Co. v. Saxon,
142 S. Ct. 1783 (2022) 217

Spencer v. JRN, Inc.,
No. 3:22-CV-00024-GFVT, 2023 WL 2278644
(E.D. Ky. Feb. 28, 2023) 236

Spikes v. Schumacher Auto Group, Inc.,
No. 21-81223-civ-SMITH, 2022 WL 18402565
(S.D. Fla. Dec. 20, 2022) 139

Sr. Ozzy's Franchising LLC v. Morales,
No. CV-23-00238-PHX-GMS, 2023 WL
2601258 (D. Ariz. Mar. 22, 2023) 91

Star Houston, Inc. v. Volvo Cars of North America, LLC,
No. 03-21-00239-CV, 2023 WL 3639585 (Tex. App., May 25, 2023) 29

In re Start Man Furniture, LLC,
No. 20-10553, 2023 WL 2717662 (Bankr. D. Del. Mar. 30, 2023) 130

Stauffer v. Innovative Heights Fairview Heights, LLC,
No. 3;20-CV-00046-MAB, 2022 WL 3139507
(S.D. Ill. Aug. 5, 2022) 101

Ste. Michelle Wine Estates, LLC v. Tri County Wholesale Distributors, Inc.,
No. 4:22 CV 1702, 2022 WL 17617319 (N.D. Ohio Dec. 13, 2022) 32

TABLE OF CASES

Stingray IP Solutions, LLC v. TP-Link Technologies Co., Ltd.,
Nos. 2:21-CV-00045-JRG, 00046-JRG, 2022
WL 17357774 (E.D. Tex. Oct. 13, 2022) 194, 207

Streedharan v. Stanley Industrial & Automotive, LLC,
No. 5:22-cv-0322-MEMF, 630 F.Supp.3d 1244
(C.D. Cal. Sept. 27, 2022) 140, 225

Strickland v. Foulke Management Corp.,
No. A-0455-21, 475 N.J. Super. 27, 290 A.3d
1259 (Mar. 3, 2023) 229

Sungyou Enterprise Co. v. Ghirardelli Chocolate Co.,
No. 22-CV-05306-TSH, 2023 WL 3134207
(N.D. Cal. Apr. 26, 2023) 231

Super 8 Worldwide Inc. v. Nirgam Enterprises, LLC,
No. 2:11-CV-06447 (WJM), 2023 WL 1360135
(D.N.J. Jan. 30, 2023) 250

Synlawn of Northern Nevada LLC v. Synthetic Turf Resources Corp.,
C.A. No. 4:22-CV-116-MHC, 2022 WL
18460632 (N. D. Ga. Nov. 3, 2022) 51

Teague v. 7 Eleven,
No. 4:21-cv-04097-SLD-JEH, 2023 WL
2072404 (C.D. Ill. Feb. 16, 2023) 141

Teague v. 7-Eleven, Inc.,
No. 4:21-cv-04097-SLD-JEH, 2023 WL
4426017 (C.D. Ill. July 10, 2023) 171

TABLE OF CASES

Terrier, LLC v. HCAFranchise Corporation,
No. 222cv01325GMNEJY, 2022 WL 4280251
(D. Nev. Sept. 2022) 51, 55, 79, 92

Tesla Inc. v. Delaware Division of Motor Vehicles,
No. 375, 2022, 2023 WL 3470406 (Del. May
15, 2023) 13, 29

Tesla, Inc. v. Louisiana Automobile Dealers Association,
No. CV 22-2982, 2023 WL 4053438 (E.D. La.
June 16, 2023)..125

In re Times Square JV, LLC,
No. 22-11715-JPM, 2023 WL 1786408 (Bankr.
S.D.N.Y. Feb. 4, 2022) 130

Titshaw v. Geer,
Nos. A23A0410, A23A0439, 2023 WL
3609488 (Ga. Ct. App. May 24, 2023) 158

Toth v. Subway Restaurants, LLC,
No. 21 MA 0084, 2022 WL 4351090 (Ohio Ct.
App., Sept. 16, 2022) 71

Track, Inc. v. ASH North America, Inc.,
No. 21-cv-786-jdp, 2023 WL 2733679 (W.D.
Wis. Mar. 31, 2023) 4

Travelodge Hotels, Inc. v. Durga, LLC,
No. 15-8412, 2023 WL 314313 (D.N.J. Jan. 19,
2023) 52

TRBR, Inc. v. General Motors, LLC,
No. 20-11269, 2022 WL 16758482 (E.D. Mich.
Nov. 8, 2022) 93

TABLE OF CASES

Tripicchio v. The UPS Store, Inc.,
  No. CV2114512MASDEA, 2023 WL 3182915
  (D.N.J. Apr. 30, 2023) 237

Tropical Paradise Resorts, LLC v. JBSHBM, LLC,
  No. 18-CV-60912, 2023 WL 1927298 (S.D. Fla.
  Feb. 10, 2023) 252

*U.S. Wholesale Outlet & Distribution, Inc. v.
Innovation Ventures, LLC*,
  No. 21-55397, 2023 WL 4633263 (9th Cir. July
  20, 2023) 126

*Udenze v. Monique Johnston, Director, Motor
Vehicle Division Texas DMV*,
  No. 03-22-00084-CV, 2023 WL 4110854 (Tex.
  App. June 22, 2023) 250

In re Vecchio,
  No. 6:20-AP-00117-LVV, 2022 WL 16828243
  (Bankr. M.D. Fla. Oct. 3, 2022) 132

Vital Distributions, LLC v. Pepperidge Farm,
  No. 2:22-cv-00319-MCE-KJN, 2023 WL
  2433362 (E.D. Cal. Mar. 9, 2023) 53

*Washburn v. One Hour Air Conditioning
Franchising, SPE, LLC*,
  No. 3:21-CV-235, 2022 WL 4481416 (S.D.
  Ohio Sept. 27, 2022) 93

Waters Edge Wineries, Inc. v. Wine Vibes, LLC,
  No. 5:22-cv-01883-SB-SHK 2023 WL 4297563
  (C.D. Cal. June 29, 2023) 53

TABLE OF CASES

Weiss v. Premier Technologies,
  No. 22-CV-6349DGL, 2023 WL 3314691
  (W.D.N.Y. May 9, 2023) 141

Wesdem, L.L.C. v. Illinois Tool Works, Inc.,
  No. 22-50769, 70 F. 4th 285 (5th Cir. June 9,
  2023) 54, 59

*Westfield National Insurance Co. v. Quest
  Pharmaceuticals, Inc.*,
  57 F.4th 558 (6th Cir. 2023) 143

Wheelmaxx, Inc. v. Mahal,
  No. 1:22-CV-01506-ADA-SKO, 2023 WL
  3224161 (E.D. Cal. May 3, 2023) 257

Whitlach v. Premier Valley, Inc.,
  86 Cal. 183

Whitlach v. Premier Valley, Inc.,
  No. 21-CV-2143 (PKC), 2022 WL 17751550
  (Cal. Ct. App. Nov. 18, 2022) 172

Williams v. D'Argent Franchising, L.L.C.,
  No. 1:20-CV-01501, 2023 WL 3059192 (W.D.
  La. Apr. 24, 2023) 237

*Window World of Baton Rouge, LLC v. Window
  World, Inc.*,
  No. 15 CVS 1, 2022 WL 17177467 (N.C.
  Super. Ct. Nov. 10, 2022) 244

Winesburg v. Stephanie Morris Nissan, LLC,
  No. 2:22-CV-04157-MDH, 2023 WL 3901483
  (W.D. Mo. June 8, 2023) 141

TABLE OF CASES

Winter v. Natural Res. Def. Council, Inc.,
555 U.S. 7 (2008) 63, 93

Wirtgen America, Inc. v. Hayden-Murphy Equipment Company,
No. 3:22-CV-00308, 2023 WL 123499 (M.D. Tenn. Jan. 6, 2023) 35

Wistron Neweb Corporation v. Genesis Networks Telecom Services, LLC,
No. 22-CV-2538 (LJL), 2023 WL 4493542 (S.D.N.Y. July 12, 2023) 54

Wistron Neweb Corporation v. Genesis Networks Telecom Services, LLC,
No. 22-cv-2538-LJL, 2022 WL 17067984 (S.D.N.Y. Nov. 17, 2022) 54, 82

Wright-Moore Corp. v. Ricoh Corp.,
980 F.2d 432 (7th Cir. 1992) 3

Yarber v. Kia America, Inc.,
No. 22-cv-03411-HSG, 2023 WL 2654186 (N.D. Cal. March 27, 2023) 60

Yogi Krupa, Inc. v. GLeS, Inc.,
No. 22-226-CFC, 2022 WL 16834164 (D. Del. Nov. 9, 2022) 19

Estate of Zamarie Chance v. Fairfield Inn & Suites,
287 N.C. App. 393, 2022 WL 17985662 (N.C. Ct. App. Dec. 29, 2022) 68

Zest Anchors, LLC v. Geryon Ventures, LLC,
No. 22-CV-230 TWR (NLS), 2022 WL 16838806 (S.D. Cal. Nov. 9, 2022) 94, 121

TABLE OF AUTHORITIES

Statutes

5 U.S.C. § 2801(7) 18

15 U.S.C. § 1222 14

15 U.S.C. §§ 2801(6)(A)–(B) 18

18 U.S.C. § 1836(b), *et seq* 114

18 U.S.C. § 1836 et seq. 115

18 U.S.C. § 1962 132

18 U.S.C. § 1965(b) 132

28 U.S.C. § 1332 228

28 U.S.C. § 1404(a) 8, 203, 204

28 U.S.C. § 2201 23

Bankruptcy Code § 365 131

Bankruptcy Code § 523(a)(3) 128

Business and Professions Code § 10032(b) 184

California Business and Professions Code §§
    20000-20043 210

351

TABLE OF AUTHORITIES

Fla. Stat. § 320.641(3) 65

Fla. Stat. § 768.72 95

General Statutes §45-345 240

Georgia Trade Secrets Act O.C.G.A. § 10-1-760, *et seq.* 114

Ky. Rev. Stat. §§ 365.800-.840 62

Missouri Statute § 407.405 199

Mont. Code Ann. § 61-4-205(1) 42

Mont. Code Ann. § 61-4-217 42

N.J.S.A. § 2A:16-51 23

N.Y. Gen. Bus. Law § 681(3)(a)(b) 11

Occupations Code § 2301.467(a)(1) 29

Ohio Rev. Code § 1333.82 31

Ohio Rev. Code § 1333.83 .... 30, 31

Ohio Rev. Code § 1333.85 .... 30, 31

Ohio Revised Code §§ 1333.82–87 30

Ohio Revised Code §4517.59(A)(14) 25

PDPA. § 23 291

PDPA. § 6 291

TABLE OF AUTHORITIES

Petroleum Marketing Practices Act, 15 U.S.C. § 2801 18

SDCL § 32-6B-45 .... 36, 42

SDCL § 32-6B-49 42

Sherman Act § 1 .... 123, 124, 223

Sherman Act §§ 1-2 124

Sherman Act § 2 .... 124, 206, 207

South Carolina Code Ann. § 56-15 .... 14, 26

Tenn. Code. Ann. § 47-25-1302 35

Vehicle Code § 3062 .... 20, 21

Vehicle Code § 3065.3 .... 20, 21

Other Authorities

16 C.F.R. § 436.1 et seq. 138

F.R.C.P 15(a)(2) 212

Fed. R. Civ. P. 8 153

Fed. R. Civ. P. 10(c) 253

Fed. R. Civ. P. 12(b)(5) 253

Fed. R. Civ. P. 12(c) 41

Fed. R. Civ. P. 15(a) 215

Fed. R. Civ. P. 23(a) 167, 170, 236

TABLE OF AUTHORITIES

Fed. R. Civ. P. 23(b) 168

Fed. R. Civ. P. 23(b)(3) 170

Fed. R. Civ. P. 23(b)(3) 236

Fed. R. Civ. P. 50 5

Fed. R. Civ. P. 59(e) 5

Fed. R. Civ. P. 60(b) 250

FRCP Rule 12(b)(6) 41

FRCP 19 .... 179, 215

FRCP Rule 23(a) 234

FRCP Rule 23(b)(2) 234

FRCP Rule 23(b)(3) 234

Rule 12 116

Rule 23(b)(2) 234

Rule 23(b)(3) 234

Rule 26 243

Rule 26(a)(1) 244

Rule 26(b)(1) 239

Rule 30(b)(6) 244

Rule 37 242

Rule 60(b)(6) 256